SIBELIUS

SIBELIUS

VOLUME III

1914–1957

ERIK TAWASTSTJERNA

edited and translated by Robert Layton

faber and faber

This edition first published in 2008
by Faber and Faber Ltd
3 Queen Square, London WC1N 3AU

Printed by CPI Antony Rowe, Eastbourne

A CIP record for this book is available from the British Library

ISBN 978-0-571-24774-5

Contents

Translator's Foreword

After the publication of Harold Johnson's Sibelius monograph in 1959 with its dark hints of hidden secrets, the Sibelius family decided that the composer should be known for what he was, and entrusted Erik Tawaststjerna with complete and unrestricted access to the composer's papers, letters and diaries. He drew on these for his mammoth five-volume biography whose Finnish edition, begun in 1960, reached completion in 1988. As I explained in the Foreword to Volume II, the first volume in English comprised the first two volumes of the Finnish and Swedish editions; and the second comprised the third. The present book encompasses the last two volumes of the Swedish and Finnish originals, and in order to accommodate them within practical (and affordable) proportions, some adaptation has had to be made. Generally speaking I have truncated or omitted altogether the analytical material concerning the Sixth and Seventh Symphonies and *Tapiola*, in the belief that the reader can examine these scores for him or herself. The widespread accessibility of the songs and smaller works on compact disc (many of those on the BIS label being annotated by Erik Tawaststjerna himself), has brought the music within the reach of a much larger audience than could have been envisaged in the 1960s when Professor Tawaststjerna embarked on his odyssey. I have, of course, retained the discussion of the genesis of the Fifth Symphony for the obvious reason that this is not available to the general reader, and adds and contributes to our understanding of this remarkable work. The 1915 version of the symphony has now been commercially recorded as part of BIS's Complete Edition of Sibelius's output.

The task of undertaking a book of these dimensions is daunting – especially when the author is involved in seeing his work through the press in different languages. Erik Tawaststjerna's original is in Swedish, the first four Finnish volumes being prepared for publication by Tuomas Anhava and Professor Erkki Salmenhaara. Only the last chapters of Volume V were written in Finnish. The English edition formed the basis of the first volume in Russian (1981) and will also form the basis of the German.

At Tawaststjerna's death in 1993 the Swedish text of the fifth volume remained incomplete, and I am greatly indebted to Fru Gitta Henning for making a Swedish-language version of the last chapters (from Chapter Sixteen onwards). Fru Henning worked with Professor Tawaststjerna for nearly twenty-four years and knew better than anyone else how his mind worked. She is currently seeing through the press the final two volumes of the Swedish language edition. Although Erik Tawaststjerna saw and approved the first part of this translation, I have had to rely on her altogether invaluable advice and guidance not only in the main body of the text but through the minefield of Sibelius's letters and, above all, diary entries. With the completion of these volumes, most of Sibelius's papers have been placed in the Library of Helsinki University, and access to the diaries and some other papers is now restricted until well into the next century.

Sibelius's diaries pose particular problems in that they are not only difficult to decipher but are often private musings that have little meaning for an outsider. They are jottings, passing thoughts, and often not syntactical. During his lifetime Sibelius kept all his correspondence with friends and publishers (there are nearly 700 letters to his wife), as well as innumerable press-cuttings. But there are few diary entries after the 1920s, and relatively little material of a personal nature from the late 1930s onwards.

There are places in which there is more than one draft of a chapter section, and I have done my best to represent the substance of both. In one or two instances (the interview Sibelius gave to an Italian critic in 1922 is one) I have restored material the author omitted from the Swedish edition. Generally speaking I have proceeded on the assumption that the English-speaking audience will have a perspective that differs from that of the Finnish and Swedish reader. Although I have made every effort to come as close to the letter of the manuscript as possible, my guiding principle has been to convey its spirit. I have aimed at a text that would come close to one which the author himself would have used, had his native tongue been English. The author had an exemplary command of English (and many other languages), and although we mostly conversed in Swedish I heard him speaking English often enough to know how elegantly he expressed himself.

I am grateful to *Suomalaisen Kirjallisuuden Seuras* (the Finnish Literary Society) for an Award in support of this project, and to Marja-Leena Rautalin of the Finnish Literary Centre; to the Finnish Embassy in London and H.E. the Ambassador, Mr Ilkka Pastinen; to Mr Frank Hellstén, Counsellor for the Ministry for Foreign Affairs Department for Press and Cultural Relations in Helsinki, and Mr Heikki Reenpää of Otava Press.

Robert Layton, London, 1997

Projected themes for the Fifth Symphony

Sketches for the Sixth Symphony over which the composer has scribbled 'Violin Concerto II/Concerto lirico'

CHAPTER ONE

War and Isolation

Three years had now passed since the Fourth Symphony. The allure of expressionism had begun to fade for him. Indeed, it had produced a reaction in the impressionist colouring of *The Oceanides*. Sibelius had long pondered over plans for a new symphony. Once again his future artistic direction posed a stylistic dilemma. While working on the final version of the Fifth Symphony in 1918, he found it taking the path of classicism; that was the direction which the ideas themselves dictated. But the motives which were occupying him then were the same as those with which he had been wrestling in August 1914.

However, his immediate problems were more practical: how to buy himself the time and peace he needed to write it? The outbreak of war presented him with alarming prospects. His bent was for the symphony, but the day-to-day realities of life necessitated the composition of lighter trifles that would prove lucrative. The conflict between real composing and making a living, always acute in his career, sharpened still further.

There were three possible ventures afoot, all of them unappealing in one way or another, but all offering immediate rewards: a ballet for London; a choral piece for the male choir, MM (*Muntra Musikanter*); or an opera for Aino Ackté. The dancer Maggie Gripenberg had revived an idea for a ballet, which had first surfaced five years earlier, based on *The Bears' Death Rituals*, a re-working by Juhani Aho of material from the *Kalevala*. Sibelius sought Axel Carpelan's views: 'But what of my own work! It seems to me that I'm binding myself hand and foot. A ballet is something I could do well and it could be a success. But what do you think? I can't just become a *vielschreiber*. That would damage both my reputation and my work. The only thing, as I see it, is to extricate myself. Don't you agree? I would value your views. Perhaps I am too negative, but to throw away on some *pas* ideas that would sit marvellously in a symphonic setting . . . No! No!' (27 July 1914)

Carpelan's response was immediate: 'My firm advice would be to listen to your inner promptings and not to commissions from left, right and centre. Follow your own star and stick to the symphonic path, be it orchestral or chamber. That is now your secure field, your real world. The present times are not the most propitious for opera or ballet. To compose *pas* to the accompaniment of cannons would be bizarre.' (30 July 1914)

This, needless to say, was exactly the sort of thing Sibelius wanted to hear, as he notes in his diary: 'I've had a wonderfully understanding letter from Axel. He is quite unique – but does not realize that my financial burdens (nearly 90,000 marks in debts) are a terrible strain.' (1 August 1914) He returned the libretto to Aho on 8 November, with his regrets, though it is clear from his diary that he did not find the subject uncongenial. He felt much the same way about the stream of commissions for cantatas. MM tried to persuade him to set Runeberg's epic poem *Kung Fjalar* for chorus and orchestra and offered a tempting fee. But though the sum figured in his budget calculations for that year, the project came to nothing.

And then there was *Juha*. This had been hanging over his head since 1912, when he had promised Aino Ackté, whose libretto it was, a firm answer within two years. Just before the time-limit ran out, he wrote to Carpelan: 'To take on *Juha*, is not, I think, a good idea for me.' When in the middle of October, Ackté pressed him for his final decision, he turned her down. Thus, in the end, Sibelius turned down all three commissions so as to concentrate on the new symphony – a decision that was both wise artistically and singularly bold, given his fears of losing his income from the continent.

Fortunately things did not turn out so badly. In the autumn of 1914 *Det Skandinaviska Musikförlaget* in Copenhagen established contact with Breitkopf's Head Office in Leipzig and through their good offices Sibelius's royalties continued to arrive. A present-day observer having vivid memories of the Second World War might be astonished to discover that post could be sent at all without being opened by the Russian-controlled Finnish censor or his German counterpart. But the route over Copenhagen took time and Sibelius's need of money was acute, so he turned to two Helsinki publishers, Lindgren and Westerlund, and later on to Wilhelm Hansen in Copenhagen, albeit not without some pangs of conscience as he felt a bond of loyalty to Breitkopf. All three gladly accepted smaller pieces, not only piano miniatures but songs and instrumental pieces. But, in the present climate, symphonies and orchestral poems were less attractive propositions. More than ever before Sibelius poured out small trifles while at a deeper level he was occupied with other matters: 'The symphony is playing in my mind. Am working on and moulding the themes. As usual consumed and burdened with small pieces. When will all this uncritical *naïveté* come to an end. How impossible it seems to change my circumstances for my few remaining years. But are they so few? I doubt it.'

Carpelan advised him to bury himself in the wilds 'without newspapers and emotions . . . Listen there to your inner voices and pretend that you are no longer part of this world of the present anguish and misery.' Sibelius without newspapers? The very idea is unthinkable. He had to have his daily dose of war news and politics, and follow the way in which Kajanus's and

2

Schnéevoigt's shares were rated on the critical stock exchange by *Hufvuds-tadsbladet* and *Uusi Suometar*, and get himself worked up by Eino Leino's articles on the arts in *Helsingin Sanomat*. Above all he missed the foreign press, the *Berliner Tageblatt* and the fresh air from abroad. And a dispassionate Sibelius was an impossibility. On one of his more difficult days, his diary reads: 'Am in a terrible state and ought to be left to myself . . . My nerves are in tatters. Why? Everyone is after me. Why should I, having a composer's cross to bear, have loans to repay, living expenses and no income? Interest repayments – interest and more interest! In the house four servants, one gardener, guests etc.' (8 November 1914)

In the end he promised a new piece, *Herr Lager och Skön Fager*, to MM: 'A commission – but it will be of some interest! The day is cloudy and rather cold. My spirits are not high – the war and all its consequences. And I'm a bit depressed about the way my work is developing. But that's necessary for the symphony on whose themes I labour.'

But the next day he thought he saw things more clearly: 'I cannot always be prepared to be accessible. Everything in my art must be cleansed and purified. But, it seems to me, my creative work has had so little effect on the world at large. Perhaps in time it will, particularly when I think of the influence my work has had on my contemporaries here (both their musical ideas and the orchestral sound). But that aside, I think I'm largely right. What melancholy thoughts. All things come from the undemanding nature with which I was born, my great defect. In many cases one consoles oneself with the thought that *es genügt das Grosse gewollt zu haben!* But for me the result is the main thing. I think I have the right – if it is permissible for me to use the word – to this pride.' (Diary, 1 August 1914)

True, no school had formed around him as it had grown up around Debussy and Schoenberg. At this time his work exercised scant influence outside Scandinavia, and even there was confined to Stenhammar and a handful of Nordic contemporaries. Some years were to elapse before he was to exercise any considerable influence in the English-speaking world. But no one, not even his favourite pupil Madetoja, had taken his symphonic principles further. Small wonder that he felt a sense of isolation in a small country cut off from the world by war.

Perhaps Sibelius still saw the world stage partly through the sensibility of *art nouveau* and its climate of *angst*. Towards the end of August he wrote to Carpelan: 'How great is the pathos and anguish of our times! We approach the long prophesied religious age. But it's a religion impossible to define – least of all in words, but perhaps music is a manifestation of it.' Was his symphony and the undoubted awe of nature that it exhibits, a religious or pantheistic manifestation? Or did he have Scriabin in mind? Only a year earlier he had written to Rosa Newmarch: 'As far as Scriabin's music is concerned, I believe that the religious music of the future will develop from his work and from opera.' (18 April 1913) Scriabin's mixture of ecstasy and

3

mysticism exercised a strong fascination at this time, and one might say that the tritone figure, so dominant a role in the Fourth Symphony, shows a certain parallel between them. Among the few modern scores he had added to his library was *Prometheus*, and not long before he had made the acquaintance of *Le Poème de l'Extase*.

It is clear from a study of a block of sketches, to which I will return in the next chapter, that Sibelius was at work not on one but two symphonies, for the basic thematic substance of the Sixth was already beginning to take shape. Of course, he had constantly to turn to the smaller pieces that brought in some income, if he was to settle at least some of his bills. These worries loomed large on his horizon, as did the continued isolation of the war and the inevitable approach of old age. The creative years from 1910 to 1914, after his throat operation, when one key work seemed to unleash the next, were on balance rich and happy. The shift towards impressionism that can be discerned in *The Oceanides* could have proved decisive in changing his creative course. But this was not to be: indeed, during the ensuing eight years, through to the autumn of 1922, he completed only one large-scale work, the Fifth Symphony, and then only after two extensive revisions. Otherwise there are the *Six Humoresques* for violin and orchestra, master-pieces in a smaller form; a work for the theatre, closely tied to the spoken text; a number of smaller instrumental pieces and songs of some distinction; and a larger number of miniatures of the second rank. In all, not too bad a result, but pretty meagre when put alongside previous eight-year periods in his career, and even the last creative years (1922–30).

With the autumn of 1914, Sibelius could be said to have entered his years of crisis. One's thoughts turn to the years 1813–18 in Beethoven's life, which Leopold Schmidt called 'something approaching an intermezzo',[1] when, following almost a decade of masterpieces, suddenly the number of great works falls off to an extraordinary extent. Life makes its inexorable demands and takes its toll with increasing severity, and for the first time forces its way into the foreground. Schmidt, in my view one of the most searching and underrated commentators on the composer, relates how the difficult side of Beethoven's nature is accentuated, how he adopts a combative attitude to others, neglects his appearance, is consumed by the lawsuit concerning his nephew and makes life impossible for his servants. One might ask how much is cause and how much effect? Could it be that the slackening of the creative fires itself unleashes destructive forces in the personality? Does the creative development bear any immediate relationship to biographical events? If you look at the daily events at the surface of Beethoven's life, it would seem they bore little relationship to the realities of his inner life.

In Sibelius's case the difficult years began six years later than they had with Beethoven. His birthday that December, the last before his fiftieth, found him on the threshold, though his signs of crisis were quite the opposite of Beethoven's. He paid increasing attention to his appearance. Now that it was no longer possible to order his suits and shirts in Paris, he turned to the most exclusive Helsinki tailors. His handmade shoes were the last word in elegance. He spared no quantities of water in his daily ablutions – although, as was common at this period, there was no public water supply installed at Ainola – and spent hours in the sauna. His daughters always recalled the discreet hint of *eau de cologne* after his morning shave. He became equally meticulous at table. Not the slightest stain was permitted on the tablecloths or serviettes. If there was the faintest food stain on a napkin, it was immediately sent back to the kitchen.

He guarded his privacy with increasing zeal, whereas Beethoven rebelled against his isolation. Of course, it would be folly to pursue the parallel too far, as Beethoven's deafness inevitably posed altogether special strains and frustrations. Sibelius's dealings with his publishers did not lead to ugly outbursts; though his pleas for more generous terms more often than not prompted them to take an even tighter grip on their wallets. However, his complicated financial problems were all eventually (and harmoniously) resolved. But, needless to say, his retreat into solitude – he abstained from concert going and grew away from his old circle of friends – brought its own pangs.

The autumn of 1914 was a constant struggle between the symphony and 'bread-and-butter' music. To atone for the disappointment he had caused MM over *Kung Fjalar*, he planned no fewer than three pieces for chorus and orchestra, all based on ideas that were later to surface in the Fifth Symphony: first, *The Sea*, to words by the Fenno–Swedish poet, Jakob Tegengren; second, *The Song of the Goths;* and lastly, *Bacchanal* to words by Viktor Rydberg. The Goths were to sing their menacing warrior song to a melody which subsequently appears as the pizzicato theme in the *Andante mosso, quasi allegretto* of the symphony. None of these projects actually came to anything. At the same time he began to pour out instrumental pieces: 'This genre – the piano miniature – is something I have to cultivate. Perhaps also violin and piano. I suppose that with these plus the songs, I could just keep my head above water. My bigger debts will have to be dealt with in some other way.' (1 October 1914) He made a start with six piano pieces: *När rönnen blommar, Den ensamma furan, Aspen, Björken, Granen* and *Syringa*. He reworked the last in 1919 before publishing it as the *Valse lyrique* for orchestra. Work of this kind was something of a strain and he wondered, along with a cartoonist in one of the Stockholm dailies, whether it was only pregnant women who threw up every morning!

But suddenly everything changed:

[17 September 1914] Laboured over the piano pieces. Sym. 5 is beginning to grow. Wonderful day. Am living life to the full – enough for two!

[19 September] Worked yesterday on Sym. 5. Whatever is going to become of this offspring? Worked really well! But my way of working, based as it is on inspiration, has nothing to do with the conventional kind of composing. As a result I cannot always see where I am going in all this wilderness.

A letter to Carpelan a few days later reads: 'I am still deep in the mire, but I have already caught a glimpse of the mountain I must climb. Strange. The opponents of militarism allow the military to determine whether ordinary people live or don't live.' And in a postscript he adds, 'God opens his door for a moment, and his orchestra is playing Sym. 5.' (22 September 1914)

There were practical matters to attend to: he had to go into Helsinki a number of times to negotiate terms with his publisher, Westerlund, for some new piano pieces. But, in spite of everything, he felt on the crest of a wave: 'Worked away on the new piece. In the morning a terrible depression, but during the day bathed in the new symphony and all my spirit grew lighter.' (2 October 1914)

He spent the next few days in bed with an infection and the next mention of the symphony does not come until 10 October: '*Alleingefühl* once more. Solitary and strong . . . the autumn sun is shining. Nature is pervaded by a sense of farewell. My heart sings full of melancholy – the shadows lengthen. Adagio in Sym. 5? That I, poor mortal, should have such wonderful times!'

He presumably alludes to the melancholy adagio theme, which appears in the sketches but was subsequently eradicated. There were also reminders of his alternative musical life. He had to correct the proofs of two scenes from the ballet *Scaramouche* in the piano reduction and send them off to Hansen in Copenhagen. To his Helsinki publishers, Lindgren and Westerlund, he sent two piano pieces each.

[14 October 1914] Worked on small things . . . *Difficile est satiram non scribere*. But why do you say such things, Jean Sibelius. Shame on you!!

[18 October] On top of the world. God knows . . . But – to me it seems that the real Jean Sibelius is only just beginning. Wonder whether the name 'symphony' has harmed my symphonies more than it has helped them. Have determined to let my inner self – my fantasy – have its say. What has to be done, must be done soon. Life is so short!

From the diary we see that he continued to compose four small pieces each month, to work on an orchestral suite for Hansen (in his haste he spells it Hamsum) as well: 'Begun in earnest with the Symphony No. 5. In a state of exhilaration when working over these themes. *Hier stehe ich und kann nichts anderes, Gott helfe mir, Amen!*' (26 October 1914)

This passage probably refers to the sketch block where he has noted down a table of themes for a four-movement symphony. But it was not long before he was forced to break off from his work. His debts, at this stage

83,000 marks, forced him to turn out more small pieces. At the beginning of November he sent Westerlund three small piano pieces for 700 marks each. Only two weeks previously his offerings had brought him 1,000 marks from Westerlund and 600 from Lindgren. But the situation was still pretty desperate:

> [4 November 1914] Am I going to be able to struggle on? Can I go on living here? *Ich glaube es wohl. Aber . . .! Das Leben muss lang genug werden!*

From August through to early November, he had managed to write sixteen small pieces and he continued to produce them at much the same pace. But in the middle of his work for Westerlund on *Couplet* and *Badinage* (the title was eventually changed to *Boutade*), he again became caught up with the symphony:

> [13 November 1914] I have had a wonderful idea. The adagio of the symphony – earth, worms and heartache – *fortissimos* and muted strings, very muted. And the sounds are godlike. Have rejoiced and revelled in the rushing strings when the soul sings. Will this glorious inspiration fall victim to criticism – my self-criticism?

The sense of autumnal decay with muted strings and *fortissimo* point towards the E flat minor episode in the finale. Its embryo is to be found on page 14 of the sketch block, surrounded by sketches for the Adagio. Two days later he put the idea to one side. Some time later, on 2 December, his diary records that the Adagio will be finished but in a different form. In fact it wasn't, but Sibelius did use this passage with its powerful dissonances in the Fifth Symphony, even though he had at one time placed it in the Sixth. Judging from the sketch block and the diaries he continued work on the symphony for about a fortnight before other projects claimed him.

He started work on two new pieces, *Laetare anima mea*, originally *Song of Praise* or *Lauda Sion*, for violin (or cello) and small orchestra. He finished it on 1 December and sent it off to Lindgren immediately. A few days earlier he had sent the same publisher a *Capriccietto* for piano for the sum of 300 marks. The same day his diary records a terrible battle for money. 'A matter of life and death. Will it be my end as an artist?' He never expressed such bitterness at his financial worries than he did now, when new ideas for the symphony were bursting forth but were constantly stifled by other musical obligations:

> [2 December 1914] Wonderful day. Sunshine. Went for a walk with Aino. New plans for composition.

> [3 December] Have caught a cold. Aino is in Helsinki . . . Once again money matters. Must write small pieces. When can I get on with my big plans? Presumably when I'm dead. What is the purpose of it all when it leads to nothing. Bankruptcy would be better.

[4 December] Worked on the *Rondoletto* . . . and also *Boutade* (both for piano).

[5 December] The day is grey, cold and gloomy. Had a phone conversation with my publisher which put us all in a filthy temper. What are we to do! Manage as best we can! The worst is that publishers can't bring anything out! The war!!! It seems as if my labours in the musical world are to no avail.

[7 December] *Ora et labora!* Pondered on life's evanescence. And other original things. Worked at the piano, i.e. piano pieces.

[13 December] Planned new pieces for violin with orchestral or piano accompaniment.

[14 December] Wonderful snowscape. Branches heavy with snow. White upon white! Worked on violin pieces for Hansen.

[15 December] Worked on the new piece. Everything still in its formative stage.

What was this new piece about which he is so unforthcoming and first mentions on 2 December? The explanation comes the following day:

[16 December 1914] Worked on *Fantasia I*.

There can be little doubt that this '*Fantasia I*' is none other than the Sixth Symphony. On pages 22 and 23 of his sketchblock Sibelius worked, presumably at the turn of the year, on the first, albeit far from definitive, form of its themes. On 15 January 1915 his diary records that the symphony is 'maturing slowly'. At this stage it would seem that he was working on both works simultaneously, since a table of themes for the Fifth Symphony on page 24 of the sketchbook is dated 12 January and on the 17th of the same month he returns to the ideas of the Sixth. Nor should his mention of *Fantasia* occasion any surprise. As early as May 1912 he had started planning an '*Erste*' and '*Zweite Phantasie für grosses Orchester*', having spoken only some weeks earlier of '*Sinfonie*' V and VI. As late as November 1914 he had complained about the inadequacy of these titles: 'But they are after all symphonies. The term must be broadened. At least I have played my part in this.' (Diary, 26 November 1914)

But pressures were mounting inside him:

[17 December 1914] How impossible it is to be creative at a time when it is only the work of others which counts! If only I, who really am producing something new, wrote like, for example, Metastasio, I would be all right. Dinners, speeches, etc. No only solitude. I alone, alone, alone! Work at my symphonic fantasy. How close to my heart this form is! *Ars longa, vita brevis.* How bitter our path in this world can be – and most often is. Have written to Stenhammar and suggested some concerts . . .

[19 December] The young are on the way up. My natural enemies! But all the same I am with them. I can't be otherwise. Things that don't come to fruition. But I can't do other than I am. Alone, alone, alone. My lot!

[21 December] Worked on the orchestral fantasy. That I'm moving towards hard times both artistically and in practical economic terms, is certain. And in order to complete this, my orchestral fantasy, I must live on advances and loans. Uncertain if I can get it published when B&H are in an enemy country.

Such were his thoughts as 1914 moved towards its close. They inevitably relate to his outer rather than his inner life. Sibelius felt the isolation of the war years acutely as if his world was ghost-ridden rather than real. The pessimistic, negative side of his nature was highlighted; he imagined all sorts of slights and saw himself as forgotten and ignored, a lonely beacon of light in a deepening winter darkness. He became increasingly oversensitive about concert invitations and complimentary tickets. He notes in his diary: 'Young talents are performing. I was deeply hurt that [Ilmari] Hannikainen did not want me at his recital.' (Diary, 4 November 1914) Of course, Hannikainen, who was only twenty-two, would have thought it presumptuous to have sent tickets to Sibelius. He was incidentally to be Alexander Siloti's duo-partner in London after the war, and one of the finest Finnish interpreters of Sibelius's piano music as well as a personal friend.

It was the same story with Kosti Vehanen, who later became Marian Anderson's accompanist in, among other things, Sibelius's songs and also partnered Aino Ackté. Sibelius felt obliged to stay away 'as there was no invitation at all'. Other concert artists, however, were not so inattentive: 'In Helsinki, [the young tenor] Väinö Sola sang beautifully: *Jubal*, etc. I have no success with the masses. This does not worry me since the other day when I went to hear the Helsinki Orchestra play, among other things, Tchaikovsky's *Francesca da Rimini*, I realized the sureness of my artistic grip. Not least that my songs – among them, *Våren flyktar hastigt* (*Spring is Flying*), written in the 1890s – sound thoroughly modern and true; also my orchestral technique and colour sound fresh even today. That gave me deep satisfaction.' (1 November 1914)

Aarre Merikanto, son of the composer of popular songs and opera and a disciple of Reger, had 'the good taste' to invite Sibelius to the first concert of his own compositions. 'A promising début', he recorded in his diary (6 November 1914) and in an undated letter to the young composer written a few days later, he spoke of him achieving great things in the future. It was a relatively conservative début in spite of some Regerish harmonies. The concert was given a second time. 'Merikanto, the admirable boy, celebrates his triumph. So he should.' (10 November 1914) After further studies in Moscow, Merikanto was to enrich the literature of Nordic opera in the early 1920s with one of its finest works, *Juha,* on the very same libretto that

9

Sibelius had returned to Aino Ackté a few weeks earlier. Merikanto could also reckon on Sibelius's friendship and support in future years.

Critics were another matter. In a small country an established composer of international standing has to tolerate the spectacle of up-and-coming rivals enjoying critical encouragement and better reviews than he does. This he found difficult to stomach. He thought that both Selim Palmgren and Moses Pergament, the latest young composer to make his début, were puffed up by *Hufvudstadsbladet* while he was taken for granted as a has-been, 'a *fait accompli*'. No doubt Sibelius was partly over-reacting, but his impatience was partly justified. His obvious eminence both in Finland and on the international scene prompted certain critics demonstratively to bestow more generous praises on others. This did not escape Erik Furuhjelm's notice: '[Herr Pergament] captivates the public with his bargain-price stuff – and our Swedish-language press puff up the concert as if it is an event of some significance . . . The real figure of stature has difficulty in winning through. This kind of criticism is in its lack of judgement damaging for our musical life.' [2]

A month or so after Furuhjelm's article, Sibelius was again ignored. Anna Hagelstam gave the première of two of his songs, *Maj (May)*, Op. 57, and *Romeo*, Op. 61, and much to his mortification, the event passed unnoticed in the press: 'Neither before nor after the concert was there a single word about them . . . I ask you, if one of our dilettantes came with new songs, what a fuss would be made of them . . . All that and the whole wretched set-up makes me feel bitter and makes it impossible to work.' (Diary, 16 January 1915)

Much the same thing happened a few days later when Sigrid Schnéevoigt presented the *Two Rondinos*, Op. 68. The critics did not have the slightest idea that these were first performances. But Sibelius also had himself to blame if the press had less to say about him than before. He had not given a concert of his own works in Helsinki since the spring of 1913, a fact which was pointed out by Bis in *Hufvudstadsbladet* in an open letter to him: 'We have become accustomed in this country to finding a season without Sibelius incomplete, he who has brought us courage with his music. Most recently the American press has been able to report on Sibelius's concert success in the New World. Now it is surely the turn of his own country.' [3]

In a time of crisis this letter testified to a longing for a national rallying point. Had Sibelius announced a concert with the Second Symphony and *Finlandia*, it would have been immediately sold out. But Sibelius saw it as a matter of honour to present new works, and noted Bis's 'well-meaning but tactless' letter with some measure of irritation. However, a few days after his birthday he wrote a friendly letter to Wasenius.

One writer who had never given him (or anyone else for that matter) cause for complaint was the columnist Guss Mattsson. A doctor of chemistry by training, Mattsson had something of Karl Kraus about him, though his satirical bite was softened by a typically Fenno-Swedish humour, which with its quiet irony could be very telling. Mattsson had condemned Kajanus's manoeuvres in St Petersburg with Kokovtsev at the time of the problems with the Helsinki orchestras (see Vol. I), and when Kajanus had complained of attacks by the Fenno-Swedish lobby because of his strong support for the Finnish language, Mattsson was quick to point out that no one had received stronger support in the Swedish-speaking press in the past than Sibelius, also a supporter of the Finnish language, and for that matter Kajanus himself. His early death in November 1914 at the age of forty-one came as a shock to Sibelius, who wrote in his diary in the same terms as he did on Strindberg's passing: 'Gustaf Mattsson's death has shaken me. He was the conscience of the journalistic world, a man with a strong ethical feeling in all his writings.'

But Sibelius's 'Fennomania' was more subtle than that of many con-temporaries, as indeed was Mattsson's allegiance to the Fenno-Swedish cause, which did not fit into any hard-line pattern. Both were able to per-ceive the situation in Finland in terms of a wider European perspective. At that time Sibelius must have understood that his position on the language question – a single, united Finnish nation with two languages – was no longer wholly realistic. Partly in response to the increasingly aggressive Finn-ish nationalism, Fenno-Swedish circles began to advance the thesis that there was a separate Swedish sense of nationhood, language and culture in Finland. As early as 1910, the poet Eino Leino, cosmopolitan in outlook and of liberal tradition, noted the growth of what we would now call a backlash: 'Our Swedish upper class are no longer Fennicized as they were during the years of growing national self-consciousness but rather the opposite . . . We have two cultures and nations, one Finnish, the other Swedish, which are moving fast apart.'[4]

Therefore pressure increased in the Finnish-speaking community towards the creation of a completely new culture, despite the inevitable risk of appearing brash. It was no longer mandatory to love Runeberg and Topelius as much as one did the *Kalevala* and Kivi. In February 1912, for example, the Finnish-language student choir refused to take part in the traditional ceremonies honouring Runeberg, the national poet. This shook Sibelius to his roots. He felt the very foundations of his view of Finnish nationalism tremble. He telephoned Heikki Klemetti, the fanatical Fen-nomanic conductor, to give vent to his indignation and (according to Klemetti) said there was no question of his allowing them to take part in his next concert. Klemetti dug his heels in and countered with the threat that if they were to be banned, he would have no part in forming a choir for Sibelius's forthcoming concert, which was to include the *Impromptu* for women's voices and orchestra, and even hinted that, were Sibelius's attitude on this issue to become public, many of the women in the *Suomen Laulu* choir would not wish to sing under Sibelius's baton! These were not idle threats made in the heat of the moment but written in black and white after a day's reflection.

Klemetti went on: 'How in present circumstances can [Runeberg] stand as our national poet, when he is worshipped above all by those elements who have turned their backs on national unity with us. It is at Kivi's grave and Lönnrot's statue that Finnish students should assemble, undisturbed by Swedish nationalists.' Klemetti forgot Runeberg's role as a rallying point during the nineteenth century when he provided the nation with moral backbone during some of its darkest days. The same day that Sibelius received Klemetti's letter, he read Mattsson's denunciation: 'These students are no longer the noble guardians of freedom, and when the great threat from the east engulfs them they should not complain.'

It was for these students and Klemetti that Sibelius composed his finest *a cappella* songs in the earliest years of the century, and as usual he soon rose above this particular quarrel. He had a high opinion of Klemetti's powers: he had proved an inspiring interpreter as a conductor, and had presented such songs as *Båtfärden* (*The Boat Journey*), *Den brustna tonen* (*The Broken Voice*), *Det brinner på ön* (*Fire on the Island*) throughout Scandinavia, the Baltic countries and central Europe – and was later to take them to England. Whatever his reactions to the Fennomanic whine, he held no brief for the Swedish upper-classes who turned up their noses at the upstart culture of the Finns. He, like Mattsson, was fully aware of the inherent dangers if the pendulum swung too far one way or the other.

Earlier that autumn, Sibelius had spent some days in the capital:

[30 September 1914] In H. A strange atmosphere difficult to define. My complete isolation from people grows. Is this pure misanthropy on my part or touch-me-not? Cold, rainy, miserable.

[1 October] The Helsinki visit has been demeaning. To meet these wretched, small-minded people. Ugh!

Presumably Sibelius had been working hard to persuade these wretched, small-minded people they were important and talented! He was more of a touch-me-not than a misanthropist – even when he thought he had been treated with disrespect by a cashier at the Academic Book Shop, or he imagined cold, malicious stares following him at the Finnish National Theatre when his daughter was on stage. On another occasion, when as usual he found people in Helsinki 'grudging and petty', his temper was fired by a genuine grievance. He had heard a 'dreadful, dilettantish attempt' by a café musician to arrange his *Berceuse*, Op. 40 No. 5, for violin: 'Is there no law, no parliamentary law to protect the rights of artists to keep their work free from molestation. If this arrangement were published, my reputation – my dearly bought reputation I might add –will be zero.' But he had to admit that Aino was right in saying that his threshold of tolerance was too low.

But he was by no means always at odds with the world. Far from it. One glorious day he went for a walk with Aino and felt the 'rays of sunlight' both from without and within. He read with delight of other men of genius, whether real or fictional, Eckermann's *Conversations with Goethe* and Romain Rolland's *Jean Christophe Part III*. Eckermann he thought 'naïve and concerned for his own advancement – so unlike me. But he was a good person and that means a lot to me.' Was he not lacking an Eckermann in his own circle? Carpelan would never manage to put together a collection of *Conversations*.

Sibelius's intuititive feeling for people rarely failed him. Among the young people in their circle of friends was a young biology student, a classmate and close friend of Eero Järnefelt's son Heikki. Järnefelt had used him as model for a wall painting at the Ceremonial Hall of the University. Sibelius himself had noticed him and wrote in his diary after taking his walk on a sunny October day in 1914: 'Met young Mr Sillanpää who looked like a gnarled pine. What poetry there is in our people. He gave me a quizzical, enigmatic look.' The young biology student was to be the Nobel Prize winner for literature in 1939, but had at this time shown nothing of his literary prowess.

A performance of *Carmen* in Helsinki captivated Sibelius and rekindled his operatic enthusiasm. A page of his sketchblock with ideas marked 'For the opera' could refer to *Juha*, were it not for the annotation ('an exotic nuance from the sea') which rather suggests Boldemann's libretto, set in Villafranca on the Mediterranean rather than in Karelia. His impending birthday and his mounting debts prompted darker thoughts. His mood shifted from elated inspiration to depression. After 'a night with dreadful nightmares', he enjoyed a 'glorious day in the wintry countryside' and 'worked well'. But the approach of his forty-ninth birthday prompted a quick change of mood:

[6 December 1914] The day is dismal and dark. How little interest there is in my music among the wider public and the critics to judge from the press here and in Sweden.

[7 December] Am alone, alone, and again alone! We all live together in our home country and manage to get on famously. Yet underneath it all, we hate each other good and proper. It's my last day at 48.

[8 December] Today is my birthday! 49 years of age! My birthday as usual: no telegram, no letter, no flowers, no greetings (apart from a telephone call from Ruth), a veritable prophet in his own country *'poeta in patria'*. Mind you, people have other things to think about these days other than birthdays. Now one is buffeted here and there – I fear that connections with Denmark will be cut off in the near future, now that three Swedish steamboats have been mined. A day with some sunshine. But December all the same and on top of that the eighth!

The prospect of Christmas lightened his spirits. He laboured hard at the new work and surrendered himself to childhood memories:

[24 December] Typical Christmas weather. Dark and full of poetry. All is full of expectation. The new work is already beginning to take shape, though there is much to be done. Written to Hansen about it.

[25 December] This morning went to the Christmas service – full of atmosphere. Today family dinner.

It was while he was on his way to church that the first ideas came to him for 'a sonata for violin with piano accompaniment' that he planned as Op. 78: 'The idea has lain dormant inside me for a long time – as long ago as the 1880s, when I wrote two pieces like it.' (Diary, 25 December 1914) But the 'Sonata No. 1, Op. 78' was to become the Sonatina, Op. 80.

As dusk began to fall, the guests started to arrive: the Järnefelts (Eero and Saimi and their children) on foot from Suviranta, and by horse-drawn sledge from Kuninkala came Sibelius's daughter Eva and her husband, parents-in-law and four brothers-in-law, very much as in the introductory scene of Tchaikovsky's *Nutcracker*. They were greeted by an enveloping warmth, the scent of burning birch wood and appetizing aromas from the kitchen where a huge woodcock was roasting in the oven under the watchful eye of Aino, whose cuisine was schooled in the best Fenno-Swedish and St Petersburg traditions. After dinner the Christmas tree lights were lit, and the children sang papa's Christmas songs, first *'Om hanget korkeat nietokset'* to words of Wilkku Joukahainen and composed in all probability in 1901.

Simple though it may be, it is a song that reveals its provenance in a subtle way. These were the years of the worst Tsarist oppression and although the key is F major, dark minor keys cast their shadow as the bitter cold and winds are evoked and only the plea in the last strophe entrusting the people to God's protection returns us to the major. As usual in the Scandinavian countries, presents had been exchanged on Christmas Eve – Katarina had no fewer than thirty packages! After that there were party games: 'the aeroplane game' where the victim is blindfolded and swung through space on a plank, an example of the Nordic Biedermeier period's childlike naïveté that survived in Finland well into the present century. Sibelius wandered from room to room with the new violin sonatina in his thoughts. On Boxing Day the children enjoyed tobogganing and there was a traditional sleigh ride. The holiday ended with a splendid evening at the Järnefelt's. After the seasonal festivities, it was not easy to return to work.

CHAPTER TWO

The Genesis of the Fifth Symphony

At some time during the late summer or early autumn of 1914, Sibelius began to note down drafts of important themes in a sketch block with large pages but no printed staves. He freely sketched rolling, spacious note-systems and filled them with motifs which are often difficult to decipher. The first thirty-seven pages cover the period from about August 1914 through to the middle of the following June. In the summer of 1916 three additional pages were added. Generally speaking they comprise motifs for the Fifth Symphony but there are also some ideas that surface in the Sixth. Two pages are devoted to an operatic project which cannot be identified with any degree of confidence, and there is a page of sketches for the Sonatina in E minor for violin and piano, Op. 80. From January 1915 onwards he adds dates to some of the sketches.

Some ideas were soon to perish by the wayside but others were worked and reworked many times, and developed into more comprehensive structures before being discarded or further reworked. Visually the sketchbook gives an impression of struggle and demonic possession reminiscent of Beethoven. The sketch throws fascinating light on the conception of the Fifth Symphony, whose progress we can follow from the first embryonic motifs in the summer of 1914 right up to the end of June 1915. Once his ideas have ripened, Sibelius sets out several dispositions of movements: ten or so for the Fifth Symphony, three for the Sixth, with thematic tables for the individual movements.

The three versions of the Fifth Symphony

Before going any further into the question of the Fifth Symphony's conception, a reminder of certain facts is necessary.[1] The first version (1915) is in four movements, and differs from the definitive published work (1919) in many important respects, even if it is built from many of the same thematic building blocks. The first movement, *Tempo moderato assai*, is clearly separated from the second, *Allegro commodo*: together the two movements correspond to the *Tempo molto moderato – Allegro assai* in the definitive score.

The 1915 score itself does not survive, but after Sibelius's death a complete set of parts was discovered among the composer's effects and a reconstruction made.

Nothing, neither a set of parts nor a score, survives of the 1916 version save for a double-bass part. In addition, there is another set of parts, used for the première of the definitive 1919 version, on which the changes have been written in or pasted over the original. In the *Andante* movement and the finale several pages have been torn out and new ones inserted, the actual number varying from part to part. The rest between the first and second movements has been removed and the transition would seem to be close to what we know. The *Andante* differs greatly from the 1915 version but has by no means reached its definitive form, while the finale's progress reveals both gains and losses. In discussing the work's growth, any reference will necessarily be to the definitive 1919 score, the only one which is accessible to the general public.

In examining the sketch block one can discern four distinct phases in the symphony's genesis during the autumn of 1914 and the subsequent spring. First, the composer sketched out the primary thematic elements including two key figures and one adagio theme. Secondly, he continued to conceive new themes and to weave them into the early material in tables of motives for specific movements. Thirdly, he sketched out a basic scheme comprising four movements with thematic tables for each. Finally, he revised and finished his basic project in a variety of different ways, for by now ideas for the Sixth Symphony were beginning to inhibit the completion of the Fifth.

When he was working on the *Kullervo* Symphony in the spring of 1891, Sibelius spoke of having a strong sense of the symphony's atmosphere without any concrete idea as to its musical expression. The conception of a major Sibelius work often took place during a transparently unproductive period, during which the first unformed visions began to take more specific shape in his imagination. This phenomenon is not uncommon in the other arts; Alvar Aalto once said, 'Sometimes, when you are in the grip of an important project, you make one exploratory sketch after another; but it never works out if you proceed piecemeal. First, you must have a complete vision.' During the turbulent summer of 1914, Sibelius began to get the first glimpse of the new symphony, and gradually, as it came to take shape in his head, he came closer to a complete vision. The sketches of the various motifs would seem to come as early as late July, since a diary entry from that time speaks of 'a wonderful theme'.

THE FIRST BASIC MOTIF
The first basic idea is stepwise. The first embryonic cell crystallizes in a simple, rhythmic motive. The composer gropes his way forwards in D minor, albeit with a B flat minor inflection.

EX 1

And in a Lydian F major.

EX 2

Then the idea gradually takes shape as the 'first basic theme' in D flat major.

EX 3

The rhythmic motif became the fundamental impulse of the symphony. It influenced not only the theme of the finale we have mentioned but also a whole group of other motifs, characterized in the main by a wave motion that proceeds stepwise. Later it is to figure as one among many candidates as the dominant theme of the first movement. Even if in the end this was not to be, the basic idea lived on to play a key role in the finale. Sibelius worked out the first main theme in sequential fashion.

EX 4

As is obvious, this is the precursor of the wind idea, first conceived *after* the sketch block stage, when the first basic theme's syncopated thirds are found.

EX 5

THE SECOND BASIC THEME

On the fifth page of his sketch block Sibelius has noted down a second basic idea, here in A flat, and familiar from the last movement of the final 1919 version.

EX 6

Three pages further on in the sketch block, he puts it into his thematic table for the scherzo, though it is soon moved on to the finale. This second swinging 'Thor's hammer' theme[2] makes a good foil to the first. The melodic line winds in ever wider intervals, beginning with a fifth and ending up with a ninth. No sooner has inspiration taken wing and the idea been fashioned into shape, than it is subjected to strong critical scrutiny. Sibelius first toys with one idea and then another, but only three really took off during the sketch block stage: the two basic ideas and an adagio figure which survived for a time only to be eliminated afterwards. This would seem to have been a decisive step in the symphony's genesis.

In both basic themes there is a kind of genetic power which is a driving force in the composer's imagination: 'I propose to let these musical thoughts and their development in my spirit fashion the formal shape of the piece.' It can seem an oversimplification to argue that the whole symphony grows out of the two basic themes, or rather from the impulses they set in motion. But in the case of the Fifth Symphony, however, it holds good in the sense that every musical idea is influenced by one or other of those ideas. Much the same duality can be found in the sketches for the Second Symphony.

In a diary entry on 10 April 1915 he was to liken the creative process to solving a puzzle: 'Spent the evening with the [Fifth] symphony. The arrangement, make-up and grouping of the themes: with all its mystery and fascination this is the important thing. It is as if God the Father had thrown down mosaic pieces from the floor of the heavens and asked me to put them back as they were. Perhaps that is a good definition of composition – perhaps not?'

The two basic themes derive from the same pattern. But it was only after June 1915 that he realized what their real significance was, and that the two pieces of the mosaic had originally lain side by side on the floor of heaven! Once the two basic themes were in place, the decisive step towards the fulfilment of his creative vision had been taken.

The second phase: the separate movements

In the next stage Sibelius began to draw up tables of themes for individual movements; first, for a scherzo, the second (originally third) movement in his projected scheme. It is in D minor; E flat is yet to emerge as the main key of the whole symphony. Under the heading 'the scerzo' [*sic*] Sibelius later added in green crayon, 'in E flat'

EX 7

Here we find (i) an unidentified theme which also appears in later tables; (ii) the bucolic horn call, the introductory theme of the *Tempo molto moderato* of the definitive version; (iii) the woodwind figure in thirds, which appears three bars after letter A in the *Tempo molto moderato*; (iv) the swinging ('Thor's hammer') theme from the finale. At this juncture the projected scherzo comes to occupy a central place in his planning. And in the bucolic horn call and the wind figure in thirds, Sibelius has fashioned two of the key elements in the exposition of the first movement.

THE LENTO MOVEMENT
A beautiful *cantabile* theme in 7/4 time and in D major (see page 8 of the sketch block), already conceived during the first phase of the symphony's

conception when it was in D flat major (see page 5), has been placed under the heading 'Lento movement'.

EX 8

Even though it was removed later, during the early stages of the symphony, it still attracted other thematic ideas into its orbit and served as a catalyst in the evolution of what was eventually to become the slow movement, the *Andante mosso, quasi allegretto*.

THE FIRST MOVEMENT: INTRADA (IN PASTORAL MOOD)

The first movement was the stepping stone to the whole project. For his 'Intrada – In Pastoral Mood' Sibelius sketched out, among other things, three ideas.

EX 9

We recognize in the first the pizzicato theme from the definitive slow movement; the second, rather ordinary idea was for a short time to function as a main theme in the finale until it was discarded towards the end of April 1915. In the third, behind the repeated notes, we have the outline of the second group of the first movement (nine bars before letter B).

EX 10

With these themes, Sibelius had taken two important steps. But the overall picture of the *Intrada* still remained uncertain. Already in the same sketch block he had assigned the pizzicato theme to another work he was planning at the time and which came to nothing: *Goternas sång* (Song of the Goths).

THE FINALE ('BACCHIC PROCESSION')

At this stage Sibelius thought of the finale as a 'Bacchic Procession'. The title clearly alludes to a passage in 'The Young·Greeks', the second canto of Rydberg's poem *Livslust och livsleda* (*Love of Life and Weariness of Life*) on whose text he had drawn for the *Impromptu* for women's choir and orchestra. The theme pours out in a headlong 6/8 rhythm.

EX 11

The general shape and character of the idea calls to mind the scherzo of the Second Symphony. The idea itself was discarded but something of its momentum and character survive in the 1919 finale. The Intrada and Bacchic Procession were probably sketched on or around 11 September 1914.

The original plan set out in four movements

The first two phases in the work's conception culminated in a new set of sketches with the heading 'E flat Sym V in four movements'. Now that most of the more important themes have been sketched, Sibelius turns his mind to the content of the individual movements. He no longer thinks of the *Intrada*'s pizzicato theme but rather the first basic motive, which – at least in its original form – was destined to disappear from the symphony. The second group, which had already figured in the scherzo in D minor, now comes in E flat minor.

EX 12

The E flat minor tonality is destined to give a curious impulse towards the birth of the Sixth Symphony. This diverges completely from the earlier *Intrada* plan. Progress on the first movement is already faltering ominously.

THE SECOND MOVEMENT: SCHERZO AND TRIO

The shape of the scherzo-plan comes into sharper focus. The two main motifs, the bucolic horn-call, and the woodwind theme with its final triplet turn up transposed into E flat major. The swinging 'Thor's hammer' theme is still present, but a query has been put against it.

EX 13

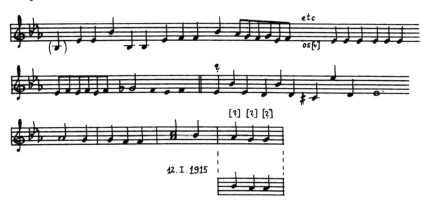

In the next motif-table, which bears the date 12 January 1915, he added the word 'Trio' above this theme. In the definitive version it leads into the B major *Allegro moderato* section. A second Trio theme is to be found on page 30 of the sketch block.

EX 14

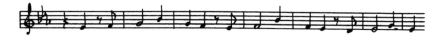

This appears a little further on in the *Allegro moderato* section, at letter D in the score. Up to this point it is obvious that Sibelius thought of the second movement as a scherzo and trio. His original point of departure was clearly a construction of the type A–B–A, in which the principal section A is built on the bucolic horn-call and the woodwind theme in thirds; the trio section B contains both trio themes; the final A section puts into effect in some way the recapitulation of the scherzo form. On the basis of this we can establish how the 'first movement', that is, the *Tempo molto moderato – Allegro moderato* group in the definitive version, emerged from the scherzo plan.

SCHERZO PLAN: DEFINITIVE VERSION

And so it is genetically justifiable to regard the *Tempo molto moderato – Allegro moderato* as a single united movement. In the 1915 version the pause between the *Moderato* introduction and the following *Allegro* is clearly a relic of the customary break between principal section and trio. In the 1916 version the pause has already been bridged over.

THE THIRD MOVEMENT: ADAGIO, B MAJOR

The beautiful principal theme in 7/4 had already been sketched before the original plan. Here Sibelius gives it in B major, with the tonic a major third below the symphony's tonal centre.

EX 15

Judging from the number of times this theme was reworked, it was close to Sibelius's heart. But he eventually gave it up because it did not harmonize with the overall spirit of the symphony.

THE FOURTH MOVEMENT, E FLAT MAJOR

The figure marked 'a' derives from the motif-table of the *Intrada*. It is hardly one of Sibelius's greatest inspirations and later on will disappear altogether. For the idea marked 'b', the composer indicates the swinging 'Thor's hammer' theme (at this stage with a query but later on without), and with this a cornerstone of the finale is laid. Sibelius also moves the theme with the descending fifth from the *Intrada*.

EX 16

As we have said, this was later embodied in the first movement, but in the 1915 version it turns up notwithstanding in the introduction to the final climax of the finale.

The second conception phase

When in the late autumn of 1914 Sibelius set out the original plan in four movements, the first phase of the work's conception was complete. The Fifth Symphony did not advance much from this stage during the following spring. Although the composer made additions, crossed out, revised and rearranged the thematic table, the original plan was not substantially altered. Of the newly-added material, only two ideas were to gain a firm footing in the symphony. One is the 'second trio theme'. The second idea spins out further the *Intrada*'s pizzicato theme and appears for the first time in – *mirabile dictu* – the Sixth Symphony, sketched probably in December 1914.

About a month later the theme – now in G flat major –was moved to the Fifth Symphony's adagio plan where it functioned as main theme, while the original adagio theme in 7/4 became a subsidiary theme in G major. With this both the pizzicato idea and the key of G major enter the slow movement. This step can be regarded as the birth of the definitive *Andante mosso quasi allegretto* movement –the pre-natal stage was when the pizzicato main theme itself was sketched for the *Intrada* plan.

In the spring of 1915 Sibelius was working hard to bring the Fifth Symphony into a more coherent shape. But the picture was complicated by ideas that were to find their way into its successor. In fact, the origin of the Sixth Symphony is interwoven with that of the Fifth, and as he finishes, revises and polishes the Fifth, ideas freely wander back and forth between the two symphonies. (It is at this point that he made his reference to the floor of heaven and putting together pieces of its mosaic in the puzzle.) The sketch block shows many surprising connections: for example, on page 14 there is a variant of the Fifth Symphony's basic figure with a characteristic touch of dissonance in the harmonic underlay.

EX 17

That is the embryo of the finale's E flat minor episode. Strangely enough, Sibelius allowed this same embryo to grow in D minor, assigning it to the finale in the table of motifs he drew up for the Sixth Symphony on 17 and 18 January 1915 (sketch block pages 28–9).

EX 18

As you see, this idea which forms the E flat minor episode in No. 5 is to all intents and purposes now in its finished form, and would seem to have flourished in the milder environment of D minor.

The pizzicato theme of the Fifth Symphony also seems to have flourished in these gentler climes. This working-out of that theme[3] appears in the table of motifs for the second movement of the Sixth Symphony.

EX 19

But after a while Sibelius realized that what he had in fact been working on was an idea for the Fifth Symphony, and he returned it to the Fifth, placing it in the table of themes for the Adagio in C flat (B) major.

EX 20

The original Adagio was demoted to a secondary role in G major. The resulting tonal plan which now emerged was E flat – G major – B (or C flat). Yet again the environment of the Sixth Symphony was serving as a kind of hothouse for the ideas of the Fifth. Conversely one finds among the sketches to the Fifth Symphony, the second, ascending figure from the finale of the Sixth, here in E flat minor.

Genesis of the Sixth Symphony

Although the origin of the Sixth Symphony is interwoven with that of the Fifth, the sketch block offers relatively little evidence of how it developed. The various phases of its conception are by no means as clearly marked as in the Fifth. All the same, we do know when his thoughts first turned to it. There is a diary entry from mid-December 1914 mentioning that he began work on 'Fantasia I', i.e. the Sixth Symphony, and there are many surprising connections with the Fifth. The following idea in E flat minor was destined to become the second theme in the finale of the Sixth. It would appear to have been written in the latter part of November, and is to be found among various workings-out of the Fifth Symphony's basic rhythmic motive.

EX 21

Both its key and context indicate that it was originally earmarked for the Fifth Symphony, though it does not harmonize completely with the other thematic material for that symphony. On the other hand, it gives a glimpse of the fundamental character of the Sixth Symphony: its Dorian mode; its predominantly stepwise melodic substance; and the fact that its theme ascends from the tonic to the flattened seventh and subsequently settles on the dominant.

This is where the material for the Sixth differs from that for the Fifth, where modal ideas are uncommon and stepwise melodic movement is generally counterbalanced by swinging interval leaps. E flat minor belongs to a different symphonic world. In this connection one's attention is drawn to a strange circumstance: the two other E flat minor themes in the original ground plan were first sketched in D minor. It would seem that during this time Sibelius was pulled between two different worlds: the Dorian D minor sound world of the Sixth Symphony-to-be, and the wilder, more thematically structured Fifth which had yet to find its tonal centre. And that no doubt explains how he tried to fill the tonal landscape of the Sixth with themes from the Fifth.

Key apart, the E flat minor theme is the fundamental idea of the Sixth Symphony. And when Sibelius, a little later in mid-December, temporarily gave up work on the Fifth Symphony and plunged into the D minor world of the Sixth, he took this E flat minor theme with him. Four pages further on in the sketch block, Sibelius begins to work out a thematic scheme for the first movement of the Sixth. In the draft of this idea for the first movement we can recognize the main theme of the completed first movement and something of its development, including the arpeggios in the repeat section (page 17 of the printed score).

EX 22

The sketches for the second movement, in G major, provide fresh evidence of how Sibelius's creative imagination, perhaps subconsciously, oscillates between the two tonal planes of the Fifth and Sixth symphonies. He notes down a theme which is quite obviously influenced by the principal pizzicato theme of the projected *Intrada* of the Fifth. In the definitive *Andante mosso quasi allegretto* movement, this theme is in fact found again as the final variation on the pizzicato main theme itself (page 83 in the score). It came into existence within the framework of the Sixth Symphony, even if it did not long remain there – it was soon moved into the motif table for the adagio.

The third movement in the Sixth Symphony's original plan was eventually to form the springboard of the finale. The 'fundamental' idea functions as principal theme in the plan, only to become later on the second theme of the definitive finale.

27

EX 23

Other material connected with the same theme is also to be found sketched out *inter alia* with the following decisive change:

EX 24

its tentative continuation:

EX 25

and the theme's descending form:

EX 26

Sibelius first planned a finale in D major with a playful main theme. This would soon be transferred to the Sonatina for violin and piano on which, as we have seen, he began work during Christmas 1914 and finished three months later.

EX 27

On a page of the sketch block dated 17 January 1915, the composer began sketching material for a new finale for the Sixth Symphony, surprisingly enough first in a Dorian E major.

EX 28

This motif was eventually to find its way into the finished symphony's third movement. Finally, on the same and on following pages, we find a new example of oscillation between the two symphonies. Among the material for the Fifth I have already mentioned is a harmonized motif in G minor, the embryo of the finale's E flat minor episode. Now, in connection with the conception of the Sixth Symphony, Sibelius begins to develop this fragment in D minor, retaining the harmonization 'as a finale theme?' for the Sixth.

EX 29

It is striking how near in this sketch he comes to the E flat minor episode in the finale of the Fifth Symphony. Among other things we find the zigzag movement with wide intervals, a reflection of the swinging 'Thor's hammer' movement and the pathos-laden final formula. Thus an embryo created in the first momentum of the Fifth was nurtured in the Sixth's sphere of influence into a striking figure, and then drawn back into its original habitat.

It seems that after January 1915 Sibelius temporarily left the world of the Sixth and the Fifth came back into the foreground. But as an epilogue, in June 1915, Sibelius put down the last notes in the sketchbook for that year: a motif table for the Sixth Symphony, which he here called the Fifth, and another for the Fifth, to which he gave the number VI. He first thought to put the swinging 'Thor's hammer' theme into the D minor Symphony (i.e. the definitive Sixth) but then changed his mind and returned it to its proper place by means of an arabesque-like arrow in red crayon.

The sketch block shows to how great an extent Sibelius was governed during the conception of a work by an intuitive vision of the whole. It was probably in August 1914 that he began to have a presentiment of the Fifth Symphony's basic dialectic, which is reflected in the two original themes, but it took him many months to arrive at the four-movement original plan and arrange the preliminary thematic material. Throughout the spring he worked to clarify his vision. The motif-fragments he finally selected all derived from the same mosaic figure, even if he did not know at first where to fit them in. He could even see several patterns before him at the same time, as when he worked on the Fifth and Sixth together. Then the puzzle became more difficult.

A question which naturally arises as one studies the sketch block is whether Sibelius had begun to write out the Fifth Symphony in the autumn of 1914 and spring of 1915, at the same time as he was working out the motif tables for the different movements, or whether he waited until the motif tables for the various movements had been established. The second alternative seems the more likely. No score sketches exist for the eventually discarded plan for the first movement and the Adagio. Of course, they *may* have been written and destroyed, but it looks as if Sibelius first worked towards a complete thematic plan before he began writing out the full score. Several years later he was to declare in an interview, 'I am the slave of my themes.' The composer also defined his 'slavery' in another way: 'I allow the musical thoughts and their development in my psyche to determine the form.' His first two musical thoughts for the Fifth Symphony were certainly decisive in determining the internal tension of its structure. The scherzo plan furnishes a concrete example. Originally Sibelius had planned a typical second movement with a fairly uncomplicated design from the formal point of view. But under the influence of the 'development in his psyche' of the motifs, the movement came to be a highly organized, totally unprecedented formal construction which constitutes the symphonic centrepiece of the whole work. The first thematic inspiration for the Sixth Symphony is also an instance of the generative power of one of the original motifs, and is reminiscent of Busoni's thesis, 'Every motif carries within it its own pre-destined fully matured form.' Besides motifs, key relationships were also a generative factor. Once the Fifth Symphony's basic key of E flat major had been established, the original plan began to move inside the major third circle: E flat – B major – G major. The D tonality and the strong Dorian element began the first harbinger of the Sixth.

Yet another sound world was to obfuscate the Sixth's genesis: Sibelius's fascination for the violin and cello as solo instruments was rekindled. During the period December 1914–January 1915, while his thoughts were occupied with the new symphony, he composed *Laetare anima mea, Romance* and *Rigaudon* for violin or cello with piano or orchestral accompaniment and worked on the Sonatina for violin and piano.

At about the end of March or beginning of April, Sibelius scribbled in ink over the pencilled sketches of the Sixth Symphony the title, 'Violin Concerto II / Concerto lirico'. Could this mean that the material he had intended for the Sixth Symphony could have been intended all along for a new concerto? Hardly, since the sketch block specifically states 'Sinf. VI' on pages 22 and 28. Doubtless he had in his mind the prospect of a concerto, and was perhaps exploring the potential this music might possess in a concerto rather than symphonic context. As we shall see, he went so far as to write to Breitkopf & Härtel about his stillborn concerto.

The sketch block reflects the changing development of ideas in Sibelius's musical imagination, his capacity to generate individual thematic motifs. As early as 1902 Richard Strauss had noted Sibelius's prodigality of inspiration: *'Seine Musik hat die Frische einer fast erschöpfenden Erfindung'*. His abundant thematic fertility is evident in this sketch block. Many in themselves excellent ideas are discarded, among them the Adagio theme for the Fifth Symphony. But of course, the capacity for melodic invention is not in itself the only or even the most important factor in the creative process. It is the potential of each idea that is vital. As Philip Barford put it in his remarkable essay *Beethoven as Man and Artist:* [4] 'In the imagination of a composer, the tonal idea or image is the essential datum. In his musical intellect thought is the force which binds tonal images together in structural and formal relationships.'

CHAPTER THREE

'My best years'

Sibelius began the new year on a note of optimism. His first diary entry for 1915 reads, 'These are my best years!' Nevertheless, New Year came in shrouded in fog, which in folk mythology portends frost in July. Be that as it may, both fog and frost were safe portents in the world of publishing. Two symphonies were in the process of gestation, and Sibelius wanted to get down to serious work on them. But where could he place them? Hansen in Copenhagen had declined: they were only interested in small piano pieces and songs. The Helsinki publishers were not big enough to take them on, and Breitkopf & Härtel in Leipzig were an uncertain quantity and were beleaguered in more senses than one. Sibelius wondered what the future had in store for Breitkopf and Germany itself. Postal connections through Copenhagen were expected to be cut off at any time, and there were fears that the neutrality of the Scandinavian countries was itself in danger.

If these were Sibelius's best years, for most publishers they were the worst thanks to the war. For the publishing house of Lindgren he planned '*Pensées fugitives* – a new series of compositions for violin with accompaniment of piano'. These chimeric titles were much in vogue at the time – Prokofiev's *Visions fugitives* date from this period. In the end Sibelius never used the title and his projected series resulted in some eleven pieces altogether, divided between Opp. 79 and 81.

As a kind of worldly pendant to *Laetare anima mea*, he composed a *Romance* for violin (or cello) and piano, and if the publisher so desired, he was prepared to arrange it for orchestra and also transcribe the solo part for viola. His intentions were clear: he realized that the F major *Romance* had the seeds of popularity and with the dreadful fate of *Valse triste* very much in his mind, he was anxious to cover himself against transcriptions. On further reflection he decided that the *Romance* and *Laetare anima mea* did not really belong together. He substituted a new pendant, *Devotion*, which he completed in June 1915, subsequently adding the subtitle '*Ab imo pectore*'. Another miniature was the *Rigaudon* for violin and cello, which he completed on 23 January. In his diary he designated it Op. 77, No. 3 but in his definitive catalogue it became Op. 78, No. 4. It appears as if he was uncertain how he should group these miniatures. Ideally he wanted to change the opus numbers to 29 and 30 but was unsure whether this was viable. Inspiration came early in the new year:

[11 January 1915] In an elated state all evening. Youth, inspiration and the future before me. It is as if my heart will break. This gentle New Year fragrance!

[12 January] I am torn between composition plans. I don't know which way I will turn. The symphonies are developing slowly. But I'm still uncertain about them. My small pieces for various publishers are wearing me out. How best to proceed? I am now really anxious about my artistic future. There seems no end to the amount of insignificant trivia I have had to occupy myself with since the outbreak of war. Oh well! And how happy I am with my symphonic work.

Glazunov was about to make another guest appearance in Helsinki, and Sibelius was already preparing himself for possible slights! 'Presumably I will not be invited as usual. I must be about the only musician in the world who is treated in this fashion. Strange!' Glazunov's love of Finland had remained steadfast. In 1909 he had written his *Finnish Fantasy* for orchestra, Op. 88, and five years later his *Finnish Sketches*, Op. 89. Finnish musicians could count on his goodwill in Petrograd and he always maintained close contacts with Kajanus. He arrived on 12 January and began immediate rehearsals with the orchestra. Sibelius came to Helsinki at the same time. Together with Aino Ackté, he was invited for a dinner party at Aline Borgström's, wife of Arthur Borgström, the businessman whose poem *Thaïs* he had set. Afterwards he popped into the Kämp and saw 'Glazunov and Kajanus huddled over a bottle of champagne'. The way he records the event in his diary suggests he felt, rightly or wrongly, that he was unwanted and excluded. Kajanus adored Glazunov and probably wanted to keep him to himself, or perhaps Sibelius was diffident about joining them.

Sir Henry Wood was fond of telling how Kajanus and Sibelius were sitting with Glazunov at the Kämp. The wine flowed and Glazunov, doubtless in his cups, pointed an accusing finger at Sibelius and berated him for making all too frequent recourse to ostinato figures: 'That's a drunkard's music, that's what it is!' Of course the significance of such incidents should not be exaggerated. After all, Glazunov had admired *Nightride and Sunrise*, which makes unusually extensive use of ostinato figures – and Sibelius was aware of this. On 18 January Glazunov conducted his oratorio *The King of Judea* and one of his piano concertos. The selfsame day Sibelius's diary notes: 'A wonderful winter day. Sun. Out for a walk. In a highly receptive mood. Have worked out a new theme – *all' antiqua*. Worked hard. I'm not completely well. This evening Glazunov concert in Helsinki.' He didn't go to the concert and felt uncomfortable about his absence. But later that year on

10 August, when Glazunov celebrated his fiftieth birthday, Sibelius noted in his diary 'a toast for him, the friend of Finland!'

From his friends abroad he had no news. Busoni had remained in Berlin ever since the autumn of 1914, but a Bach recital which he gave for charity was ungraciously received (he was, after all, Italian). In January 1915 Busoni set off for America and his New York concert was full of pianists – Josef Hofmann, Harold Bauer, Carl Friedberg and Percy Grainger. But after a tour of the West Coast, he ended up back in New York without any definite engagements for the autumn. Disillusioned, he returned to Europe and disembarked at Genoa, where he encountered more disappointments. Italy, now on the side of the Allies, had no position to offer him and, torn between the two great power blocs, he was in a desperate position. In great distress he turned for help to Volkmar Andreae in Zürich who found a post for him at the Conservatoire. Stenhammar, who wanted to engage Busoni for some concerts in Gothenburg, asked Sibelius to put in a good word for the Gothenburg Orchestra. This he did more than willingly. He sent a strong recommendation to Stenhammar for him to forward to Busoni, but whether it ever reached him is another matter.

One wonders whether Sibelius ever grasped how fortunate he was by comparison with his old friend. In spite of his extravagance, Sibelius's practical bourgeois instincts were strong and in building Ainola, he had safeguarded his future. Busoni, on the other hand, had never bought a house or a flat in his life; he had sold his Bach editions outright; his generosity was boundless, not least to his pupils, and was never offset by his large fees. His birthright and lifestyle were those of an itinerant artist, and his half-German, half-Italian inheritance made him more than ever rootless. Even if Sibelius was obliged to turn out instrumental trifles to keep the wolf from the door, there was at least a door to keep them from. Never did he just have to live out of a suitcase.

In March 1915 the faithful Bantock gladdened the heart of his 'dear Väinämöinen' with a letter. He had conducted the first two movements of the Third Symphony in Birmingham with his students – the finale was too difficult for them – but the war imposed special difficulties: 'In the present conditions, of course, there is comparatively little going on in the way of art: & it must naturally be the same with you. Everyone's energies are concentrated upon maintaining a place in the world where we can live & work in our own way, without being dominated by an alien & brutal ideal. When it is all over, we hope we shall be rid of a nightmare. And then the time may come again when we shall see you over here once more.' (23 March 1915)

Bantock was surely right: art was hard pressed among the warring powers. As far as music was concerned, programme policy was determined more or less by nationalist considerations, though the English seem to have been more liberal than either their French allies or the German enemy. Before the war Sibelius had complained that he stood in the international critics' firing-line. Now his music was out of range and, except in the Scandinavian countries and America, he was little played. Karl Muck conducted the First and Fourth symphonies in Boston, and the cellist Herman Sandby asked him to write a cello concerto, as he noted in his diary on 16 January. But the steady stream of press cuttings from Germany and England dried up. Life felt empty.

'Will my torment begin all over again? And what then! Become forgotten,' Sibelius asks. This idea of becoming forgotten was merely one of his torments. When Ida Aalberg, the great Finnish tragedienne, died, he dwelt on his own mortality: 'My generation is disappearing. And all of us can be replaced, they say! God only knows!' All this maudlin self-absorption becomes more digestible when it is tinged with self-irony: 'Where will all this boundless arrogance and mighty self-esteem lead to? Let it be and pray that you have inspiration. In spite of it. Poor Aino! That infinitely sensitive being. Must she be a sacrifice. It always seems so! It's terrible.'

He harps on this theme with numerous variations: 'It seems to me as if all I have accomplished is of no significance. As if my life is completely flawed. And Aino who has sacrificed everything on that altar.' (Diary, 16 February 1915) And a few days later: 'Aino in Hlk. Heard her voice in the telephone and became sentimental. How hard it is for people of her stock?' Yet Aino did not sacrifice herself but offered herself voluntarily. Margareta remarked in a retrospective article of 1972, 'When she was young, Mama read Tolstoy, but later she devoted herself entirely to Papa,' and it was not intended pejoratively. Aino did not cut herself off from the outside world but continued to read Tolstoy and other authors and generally kept herself abreast of what was happening in the cultural and political field. But instead of becoming a Tolstoyan prophet in the same way as her brother Arvid or, for example, setting up a Tolstoyan women's movement, she practised the ideals of love and service in the home, not demonstratively but unostentatiously. The relationship between the two was subtle, and with an infinite number of overtones, even if his appalling sense of money drove both Aino and Eva to distraction. Eva was expecting her first child and while her husband was in Petrograd for two months to lay the foundations of his business there, Eva stayed with her parents.

Sibelius was ashamed of his ineptitude in money matters: 'I lack any practical capacity to handle day-to-day expenses. I must earn about 3,000 marks a month but that never seems to go far enough. And I see no light at the end of the tunnel and there's no one left to turn to for help as they have all done so in the past and can't be expected to again. The reality of the situation is frightful. But it would hardly be manly to worry Aino when she makes such superhuman efforts to be economical.' (Diary, 20 January 1915) But the next day he had to find a further 200 marks, which led to a new outburst: 'For the woman of today love and happiness etc. depend on money and more money! There is no peace, no happiness when they can't have everything perfect in the home just as others have. To live for "ideals" these days is an anachronism.'

Not for Aino, who lived for his ideals, which she made her own. That their lifestyle called for money was not entirely their fault. Their daughter Ruth, now twenty, didn't give money a passing thought. She was an actress at the Finnish National Theatre and was often seen in the company of Jussi Snellman, who was fifteen years older and a theosophist. From an early age she had assumed that her father and mother existed for the sole reason that she needed a father and mother. She never saw Jean Sibelius as the focal point of the family only herself as the centre of the stage. She left school before her final year was over, auditioned for the National Theatre School and was accepted. 'Give it three years,' her father said, 'and if nothing comes of you, leave the stage.' Her response was nothing if not firm: 'Even if I spend the whole of my life doing walk-on parts, I shall never leave the theatre.' She was soon given one *ingénue* role after another, and during the spring of 1915 brought Jussi Snellman home to Ainola to meet her parents. Sibelius was initially worried by their age difference but soon formed a strong liking for his prospective son-in-law.

Sibelius possessed a quiet, reluctant admiration for those who managed to overcome life's problems: 'Erik [Eero Järnefelt] is doing very well and so are all the others! But you are suffering from the war – and acutely!' Indeed, his position was acute. He sent two piano pieces to the publisher Lindgren and asked their director, Lennart Blomstedt, to send his honorarium of 800 marks, together with an advance of a further 300, to the solicitor who handled his affairs. A loan was due for repayment, one among many; that serves to indicate his position. What pained him most, however, was the necessity to sell himself. Even the beautiful F major *Romance* prompted afterthoughts: 'Maybe it is too traditional. But *was zu machen?* . . . The fact that all this stands in the way of the symphonies depresses Aino.' (Diary, 31 January 1915)

Richard Burgin, the new leader of the Helsinki Orchestra, who was to become Koussevitzky's 'concertmaster' in Boston, played the Violin Concerto in Helsinki. Aino and Eva went into town for the concert. At this time Sibelius could not have had many opportunities of hearing an artist of international calibre play the concerto but unaccountably he remained at home. He was delighted with the success Burgin had with the work and noted that it was now 'as if Bis's and others' ears have at last opened to the concerto'. Aino was transported. Sibelius comments in his diary: 'Strange how Aino understands my pieces and how sound is her artistic judgement! Well, perhaps it is not so strange really since she has been with me in its creation.' (Diary, 2 February 1915)

In spite of this success, he remained in a deep depression, not rising until late in the afternoon so as to put off getting up to face life: 'I will never become the great composer Aino and I dreamt of. I have too many characteristics working against me – a strong and irresistible sense of isolation and disappointment at what I have actually accomplished.' (Diary, 11 February 1915) He even wonders whether he isn't played out. '30 bagatelles in year + a symph. poem. Life is running away like sand through one's fingers.' It is not always easy to decide what was cause and effect: was it the bagatelles which inhibited the flow of his symphonic inspiration? Or did he turn to the bagatelles because of a hold-up in the symphonic flow?

He now chose the middle way between the miniatures and the symphony by taking up the Violin Sonatina again. The middle of February finds him engrossed in the first movement: 'Dreamt I was twelve and a virtuoso. Childhood heavens and stars. Many stars.' (Diary, 12 February 1915) The next day he felt that he had to 'battle for life', i.e. to be able to write his new symphony. But in any event he continued with the sonatina, working on the second movement in a mood of 'loneliness and dejection'. After a good deal of writing and rewriting, he finished the whole piece in March.

'When my work is going well, I don't give a hang for what any Tom, Dick and Harry thinks.' (Diary, 17 February 1915) Other diary entries show that he thought it was high time to turn to bigger things: 'Best to get out of the world where I am working only to pay off bank interest. The worst is that my nerves have gone to pieces. To go to Helsinki in this state would be a drain on my resources. How will Aino cope with it all? If only I could keep it from her as I did in former times.' Where was he to turn? Scandinavia was the only real possibility. But Tofft's and Hecht's attack on the Fourth Symphony in Copenhagen in 1912 had left a sour taste in his mouth, and more recently the Norwegian critic Hjalmar Borgström had made a slighting reference to him when Selim Palmgren had visited Christiania to play his Second Piano Concerto (*The River*): 'Palmgren composes more sensitively but nonetheless with as much power as his celebrated countryman Sibelius.'[1] Peterson-Berger in Stockholm was unpredictable, and the following year sharpened his pen on both the Violin Concerto and the Fourth Symphony.

But Gothenburg was different. There lived Wilhelm Stenhammar, as Sibelius put it in his letter to Busoni,[2] 'a great artist and a gentleman to his fingertips; his expertly trained orchestra and their musical public have no rivals in the North'. That the Fourth Symphony had been greeted with little understanding by the Gothenburg public was understood and forgiven. He had set his sights on Gothenburg but his indecision had sorely tried Stenhammar's patience (and exasperated the orchestra's management). They had begun negotiating his visit as early as January 1914, when Sibelius had promised to come in March, only to withdraw at the last minute: 'It is impossible for me now. My conscience forces me to this. But when I have some new works ready next year, as I hope, it would give me great joy to perform them in Gothenburg.'[3]

Sibelius saw it almost as a matter of honour to come with something new in his baggage. Stenhammar did not give up and a new agreement was reached for two concerts in February 1915. Of course there were practical difficulties. Sibelius asked Stenhammar to get the orchestral material of *The Oceanides* and *The Bard* from Germany: 'I still have no new symphony *pauvre diable*. But soon!'

However, on 1 December he wrote another somewhat laconic letter to Stenhammar: 'Yet again I am forced to withdraw from the forthcoming engagement in Gothenburg. I must have my new work ready. Only then can I come.' And in his diary he notes: 'Have written to Stenhammar. Am going back into my shell for a bit.'

As Stenhammar pointed out in his reply, this put him in a highly embarrassing position: 'You seem to have got it into your head that you cannot come to us without bringing a brand new symphony. This thought may be enormously flattering for Gothenburg but under present conditions is completely impractical . . . you have nevertheless an abundance of new works to bring, and you must understand that for the moment our public will prefer to hear the old ones. However, I assume that your cancellation could have other reasons, as was the case last season, and a reason which I need hardly say that I fully respect, your overwhelming need for time and freedom to work. But is it not possible that this need can itself be too powerful and indeed become tyrannical. In fact, when you are engrossed in a major undertaking, it can be directly beneficial to emerge from isolation and show yourself to the public . . . You cannot come before your new piece is ready. Then you can come. But are you sure of that? Are you certain that, when that day comes, there will not be new plans for new works, which will have a similar hold over you and must also be finished. That seems more than probable to me.'

Stenhammar did not pass on the news to the orchestra's management and ended by asking him 'to take this chalice' from him. He was rewarded by an about turn: 'From my heart I thank you for your letter. In each line I see yet again your great sympathy for my music. I shall come. I hope to have a novelty with me for a first performance.'

The concerts were agreed for 22 and 24 March, but to raise money for the fare he had to finish the Violin Sonatina! It was ready by the 12th; on the 13th he collected his fee from Lindgren in Helsinki, and on Sunday the 14th set out on his journey to Gothenburg. He bade farewell to Aino and his little twelve-year-old daughter Katarina, who was reading Strindberg's *Inferno*, playing the piano and enjoying sleigh-rides in the moonlight!

It was now nine months since he had raised a baton. The rapturous ovations in the Shed in Norfolk were becoming dim memories and he longed for new ones. Now once again he was an artist on tour – and even if he did not have a brand-new work in his briefcase, he would at least give *The Oceanides* its European première. The pea soup he ordered in Riihimäki while waiting for his connecting train to the north tasted like nectar. Even the monotonous journey round the Bothnian Gulf (the ferry between Turku and Helsinki was hazardous on account of ice and wartime conditions) seemed like an adventure. Karunki in northern Finland struck him as a kind of Klondike; northern Sweden he saw as 'sunshine and its streams full of trout'. In Stockholm he had a splendid time with Armas Järnefelt and Liva, his second wife. At his favourite restaurant, the Operakällaren, whose interior remains one of the finest examples of *art nouveau* in Scandinavia, he stumbled quite unexpectedly upon his old friend Adolf Paul in a telephone booth. Paul held Swedish citizenship and had decided to leave the rigours of wartime Germany for the calmer environment of neutral Sweden. Paul impulsively changed his plans to go to Gothenburg for Sibelius's concerts.

The day after his arrival Sibelius wrote to Aino: 'I spent yesterday with Stenhammar, my old friend and admirer of the Fourth Symphony. A wonderful understanding. We talked a great deal about you. Today – that's to say, just now – rehearsal of *The Oceanides*. Later, dinner at the Mannheimers . . . I haven't bought an overcoat yet. It's cold but the weather is already turning towards Spring.' (20 March 1915)

He had taken Stenhammar's advice about the programmes: for the Monday subscribers who had hissed the Fourth Symphony in 1911, he took the Second Symphony preceded by the Second Set of *Scènes historiques*, two movements from *Swanwhite* and *The Oceanides*. One can sense a touch of stage fright in his next letter: 'Soon the concert. I have been with all sorts of people – *The Oceanides* sounds glorious. Stenhammar is very taken with my pieces. He is such a refined person.' (22 March 1915)

After the concert he could relax a little: 'Great success (although I was nervous). Stenhammar was captivated by *The Oceanides*, which is really something wonderful. Yesterday I was at a large supper party at the Bratt's [Stenhammar's sister-in-law] and was presented with a walking-stick of Spanish reed with a silver handle, and very rare – 200 years old, as well as roses and much else.'

The second concert was for the more sophisticated Gothenburg public. His diary records: 'Conducted excellently. Programme well chosen with a first half of more brilliant pieces: the first set of *Scènes historiques*, the *Nocturne* from the *King Christian II* suite, *The Path of the Lover* from *Rakastava* and *Lemminkäinen's Homeward Journey*. In the second half the Fourth Symphony and *The Oceanides* – the last wonderful! After the final number there was a deafening torrent of applause, stamps, cries of bravo, a standing ovation and fanfares from the orchestra.'

While the descriptive tone-painting of *The Oceanides* struck a responsive chord from both the public and critics, the Fourth Symphony still posed difficulties. But Sibelius's conducting won high praise: 'Our orchestra has been inspired by a dedication and spiritual power with which we have not been spoilt in recent times ... the orchestra seems to have undergone a refreshing renewal.'[4]

Sibelius had set a number of Ernst Josephsson's poems; indeed, these settings must be numbered among his finest songs. So while he was in Gothenburg he took the opportunity of paying a visit to the Art Gallery, where some of Josephsson's paintings are hung. Although he started as a follower of Courbet and Manet, Ernst Josephsson (1851–1906) became something of a symbolist visionary and among his most celebrated works is *The Water-Spirit*, who stands as a symbol of the creative artist. Towards the end of his life Josephsson suffered from mental instability and it is from this period that some of his most powerful works come. They evince a highly developed feeling for contour and it is said that they exercised some influence on Picasso.

What did he think as he stood before Josephsson's *The Water-Spirit*? Six years earlier, in 1909, he had set Josephsson's poem of the same name; now he saw the 'black-haired youth as pale as a ghost', but the water-spirit who inspired the boy with his 'bejewelled harp' is not in the picture – its disappearance is already hinted at in the closing lines of the poem.

> The youth was only my fantasy
> The Water spirit the waterfall that fell nearby
> Caressing my cheek with its spray.

Josephsson's concept must have meant much to Sibelius. In the song the tritone which was to be the kernel of the Fourth Symphony appears, and Josephsson's poem may have contributed something to the inspiration of the inner landscape of the symphony itself.

It is not known whether Sibelius ever saw Josephsson's drawing *Jubal*. If he did, this too should have given him much the same feeling of artistic and spiritual kinship. The harp strings, the curving lines of the swans' necks, the rising curves of the sunflower stalks are all there in the contours of Sibelius's vocal line and piano figuration. But among the works from the period of Josephsson's illness is an illustration of another poem which Sibelius had set, *Duke Magnus and the Mermaid*. For anyone knowing only the poem and the Sibelius setting, Josephsson's water-colour would come as something of a shock. There is no question of any friendly creature from the waters bearing her nobleman through the night till at daybreak he is 'found among violets, unharmed, slumbering by the river bank'. Far from it; Duke Magnus is shown ensnared between two huge mermaid tails, rigid and taut like a bow, listening in ecstasy to her harp playing. Josephsson's biographer Erik Blomberg rightly sees this water-colour as an expression of his maternal bond. As a ten-year-old the poet and painter had lost his father, symbolized in the drawing as the sun. As a boy he was full of vitality and had a strong appetite for outdoor life, though he was prone to sentimentality and had a weaker, dreamier side to his nature. Later on he shrank from declaring himself to the woman he loved because of an illness. His Oedipal inclinations became further accentuated and a tendency towards homosexuality surfaced.

Sibelius was fascinated by the Josephsson phenomenon, for their lives betrayed strong parallels and differences. Sibelius too had lost his father in childhood, at an even earlier age than Josephsson, but had a strong surrogate father figure in his down-to-earth, straightforward grandmother, at whom he could let off steam. He freed himself at an early stage from his mother's dominance and turned to his aunt Evelina, but theirs was an uncomplicated relationship and her feeling for him was not possessive. When, after a number of escapades, he married Aino, he achieved a fulfilled, happy relationship: 'You are the delight of my eyes, my heart's repose – the object of my love and its life-giving force . . . never could I have dreamt that I could partake in such happiness,' he wrote at the beginning of their marriage. For Sibelius the young Josephsson's poetic vision of the mermaid who cushions her knight among the violets was close to his own. The dominating masculine qualities of the mermaid of Josephsson's water-colour were for him alien, yet he sensed in the feverish sensibility of Josephsson qualities in his own psyche – fear of the mental disturbance that had afflicted his sister, and his craving for alcohol which was to hold him in thrall. His visit to the museum made so strong an impression on him that he wrote of it in his diary.

This is the only occasion save one when he records his impressions of a foreign art collection, the other being his visit to an exhibition of French painting in Christiania in the autumn of 1910, when he muses on Matisse's influence on Norwegian painting. The following month he looked back on his travel impressions: 'I am really pleased that I went to Gothenburg. And to such good purpose. How near I was to pulling out of it. And what a glorious sea of orchestral sound. Stenhammar did me an enormous service by doing all he did.' (29 March 1915)

Opus Numbering 1909, 1911 and 1915

Before proceeding any further, it may be useful to clear up the vexed question of Sibelius's opus numbering. He never followed up the notion outlined in his diary on 10 January 1915 of changing the Opp. 76 and 77 to 29 and 30. They were to remain in their rightful chronological place in his opus list. But the two series of piano pieces he had written for Westerlund, the first begun in November 1912 and the second a year later, were both assigned low opus numbers (40 and 34 respectively) and thus placed close to the First Symphony, Op. 39 (1900), and *The Rapids-Riders' Brides* or *Ferrymans' Brides*, Op. 33 (1897).

But these are far from being the only misleading opus numbers in Sibelius's definitive catalogue. For example, *Kullervo*, Op. 7 (1892), is flanked by the *Cassazione*, Op. 6 (1904), and *The Lizard*, Op. 8, of 1909. However did these bizarre numbers arise? It has been suggested that Sibelius clearly thought that his list of works looked better if such bagatelles as Opp. 34 and 40 were placed in the more modest context of the 1890s rather than the more exalted company of the Fourth and Fifth symphonies. But if this were the case, why would he make no effort to hide their date of composition? Besides that, had he not planned to move back such masterpieces as *Teodora* and *Jubal* from their originally low opus number 45 to the even more misleading 35, and *The Bard* from the correct 70 *bis* to 64? But the changes were not intended to sow confusion about the chronology of his work but had a much simpler function. Sibelius's intentions were quite straight-forward: to eliminate earlier works from his opus list and insert in their place compositions which enjoyed his imprimatur. This inevitably gave rise to chronological inconsistencies.

OPUS LIST 1909 (OPP. 1–58)

Up to 1905 Sibelius did not assign opus numbers to his works, either in manuscript or published form. The question of opus numbers first arose in February 1905, when Sibelius signed his contract with Lienau. But already by the end of May, Lienau was asking what opus number he should give the *Pelléas et Mélisande* music. In the agreement of 20 July 1905 between Fazer (Helsingfors Nya Musikhandel) and Breitkopf & Härtel, when the Leipzig firm took over the catalogue, the published works were referred to solely by their publisher's catalogue number; manuscripts had no number at all. Subsequently Breitkopf received a catalogue covering only those works from Op. 5 through to Op. 45, which Sibelius had up to this point assigned to Fazer and his other Finnish publishers, Wasenius and Lindgren. There were gaps where an opus number existed but no work was attached. Later in the year, on 4 November, Breitkopf wrote to Sibelius asking about these missing pieces. About them, however, Sibelius kept his silence.

A numerical opus list in Sibelius's own hand from the late summer of 1909 gives some ideas about these gaps. It comprises 58 opus numbers, set out largely in chronological order from the C sharp minor Variations, Op. 1, through to the Ten Piano Pieces, Op. 58 (1909), together with some thirteen unnumbered works. This list gives a far better idea of their actual sequence of composition than the three later work lists (1911, 1915 and the definitive one). Take for example the first ten items:

Op. 1   Variations in C sharp minor for string quartet (1888)
Op. 2   String Quartet in A minor (1889)
Op. 3   String Quartet in B flat (1889 completed 1890)
Op. 4   String Trio in A (1889)
Op. 5   Six Impromptus for piano (1893)
Op. 6   Overture in E major for orchestra (1891)

Op. 7   *Ballet Scene* for orchestra (1891)
Op. 8   *Kullervo*, symphonic poem in five parts for soloists, chorus and orchestra (1892)
Op. 9   *En Saga* for orchestra (1893 rev 1902)
Op. 10   Piano Quintet in G minor (1890)

That gives a more accurate picture of Sibelius's development as a composer from his last two student years through to the first two years after his initial breakthrough. It is only the printed works that disturb the chronological order – had he reversed the positions of the published *Impromptus* and the unpublished Piano Quintet, the sequence would be more or less accurate.

But the longer Sibelius pondered over this list in 1909, the greater his unease. He began to regret that he had included some of his youthful indiscretions and occasional pieces. And so he put blue crayon marks in the margin beside some twenty works that he intended to remove or revise. Of the first ten, six were to lose their place: four chamber music pieces from his student years in Helsinki (Opp. 1, 2, 4 and 10) and two orchestral pieces written in Vienna (Opp. 5 and 6). Later on in the catalogue he removed the *Ceremonial Cantata* of 1894 (Op. 15), the *Coronation Cantata* (Op. 19), his opera *Jungfrun i tornet (The Maiden in the Tower)* (Op. 20), the *Serenade* for baritone and orchestra to words of Stagnelius, along with a number of smaller pieces. Then the question arose of how to fill the gaps that inevitably arose. Quite a few opus numbers referred to published works and these could not be moved. And so Sibelius could only make use of so far unpublished works. These, of course, provided a strategic reserve of uneven quality. To them he added, presumably by accident, *Kyllikki* – three piano pieces which he had already listed as Op. 41, No. 1 to Breitkopf. *Kyllikki* displaced the choral song *Har du mod?* from Op. 41 to 31, where it now kept company with, among other things, *The Song of the Athenians*. A more questionable notion was the insertion of the funeral hymn *Natus in curas* in the space previously occupied by the Overture in A minor (1902), which had curiously been allotted Op. 21 just before the much earlier *Lemminkäinen Suite*.

Of course, the reserves of unpublished music were limited, and another possibility was to make use of newly-composed works to fill in these gaps. And so in order to avoid too great a chronological discrepancy, Sibelius would remove a not-too-distant work in its favour, then place that further back in his opus list, and so on until he encountered one that he could remove altogether. Another means was of course to revise an older work so as to make it worthy of inclusion in his opus list. A diary entry of January 1910 lists some eighteen works under the title 'Old Pieces to be Rewritten', among them the two hitherto unpublished *Lemminkäinen Legends* (*Lemminkäinen and the Maidens of the Island* and *Lemminkäinen in Tuonela*) and surprisingly enough, the second, fourth and fifth movements of *Kullervo*.

43

Later that year he managed to complete two of these revisions: the *Impromptu* for women's voices and orchestra and *Tulen synty (The Origin of Fire)*.

In the summer of 1911, after the completion of the Fourth Symphony, his plans to revise his earlier works and overhaul his catalogue had advanced far enough for him to make a new list of compositions. Compared with the 1909 list, there are many deletions, revised dates and additions, but even so there are still significant differences from the next complete list of 1915. The catalogue would seem to have gone as far as Op. 64, the *Wedding Procession* from the incidental music to Adolf Paul's *Die Sprache der Vogel* (1911). Later on, it seems, he added the Three Sonatinas for piano, Op. 67 (1912). Some twenty-one items are listed as being without opus numbers, among them 'The Miller's Song' (English text), presumably a commission from America. How far these concerns were preoccupying him can be seen from further diary entries: in the middle of August 1911, he lists 'Further suggestions for incorrect opus numbers', and adds sixteen numbers – which he later changed.

Both the 1911 catalogue and the diary entries paint a pretty chaotic picture. With their countless changes, underlinings and crossings-out, additions, rings made with pencil or pen, red, green or blue crayon, they represent a strange mixture of doubt and frustration. He was undoubtedly in the grip of a compulsion to sort out these matters once and for all, and his zeal at times assumes almost manic proportions, when he worries about a relatively insignificant song like *Har du mod?*. He even allowed it to disrupt work on the Fourth Symphony in September 1911, when he turned to the Pageant music he wrote for the Press Pension Celebrations of 1899, and compiled from them the first set of *Scènes historiques*. At the same time he moved them from Op. 26, where *Finlandia* remained – back one opus number to 25. The *Fantasy* for cello and piano, Op. 25, was then renamed *Malinconia* and moved back to Op. 20, thus displacing *The Maiden in the Tower*, which disappears altogether from the opus list. As his Op. 1 Sibelius now gives two representative pieces from his study years, the Romance (1888) and the *Perpetuum mobile* (1891)[5] for violin and piano.

The provenance of the song *Arioso*, Op. 3, is another puzzle, and the more I have looked into its genesis, the more convinced I have become that it was not composed 'before 1890' or 'in 1893' or 1897 – as Sibelius has variously said, but was *composed* and not *reworked* in 1911. A later date of 1913 given in some sources is incorrect. The evidence for this can be briefly enumerated.

First, *Arioso* is not mentioned in any earlier list. It is not in the 1909 list of 'Old pieces to be re-worked'; nor in the list of August 1911, 'Further suggestions for incorrect opus numbers', Sibelius made in his diary. In the 1911 list, the title *Arioso* has been inserted in pencil in Op. 3, covering the earlier entry in ink, which was the Scherzo from the B flat String Quartet.

Secondly, there is further support for this view in his diary entries:

[14 October 1911] Worked on the cantata *Men from the plains* etc, and a little on *Arioso*.

[15 October] Worked on *Arioso*.

[17 October] Scored, made piano arrangement, and a fair copy of *Arioso*, Op. 3.

[18 October] In Helsinki. Sold Op. 3.

He 'worked' on *Arioso*. Nowhere does he say 'rework' or 'revise', as he had done about the *Romance* and the *Perpetuum mobile* or *Epilogue*.

But if *Arioso* was a brand-new work, why did he give it so misleading an opus number? The answer is to be found in the contract he had with his publisher. He sold *Arioso* – as he had the *Romance* and *Epilogue* – to Apostol's representative Zucco, 'a devil to deal with about money'. Strictly speaking, he should not have done so, as he had promised Breitkopf in September the right of first refusal for 'every new or even older and unpublished work'.

Apostol immediately offered Breitkopf *Arioso* for an exceedingly large sum. As early as 24 October (only a week or so after the sale) Breitkopf made discreet enquiries from Sibelius 'whether this perhaps concerned an earlier composition? Otherwise you would surely have turned to us directly, as indeed you have been accustomed to do, to our great pleasure, for so long a time'. This gentlemanly reprimand, though wrapped in cotton wool, at the same time gave Sibelius his cue. According to a draft he made on 31 October, Sibelius answered: '*Arioso* is an old work, written before 1890. It is listed as Op. 3 in my opus catalogue. I received a relatively high sum for it, as Apostol belongs to those publishers – among them some German houses – who bombard me with offers of all kinds. My fee went to offset some outstanding bank debits.' One could well imagine that Zucco had trapped Sibelius with an advance, which the composer had paid for with *Arioso*. However, so as not in any way to endanger his relations with Breitkopf, he camouflaged the piece with a low opus number, in the knowledge that they would more easily overlook him parting with an early work than a brand-new one.

Furthermore, the late date for its first performance (18 September 1913) with Ida Ekman points to 1911. Had an earlier version existed, Sibelius would hardly have withheld it from Ida Ekman or Aino Ackté, who were busily championing his songs at the turn of the century. Stylistically though, at first glance the matter seems more problematic. The harmonic simplicity of the song is matched in the earlier Runeberg settings. Yet it is also to be found in later ones such as *Fåfäng önskan* (1910) and *Vem styrde hit din väg?*

(1917). But the refined string writing surely points to the later date, though the piano accompaniment could well be earlier – just as *Rakastava* (transcribed for strings in 1912–13) went back to a choral piece.

However, there is one stylistic factor which is decisive, and that is the vocal tessitura. Sibelius never composed such wide-ranging vocal lines during the 1890s but only much later in *Höstkväll (Autumn Evening)* and *Luonnotar*. But could these also not have come into being as the result of a revision? *Rakastava* shows that the composer left the vocal line largely intact, except where he replaced it with completely instrumentally-designed material. You can say with some degree of certainty that a line which had been determined by words remained an invariable ingredient in a Sibelius reworking.

There is an interesting postscript. At the request of the publisher Westerlund, into which Apostol was incorporated on the owner's death, Sibelius testified on 28 April 1942 that he had sold *Arioso* to Apostol in the year 1893. But at that time Apostol was a military bandmaster and it was only after he retired that he founded his publishing house. Even if it had existed in the 1890s, it is surely unlikely that Sibelius would have sold *Arioso* twice to the same publisher! No, the evidence points to 1911 as the date of composition with nothing to point to an earlier date.

THE 1915 OPUS LIST (OPP. 1–82)

Opus numbers again rear their head in the autumn of 1915, when Otto Andersson suggested a work list to mark the occasion of his fiftieth birthday. A fair copy was made by his small daughter Katarina and given to Andersson on 27 November 1915. Unlike the two earlier lists, it includes the date and place of compositions, but omits works without opus numbers. This goes up to Op. 82, and offers yet another Op. 1, the *Five Christmas Songs*.

To return to the two series of piano pieces which Sibelius completed in 1914 and placed in the chronologically misleading places of Opp. 35 and 50 – he could only do this at the cost of some disruption and, as part of what we might flippantly call 'Operation Lizard', *Ödlan (The Lizard)* had originally been moved from Op. 59 to Op. 40, moving its occupant, the *Cassazione*, back to Op. 34, and the *Impromptu* for women's voices back to 19, and pushing the *Coronation Cantata* out into the cold.

It would appear that Sibelius was not pleased with the idea of the three 'improvisations', *Sandels, Snöfrid,* and *Islossningen i Uleå älv (The Melting of the Ice on the Uleå River)* appearing under separate opus numbers (28, 29 and 30), and decided to bring them together under one umbrella, Op. 28a, b and c. So he needed two new works or sets of pieces to put in their places. One knocked *The Lizard* from Op. 40 down to 29a, and the other moved the *Cassazione*, Op. 34, down four points to Op. 30. Another source of dissatisfaction was the *Wedding Procession* to Adolf Paul's play *Die Sprache der Vogel*, which had an opus number all to itself. He therefore moved *The Bard* –

correctly given in his diary as Op. 70b – into its place, moving the Wedding Procession into Op. 29b, alongside *The Lizard*.

Now we come to the 1915 catalogue, after three years and many agonizing realignments. At this point Sibelius decided that he did not want the *Kullervo* Symphony, now Op. 7, flanked by the E major Overture from his year in Vienna and the Six School Songs, Op. 8. And so both of these went, and the *Cassazione*, Op. 30, was unceremoniously moved into the place of Op. 6 and *The Lizard*, Op. 29a, moved down to Op. 8. At the same time the *Wedding Procession* was sent into disgrace as part of the Works without Opus Number list! Now Opus 29 and 30 were again 'free'. At one time he had thought to fill them with Opp. 76 and 77 but thought better of it and instead took pity on *Snöfrid* and *The Melting of the Ice on the Uleå River*, which reverted from their Op. 28b and 28c back to their original home. All this juggling resulted in the removal of the *Coronation Cantata* (1896), the *Ballet Scene*, the *Carminalia* arrangements and other pieces from his catalogue, and a good deal of chronological confusion in what remained.

The 1909 work list gave a more or less chronologically accurate picture of Sibelius's output up to Op. 58. Important early works occupy their rightful place even if they may not hold their own artistically with later compositions. But later, when he began to feel uncomfortable with (or not to put too fine a point on it, ashamed of) his earlier works, chronological exactitude became a secondary consideration, artistic quality the first. But this revision was basically an unsatisfactory compromise: true, he managed – unfortunately – to get rid of a number of pieces, but the compositions with which he plugged the gaps were by no means always of the highest quality. Moreover, there were a number of works of lesser importance already in print that he could do nothing about. Indeed, he lost sight of the fact that in a true historic perspective, these early works were nothing to be ashamed of. He could well have used the 1909 catalogue as a basis on which to build.

But perhaps all this served as a kind of creative stimulus, for in the 1909 catalogue the choral suite *Rakastava* is listed as Op. 18, No. 1, without any blue marks, underlinings or crossings in the margin. Only as late as the autumn of 1911 did it come under the by now familiar scrutiny. This decision to look at the work again resulted in the suite for strings and timpani, with which we are now so familiar as Op. 14. The result of this was the loss of the previous Op. 14, the *Ceremonial Cantata* of 1894, and its removal from its proud place in his opus list.

CHAPTER FOUR

1915

After his trip to Gothenburg, Sibelius felt on top of the world. The change of scene and the excitement of the concerts spurred him to return to the challenge of the Fifth Symphony: 'The symphony continues to consume my thoughts. When will I again be engulfed in its great torrent?' That same day, 30 March 1915, he sketched out a new thematic table for it. But the first movement continued to trouble him. On top of that there was another project looming into view.

At the beginning of April he wrote to Breitkopf & Härtel offering them a new violin concerto: 'But before embarking on this project, I would like to know, should you approve the work, whether you would be willing to pay me five thousand Reichsmarks for an edition of 10,000?' Among the sketches for the Sixth Symphony (on page 22 of the sketch block) Sibelius has scribbled *Violin Concerto II / Concerto lirico*. But almost immediately he was seized with doubts, and on 10 April appended in green crayon a question mark after the title. Of course, the notion of turning a symphony into a violin concerto is not out of the question. Brahms's D minor Piano Concerto began life in this way.

The ball was now in Breitkopf's court. Their reply was as courteous as it was cautious. They would best be in a position to make up their minds when they had seen the concerto, then the question of an honorarium could be resolved to their mutual satisfaction. An advance of a few thousand inflation-ridden Reichsmarks would merely have been soaked up by Sibelius's debts, and he would have been under an obligation either to proceed with adapting the material of the Sixth Symphony into a violin concerto or composing an entirely fresh one. But Breitkopf's cool response gave the composer time for second thoughts; on 28 April, the day he received their letter, his diary summed up his composition plans: 'Song for B & H, *Kyssen (The Kiss)* Runeberg, [Op. 72, No. 3]. The new violin concerto. Fifth Symphony. 'Karisto song' *Kaiutar*, [Op. 72, No. 4]. Also for chorus and orchestra, *Young Hellenes*, Rydberg.' Not long afterwards he abandoned the concerto and, according to the sketch block, the ideas reverted to their place in the future Sixth Symphony. And so Breitkopf never got their Violin Concerto

No. 2. Nor, for that matter, the Fifth, Sixth and Seventh symphonies and *The Tempest* and much else. Naturally, wartime conditions were disruptive, but a more positive response to the new concerto might well have served to strengthen the continuity of their relationship in the critical post-war years.

Sibelius registered the changing seasons with the eye of an impressionist:

> [9 April 1915] Walked and toasted the approach of the spring with the air, mist and haze.

> [10 April] There is warmth in the air and winter is in transmigration. At last it is mild, and radiates youth and adventure.

The scent of spring inspired him to resume his work on the Fifth Symphony: 'Walked in the cold spring sun. Memories of old affronts and humiliations came back. Had powerful visions of the Fifth Symphony, the new one.'(18 April)

His spirits continued on an upward curve for the next few days:

> [20 April 1915] Have been in high spirits on account of the symphony. The day is grey and cold but spring is gathering force.

> [21 April] Just before ten-to-eleven saw sixteen swans. One of the greatest experiences in life. Oh God, what beauty: they circled over me for a long time. Disappeared into the hazy sun like a silver ribbon, which glittered from time to time. Their cries were of the same woodwind timbre as the cranes but without any tremolo. The swans are closer to trumpets, though there is an element of the sarussophone. A low suppressed memory of a small child's cry. Nature's mystery and life's melancholy. The Fifth Symphony's finale theme.

EX 30

The trumpet will bind it together . . . This must now come to me which has so long resonated in the air. Have been transported today.

But the following day found him less buoyant: 'Working at the symphony which is further than ever from its final form.'

> [24 April 1915] The swans are always in my thoughts and give life its lustre. It is curious that nothing in the whole world, be it art, literature or music, has anything like the same effect on me as these swans, cranes and wild geese. Their sound and their very being. Apropos the symphonies: they are for my credo as I perceived it at various stages in my life. Which

is why they are all so different. *Nos mutamur in temporibus*. Or better still: *tempora mutantur et nos in illis mutamur*.

The diary shows that he worked on the first movement of the symphony and the transition from theme A to theme B during the next two days, but then had to turn to other things, among them the songs *Kyssen* and *Kaiutar*. The diary betrays his feelings of distaste and anxiety: 'Doubts about the future. Will I be able to row the boat back to land? Time presses. Everything is falling apart around me and I am on my own, alone.' (29 April 1915)

There were no more guest appearances abroad for Sibelius in 1915 or, for that matter, the next five years. In Helsinki he had at his disposal a much reduced wartime orchestra of some forty players, all surviving on starvation wages. The great orchestral rivalry of past years had gone. With the advent of war, the German players who formed the backbone of Schnéevoigt's orchestra had been forced to leave Finland. Instead of two, there was now only one orchestra – the Helsinki City Orchestra – the podium being shared by the two rival conductors, Kajanus and Schnéevoigt.

Of the two, Schnéevoigt enjoyed the greater international renown. He was a frequent guest in Stockholm and was soon to be the Concert Society's permanent conductor. At this time Stockholm's musical life was dominated by Finnish conductors: Sibelius's brother-in-law Armas Järnefelt was in charge of the Opera Orchestra. Indeed, Sibelius himself could have conducted in Stockholm every season had he so wished. Schnéevoigt had hoped to bring him over in the spring of 1915, but Sibelius declined the invitation. A diary entry noted: 'Of course I said no, as the Opera invited me previously and I refused.' Be that as it may, one senses that his decision may in part have been motivated by the prospect of being subjected to Peterson-Berger's barbed pen. When Schnéevoigt conducted the Second Symphony in April, the audience broke into applause after each movement and Peterson-Berger's review was highly respectful: 'Sibelius is . . . a kind of Finnish Byron in music, with an attitude of Romantic dandyism and behind that something atavistic, east European, *zigeuner*-like. When he reveals himself it is as if he unfurled his fine linen shirt tails, to show motley wild figures engraved on his shaggy chest . . . in its psychological richness, this is decidedly music of the future.'[1]

The review did not escape Sibelius's eagle eye: 'Petterson [*sic*] Berger wrote a strangely interesting definition of me and my art.' (Diary, 1 May 1915)

America loomed like a far-off Eldorado. He corresponded with Stoeckel and was sent reviews, good and not so good. But an unfavourable notice could ruin his day:

[8 April 1915] As far as America is concerned – now doubtful whether I will ever go there again. Presumably they are scheming against me. Think so on account of a particular review, sent to me from Norfolk, won't think of it any more. In any event won't go there unless there is a lot of money in prospect. How strange it is with all these intrigues! One laughs it off but they hurt for a long time. Yes, maybe always.

Sibelius drank black coffee, one cup after another, to the point where he began to feel shaky: 'Is it going to be impossible for me to give it up? But everyone must have some kind of poison.' Once his fear of cancer receded, he found it more and more difficult to resist wine and cigars. Even before his trip to Gothenburg he had spent a pleasant February evening in the comfort of the library with his son-in-law Arvi when he had succumbed to temptation: 'Arvi was here unexpectedly. Had a cigar with him and drank a tiny bit of red wine. The tobacco tasted excellent. But I don't think I'll ever be able to smoke much. Felt it immediately in the throat.'

His spirits immediately picked up and persuaded him to 'have high hopes of the violin sonatina' on which he was working. His fall from grace, the first since 1908, was followed by others. As far as wine was concerned, he was very cautious to start with – he knew his own weaknesses. 'Tippled a little wine. But the old spirit is gone,' he noted. Tobacco may have irritated his throat but was otherwise less dangerous. By early May he was puffing away full blast with his cigars: 'It is as if I have my youth back – I can work better if I have the house to myself. Why, I wonder?' He continued with his smoking and told himself that his 'throat would last for a long time to come', and that it would help cure his 'hypochondria'. His doctor had forbidden smoking until after midsummer and even went so far as to threaten to extend the ban to coffee, which Sibelius was drinking in inordinate quantity.

The next day his diary mentions that he met Eero Järnefelt looking 'young and elegant', which prompted him to muse on how shabby and old he was looking himself. With Järnefelt he discussed what was for both of them a topical issue: age and rejuvenation. With the approach of his fiftieth birthday, these matters, and life's evanescence, were in the forefront of Sibelius's mind. In Gothenburg he was still able to play the part of a young man to Stenhammar's sister-in-law Olga Bratt, whom he admired – at a respectful distance. But the day was approaching when he would be a grandfather, which prompted further musings on age. He found scant consolation in the traditional belief that you are as old as you feel, and that it is your mental outlook that determines your age: 'This is not so. Our bodies are to a large extent the decisive factor. These old bald turkey-cocks that go around thinking that they are loved. They are, to say the least, sad wretches. Every age, like every season, has its special distinction. My goodness, how wise, intelligent and above all young I am! . . . The sap still rises in you just as it does in other fifty-year-old trees. But alas, the days when one sat on a bank, held hands and swore eternal fidelity are over. I say that in the hope that it is so. But the *wiederholte Pubertät* among geniuses, of which Goethe spoke, flatters me.' (4 June 1915)

A letter from Adolf Paul delighted him: 'Thank you for your wonderful music in Gothenburg, on which I will feast for many months to come. I cannot show as much as I would like how and what I feel, and perhaps at times seem a little crabby since things have not turned out quite in the way I had wanted. But you know none the less that a large part of my life is called Janne and another equally large part is filled by his music . . . My belief in happiness was restored once more, when my wild journeyings brought me together with you again, my glorious friend . . . The *Nocturne* (from *King Christian II*) made me feel young again.'

The younger generation of composers was also making headway: Heikki Klemetti conducted the first performance of Madetoja's *Sammon ryöstö* *(The Capture of the Sampo)*, whose success Sibelius duly noted as a challenge, almost as a threat. Now he must make sure that he in his turn came up with a masterpiece. His neighbour, the painter Pekka Halonen, put on an exhibition which also enjoyed great success: 'To my sorrow I have noticed that success seems to change one's old friends.' This notion seems to have persisted, as ten days later he added, 'Halonen's changed manner distresses us all. How dangerous success can be if it is not balanced by a deep and refined sensibility.'

To raise money, Sibelius had turned to a setting of Rydberg's *Unge hellener (Young Hellenes)*. Perhaps he had hoped to make this commission more congenial by choosing a text that dealt with love, wine and orgies. But he became increasingly unsure of it and abandoned the project. His moods changed with the April weather: 'Am again over-sensitive. How is it possible? I thought I had grown out of these debilitating bouts.' On such days he saw life through jaundiced eyes. With a certain distaste he notes that his son-in-law Arvi came to Ainola 'full of Helsinki gossip'. No doubt Arvi radiated the confidence of a young, successful businessman which made Sibelius feel somewhat put in the shade: 'I have difficulty in asserting myself. Now the latest is Arvi, whom we are all fond of. I am hardly an ideal father-in-law. In fact quite impossible. I have to confide all this rubbish to my diary as I am no good for anybody or anything.' (10 April 1915)

Sibelius was not alone in his preoccupation with his forthcoming fiftieth birthday. Akseli Gallen-Kallela (Axel Gallén), Sibelius's friend and drinking companion from the Symposium years, was fifty on 26 April. The two friends had not met since Gallén's return from his trip to Africa (1909–10), an enterprise which Sibelius had much favoured. 'Your journey to Africa is about the most sensible thing I have heard of for ages,' he told him. Sensible may not perhaps have been the right word, but in one respect Sibelius had been right, for the visit to Africa served to resolve Gallén's long artistic crisis, so much so that his output rose to almost manic proportions. He painted a large number of richly-coloured canvases, at times full of an impressionistic fervour, at other times with an eruptive and expressionist force reminiscent of Nolde or Kirchner. They could have been the beginning of a new and fruitful period in his development, but neither at home nor in Sweden were they well received by the press. When the so-called Group of Seven (*Septem-gruppen*) mounted an exhibition in Helsinki in 1912, neo-impressionism with its species of *pointillisme* triumphed; its musical counterpart is best found in *The Oceanides* two years later. A little later came the expressionist 'November group', and many saw the Gallén exhibits as worshipping at the altar of an archaic nationalism. Others, of course, regretted that he had not continued along the lines he had explored in his youthful work.

Gallén sank into deep depression: 'I am now the equal of the other has-beens; no better nor worse than any of them.' But outwardly he retained his old Renaissance Man profile with Nietzschean overtones; he kept his sensitivity and pessimism hidden behind an outgoing, ebullient mask. Gallén continued to meet Robert Kajanus, as in days of old, and Eino Leino also belonged to his circle; but he no longer saw anything of Sibelius. Where money was concerned, Gallén showed princely abandon. By his side, Sibelius was a model of the domestic virtues. His Paris years and his journey in Africa consumed his resources; the first thing to greet him on his return home was an order of distraint left on his wife's piano by the bailiffs. But driven on by grandiose visions he built a palatial studio at Tarvaspää, some distance west of Helsinki, while Kalela, his old home in Ruovesi, fell into disrepair and dilapidation. One wonders whether he sought sanctuary from mankind within its grey walls and kept watch in its battlemented towers, of which he had always dreamt in his childhood. He never completely fitted out or furnished the place properly, and in the end only lived there for very short periods. Like Sibelius, Gallén dwelt morbidly on negative reviews and the controversy that inevitably surrounds a celebrity. In fact he believed that he was an outcast, boycotted in Finland, and affected, with all the hyperbole of a diva, to believe that his fiftieth birthday would pass unnoticed. Needless to say, the celebrations were far from modest. In the morning Kajanus and the Helsinki Orchestra serenaded him with *Finlandia* among other things, and the whole of the cultural establishment paid their respects during the day and later at a civic dinner in his honour. Sibelius partook in neither celebration but contented himself with a letter:

> With deep emotion I pen these lines to you, dear Gallén. Fifty years, to be sure, is in itself nothing, but it does afford an occasion to take stock of one's achievement. And what, Master, have you not given us all, your country and the whole world? Receive our thanks for it all and, from the bottom of my heart, sincerest good wishes.
>
> In enduring friendship and gratitude, your affectionate admirer, Jean Sibelius.

There was no word of regret at his absence. His diary reveals his state of mind: he felt that he had been left out of the picture. On 24 April the diary records: 'Worked on the first movement. Newspapers full of Gallén. Full of pompous sentimentalities.' And on the actual birthday he continued working, still struggling with the transition material from theme A to theme B in the first movement. When his letter was published in the press, he feared that it might reflect badly on him, or that he might seem ungracious; and later he appears to have had pangs of conscience about his absence from the dinner. His diary notes: 'Eero and a number of my friends are unhappy that I did not go to the Gallén dinner. But my work on this symphony makes me impossible. And just at the moment I am not sure whether I have the strength to carry on with this symphonic credo – judging from the countless changes and corrections. And there are always money worries in the background. And I have so little time in which to get it ready. Well, Jean Sibelius, you have only yourself to blame. If I can't appear in good spirits at the dinner, I think it better manners to stay away. That my absence will be interpreted as "envy" or God knows what by the ill-disposed and by a stupid, really stupid, public is certain.'

But the public did not have to be particularly stupid to note that Sibelius and Aino were conspicuous by their absence. The festivities over, Sibelius went through the newspapers with characteristic thoroughness and found plenty of things to fuel his insecurity. Allusions to Gallén's role as an inspirer, almost progenitor, of Finnish music. In his festive poem Eino Leino had written, with the extravagance such occasions induce: 'Our arts, paintings, temples, statues, music, song, all pay their tribute'; and Kajanus had spoken of Gallén's work as giving 'rich inspiration to all the other arts'. These were easily construed as subtle intimations that Gallén was the key figure in the Finnish artistic world. It was he who had given inspiration to 'our Finnish music, and Kajanus who has given it an international reputation'! Could Sibelius have sat there while Leino and Kajanus deprived him of his role as the founder of modern Finnish music?

But this was only part of the problem: his basic preoccupation was with the transition in the first movement. The first theme must be got rid of; the whole movement was doomed. Wrestling with these problems was all-consuming. Moreover, he had come to feel a certain wariness of the great painter and perhaps felt ill at ease in his presence; an outsize renaissance personality was one thing but he had over the years developed a certain bitterness. After the festivities, Gallén longed for the wilds of Kalela; listening to the tributes was like reading one's own obituary. A week or so later he replied to Sibelius's greetings:

Dear Sibelius!
Forgive the typewriter, but you of all people will know what a strain my handwriting is. You wrote on my fiftieth birthday an introduction to the immortals' house of nobility, a right royal letter of honour, that calls for no further words, and with whose blessing I could rest on my bed of laurels undisturbed for many years to come – but as you best know yourself, how demanding we are at our age; that we prefer to be con-

sumed by the orgies with which our work beguiles us, concerned by nothing other than artistic conscience. Our muses, since we have them, are as impatient of acclaim as the victor's white mare is tired of dancing in his curved bridle and longs for the free pastures.

You, Sibelius, were an equal and close comrade-in-arms at that time when we embarked on our respective paths, and since then you have been for me an admired paradigm. We both have so much work to do that we have no time to spend in each other's company, but it often seems to me that our emanations meet.

At the dinner on 26 April, at which I had vainly hoped to welcome you and your wife among my nearest intimates at table, I was able to survive the flood of greetings by the thought of Cervantes' wonderful hero, who remained undaunted . . . The enchanting people did all they could to ruin my innate modesty.

Soon it will be your turn, and then watch out!! At least you will escape comparison with the knight of La Mancha, since you have no windmills or wine sacks to defend yourself against. Your letter was so touching that I must clothe my deep emotion and gratitude to conceal the depth of my feelings.
Your Gallén

For all the compliments and flattery, it had become difficult for them to restore their past intimacy. Sibelius was naturally on the lookout for any hint that Gallén had taken offence: 'From Gallén a strange letter. He speaks of me as his "equal" when we set out at the beginning of our career. But later?' Reading his letter, it is clear that, for Gallén, Sibelius was by now the paradigm whose achievement he had not matched. 'Misunderstand me correctly', Sibelius was fond of saying, but was less able to apply it himself. It was just as well, perhaps, that Sibelius and Gallén did not see much of each other in the real world, fiendishly sensitive and conscious of their own genius as they both were. Their emanations often met in a harmonious, irrational sphere. In the 1890s both had their visions of the dark waters of the river of Death in Tuonela, of the Swan and Lemminkäinen's mother in their respective media. And this imaginative world forged bonds that could never be undone.

Sibelius's thoughts now turned to his friend Axel Carpelan, to whom he wrote: 'Yesterday I sent you scores of *La Chasse* and *At the Drawbridge*, and I want to ask you if I ever sent the *Bard*? Have gone through a very dark period. Heavy in spirit because I am so alone. I have many new works on the stocks.'

Carpelan was too exhausted by illness to reply with more than a note of acknowledgement and thanks. Sibelius detected a lack of warmth: 'Axel Carpelan has written with his hand but not his heart.' When Sibelius wrote a couple of weeks later, his commentary on the war was very much in

Carpelan's manner: 'Italy is now in the war. Those villains who have betrayed their allies under whose protection they had grown strong. And people can speak of this treachery as if it were the normal way to behave and even applaud it. What passions this all rouses. And mankind seems to descend more and more into barbarism.'

Aino 'frail yet so strong,' he observed. 'Not even carefree words could disguise her real feelings of sorrow.' After the fiasco with the choral pieces he thought Aino 'took things more to heart than they were worth. She is used to looking up to me as the master and sees me struggling – again and again fighting for survival.' His luck seemed to have run out. Everything seemed to conspire against him – even the potatoes he had specially procured from von Konow. His major-domo Heikki Sormunen informed him that the Järnefelts' potatoes were better than his. 'That's the limit. Beat that. And this is the sort of pettiness that I have to put up with. Now I am slowly steeling myself to sell off the property. But is that sensible? Having land has its points. Have tried to bite off more than I can chew. And now I am finished and worn out. Completely finished.'

His state of mind changed with kaleidoscopic frequency:

[30 April 1915] Had a bad attack of nerves and have stayed in bed all day.

[1 May] Poul Knudsen sent me a new libretto for a pantomime, *En moder (A Mother)*, based on Hans Andersen.

[2 May] Feeling a bit better, though many things upset me so much – it can't be normal. The day is like winter and it snowed in the evening – 1 or 2 degrees below. Cold.

[3 May] Worked on *Kyssen (The Kiss)*, the song, by the grace of God. Cold.

[4 May] It is not my lot to follow the sure, broad path that the artist slowly and steadily treads. And where one rises in social status and achieves financial success. No! The musical world at large realizes I am a great artist, but what about here at home? My music doesn't make any money at all. And nothing that doesn't make money is any good in the eyes of people in Helsinki. That is what I have to put up with. And see how others put what I have done to their own uses. Today sunshine, but it is snowing and cold. Work away at the symphony and songs and new pieces.

[5–6 May] Nature is beginning to come to life again. Warm – about 8 to 10 degrees. Work on the songs . . .

[7–8 May]. *The Kiss* is now ready in sketch form. Also *Kaiutar* (Larin Kyösti) which I think will be something . . . Wonderful day – in the morning some rain and later sun – about 13 degrees.

The poet Larin Kyösti was one of the few people from his home town with whom Sibelius had kept in touch, and one of the few Finnish-language poets to whom he turned. Kyösti had often asked Sibelius to set his poems and some years previously, at about the time of the Fourth Symphony, had asked him to write music for his symbolist play *Ad astra*, but the composer had always declined, albeit in the friendliest of terms. He had written to Kyösti: 'Just got home – everyone is so excited about *Ad astra*. Have already read your work in Finnish and admire it. In my view it is a strong foundation stone on which you will build a grand and magnificent edifice. But I can't write any music for it. I am so preoccupied with other projects. It pains me to have to write to you like this.' (15 July 1911) Their friendship survived, and a couple of years later the poet visited Ainola. He was overjoyed that Sibelius was now setting *Kaiutar*.

Sibelius's May diary continues:

[9 May 1915] Things are not getting better for Aino. Her heart! The day is chilly, though the clouds have been strikingly beautiful.

[10 May] Made a fair copy of the songs . . . Sunny but cold. Wind from the north.

[11 May] Sent the two songs off this morning. Selim Palmgren has refused to pianofy [his slang for 'transcribe'] *Älskades väg (The Way of the Beloved)* from *Rakastava*. Aino better.

[13 May] Rapallo [the name Sibelius gave to the south-facing part of his garden after his 1901 stay in Rapallo] is now planted with fruit trees. The day is rainy and cold. Worked on Op. 79.

[14 May] Money troubles continue to pour down. It looks as if Gidi's [Gideon Järnefelt's] office [which looked after his affairs] are fed up with the whole wretched business.

For the next few days the diary concerns itself with charting progress, or rather the lack of it, on the cantata *Young Hellenes*, which he had been planning for the male choir MM and to which he had provisionally assigned the opus number 79. He became furious with himself over the difficulties he was encountering with it, and some days later decided it was to be renamed *Backosotåget (Bacchic Procession)*, Op. 79. By the time summer had come, he had given up the idea altogether and the opus number was allotted to the six violin pieces.

On 23 May, Eva was delivered of a daughter. 'So I am now a grandfather. How extraordinary!' – particularly in view of the fact that Sibelius's 'snow buntings', as he called his two younger daughters, were still in the nest. Heidi was four and Margareta six, so that they were better suited to be the sisters of the newcomer rather than the aunts. By their side, the twelve-year-old

Katarina was a young woman and at a difficult age. 'Yesterday,' she noted in her diary, 'I had a terrible row with papa. We both of us lost our tempers. Mother said that I must humbly apologize, but it will be a long time before I shall humble myself.' The following day 'Kaj's' father noted: 'Aino has gone into town with Kaj, who is difficult to bring up.'

Aino's code of etiquette was closer to that of the Winter Palace than of Helsinki, and she tried to impose it on her daughters and their friends. One evening when Katarina was visiting her cousin Marjatta Sibelius, they both took it into their heads to telephone the youngest of the Paloheimo boys in Järvenpää. While Marjatta was talking, Katarina interrupted to ask where the washbasin was – and spoke so loudly that the question could be heard by the young man at the other end of the line. Some days later, while in the sauna, Katarina was mildly admonished: 'You know, it isn't really ladylike to speak of such things as washbasins in that way; it is just a shade indelicate!' Katarina had begun to take piano lessons with Martha Tornell, to whom Sibelius dedicated his Sonatinas, Op. 67. But practising at home posed problems, as it prevented Sibelius composing.

Aarre Merikanto dedicated his new work *Theme, Five Variations and Fugue* to him. Sibelius was very taken with the gesture: 'I have hopes of that man. What he can achieve, if only he is granted enough time . . . !' (27 May 1915)

At the end of May the morels were ripe for picking. Sibelius stayed indoors and worried about bagatelles: 'My colleagues Kuula, Melartin and the others are writing one big piece after another, while I am rummaging through the ashes. Are things never going to get any better? Should I throw in the towel? Never! Aino wants me to go mushrooming but I am impossible at the moment.'

All the same, Aino managed to lure him out into the forest: 'Forced myself and went picking mushrooms and had a lovely time in the country-side.' Not that Sibelius managed to gather many mushrooms. He picked a morel, lifted it to his nostrils and put the little thing in Aino's basket. Then he brushed a few pine needles from his cuffs and went off home.

CHAPTER FIVE

Fiftieth Birthday: *'Difficile est satiram non scribere'*

n June 1915, at the height of the war, Rosa Newmarch unexpectedly
irrived in Helsinki together with her daughter Elsie and Otto Kling and his
wife, whom Sibelius had met in London. They were on their way to Petrograd on a half musical, half political goodwill mission. During their crossing
rom Newcastle to Bergen they had caught sight of several shipwrecks, and
n Stockholm they had been courteously but not warmly received. In Fin-
and, however, their welcome was altogether different. Sibelius and Aino
went to meet them in Helsinki and took them out to Järvenpää: 'Sibelius
ind his family received us with all their usual warmth and hospitality.'¹

Mrs Newmarch was not one to keep her views to herself, and it is clear
rom his diary that Sibelius found her hatred of the Germans and the strain
of talking French all day onerous. He did not involve himself with the
lelicate question of German–Russian hostilities, for his perspective was of
course very different. On the whole, however, with his English sympathies
ie had little difficulty in understanding Mrs Newmarch's point of view. She
hought Helsinki had lost none of its charm and most of all that it resembled
1 pleasant English bathing resort transplanted to more northerly latitudes.
3ut beneath it all she could sense the underlying disquiet and sense of
mpending revolution. Out at Ainola everything was peace and quiet, and
ier only disappointment was that she was not able to see her favourite,
Katarina, who had measles.

Otherwise, the summer unfolded without Sibelius managing to make
ierious headway on the Fifth Symphony. He luxuriated in the warmth of
he late spring, full of nostalgia for childhood summers, and occupied him-
ielf with various smaller pieces, such as *Devotion*, Op. 77, No. 2, for violin or
cello and piano (later orchestrated) and *Tempo di menuetto*, Op. 79, No. 2,
both of which were ready in June. What did it matter that the house was
lisrupted by Katarina's measles, that it was being spring-cleaned and turned
ipside down, and that he himself was consumed by financial and practical
worries! 'In spite of everything, life is still glorious! These clear spring days
lrive me insane! It is like perceiving everything with heightened clarity.'
(7–8 June 1915)

Eero and Saimi Järnefelt celebrated their silver wedding, and Sibelius marked the occasion by the composition of a duet for two sopranos, *'Tanken'* ('The Thought'), which was performed by his own daughter Ruth and Eero's daughter Lena. The duet, with its note of anxiety, harmonizes perfectly with the Järnefelt's own ambience:

> Thought, see, how the bird glides
> Light and free under the clouds.
> You also have your wings,
> And the space in which to fly.

On Midsummer's Eve the Järnefelts, the Sibeliuses and other members of the artists' colony assembled for the customary festivities, and Saimi declaimed her traditional rhyming chronicle of the past year's events. Neither Sibelius nor Katarina responded to her sense of humour, and thought some of her couplets were directed against them. And when on the following day Katarina returned home in tears after playing with the Järnefelt children, Sibelius was quite incensed: 'Kaj has the misfortune of not being able to fight back. She takes after her mother and father. We shrink from such things and have to take the consequences.' But later on, in August, he was at pains to note Saimi's good points and, as so often in his diaries, endeavoured not to give too one-sided a picture.

At the end of June he spent a day in Tavastehus (Hämeenlinna) with Walter von Konow to relive childhood memories. He had a feeling, as he did with childhood friends from Lovisa, that Walter did not quite understand why Sibelius enjoyed an international reputation while he did not! 'This comes through in his attitude and makes me depressed. And yet we are good friends!' From Tavastehus he returned home via Helsinki, where he 'made merry with Favén, etc'. On returning to Ainola he began working on the symphony again, but broke off to complete some more small pieces. Looking round him at home, he realized that he was no longer satisfied with the state of Ainola: 'The house needs smartening up.' (Diary, 7 July 1915).

His thoughts turned next day to the violin and to the sound of Italy: 'Padre Martini! His bel canto! Violin pieces. Melancholy and sense of farewell – the future looks bleaker.' But life had its turbulent side too: 'More storms here in the house. Different lifestyles and ways of thinking.' And the wider world troubled him too: 'The silence of my enemies does not bode well. Must have something new ready for Lindgren. Composition comes quite easily to me just at the moment. But all the threads lead to the Fifth Symphony. Spent a lot of time with Kitti. Smoking in spite of everything.'

Christian (Kitti) Sibelius was convalescing in Järvenpää after an illness. Aino accompanied his cello playing. Early in July Kajanus wrote to announce that *Snöfrid* was to be one of the attractions of the coming season. However, as no one could find the score, Kajanus asked whether Sibelius himself had a copy and how they should proceed in the matter. Sibelius replied immediately to his friend's summer greetings: 'Thanks for your card with the pleasing news. So far as the score of *Snöfrid* is concerned, I have not been able to find it in spite of an intensive search. But both the orchestral and choral parts are here, so if the worst comes to the worst, the score can be reconstructed, particularly as there is still plenty of time. With all our old friendship I wish you a pleasant and happy summer in your beautiful Obbnas.'[2]

The friendly tone of his note mirrors Sibelius's feelings for Kajanus at the brighter end of his psychic spectrum: 'The days are major and minor, my thoughts major and minor, and my work major and minor.' Sibelius could think of nothing better than to buy some wine and come down to earth. So as to compensate MM for the cantata he failed to deliver, he revised *Sandels* for chorus and orchestra. He had originally planned – in his diary of 23–9 July 1915 – to leave this piece to slumber undisturbed as 'a kind of "*document humain*" of 1898 – or 97 to be exact!' In addition, he wrote two *a cappella* songs for them, *Ett drömackord* to words of Fröding and *Eviga Eros (Eternal Eros)* to a poem of Bertel Gripenberg. The summer also saw the completion of some other miniatures: the *Impromptu*, Op 87, No. 1, for violin (alternatively cello) and piano; two additions to the Piano Pieces, Op. 40, *Scherzando* and *Petite sérénade;* and the song, *Der Wanderer und der Bach*, Op. 72, No. 5. Another piece from this summer is the *Romance* for violin and piano, Op. 79, No. 2, presumably identical with the *Souvenir*, Op. 79, No. 1.

In June, Breitkopf & Härtel wrote to tell Sibelius that *The Oceanides* had been published and that a piano arrangement of the score had been prepared by Hermann Gärtner, who had also made a piano transcription of *Luonnotar*. Sibelius approved the arrangement of *The Oceanides*, but decided to make his own transcription of *Luonnotar*. The result is highly effective pianistically and testifies to his considerable skill in this art. Breitkopf & Härtel accepted his arrangement for publication and at the same time asked him to send back the full score, which they had returned to him the previous year. But Sibelius made no response. Three years later they repeated their request, and added that they would be quite happy to work from a copy if the original was no longer to hand. Even as late as 1978, when these lines were written, the score of *Luonnotar* remains in manuscript![3]

His untiring productivity in the field of miniatures filled him with distaste: 'All these days have gone up in smoke. I have searched my heart. Become worried about myself, when I have to churn out these small lyrics. But what other course do I have? Even so, one can do these things with skill.' (25 July 1915) Skill, however, was not the question; it was on the symphony that he was longing to show his genius. The high point of the summer at Ainola was a performance of *Salome*, a play by Kerttu Paloheimo, mother-in-law of his daughter Eva. The incidental music had been composed by a young and controversial figure, Moses Pergament, whose début

61

as a composer the previous autumn had caused such a stir in Helsinki. Bearing in mind Furuhjelm's comment on the lack of judgment exhibited by the Swedish-language press in hailing Pergament in such extravagant terms, Sibelius must have wondered whether his own daily, *Hufvudstads-bladet*, would use Pergament as a stick with which to beat him. But after he had seen a performance with his daughter Ruth playing the title role, he was won over by the younger man's score: 'Moses Pergament did himself credit with his music.' Though he complained about all the comings and goings at Ainola, Sibelius found time to be a good host and made a punch consisting of pineapple, three bottles of Sauternes, two bottles of hock, ten lemons, lemonade and Lacrimae Christi!

Almost in desperation he composed a humorous song, only to destroy it immediately: 'My spirits are so low that I can barely describe it. I suppose I must give up smoking. See everything as black again. Have at the back of my mind a number of new works, but I can't write them down. Can't address myself to anything – very strange!' It was well into August, the weather was cooler and autumn was approaching, but still the Fifth Symphony was a long way off completion. It was in this despondent frame of mind that he read a report of an article by the French critic Touchard in *La Revue bleue*, which came like salt in his wounds. 'Sibelius,' wrote Touchard, 'has dressed the folk song in a toga. He is simple and unsophisticated; he is the people.' In the symphonies Sibelius shows himself more as 'a good craftsman than a master'. His originality, according to Touchard, best emerges in the piano pieces and songs, even if some of them appear as 'directly banal, designed for a public that is musically uneducated'. Touchard said in French much the same as Niemann had said in German, namely that Sibelius's music is a kind of folksy, home-made music.

Sibelius wondered whether the article could have been inspired by Minnie Tracey, the American singer who had wanted to champion his songs in Paris – a project he did not encourage, on the advice of Mrs Newmarch. He was disgusted both on account of the article's substance and the fact that it had been widely quoted in the Helsinki newspapers: 'In this I can see clearly that there are also those here at home who want to denigrate me. Everyone else has recognition heaped on them but not, I'm sorry to say, me! What a vile world we live in! And poor Aino who, however tough, is not made to ride this kind of storm. But shall I go under because of this Minnie Tracey . . . ? I shall shortly be fifty. Poor – so poor that I have to compose small pieces. Insulted – and in spite of my achievements, recognition goes to others. How can I bear all this? Only with solitary dignity. Martyrdom is not the sort of thing I go in for.'

To make matters worse, Touchard had included *Kullervo* among Kajanus's works! 'What other works are they going to include in his worklist?!' But as on other occasions, Sibelius consoled himself with the thought that so long as his works are published, they will eventually come into their own: 'Why should fame bring so much suffering? Jesus Christ!' (Diary, 15 August 1915) The next day finds him wondering why his hair hasn't turned white after such a night: 'How well I understand the word "chagrin"? Will the sun shine no more? How to restore my equilibrium, desire to work and joy in working. Only by treating my fellow men with contempt. But to cultivate this at fifty and with my temperament – that's another matter!' About one thing he was certain: that under no circumstances would he permit his fiftieth birthday to be an occasion for celebration.

With his spirits low, he turned for contact to his old friend who had proved an anchor in his life:

Dear Axel,
Herewith a sign of life. Hope that you are in reasonable shape in these dreadful times. I am worked up about many things. Intrigues against me, etc. I've composed quite a number – nearly forty – new works, and feel quite written out. Aino is suffering from insomnia. You see that things are going downhill in every way. The children are well and often speak of you.

This time Carpelan did not have the strength to respond immediately to Sibelius's sign of life, not even with a card.

In Järvenpää as in the rest of Finland, life went on very much as if there was no war. However, recruitment was under way. Of the male students newly enrolled in Nylandsnation,[4] Sibelius's own alma mater, some 27 per cent were called to the colours. But any signs of what Sibelius and his circle were hoping for, namely the disintegration of the Tsarist régime, were hard to detect. On 9 March his diary records Nicholas II's visit to Helsinki, and the fact that he travelled incognito and was heavily guarded. Many years previously, as part of his duties at the university, he had composed a Coronation Cantata in Nicholas II's honour. On this occasion, when the Tsar passed the university the staff and about a hundred activist students stood in homage on the steps. Some token of enthusiasm was mandatory, but no cheers were raised; those present uncovered their heads in demonstrative silence. Of increasing concern to Sibelius during the summer of 1915 was the fear that Sweden would be drawn into the war. His diary voices his anxiety in both June and July, for had Sweden been sucked into the maelstrom, his window on the west would have been closed.

With Sibelius's fiftieth birthday fast looming on the horizon, two biographies – one in Swedish, the other in Finnish – were planned. The Swedish volume was to be by Erik Furuhjelm, the Finnish by Leevi Madetoja. As usual in Finland where such matters are concerned, preparations were begun far too late in the day. In the middle of June, Sibelius makes the first mention of Furuhjelm's project in his diary. His biographer had already written the first chapter, but was unable to proceed further without studying the score of *Kullervo*, of which there was only one extant copy. Sibelius himself did not have it. Presumably it had been deposited in the Phil-harmonic Orchestra's library after the first performance in the 1890s. Prompted by Furuhjelm's inquiry and still smarting from the article in *La Revue bleue*, Sibelius turned to Kajanus: 'Have just read in *Suometar* about your *Kullervo* symphony and came to think about my own. Is it impossible for you to get the score to me?' This was not the first occasion he had asked for its return. Two years earlier in 1913 he had written in rather sharp terms calling for its return 'as quickly as is practical'.

The ensuing search proved quite nerve-racking. After having turned the libraries of both the Music Institute and the Orchestra inside out to no avail, Kajanus was faced with a barely credible possibility. Had some fanatical autograph collector gone off with the score? 'When I have found your *Kullervo* I shall put on a special train of jubilation to Järvenpää.' His note ends by thanking Sibelius for 'what is, to say the least, monumental patience'.

So we are faced with the fact that in the summer of 1915 two important Sibelius manuscripts, *Snöfrid* and *Kullervo,* had gone missing. It would seem that neither Sibelius himself nor Kajanus – nor, for that matter, anyone else – had realized their importance or had any idea of their real worth. Sibelius's patience was beginning to run out: 'Letter from Kajus. He has not taken the slightest care of *Kullervo* or – this is more likely – one of the orchestral staff who belongs to the clique around him has burnt it.' Second thoughts only fuelled his suspicions, for a day or so later he adds: 'Almost certainly!' Furuhjelm was forced to break off work on his book. Some months later, at about the time of Sibelius's fiftieth birthday, Kajanus came across the score in his own library, and Furuhjelm was able to resume work. His book first appeared in the following year.

Madetoja's venture proved ill-fated. From the isolation of his island in Lake Keitele, he writes in 1915: 'I'm composing a symphony, but it makes slow progress as the beauties of my surroundings here are all too consuming. But *ça viendra* – I hope . . . Next Christmas – when you celebrate your fiftieth birthday – I plan to write a book about you and your musical achievements up to the present. Would you have any objections to this? Or would you not consider me suitable for such a task? I appreciate that this is a delicate matter – it would in fact be the very first attempt at the subject in the Finnish language, and I can assure you that I would try my very best to do justice to it.'

Sibelius gave his consent, but when Madetoja visited him at Ainola to talk about his biographical project, he was gripped by doubts: '*Muss es sein?*' Admittedly, his reservations concerned the prospect of *any* biography rather than one by Madetoja, for he realized that he could not hope for a more sensitive biographer. Subsequently Madetoja sent him a list of questions, which reveal how little was known at this time about Sibelius, even among the intelligent and well-informed. 'Did you receive any music tuition in

Hämeenlinna? How old were you when you began to play the violin and compose? Who was your violin teacher in Helsinki?' – and so on! All the same, when Madetoja next visited Ainola, Sibelius was reassured and in better spirits: 'We had a splendid time. He's a good fellow.'

Madetoja continued to work on his Sibelius book in Viipuri, where he held a conducting post, but in the middle of October he was forced to send Sibelius humiliating news: 'I have now received refusals from every publisher. For me this is totally incomprehensible. Things have come to a pretty poor state when our publishers are so cautious, and think only of their wretched balance sheets, when a project of this importance concerning our greatest composer is proposed. I hope, however, you won't be angry with me, even though I have troubled you so much over this project.'

If Madetoja's biography came to nothing and Furuhjelm's was held up, one book did at least appear in time for the great day – this was by the Danish writer Gunnar Hauch. As early as August 1915 he had sent Sibelius a long and well thought-out article, which the composer thought 'outstanding'. A little later, in the autumn, he published it as a monograph, which drew an appreciative response from the composer.

The autumn season was fast approaching. Sibelius went to Helsinki but returned in a tired and nervous state. He began to smoke heavily: 'I am not at all well. I am a hypochondriac – if it really is hypochondria?' He had three months before him in which to finish the Fifth Symphony.

'Saw the cranes flying south in full-throated song. They have taught me about sonority all over again.' The 5 September dawned like a summer's day, but the weather soon broke and the following day was cold, rainy and desolate. Sibelius had several small pieces under way in his head, but could not bring himself to write them down. He smoked and was oversensitive as never before. The following week brought relief: this was what he had been waiting for. 'These days immersed in the symphony, whose ideas flow into me.' The final stages of the Fifth Symphony's first version were a fight against time. He leafed through his diary, only to realize that too much of his nervous energy had been absorbed by money worries: 'Can I get the symphony ready for 8 December? The prospects look bleak! *Mais nous verrons.*' But then his spirits soon soared:

> [26 September 1915] Have been on the crest of a wave. Or rather still am. However, now on the way down again. A reaction against the powerful atmosphere in which I have been caught up during the last few days . . . My symphony must see the light of day. Money and practical matters will have to look after themselves.

Fears that he would not finish in time brought fears of ill health and phantom symptoms:

'Worries about my throat have drowned inspiration. Have I become hoarse or not? I can't remember a time when everything seemed so black. If

I have cancer of the throat, then I think a bullet in the temple is the only way out. Up to now I can't get to the end. After this something light; a light opera or operetta. But it won't turn out that well!'

Aino found it painful to watch his agony, and Sibelius himself thought her painfully scarred by the nervous tension which he generated: 'It breaks my heart to see her like this. She is so alone, and has to cope all by herself. How can one work in these conditions? I hardly sleep these days without recourse to sleeping tablets. For several days now I've taken Adalin. But I have worked so hard.' Of course there were brighter moments: they took their morning walk together at about ten. Katarina knew that she must be up and dressed by then so that she could practise the piano until half-past eleven. And at the end of September they celebrated the anniversary of their engagement by harvesting the apples from their garden. Admittedly Sibelius did not do the bulk of the work, but did enough to taste the fresh air.

In Helsinki the new concert season began auspiciously. The number of musicians in the Helsinki Orchestra had grown to more than fifty and their salaries had been increased. Kajanus was to conduct Sibelius's four symphonies, the First and Second before the birthday celebrations and the Third and Fourth in the spring. Schnéevoigt had embarked on another Beethoven cycle. The rivalry between the two maestros was strong. After Schnéevoigt had given the Fifth Symphony on 7 October, Kajanus immediately put on an extra concert six days later at which he repeated it 'by public request'. The city authorities clearly favoured Schnéevoigt. He conducted the lion's share of the season and received an annual fee of 12,000 marks as opposed to Kajanus's 8,000! But by the spring of 1916 Schnéevoigt had come to play a less prominent role, for he was already preparing himself for his move to Stockholm.

Conductors' fees throw some light on Sibelius's own plight. His own basic income was the State Pension of about 5,000 marks a year. Kajanus had the same pension plus his 8,000 from the Orchestra and in addition a salary for his duties at the university where he was in charge of music – in all, something like 20,000 marks. Schnéevoigt's total income in Helsinki and Stockholm was certainly considerably more. On top of this Sibelius was burdened by debt. In order to struggle on, he had to produce bread-and-butter music, such as the *Mazurka* for violin and piano for which Westerlund paid him an honorarium of 1,000 marks. Thus when Armas Järnefelt wrote from Stockholm in early October inviting him to conduct one of the Royal Opera's concerts during the coming spring, Sibelius's telegram merely read '*Avec plaisir*'.

At the end of the summer season Richard Burgin, who was to become Koussevitzky's concert master in Boston, played the Violin Concerto. When he first tried the work in Pavlovsk in February, it was with limited success; Sibelius described the reviews as 'sweet–sour'. But Burgin had the bit between his teeth and returned to the score, again with Schnéevoigt as conductor. It was sandwiched between Beethoven's Fourth and Fifth symphonies, and on this occasion Sibelius was in attendance: 'Not at all bad, but somewhat on the slow side and the orchestral accompaniment was not well prepared.' A week after this concert, Sibelius could comment on the progress of the new symphony: 'Everything now in broad outline. Worried that I won't have time to work on all the details and make a fair copy. But I must.' (13 October 1915)

On an adjoining page he notes: 'A strange phenomenon that I have to compose – and compose well – in the eyes of the public. They are not content with what I have done but demand more and more masterpieces. It is a thankless existence, my life and composition – and without joy!' It didn't need much to send him into another depression:

[14 October 1915] There are so many, so many who try and belittle what I have done. Very few who give me my due. Am in a dreadful state just now. It is as if everything that I have composed up to now, all my work, equals nothing. And am put into a bad humour on account of Bis's usual impertinences. That base, perfidious creature! Aino said that life is hard. How many times have I not thought this? What joy it will be to leave it! Yet the responsibility, the prospects for the children. That weighs at the moment of death. What agony it all is. And there seems no prospect of light in all this darkness.

At the turn of the months of October and November, *Snöfrid* was given twice under Kajanus's baton. Sibelius, it would seem, attended neither performance, but noted with pleasure that on each occasion it was encored: 'What is one to make of it? A youthful piece after all.' As had been the case during the gestation of the Fourth Symphony, there are big gaps in the diary. During the latter part of October there is not a single entry. By the beginning of November the symphony had progressed to the fair copy stage and was ready to be sent off.

Katarina was plagued by earache, and in the end Aino was forced to take her into Helsinki where she was admitted to hospital. Sibelius was left on his own for a couple of weeks. He remained perturbed by adverse criticism: 'The first movement of the symphony is now with the copyists . . . The belittling of my work infuriates me. They are hounding me – to death?' (2 November 1915)

On the 8th he reports that the second movement (which corresponds to the *Allegro moderato* section of the first movement in the definitive version) is with the copyist. By the 11th he is again plunged into gloom and wishes he might cut himself off and disregard criticism. 'It is as well', he notes in his diary, 'that Aino isn't home and can't see for herself my time in hell.' By the middle of the month he notes that the third movement is finished and with the copyist. 'Yesterday Katarina came safely back home. Aino is poorly and

in bed. I am in my usual regular state. Am working on the last movement.'
(17 November 1915)

At about this time Carpelan left Tammerfors (Tampere) for good and
returned to his childhood home Åbo (Turku), where the past sighs in the tree-
tops and the cathedral spires soar up unchanging in the midst of life's bustle.
There he heard Sibelius's Violin Concerto for the first time, though he had
gone through the score on countless occasions. Again the soloist was Burgin
and the performance was technically flawless. 'Well played by soloist and
orchestra, the concerto is without question one of the greatest works in the
literature of the violin.' That was his verdict, which he hastened to deliver to
the composer. A few days later he received the scores of *The Oceanides* and
The Bard, into which he immediately threw himself. *The Oceanides* drove
everything else from his mind: 'A new breakthrough, a new style and technique, and such sonorities and harmonies I have never heard before.'

In Helsinki there were arguments about the Sibelius birthday concerts
and festivities. The choice of venue for his birthday concert, for example,
was controversial. Sibelius had originally decided on the Finnish National
Theatre, whose acoustic was not particularly well suited to orchestral music.
It was unlike him to make such a choice, but no doubt he was swayed by the
keen Finnish-language sympathies of the rest of the family and the fact that
his daughter Ruth was a member of the National Theatre company. However, at the beginning of November he changed his mind and decided that
the birthday concert should take place in the Great Hall of the University.
Ruth and Katarina were absolutely furious at first, but soon accepted their
father's decision. It should have been obvious from the start that Sibelius
wanted to celebrate so important an occasion in the same hall where Kajanus had in 1882 opened the very first concert season of his orchestra with
Beethoven's Fifth, and where nearly all of his larger works from *Kullervo*
onwards had received their first performances. The Great Hall of the University was to Helsinki what the Musikvereinsaal was (and still is) to Vienna,
and it was equally a gathering place for both the Finnish and Swedish-
speaking factions.

Katarina gives a good picture of life at Ainola towards the end of
November: 'Mamma is with her friends sewing and uncle Pekka (Halonen)
is here, though I don't think that papa is at all pleased that he is here, because
these days papa is in a dreadful hurry with his fifth symphony. Everything
here is upside down . . . Papa is awake every night until five in the morning
and then stays in bed, and pretends he is working there, and doesn't get up
before twelve or half-past.' So it was Aino who was left to answer the
telephone and deal with all the practical matters, among them the sensitive
issue of placing the guests. This time she did not forget Carpelan – who
with perhaps the slightest streak of irony, thanked her for 'this undeserved
kindness towards my unworthy person'. On 1 December Sibelius left for
Helsinki to begin the orchestral rehearsals. A whole series of events had

been arranged in connection with the birthday, heralded on the 6th by a chamber music concert at the Music Institute. Richard Burgin and Ilmari Hannikainen played the new violin sonatina (then still called sonata). The critic Katila thought that the usually reliable Burgin did not manage to convey all its finer dynamic shadings and nuances.[5] The sonata, Sibelius had told Furuhjelm a few days earlier, 'should ideally be played by a sixteen-year-old girl!' Then followed two movements from the B flat Quartet, Op. 4, a reminder of the time when Sibelius himself played the violin in the Music Institute's Quartet; after which Ilmari Hannikainen gave a brilliant account of *Kyllikki* which should have persuaded the composer that his piano music had found a powerful advocate in Hannikainen. The final work on the programme was *Voces intimae*.

When on his birthday Sibelius opened his copy of *Helsingin Sanomat*, the Finnish-language daily, the first thing he saw was Eino Leino's dithyramb in his praise. It was as if the poet had been inspired by the aphoristic quality of Sibelius's art; seldom has any Finnish poem achieved such lightness of touch and texture. The paper also ran a remarkable article by Madetoja in which he argued that many critics had set too much store by the nationalist colouring and programmatic nature of Sibelius's music and overlooked its qualities as absolute, pure music; an argument no doubt intended to counter the views of Nieman, Touchard and others. Later, on his way to the morning rehearsal, he could see that his portrait adorned most shop windows, and afterwards he was fêted by the Finnish-speaking academic community. Suomen Laulu (Finland's Singers) sang the festive march from the Ceremonial Cantata of 1894, something of a rarity, and the YL Singers gave *Båtfärden (The Boat Journey)* and *Till fosterland (To My Country)*. The Swedish-speaking academics were not represented. Presumably they had not been asked. Feelings ran high at this time in the language war. Later on in the afternoon he repaired to his hotel, where he received a constant flow of congratulatory messages and presents. Carpelan had taken the precaution of sending his congratulatory letter well in advance – 'Now at last you stand at the brink of your brightest and greatest creative epoch' – and went on to speak of his serene, masterly powers. Nor did his message omit to pay tribute to Aino, whose supportive ministrations had protected him for us . . . she has earned eternal honour and eternal gratitude. He also paid his respects in person during a pause in the celebrations, and their conversation touched on Sibelius's beloved swans and cranes.

And so it was time for Sibelius to don his tails. There was a real sense of occasion at the concert, whose programme was completely new for Helsinki. After *The Oceanides*, which opened the proceedings, Kajanus presented Sibelius with a ceremonial wreath of honour 'from his old fellow comrade-in-arms'. Then Richard Burgin was the soloist in the two *Serenades*, the second of which had to be repeated, after which Sibelius was presented with a civic address bearing 15,000 signatures. Carpelan's words to him after the

death of Edelfelt – 'You are now our pride and our hope' – had truly come
to fulfilment.

After the interval came the first performance of the Fifth Symphony.
Present-day listeners accustomed to the final version of the work would
have found much to surprise them on this occasion. The broad outlines
would be familiar but at many places a modern listener would be taken
aback. In the first movement, *Tempo molto moderato* (in the 1915 version
Tempo moderato assai), where the B major transition to the *Allegro moderato*
would be expected, a pastoral section in E flat occurs with the main horn
figure played pizzicato on the strings. Even more surprising would be the
fact that the musical argument is interrupted by a long *fermata*. Only then
does the *Allegro moderato* (then called *Allegro commodo*) get under way. Much
else is different, notably the fact that the last forty bars, which bring the
present first movement to a climax, are missing. In the *Andante mosso* movement there is a 'strange pizzicato song [*sic*] which with the exception of a
few short rests and bowed sections, continues for the whole of the movement' (the quotation comes from a contemporary review by the composer
Otto Kotiläinen).[6] The modern listener would be able to navigate the finale
without much difficulty. After the celebrated 'Thor's hammer' theme on
the horns in E flat, the same theme continues in C major, and against a
backdrop comprising the three descending notes of the first movement's
second group (A flat, E flat, D) a trumpet call is heard, having a positively
bitonal effect rather like the cries of the crane. ('A strange trumpet note sears
right through the theme making an altogether fearsome impression' was
how Kotiläinen put it.)

EX 31

After the G flat episode, *misterioso* (from letter I to N in the definitive
score), the music continues with a mysterious passage and the 'Thor's hammer' theme in E flat over the double basses alternating A flat–D flat.

EX 32

The present-day listener would have had to wait rather longer for the E flat minor episode, *Un pocchetino largamente*, and when it comes, followed by the magnificent closing climax, the final bars would take them aback. Instead of the six final chords there are only five, and four of these are sustained by wind, horns and strings. The total duration was thirty-five minutes as opposed to the thirty of the familiar final version.

Rolf Nevanlinna, mathematician and keen chamber musician, gives an eye-witness account of the composer from his vantage point close to the podium. Sibelius grew pale and drawn; his aquamarine eyes shone with great intensity, and the tremulous movement of the baton had by the end of the performance been matched in his whole body. It was only a few steps from the University to the Bourse – designed by Lars Sonck, who had drawn up the plans for Ainola – where the banquet was to take place. In Europe the cannons were thundering, while in Finland no one could foretell the fate that awaited them.

Kajanus, proud and erect, spoke of Sibelius in a way that the composer could never have expected: 'As far as our Finnish music is concerned, it scarcely existed when Jean Sibelius struck his first mighty chords. What little there was before him was but a weak offshoot of the German school, with a little ethnic colouring from Finnish folk music.' The next sentences have assumed almost classic status in Finnish musical history: 'Barely had we begun to till the barren soil when a mighty sound arose from the wilderness. Away with spades and picks. Finnish music's mighty springs came bursting forth. A mighty torrent burst forth to engulf all before it. Jean Sibelius alone showed the way. In *Kullervo* he had with one stroke realized the dream of a genuine Finnish voice.'

Where did Kajanus see himself in this picture, with his symphonic poem *Aino*, *Finnish Rhapsodies* and *Sinfonietta*? Sibelius unleashed the floods of genius – he, Kajanus, had merely prepared the frozen soil with the spades and picks of talent. He ended with a vision of a music of the future that would build its aesthetic on Sibelius's achievement. What did Sibelius make of this prophecy? He knew what his standing was in central Europe and France. Yet strangely enough, during the previous year he had written from Berlin – without having seen Mahler's now famous words – 'my time will come'.

The Helsinki public was now in the grip of Sibelius fever, and there was a profusion of concerts devoted to his music. Schnéevoigt and Kajanus shared a concert conducting the First and Second symphonies respectively, separated by a group of songs with Ida Ekman as soloist (10 December). Sibelius himself conducted two repeats of the birthday programme, one at the Finnish National Theatre on 12 December, and the other at the University on the 18th. Muntra Musikanterna gave a Sibelius evening which included *Sandels* and the *Song of the Athenians* on the 14th.

The following day Sibelius went to a Schnéevoigt concert to hear the first performance of Aarre Merikanto's *Theme with Variations and Fugue*:

'Like everything I have heard of yours, this composition appealed to me on account of its magnificent control and strong poetic feeling. Perhaps you have loved your beautiful theme a little too much. You might perhaps ask me whether one can love something too much in life and I would reply that that is the prerequisite of youth – but one suffers on this account.'

When it was all over, Sibelius returned to his diary: '*Difficile est satiram non scribere* [It is difficult to take this seriously]. *Sine ira et studio.* Written hundreds of letters of thanks. Received twenty-odd paintings from Finnish artists who sent a canvas each. Also a Steinway grand piano, a Persian rug, etc. Breitkopf & Härtel sent a leather-bound formal address. But I'm tired of all this attention. Long to get to work – something which makes life worth living. Horribly cold, circa 20–30 degrees centigrade below zero. Otto Andersson has worked out my family tree so thoroughly that it makes me ill. It's as if I'm already dead.'

Otto Andersson had marked the birthday by publishing two Sibelius numbers of *Tidning för Musik*. In the first there was a genealogical table following Sibelius's ancestry on the paternal side, while the second traced his mother's side. The first went back as far as his great-grandfather Johan Mattsson, who married into the Sibbe landholding. Andersson had not managed to get very far in tracing Johan's father. He traces Johan's wife back through her father and grandfather (the two previous peasant farmers at Sibbe). The grandmother's Swedish background with the Åkerberg and Unonious families are also firmly in the picture. On Sibelius's maternal side Andersson only names, besides Maria Borg, the mother's father and grandmother Haartman. In concentrating on his forefathers on the paternal side, Andersson presents the composer as being predominantly from Nyland, Swedish in descent and language, as well as having connections by blood with the Swedish mainland, albeit modest in social standing. In his genealogical table of the maternal side, families other than Borg and Haartman do not figure, though they are to a large extent of Finnish origin. Sibelius would undoubtedly have preferred their existence to have been acknowledged, if only for the sake of ethnic balance. He immediately foresaw that the Finnish-speaking faction would be making its own researches so as to stress his pure Finnish origins, and was fearful that his family tree would become a bone of contention. That was enough to make him feel ill.

Their time together during the birthday celebrations seems to have resolved any doubts that might have strained Carpelan's relationship with Sibelius. His letter of thanks shows every sign of reconciliation: 'Aino and Janne, wonderful, good people. Receive my deepest and most heartfelt thanks for all the kindness and attention you bestowed on me, unworthy creature, during those unforgettable days in Helsinki. Everything that befell me was glorious and nourishing after the long years of privation and misery . . . I begin to believe, nay know, that I have rediscovered my true, devoted friends, never again to lose them.'

Carpelan closely followed everything that was written about Sibelius, and had recently ploughed through Erik Furuhjelm's comprehensive, somewhat high-flown essay on the composer – published the preceding year in the Stockholm periodical *Ord och Bild* – which he found too intellectual in its approach. Furuhjelm divided Sibelius's output up to that point into three periods. The first, the formative artistic years, extend to the middle of the 1890s and are characterized by subjective inner narrative, folk-like elements, the mythological and the portrayal of nature without any exaggerated tendencies. The second, from the *Lemminkäinen Legends* through to the First Symphony, is dominated by 'historic mythology'. More than in Sibelius's other work, objectivity distinguishes their expression. The third phase, marking his self-discovery, is divided into two further periods: in the first, the Second Symphony turns towards the concrete outer world, wherein the composer finds new stimulus for his inspiration; the second marks the individual's isolation within himself – 'the period of introspection and artistic asceticism which opens with the string quartet *Voces intimae* and finds its strongest expression up to now in the Fourth Symphony.' Neither *The Bard* nor *Luonnotar*, nor the stylistic change encountered in *The Oceanides*, are touched upon in this article.

Viewed from his premises Furuhjelm's postulations do enjoy some validity, but Carpelan would have none of it. His division of Sibelius's output into different periods was an abomination and did violence to the real facts. Furuhjelm he regards as 'a victim of his own abstractions' and argues that he has arranged the facts to accommodate his theories. In citing Bergson, Carpelan had been right in placing the Fourth Symphony in the spiritual and psychic context of its time. Now he was denouncing the attempt to impose on art an intellectual or logical concept and other abstractions such as number symbolism.

With the new year nearly upon him, Sibelius had still not recovered his equilibrium after the celebrations and could not settle down. He pondered further over Armas Järnefelt's invitation to conduct the Fifth Symphony at the Royal Opera. Carpelan advised him against conducting in such a provincial backwater in front of 'an incomprehending audience and ignorant critics'. Sibelius replied, 'They would quite simply be unable to grasp my Fifth in Stockholm.' In his diary he noted, 'This Stockholm philistinism in musical matters! Their Swedish insularity! Their blinkered view of everything that is not homegrown. It amazes me that Armas can put up with them. Still, there is always Stenhammar – a golden apple in that Sodom.'

On New Year's Eve he went into Helsinki with Aino, returning to Ainola to see the new Year in. He had been through the score of the Fifth Symphony again, and what had been a gnawing doubt at the concerts now struck him with the force of certainty. In its present form the Fifth Symphony would not do.

CHAPTER SIX

Interregnum

In his New Year's poem of 1916 Sibelius's friend Bertel Gripenberg wrote:

> Deliver us a year of victory,
> where years of defeat
> have laden our days
> yesterday as now.
>
> For once let the world
> move towards a miracle,
> let honest men have success,
> let the villains fall!

Sibelius's own thoughts were not dissimilar: '1916 opens with calamity, high hopes and God knows what.' He went in expectation of the unexpected. The great powers were locked in a stalemate and were tearing themselves apart to gain the upper hand at Verdun and on the Somme, in the Carpathian mountains and on the River Isonzo, but to no avail. There was always a hope that Tsarism would collapse – but could one be sure of the emergence of 'honest men' in the sense that Gripenberg and Sibelius intended?

Carpelan had given up his role as political commentator and prophet. His New Year theme did not much differ from Gripenberg's: 'We must wait and see if the age of miracles has not passed.' He threw himself with even more abandon into Sibelius's music. He had heard someone play *Boutade*, Op. 34, and wanted to have all the six bagatelles Sibelius had so far published. Of all things this delighted Sibelius: 'Axel is, it seems, livelier than ever. Occupies himself studying philosophy etc. and is much involved in musical aesthetics. Let's hope his health holds out.' (Diary, 5 January 1916)

On 9 January Sibelius conducted a concert at Folketshus, the headquarters of the labour movement. The acoustic was not particularly suitable, but apparently the city's musical authorities, as well as Sibelius himself, were keen that his birthday should also be celebrated there. The opening piece, *The Oceanides,* was disturbed by latecomers, but the birthday programme

74

was supplemented by the definitive version of *The Bard*, which was being heard for the first time. 'We know,' wrote Erik Furuhjelm, 'that Sibelius has penetrated the soul of the Nordic Bard; some chords echo from his lyre, and a romatic antiquity passes before our inner vision – it is not really a popular piece, but all the same it was encored.'[1]

Sibelius now had time to respond to Carpelan's New Year letter: 'For about a week after my concert I have been plagued by acute earache, and have now spent a week in Helsinki to get it attended to . . . I shall not go to Sweden now. There are many reasons, not least my work – and life's brevity! Have been reading about Swedenborg and have found "much grist to the mill".' Martin Lamm's book on Swedenborg had been published in Stockholm in 1915, and Sibelius eagerly devoured it. Swedenborg struck a responsive chord in his own pantheism and mysticism. His interest was certainly stimulated by his reading of Strindberg's *Inferno, A Blue Book* and other literature of occult leanings.

According to Lamm's biography, Swedenborg had already experienced mystical states during his childhood, and had acquired the capacity for 'inner breathing' during states when normal respiration is suspended. 'This induces a state of trance in which the subject feels himself cut off from the outer world and at the same time is suffused with inner light. His feelings reach a depth, his thoughts a clarity, which he does not enjoy in his normal state. This command over breathing also leads to visions of an hallucinatory character.'[2]

Perhaps Sibelius's thoughts turned to the 'moods' and 'wonderful trances' during which he experienced his own musical visions – albeit not hallucinatory, since after emerging from the creative imagination they had taken shape and been committed to paper. Generally speaking Sibelius was fascinated by the Swedenborg phenomenon. His sympathies were already enlisted by the knowledge that Swedenborg loved music above all else, and hailed his father's remark that 'in the glories of music God has made a mighty and powerful resource'. But above all Swedenborg's belief in the role of intuition must have exerted a strong appeal. Lamm quotes *Oeconomis Regni Animalis I: '*We know that poets, musicians, singers, painters, architects and sculptors are born to their respective roles, and so is the case with others of a like mind. They are born with a spiritual power, a strongly developed fantasy and intuition.'[3] Did not Sibelius himself create his themes with fantasy and intuition; and likewise, did he not use spiritual power to build them into structures of a higher order?

According to Lamm, Swedenborg's definition of knowledge in *Sapientia Angelica de Divina Providentia* 'bridges the gap between science and art more clearly . . . We perceive that the origins of knowledge are a complete and total mystery. Our understanding of knowledge is created by our selves, and the highest knowledge, Spirit, lies beyond our consciousness.'[4]

This passage could have reminded Sibelius that in the autumn of 1910, musing over the concept of music as a science, he had recorded in his diary: 'What you are doing, after all, is art not science.' (6 October 1910) To which he appended: 'God knows, incidentally, whether science is the antithesis of art.' Now Swedenborg gave voice to something he had only sensed: that science and art are not opposites, but components of one and the same mystic force.

Even if much of Swedenborg's theological outlook should have been alien to him, Sibelius ought to have been responsive to his view of a Divine Providence which shapes our ends: 'We know only that there is a divinity which is working within us, but we do not know how it works. And that it is the Divine Law that Man shall be unaware of its working, for if we knew and understood it, we would lose our independent will and would not be free agents.'[5] Perhaps Sibelius came close to that sense of God to which he gave such powerful and mysterious expression in *På verandan vid havet*. Lamm's book on Swedenborg was grist to the mill, in the sense that it echoed something of his own philosophy, centred on 'that wonderful logic' – let us call it God – whose instrument he was. To realize the divine power's commanding imperative, he must unite both the intuitive and inspirational with the conscious, rational component; his wonderful trances and his intellectual powers.

In his New Year letter Carpelan had asked whether Sibelius would object if he deposited (or possibly donated) the letters he had written to him in the archives of the Åbo Library, 'which would naturally remain unopened for say about thirty years after we have passed on'. For Carpelan this lapse of time would prove perfectly adequate, though in Sibelius's case it would not. At the time, however, any anxieties were fully alleviated: 'Concerning my letters, you can dispose of them as you think best. Your suggestions that they may be examined after thirty years is eminently acceptable.' To think in terms of an early death was part of the Sibelian psychology, though he was of course fated to live for a further forty years!

His fears for Carpelan's stamina were to be realized all too soon. Carpelan succumbed to inflammation of the lung, and in his feverish dreams heard Beethoven conducting his Tenth Symphony with an orchestra comprising flowers and trees, and thought he had assumed the shape of a dragonfly and was floating over his own funeral procession. Poised as he was between life and death, and far too frail to wield a pen, he dictated a line of greeting to Sibelius, concerned more about his hearing than his own condition. Sibelius noted with alarm: 'Axel Carpelan dying. I am going deaf.' (Diary, 21 January 1916) But more hopeful news soon came from Åbo that only one lung had been affected. When the worst was over, Sibelius wrote on 10 February: 'You cannot imagine what I have gone through since I heard the news that you were dangerously ill. The sun went down for my music. To my great, great joy, I learn that you have fought resolutely for your health, and have triumphed. I don't need to tell you how relieved and happy I am. My ears are being treated and are getting better. My hearing is now almost back to normal. Two weeks ago I was as good as deaf. As far as composition goes, I have new plans and am dying to get to grips with them.'

Carpelan never fully recovered from his illness; the last chapter of his life had now opened. Sibelius had been in a lather of indecision about his Stockholm visit and wrote to Armas: 'As far as the concerts are concerned, the prospects for my visit look black. I would in any case suggest that for the regular concert, wonder of wonders, the familiar pieces, Symphony 2 and the Violin Concerto [with Burgin] plus the unfamiliar things, *The Oceanides* and perhaps some of the *Historical Scenes* or other old favourites. At my own concert [the second one], if his lordship [Petersson-Berger] graciously permits it, I should perform among other things my Symphony 5, which will certainly be torn to pieces by the aforementioned personage.' (7 January 1916)

News of the guest appearance in Stockholm soon reached Stenhammar, who wrote inviting Sibelius to extend his visit and go on to Gothenburg. Should his Stockholm visit come to anything, Sibelius replied that he would extend it to include Gothenburg. Sibelius now had three relatively lucrative engagements in prospect, but he still remained hesitant. The Fifth Symphony, the novelty which everyone was dying to hear, had become his problem child and had to be reworked:

[5 January 1916] Have been working these past few days to get the symphony into publishable form.

But the work made scant progress, and soon a terrible reaction set in:

[17 January 1916] Am not yet satisfied with the symphony's shape. My hearing is depressing me. Kajus and other 'friends' will have a new and wonderful weapon – Sibben can't hear – which will feed the appetite of those wanting to topple the giant. But if I am toppled I shall cause quite a stir.

All Kajanus's attentiveness had not been enough to heal the old breach completely. An entry in Sibelius's diary just before the New Year suggests that tongues had been wagging behind the scenes: 'Kajus has behaved very correctly during my festivities. Some people suspect there's something behind it. But why?' (28 December 1915) His outburst against Kajanus and 'the others' prompted afterthoughts: 'Is this not bitterness? After all, they are also human. And that I stand in their way is hardly calculated to induce them to regard me with unmixed feelings? Are you, Ego, any better yourself?'

A hundred and one things were worrying him, among them the fact that he had sold some small pieces to the publisher Lindgren behind Breitkopf & Härtel's back.

[24 January 1916] Bad atmosphere at home. Money worries again to the fore. Anxiety, self-reproaches and recriminations. One thing is clear: that as things are, I won't be able to manage; either in practical terms or peace of mind. Working away on a *Liebeslied* for violin, together with – in secret – the Fifth Symphony revision.

The Royal Opera Orchestra's concert in Stockholm was planned for 18 February and a week later Sibelius was to proceed to Gothenburg. He had very little time in which to rework the symphony and get the orchestral parts copied. Both Järnefelt and Stenhammar wanted a definite yes or no, and he eventually wired regrets. In his letter of explanation to Armas he wrote:

I have already been waiting a long time on account of the slow post for news on your side, and heard from Mamma [Elisabeth Järnefelt] that you weren't altogether certain about the second concert, which finally prompted me to pull out. My first thought in coming was to give profitable concerts of my own. These days I am dependent on such emoluments and their size.

None the less, in spite of that I would have come as a favour to you, were it not for the fact that I have not been well earlier in the year – my ears! You can't imagine how it felt; for about a fortnight I was as good as deaf. And I don't think my right ear will ever be really good. Please let's keep this between ourselves and say nothing about my hearing.

From one explanation he falls back on another. But he did not give the real reason to anyone, even his brother-in-law, though he did confide the truth to his diary:

[26 January 1916] I must confess that I am working again on Sym. 5. Struggling with God. I want to give my new symphony a different, more human form. More earthy, more vibrant. The trouble was that when I was working on it I was another person.

It is obvious that Sibelius had given up hope of getting the symphony ready for the press simply by tinkering with details. He had come to the conclusion that he must in part radically recast its structure. To put some distance between him and the symphony, he puts it on one side in favour of the Sixth Symphony:

[27 January 1916] Worked on Symphony 6. Wonderful day. Walked in valedictory colourings. The trees spoke. Everything was living. No word from Axel. The pen I'm writing with is Finnish, that's to say, finished! Must begin to work things out on paper, not just in my head. According to the doctor, my ear infection is related to influenza. I must try and keep all these things in perspective.

Kajanus conducted the Third Symphony and the *Historic Scenes* in Helsinki, but Sibelius stayed at home and was represented by Aino and their daughter Katarina. After all the Sibelius celebrations the public had had enough, and the auditorium was almost empty.

– 2 –

Otto Andersson's genealogical study in the *Tidning för musik* unleashed a swift response from the Finnish side. With financial support from K. A. Paloheimo, the father-in-law of his daughter Eva, the genealogist Granit-Ilmoniemi had embarked on his study of the composer's ancestry. On 23 January the Finnish-language paper *Uusi Suometar* published the first instalment. Granit-Ilmoniemi found some inaccuracies in Andersson's account: Johan Mattsson, for example, did not come from far away but from a neighbouring farm holding – so Sibelius's fantasies about coming from distant shores went up in smoke.

The next thing was to establish where Johan came from. It was not known at this stage where his parents, Matts Mårtensson and his wife Anna, had come from before they moved to Silvastas. Perhaps it would be possible to prove that pure Finnish blood flowed in their veins. Sibelius himself had been brought up in the belief that his family name had already been in use by Mattsson of Sibbe, but this misconception was now rectified. As late as 1818 Johan had been registered in the church's confirmation book as 'Peasant. Johan Sibbe from Lappträsk'. Four days later *Uusi Suometar* published a second instalment, dealing with the Borgs, his mother's family, with names such as Haartman, Chydenius, Ruuth and others which complemented Andersson's family-tree.

To say that the composer himself was not best pleased to see all this in a daily paper would be something of an understatement. Indeed, he took it very badly: 'He has treated the subject like an oaf, crudely and crassly. Must pull myself together. I must try to be philosophical about it.' But Sibelius wasn't able to muster up quite enough philosophy: '*Uusi Suometar's* family researches have upset me so much that I can't think of anything else.' He felt humiliated to see his lineage exposed to the vulgar gaze, particularly the fact that he came from a humble background: 'A quarter of my ancestors are peasants. It is difficult for me to maintain my equilibrium. In fact, *Uusi Suometar* have managed to strike a blow home where I feel vulnerable.' (Diary, 2 February 1916)

His diary entry is in fact quite hysterical. He speaks of himself as *un homme fini*, and his nerves were obviously under great strain; he talks of suicide, and of how difficult it would be to hold up his head in public. No doubt his intemperate outburst was in part an expression of the pent-up feelings of frustration he suffered because of his inability to resolve the problems of the Fifth Symphony.

However, the birthday celebrations brought in their wake a more pleasant surprise. On Runeberg's Day (5 February) the singer Ida Ekman visited Ainola to deliver a belated birthday present: an envelope containing receipts for all his current debts, including his loan from Ramsay, and a bank credit of 10,000 Finnish marks. The proceeds of the collection amounted in all to some 30,000 marks. 'I was beside myself with joy. Had never imagined anything like this could happen.' His celebratory concerts had brought in 10,000 marks, but this was nowhere near enough to pay off more than a fraction of his debts.

After a few days working on the Sixth Symphony at the end of January, he turned again to the Fifth:

[2 February 1916] My ears are still painful. Am sceptical about their getting better. After that, my sanity! Yesterday was with Christian, a wonderful brother. Get to grips with the revision of Symphony 5. It is going slowly but well.

[11 February] Planning new orchestral pieces, with or without a vocal part; fantasies or ? This to gain peace of mind to work. Peace from all the devilry. If only I can have my capacity and appetite for work, and my powers back. Everything now is as if I am finished. Always alone. Alone at home, alone when I am at restaurants in Helsinki, alone on the road and on the train. Alone – alone.

[13 February] I am still not finding it possible to get on with work. It must be some sickness. In spite of everything I want to give some concerts this season.

[18 February] Heard the Brahms variations, Beethoven G major concerto and Tchaikovsky Fifth under Georg Schnéevoigt. Went home in high winds. Today Aino is in bed. Am in slightly better spirits concerning work – that's to say, working methods.

[19 February] In Helsinki on my own. Am like a sleep-walker.

[21 February] Today sensed the wings of death. Altogether out of sympathy with this Helsinki music life and its zealous Apostles. [Here he alludes also to the publisher Apostol, who had bought *Arioso*.]

[23 February] In a much better and calmer frame of mind. But this period of nervous strain has taken its toll and left indelible marks. Torn to shreds by the Petersburg critics. New plans for compositions.

But even if he was making some headway, Sibelius did not manage to effect the revision of the Fifth Symphony in one fell swoop. Far from having an inhibiting effect on Helsinki's musical life, the war seems to have stimulated it. During the 1915–16 season no fewer than four new symphonies appeared. In November Kajanus broke his long creative silence with a *Sinfonietta* in sober classical style. Next came Sibelius's Fifth, and then at the turn of the year Erkki Melartin's Fifth. And on 10 February Sibelius attended the première of the First Symphony by his former pupil Leevi Madetoja, a work which has its roots in early Sibelius and Tchaikovsky, but possesses all the same a strongly individual character which found favour with the critics.

Sibelius himself wrote of its beauty, but added: 'In *Hufvudstadsbladet* today Bis maintains that he [Madetoja] is influenced by me. That sort of remark will surely put paid to our relationship. I say that with some bitterness.' There is undoubtedly some truth in the criticism, which must have been a sore point as far as the younger man was concerned. Sibelius's misgivings were confirmed a few days later: 'Met Madetoja, who – I'm sorry to say – has become pretty bumptious after his latest success. Kajanus smothers him with flattery and he hasn't the breeding to see it for what it is.' A little later he writes: 'When I ran into him, Madetoja was quite sullen. That is certainly not something he learnt from me!' Yet again a prickly personal relationship. Sibelius confused, either intentionally or unintentionally, Madetoja's melancholia with sulkiness – and took it personally. Nor is it impossible that, for all his affection for Sibelius, Madetoja wanted to free himself from his influence and become his own man.

On 26 February a number of Sibelius's friends gave a dinner for him at the Societetshuset (Seurahuone) in Helsinki. Even if his diary indicates pleasure at this gesture, it did not dispel his gloom: 'All these days . . . out. Dead.' But then something happened to lift his spirits. On 2 March Kajanus conducted an all-Sibelius programme with the Fourth Symphony as the main work. 'We've gone through it several times and it now seems to me that he's got to the heart of it.' And on this occasion the symphony went down well with the public. Sibelius left his place by Aino's side, went up to the podium and shook Kajanus warmly by the hand.

Another occurrence of a completely different kind also cheered him. 'At the concert Emil Forsström, a keen music enthusiast, came with a donation of almost 13,000 marks to help with my debts. Magnificent, when I think that these friends of mine are no millionaires.' Although the symphony might have won over the public, once again it still puzzled the critics. Bis in *Hufvudstadsbladet* did not care for the first two movements: 'Is this calculated utterance, this deep-seeming prose-poem to be the chosen language of the music of the future or will the warm, God-given inspiration Sibelius gave us in *The Swan of Tuonela* and . . . *En saga* maintain its supremacy over the speculative. In this day and age, when Sibelius's *Saga* has captivated us, we love to think of the triumph of beauty, and feel that the composer himself has borne witness to this in his Fifth Symphony.'[6]

'Bis's review totally confused.' Sibelius could not even work up any indignation about it. At the same time he was uneasy at the thought that he should have abandoned the 'God-given inspiration' of his youthful works for a calculating, speculative Fourth Symphony, but turned his back on this path in the Fifth. Had he, Sibelius, capitulated to the Vienna Philharmonic or to the tastes of the Gothenburg officers? Or even worse, should he himself have come to the conclusion that the Fourth Symphony was leading him on a false bearing? No, a thousand times no! As always, he was the slave of his themes and they pointed in a more classical direction. Bis did not grasp that the Fifth Symphony was every bit as progressive in its different way as the Fourth.

Katila, *Uusi Suometar's* critic, went overboard in his enthusiasm and spoke of 'its structure and contours emerging with enormous clarity, and one is amazed at the way these forward-looking impressionistic ideas were shaped into a structure of great sophistication and drawn together into a monumental logical entity'.

Bis and Katila were at opposite poles, as they had been eight days earlier when Mahler's *Das Lied von der Erde* received its Finnish première. Bis had hailed Mahler's 'depth and imposing formal mastery, harmonic resource and command of the orchestra', while his colleague felt worn out when this 'meandering through a tonal desert was at an end, and thought with some envy of those who had the moral courage to walk out in the middle of the symphony'. Thus the battle lines between the Mahlerians and the Sibelians in 1916 were drawn here, between *Das Lied* and the Fourth Symphony. A performance of Scriabin's *Le poème de l'extase* drew similarly divergent responses. The other novelties of the season, Debussy's *Rondes de printemps* and Reger's *Romantic Suite*, seem to have passed without undue controversy. Judging from the available evidence, one can say with virtually complete certainty that Sibelius attended none of these events, which were all conducted by Schnéevoigt.

At various times in his life, most recently in Paris in 1911 and Berlin in 1914, Sibelius had deliberately sought the stimulus of new music and attended many concerts, but now that he was struggling with the Fifth Symphony, he wanted no distractions that would disturb his train of thought. However, young composers who came to him could count on his good will. As early as the summer of 1914 he had recommended Väinö Raitio, a composer pupil at the Music Institute, for a scholarship and later on went through some of his compositions with him. Now, in March 1916, Raitio was ready to put on the first concert of his compositions, with Kajanus as conductor, and thanks to Sibelius he was able to engage the Helsinki Orchestra on favourable terms.

Sibelius thought his début very promising. Some days earlier he had pondered his relationship with the younger generation of composers: 'It is very much as I had foreseen. The old ground rules seem to apply. Although my own shares have risen, so to say, I remain completely insecure. I can see how the young are coming along and holding their heads high – Madetoja higher than others – and one must admire them, but my own course demands more egoism and tenacity than I can at present muster. And my contemporaries, amongst others Abraham Ojanperä who sang in *Kullervo* in 1892, are dying off.' (Diary, 9 March 1916)

Prompted by Sibelius's successful appearances at the time of his fiftieth birthday, several influential people in the musical world approached him with a view to his giving two further concerts in Helsinki in March, and offered financial guarantees. The impresario and opera chief Edvard Fazer advised caution, and even as late as the middle of February Sibelius was undecided: 'We'll have to see, but I'm a bit dubious about the financial backing!'

Naturally, it was not easy at this late stage to fit two new dates into the orchestra's schedule: 'Conductors' squabbles are holding things up. It's all on my account. They have asked me to conduct, but I don't seem to have an orchestra.' Doubtless neither Kajanus nor Schnéevoigt were willing to give up precious concerts and rehearsal time at such short notice. The final outcome, however, was that the orchestra was placed at his disposal on 23 and 30 March.

Erik Furuhjelm wrote after the first concert:

Jean Sibelius is a very fine conductor: he appears inspired and skilful on the concert podium and is instructive in rehearsal. It is a great pleasure to watch his preparation of his own works. He is accustomed to making penetrating and telling points; and has an extraordinary capacity to draw playing of culture and nobility from the orchestra . . . The difficult passages in *Night Ride and Sunrise* received a somewhat agitated reading. This time *The Bard* was not encored but both the *Canzonetta* and *The Dryad,* as well as the encore, *Valse triste,* were presented with the utmost subtlety and finesse.

The Second Symphony was given in a surprisingly brisk tempo. I don't remember whether the composer has ever conducted it at this pace on an earlier occasion. Kajanus's performances – which can generally be regarded as authoritative – have usually been much broader in character. In any event, I was for my part very much taken with his reading yesterday. The outer movements were given with energy and speed and in the slow movement the tragic pathos communicated itself powerfully.[7]

At the other concert Sibelius conducted the Fifth Symphony in its first version for the fifth and last time. In addition, the programme included *Pohjola's Daughter* and *Rakastava* as well as, by special request, the *Valse triste.* The first cellist of the orchestra, Ossian Fohström, played two pieces which Sibelius had written for him, *Devotion (Laetare anima mea)* and *Cantique (Ab imo pectore).* Erik Furuhjelm thought them 'deeply felt, full of nobility and poise, and beautifully scored'. Afterwards Sibelius let off steam in his diary: 'I have the concerts in Helsinki behind me, together with some high times with my old drinking companions. Not bad – except that my nerves are not up to it these days. I will soon fall into a depression, And go through hell. What I haven't gone through in Helsinki during the last few days. How these Apostles have irritated me – but Kajus has taught me how to treat them. Wine and cigars with Arvi [Paloheimo]. I can't help it now; I can't manage without these oases in life.'

– 3 –

In the spring of 1916 Sibelius was widely played abroad. Oskar Fried – in whose company he had visited the Hermitage in St Petersburg in 1907 – conducted the Fourth Symphony in his enterprising series of concerts at the Freie Volksbühne in Berlin, though to no great critical acclaim. In the *Neue Zeitschrift für Musik,* Bruno Schrader doubted whether the symphony would ever gain much of a foothold in Germany, and found its substance insufficient to sustain its great length! 'A great deal of it is undoubtedly atmospheric but sounds ugly all the same. Certain ideas could be seen as national and Finnish; others are just borrowed from the French.' The symphony prompted ambivalent feelings: 'It both fascinates and repels; it intrigues at the same time as it fatigues'. Nor was Heinz Tiessen in the *Allgemeine Musikzeitung* much more positive: 'It is not compelling, though the listener who is already persuaded by his music will find many passages of real poetry and exquisite tonal refinement. In the long run a deficient creative vitality serves to leave a predominantly negative impression.' Shortly before the New Year, Joseph Stransky, whose account of the Third Symphony in Berlin had prompted such an adverse response from Adolf Paul, conducted *The Oceanides* with the New York Philharmonic, but it was by all accounts not a success, though Augeners told Sibelius that the reviews were 'respectful'.

In Rome, Toscanini conducted a magnificent performance of *En Saga* which Alfredo Casella hailed as '*poeticissimo*', while *La Tribuna* wrote that two of its themes sounded more Spanish than Finnish. At the Stockholm Opera, Armas Järnefelt conducted a belated celebratory concert, replacing the Fifth Symphony by the more familiar Second, while Richard Burgin, dependable as ever, played the solo part in the Violin Concerto, which had been introduced to Stockholm by the Swedish violinist Julius Ruthström (it was later given by its dedicatee Ferenc von Vecsay, albeit to a piano accompaniment!). The programme also included the second set of the *Scènes historiques* and *The Oceanides*.

Back home, Sibelius could read three of the reviews, among them Peterson-Berger's, which were reproduced in *Hufvudstadsbladet*. That the Swedish critic liked the Second Symphony was something he already knew, but now Peterson-Berger took 'the strong Sibelius' as a stick with which to beat the Violin Concerto, Sibelius's 'unlucky duckling, an artificial sequence of good intentions whose promise one never sees fulfilled'. *The Oceanides* was 'at best an effective and technically interesting tone picture, something in Böcklin's style,' but without any connection with antiquity.[8] For Sibelius, it didn't much help matters that Olallo Morales or others wrote with enthusiasm of the new work, for it was Peterson-Berger who counted in Stockholm and set the tone – and took his toll on Sibelius's nerves. 'Torn to shreds by the critics, who treat me as a nothing. They are beginning to hound and harass me now. Harry me to death.'

A few days later he noted that the Violin Sonatina, Op. 80, had met with success in Stockholm, 'though Peterson-Berger thinks that I have already written myself out. Really! Why is one pestered with Peterson-Berger?'

In Zürich on 15 March, Busoni, who had taken over the Tonhalle Orchestra for part of the season, conducted the Second Symphony. The rest of the programme he took over was previously planned: Tchaikovksy's Violin Concerto and Wotan's Farewell from *Die Walküre*. The latter prompted a broadside about his hatred for these gods and heroes, who had 'given him the creeps for the last fifty years'.[9]

Neither Busoni nor Sibelius were Wagnerians. With the former it was a matter of temperamental disaffinity; with the latter it was a love–hate relationship. The *Neue Zürcher Zeitungs* critic questioned whether he would not have served both Sibelius and the public better by playing one of his tone poems! 'The symphony is not really his field, for his themes are too short-breathed.' Niemann's *kurzatmig* rides again. But apart from this, the review was far from unfavourable: 'One's sympathies are consistently enlisted by his expressive language, which bestrides a pale grace, which neither in its melancholy nor in its more joyous moods succumbs to the overstatement favoured by the Slavonic races.' Busoni's interpretation of 'this noble and sonorous music' was 'beautiful and subtle in realization', even if rhythms could have been more strongly articulated. After the concert Busoni sent Sibelius a card which lifted his spirits, '*Sempre affettuosamente e crescendo,*' to which his wife Gerda added, 'The Symphony was marvellous!' In his diary Sibelius recorded: 'Busoni has performed Sym. 2 in Zürich with great success.' These foreign reviews added a certain savour to life that Sibelius needed – just as he needed other drugs: 'All this business with smoking. I simply can't stop it. I'm sure it is not doing my ears any good.'

Growing old was grounds for a pessimism that often surfaces in his diary with the expression 'When the shadows lengthen'. On the first occasion when it appears, in August 1914, it is in his Finnish persona, and stands out against the Swedish text of the rest of the entry. As we know from the evidence of the sketchbooks, he was immersed in a D minor world, which key dominated the conception of the Sixth Symphony towards the end of the same autumn. Are these ever-lengthening shadows in some way mirrored in its Dorian atmosphere of melancholy and resignation, and its pallor and delicacy, as if new horizons are opening as one passes the zenith on the wheel of life? Seven years later, when he was making a guest appearance in

Gothenburg, he used the same expression in a newspaper interview to encapsulate the mood of this symphony.

In his darker moments he had Strindberg to turn to. But Sibelius would not have been Sibelius if, on passing fifty, he had not found new verbal images to encapsulate his responses to life, some so powerful in their resonance that they could almost stand as a symbol of his personality. He wrote to Armas Järnefelt (during the war years, to judge from his handwriting): 'At my age the future pales and disillusion assumes its colours'; but in another mood perhaps, he could feel the reverse. And while the shadows lengthened over the Sixth Symphony, the sun was beginning to rise over the Fifth.

On 18 April he went to Väinö Sola's song recital, which included two songs into which he had poured his soul: '*Höstkväll* was all right, but not *Dolce far niente*. I said complimentary things, but he doesn't really have much idea of what it is all about. Sang too slowly and at the same time not lightly enough. The song should be sung in time and *sotto voce*. Have lived life to the full at these times. With a certain melancholy.'

The spring migration filled him with enchantment: 'Saw cranes. Heard their special cries that mean so much to me.' The next day he noted: 'Twelve swans are out there on the ice. Saw them with binoculars! Saw six wild geese [possibly grey geese, according to Heikki Järnefelt] as well as an eagle. A memorable day. Went to Puotinokka, a nearby promontory, with Heikki's binoculars and watched the swans. Very special, poetic! Wonderful!'

At the end of April the weather turned warmer:

[28 April 1916] 'A wonderful day. Spring and Life. The scent of the earth; muted and fortissimo. And this special light which is reminiscent of the August sun. Like a sixteen-year-old eagerly on his way to his beloved.'

In May he worked on some piano and violin miniatures, and made only two entries in his diary:

[10 May 1916] After some wonderful, warm days (26 or over in the shade), the snow has returned – we have had it now for three days! Went to Helsinki to bury old Swan [Eero Järnefelt's father-in-law] together with Gidi Järnefelt. Jussi Snellman has got a rise in salary. He will do well for himself in life.

[20 May] To our great joy Eva was here from St Petersburg with her little girl. The days are cold. Am working at times very hard on a number of small pieces. Hope they'll make some money!

As before, he now relived his youth through his daughter Ruth, since Christmas engaged to the actor Jussi Snellman. He noted all her changing moods on her visits to Ainola: 'Ruth is low today – fighting back the tears because Jussi hasn't telephoned.' At times like these Sibelius wished that she would leave the theatre and Snellman.

Meanwhile he waited impatiently for a sign of life from Axel Carpelan. But Axel, after coming so close to death, hadn't the energy to write. Yet again Sibelius began to wonder whether his friendship was going unreciprocated: 'Still no word from Axel Carpelan! So this war has also taken away a friend. And since I have no new works to show in print, my publisher is silent – not interested. At Easter I became 'professor' – what little importance I attach to that sort of thing now! But perhaps unfairly. My work? I'm soldiering on with the small piano pieces, but I'm unhappy about the slow progress I'm making otherwise. A reaction perhaps? But I should have worked my way through that already. Aino worried?! Leena Järnefelt has made Katarina a really delightful hat!' (Diary, 26 June 1916)

On 9 June he put together a collection of various smaller compositions including six piano pieces: *Iris* and *Nejlika (Carnation)* as a start for his group of flower pieces, together with the *Pièce enfantine, Harlequinade, Humoresque* and *Elegiaco*, Op. 76; as well as a couple of violin pieces, *Danse caracteristique* and *Sérénade*. Next day he sold the lot to Lindgrens for 6,500 marks.

June was like winter but without the snow. Around midsummer Erik Furuhjelm came out to Ainola to see him about his forthcoming biography: 'So many questions and answers! The day ended with a sunset which was as spectacular as in a story book! We had some superb sherry!'

In between heart attacks Axel Carpelan at last sent him a card.

[21 June 1916] That wonderful friend, weak and ailing. Today lots of clouds from the south. Poor Finland!

'Poor Finland' recurs repeatedly at this time. Presumably he identified the June cold and his own despondent condition with Finland's precarious position on the world stage. As he saw it, there could be no solution to Finland's problems while the Tsarist Empire survived. Every Russian success reduced the prospect of Finnish independence. The Imperial armies under Marshal Brusilov had launched a massive offensive in Galizia (Poland) and broken through the Austrian lines, while on Midsummer Day the Allied forces had mounted an assault along the Somme to relieve the pressure on Verdun. Sibelius perhaps feared that the Central Powers were beginning to lose the initiative, but still noted in his diary: 'I'm afraid that the war will not end for a long time. And my years are running out.'

In all this, Finland – and Sibelius – are centre stage. When would his isolation come to an end? When would he again have the opportunity of conducting his works in the capital cities of the world, and breathe in the fresh air of inspiration? At the same time he felt his own fate inextricably bound to that of his country.

His sister Linda had one of her better periods of remission and was allowed leave from the hospital to pay a two-day visit to Ainola:

[23 June 1916] Linda here. I feel very low. Why? Whenever I am with her,

I see only the failures and the hopelessness of existence and all its sorrow. All this drags me down so that I am no longer able to do anything.

Sibelius hastened to thank Carpelan for his greetings and reinforce his feelings of affection: 'My thoughts turn to you more than often, and in particular when I have completed a composition. Then one of my first thoughts is, "Hope that it meets with Axel's approval." So you see! Ruth will soon get married – 21 July. Katarina has become quite a young lady and has taken her final exams, although she still lives at home. Margareta and Heidi are busy learning Swedish for all they're worth. Aino has been very nervy but is now better thanks to her work in the garden.'

Before the war the ladies of the house busied themselves with weaving and making various household delicacies. The mistress of Ainola spent her time digging the garden, planting fruit and vegetables right up until the late autumn.

Sibelius made it a point of honour to wed his daughters in style: 'At home everything revolves round the family festivities for Ruth's wedding.' (Diary, 1 July 1916) Guests were beginning to arrive: Aino's mother and her eldest brother Kaspar, who acted as the Russian interpreter in Kuopio and was a gifted amateur painter. He was something of a character, with an argumentative streak, who had given the impression on an earlier visit to Ainola of being gruff.

All this cost money, and Sibelius worked like a blacksmith to deliver some piano pieces to Westerlund. On 3 July, the same day as the banns were first read, he had five pieces ready: *Danse pastorale, Joueur de harpe, Reconnaissance* and *Souvenir*, Op. 34, and the *Polonaise*, Op. 40. His son-in-law-to-be took the manuscripts into town and delivered them on his behalf. Sibelius followed a few days later (7 July) to pick up the money, returning to Ainola the day after with feelings of acute guilt: 'Plastered! See everything as black – without any hope.' Three days later he pulled himself together and set to work on a new project – incidental music to Hugo von Hofmannsthal's *Everyman* – in fulfilment of a promise to Jalmari Lahdensuo, head of the Finnish National Theatre. On 11 July he wondered whether anything much would come of it and two days later he put it aside, noting: 'Morning in the summer rain. The sun comes out again. *Dolce far niente.*'

The wedding took place on 21 July, and on the previous Sunday there was a ball at Ainola: 'The party for Ruth and Jussi went off well. But my punch was not to my taste. Put together in too slipshod a fashion. More care and inspiration needed.' Nor was he any more pleased with his musical concoctions: 'My work, which should develop along the lines of *quod diis placebit*, takes place *ut diis placebit*. A strange apathy has overtaken me. Perhaps it would be better if I followed the dictates of my heart. But I always have so many commissions. They govern my thinking and feeling.'

With all the northerner's sense of longing, he immersed his whole being in the glories of summer.

[27 July 1916] I am harvesting the sunshine and warmth for use in the winter.

– 4 –

At the beginning of August, Madetoja, who was just beginning his stint as critic of the *Helsingin Sanomat,* interviewed Sibelius at Ainola. After dinner their conversation turned to contemporary music, first of all Scriabin, who had recently died, then Schoenberg and the radical Viennese school: 'All these experiments which lie outside the normal domains of music should be taken for what they are worth. However, one can say that music is developing with giant strides, or to put it another way, is taking us in a direction which will comparatively soon reveal its true nature to the clear-thinking music lover. What is written today is already out of date tomorrow. Mahler's symphonies, which I thought were epoch-making some years ago, have already lost almost all their capacity to surprise.'

But he was careful to strike a note of caution: 'Of course, you must bear in mind that all I am saying now, on 8 August 1916 at about six in the evening, could take on a completely different light tomorrow, were we to touch on the same subjects.' Was he suddenly stricken by misgivings at his indiscretion? Two years earlier in Berlin he had been completely gripped by Mahler's *Das klagende Lied* and Schoenberg's F sharp minor quartet. But since *The Oceanides* he had moved away from expressionism and developed an altogether more ambivalent attitude towards Mahler. He was both drawn to and at the same time repelled by the directness of his musical expression. Perhaps his present judgement was affected by non-musical considerations. Could he have been swayed by unworthy thoughts and was reacting against Bis's extravagant praise in *Hufvudstadsbladet* of *Das Lied von der Erde* at the expense of his Fourth Symphony? One wonders too what his response would have been to Mahler's Ninth Symphony, whose *Adagio* comes close in feeling to the slow movement of the Fourth. But he was never to hear this symphony.

When Madetoja asked Sibelius about his own plans, he was greeted by a wall of silence: 'These are matters that I have decided never to talk about. I have become wise through experience. Some time ago I agreed to compose a song for Aino Ackté, a setting of Poe's *The Raven*, with a view to a projected concert tour. News of this spread immediately round the world. After I had struggled with this piece for some time, I came to the conclusion that the poem was impossible to set except as a melodrama. Nothing came of the song and I was placed in an embarrassing situation.' He made no mention of the fact that material from *The Raven* found its way into the finale of the Fourth Symphony.

At Ida Ekman's request, he began work on some songs. Quite apart from her artistry, he admired her as a person: 'This wonderful singer is also a delightful companion. She is unaffected and a good conversationalist. I can't bear the scandal-mongering of my other singers.' By the end of the month he had five songs ready: *Vårförnimmelser, Längtan heter din arvedel, Dold förening, Och finns det en tanke?* and *Sångarlön.* He published them as Op. 86, adding a sixth, *I systrar, I bröder,* to their number in November 1917.

But as is clear from his diary, it was making time for the revision of the Fifth Symphony that was now the problem: 'Thoughts of death! I'll never be able to complete the work I've dreamt about. Pins-and-needles in my hand: blood clot? . . . All my being and striving so completely unfulfilled. This is the end of you, glorious Jean Sibelius. You, a real Jean Christophe!'

Earlier in the year he had sent Carpelan scores of *The Oceanides* and *The Bard,* but his next letter makes it clear that:

Unfortunately it will be some time before I can send you more scores. The only things I can get printed – piano pieces and songs – are done in Sweden; to print music here is not profitable.

I often ask myself, shall I be condemned to live in total isolation from the great cultural centres – shall I never experience the delights that I always have when I am conducting a first-class orchestra in my music? But perhaps I am looking too much on the dark side. A composer of my temperament must always work with thoughts of the future. I shall soon be ready [with the incidental music to *Everyman*]. After that I shall subject the Fifth Symphony to a refit and then put out to sea. New plans and new ideas. Life again feels rich and deep.

Carpelan, on the other hand, had added an inflamed pancreas to his numerous collection of ailments. He anticipated death from starvation and dehydration, and wrote yet another of his numerous farewell letters!

By September Sibelius's deadline for the *Everyman* music was fast approaching: 'Think I have a hold on myself. My debts and the interest have gone down – with God's and others help – to 37,000 marks.' But people were a continual distraction. Linda expected him and Aino to go and visit her in the mental hospital: 'But how can I be of any use to her in the state I am now in?' Leena and Heikki Järnefelt turned up at Ainola late one night together with Sillanpää – who had just made his publishing début with *Life and Sun* – and a young lady to pay court to Ruth and Jussi Snellman. Amongst other things, the conversation touched on the Chinese labourers whom the Russian authorities had imported to work on their defences. The next day Sibelius betrayed impatience with his guests and in particular Sillanpää, whom he found self-satisfied and far too sure of himself. But perhaps he felt that he did not find the right tone with the younger generation.

In the middle of September Sibelius went to Helsinki for a couple of days to see Lahdensuo at the Finnish National Theatre, who went through his plans for *Everyman*. Sibelius did not find his company particularly congenial, and spent more time with Viktor Hoving from Viborg, with whom conversation and wine generously flowed. Hjalmar Procopé, for whose *Belshazzar's Feast* he had provided a score, also comes into the picture. Sibelius could not keep away from Helsinki and returned from his trips very much the worse for wear: 'Was in town yesterday. Not without drinking. Realize that this will not do. Must cut down on alcohol to as little as possible. Same with tobacco. Today am in the depths of despair. Met Kajanus yesterday and had a good time with him. He has dedicated his *Sinfonietta* to me.'

By 6 October he had finished the incidental music to *Everyman* and a fortnight later went to a stage rehearsal. The première took place on 6 November and his music met with success. Madetoja thought the play greatly enhanced by the score. But the theatre was not the only place in which his presence was felt that autumn. Ida Ekman, accompanied by her husband Karl, gave a survey of the Sibelius songs in the course of four recitals. Sibelius and Aino attended the first on 7 October, which included the five songs of his new set, Op. 86. Although Sibelius himself wrote that she sang wonderfully, Ida Ekman was by this stage past her prime. Her great days had been in the 1890s and by now she was having some difficulty at the top end of her register. Her hearing became impaired with the years and affected her intonation. Sibelius's writing in his last three sets of songs, Opp. 86, 88 and 90, was probably conditioned to some extent by her vocal limitations.

The 1916–17 season was something of a golden period for Finnish singers. The great interpreter of the Sibelius songs at this time was Aino Ackté, who had given the première of *Luonnotar* two years earlier under both Schnéevoigt and Sibelius himself. But now she was turning her attention to the younger generation, among others Erkki Melartin and Ilmari Hannikainen. Alma Kuula naturally championed her husband's songs and those of an up-and-coming *lieder* composer, Yrjö Kilpinen. Maikki Järnefelt, now married to Selim Palmgren, made a triumphant comeback with her pianist husband after some years' absence, and had given *The Rapids-Riders' Brides* in Stockholm. It did not escape Sibelius's eye that this had even enjoyed the approbation of Peterson-Berger.

Otherwise it was Palmgren who was enjoying wide exposure with his songs, which his wife was energetically promoting. On 14 November he scored a triumphant success with his Second Piano Concerto *(The River)*, which he played under Kajanus's baton in November, together with his new concerto *Metamorphoses*, a set of variations on an Ostrobothnian hymn spiced with Lisztian bravura and impressionistic harmonies. The public undoubtedly found his concertos and piano pieces, such as *May Night* and *Moonlight,* easier to assimilate than the Fourth and Fifth Symphonies of Sibelius. The critic Evert Katila hailed the new concerto in extravagant terms and called the smaller piano pieces included in the programme 'without peer in the literature of Finnish piano music'. (The author can recall conversations in his parental home during the 1920s, 'We have Sibelius and Palmgren . . . Sibelius cannot write for the piano, but take Palmgren – he is the Chopin of the North.') Palmgren expressed himself warmly about both Sibelius's music and his person in his memoirs. Concerning the piano music, he wrote: 'Even in what is for him an alien medium, the master moves with an unerring feeling for sonority.' Sibelius did not begrudge Palmgren his success, but did resent those critics who used Palmgren as a stick with which to beat him. But it is fair to say that his preference was for Madetoja, whom he thought a cut above the others of that generation.

Sibelius did not attend the Palmgren concert, nor those of other young composers such as Heino Kaski and Lauri Ikonen, but stayed at home and wrestled with the Fifth Symphony: 'Walk a lot. And am neglectful of my colleagues. Ignore their concerts. But I must get on with my own work. *Il sacro egoism.*' After *Everyman* was finished Sibelius returned to the symphony, but was not in the right frame of mind: 'I have wasted the day here at home. I can't say I am having much joy being here in Finland.' By the end of the month he was almost in desperation at his lack of progress.

Early in November he records that the first three movements are with his copyist and that he is working on the finale. As we can see, he is still speaking – perhaps out of habit – of four movements, though at this stage the first two were now linked together. 'Am in complete chaos. What a life! Agony and elation!' Reading between the lines in his diary, one can discern a certain anxiety. Would he be able to pay for the family's upkeep and pay off his loan interest by composing? 'And what then? The public here is fickle. Am writing this at midnight and am looking on the black side of things. Perhaps it will seem different in the morning. In any event I have composed too much. I need more time. No word from Axel. Now have rheumatism. Perhaps my exercise in the morning is too extreme. But it keeps colds away. And that's the most important thing for one's ears. Erik Furuhjelm is working away at his Jean S. book and has already finished it. Hope it is not a disaster.'

Sibelius's thoughts ramble from topic to topic until he confesses that he is 'writing all this rubbish' to get his depression out of his system. Not the least of his worries was the fact that his daughter Ruth was expecting her first child. Another was his dissatisfaction with the Fifth Symphony. He turned for consolation to the violin, with which he had flirted the previous year:

Am in good spirits this evening and have done well, i.e. composed full of life and wonder. Have taken up the *Humoresques* for violin (orch. or piano).

The copying of the Fifth Symphony cost 670 marks! That hurts! Money runs away! And what joy will I get out of it? Only abusive reviews etc. What a strange occupation I have chosen, composing! Such idealism in our day and age must seem quite absurd. But perhaps there will be a change of outlook soon. And I must admit that I have set my sights high and chosen something big. Am waiting for Aino and the children to come home [they had been staying with Aino's relations]. How much I love them! Come on, sentimental J. S., pull yourself together. What's the use of upsetting yourself?

– 6 –

December was a month of birthdays. Kajanus was sixty on the 2nd. Aino and Sibelius attended the celebratory dinner, though Gallen-Kallela did not emerge from his lonely retreat in the winter darkness of Ruovesi but sent his daughter instead with a beautiful illuminated address. A week later it was Sibelius's turn and he spent his fifty-first birthday at a concert in Åbo, where he conducted the newly-revised Fifth Symphony. Carpelan came to the concert and they spent some time together afterwards, before Sibelius returned to Helsinki, where on 14 December he conducted the new symphony together with the Third and the *Pelléas et Mélisande* music.

Any listener following with the definitive score would have greeted the new version with a measure of relief. The transition from the *Tempo molto moderato* to the *Allegro moderato*, formerly two separate movements, had succeeded almost one hundred per cent. To judge from the surviving double-bass part, the *Andante mosso* movement differed both from the first version and the definitive score. And in the finale, the tragic E flat minor episode from the first version is removed and replaced by a *vivace* episode in the major. Overall, the revision of the finale was not successful: the composer had taken one step forward but two back.

Afterwards Sibelius felt disappointment: 'The concert in Helsinki was not altogether to my taste. No enthusiasm. I am minded to believe that there were those who schemed against me, and I have been told that this was the case. Have even been given their names. Several of them my so-called friends. Strange are the ways of the human heart. In all events this wretched war is likely to go on, and thus my isolation too.'

Although the reviews were respectful and Madetoja's enthusiastic, Bis struck a more negative note: he was unconvinced by the transition from the first to second movements and the exaggerated dissonance of the finale. Sibelius took his review badly and was all the more grateful for a long letter from Carpelan. He thought the transition 'wonderful', and his paean of praise had only a slight reservation about the pizzicati in the second. He also had his views about conductors, and thought Schnéevoigt 'should be forbidden

93

to conduct any Sibelius work in public'. He thought him stupid and crude, with no feeling for his music.

At Christmas, Erik Furuhjelm's book at last appeared – one year late and 221 pages long. Sibelius was pleased with the result. Half was devoted to his genealogical background, childhood and school years in Hämeenlinna and his studies in Helsinki, Berlin and Vienna. The period from 1892, from *Kullervo* through to the First Symphony and *Finlandia,* occupied eighty pages and the years 1900–1915, up to the first version of the Fifth symphony, were allotted thirty-seven. The book performed a valuable function by covering Sibelius's formative years and was for a long time the only source of information about them. It says much for Sibelius's confidence in Furuhjelm that he entrusted him with a number of early scores, among them *Kullervo* and various earlier pieces, some of which he subsequently burnt. Above all, because it was written by a composer and scholar the book concentrated on musical rather than biographical issues, and challenged the arguments of Niemann and others about Sibelius's alleged folkloristic and programmatic bent.

At the end of the year his diary touched on new plans. He decided among other things to orchestrate his song *Marssnön (The March Snow),* written at the turn of the century. But when he came to look back over the year, he realised that the struggle for the Fifth Symphony had not yet been won.

CHAPTER SEVEN

1917: Year of Revolution

The fateful year of revolution was dawning. Russia, and Finland itself, stood on the brink of epoch-making events. How did Sibelius and those around him react to the unfolding drama, and did they sense what effect it would have on the future of their own country? Sibelius himself was acutely aware of looming disaster, of the approaching death throes of the pre-war era of the *Jugendstil*. How many times had he not sensed death's wings beating around him or felt himself as in a ship adrift on a windless sea? He needed suffering as a source of creative power. 'He is richest who can suffer most,' as he once wrote to Carpelan.[1]

'We, sons of the cataclysm, born to a dying sun . . .' Sibelius shared Bertel Gripenberg's pessimism and sense of darkness, and pored over *die Tragödie des Menschen*, his own tragedy when he viewed the dying embers of the sun through Ainola's windows. The evening skies glow like red burgundy. It would always be burgundy or champagne; there would be the rustling of silk and the glistening of rubies, and grief always followed in the wake of plea-sure. Gripenberg's poetic metaphors, which Sibelius set, are revealing. For behind the mask they donned of being tired of life, both artists possessed a strong appetite for its pleasures, of 'festive pomp and the captivating mid-summer nights', of Salome's, Teodora's and Lulu's followers, of hunting parties and nocturnal entertainments – just as their beliefs had always been borne aloft by a belief in a bright future, despite the long years of Tsarist repression.

It is true to say that *Jugendstil* developed quite differently in Finland than on the European continent. It was more monumental and less decadent, largely because in so many areas – architecture, music and painting – it was giving expression for the very first time to the national spirit and character. Finnish *art nouveau* was not a late flowering of an overripe romanticism but a first manifestation of national art. The leading players in its development, Sibelius and Kajanus, Gallén-Kallela and Eliel Saarinen, Bertel Gripenberg and Eino Leino, shared the same mission as creators of Finland's image at home and abroad, and this was a motivating force in their lives. Thanks to the role they played, they enjoyed a privileged position at the very summit

of the social hierarchy. Even if they were penniless and were frequent sup-
plicants at the money-lender's, their prestige as artists gave them the sure
knowledge that they belonged to the élite of the élite, adored and envied by
the public, highly regarded but poorly looked after, praised and reviled but
always at the centre of public attention. Unlike a number of the early expressionist and *art nouveau* artists, such as the members of *Der blaue Reiter*, the
leading artists of the Finnish golden age – with the possible exception of
Eino Leino – remained indifferent to social problems or to working-class
privations and concerns. From their Olympian heights they had formed an
idealized picture of 'the people' that they were quite happy with, just as the
people were largely happy with them. But now they felt the first tremors in
the order they had come to take for granted. They and their class no longer
sat so firmly in the saddle, but were threatened by an imminent working-
class uprising. What previously had been a sense of artistic decline and fall
was soon in danger of becoming a material reality.

For Gripenberg all this came as no surprise. He had seen the light during
the popular uprisings in the Baltic States as early as 1909, when freedom,
equality and brotherhood on proletarian terms meant freedom to pillage
and destroy, equality was grey prison uniforms, and brotherhood was in
butchery. This was how Gripenberg described the situation during the
years 1915–17 in Sääksmäki, Sibelius's childhood tract, where he had a small
farm holding: 'The political position here in Finland became day by day
more intolerable. Russia, now under great pressure, maintained its strong
grip on the country. But there were other sources of anxiety: revolutionary
ferment among the working masses, not least in the countryside . . . The
workers' threat against society was no longer a mild subterranean murmur,
but had come to the surface and was directed against everybody and
everything.'

Gripenberg foresaw the fall of the Tsarist régime, but feared the worst for
Finland; he did not dare to hope that 'our people . . . would take advantage
of Russia's disintegration with good sense and judgement.' Gallen-Kallela's
views were not dissimilar. Even though he did not share Gripenberg's
upper-class military background, he regarded the rest of humanity from a
lofty Nietzschean viewpoint. He may have idealized the Finnish people, but
he was more than aware of the darker forces among them.

But for Gripenberg and so many like-minded members of Sibelius's
circle, it was their national identity rather than any class divisions that motivated them. Yet they were faced with a dilemma. They wanted an
independent national existence, but a precondition of this was the collapse
of Tsarism. Yet if the coming revolution eventually led to a proletarian
take-over of power not only in Russia but in Finland as well, this would in
itself forge a link between the two countries based on class sentiment. And
so the times when Gallen-Kallela, Gripenberg and Saarinen could cheer the
radicals, as they did at the time of the 1905 general strike, and give refuge and

support to Maxim Gorky were over. Although Sibelius was a less political animal, his view of the overall situation did not basically differ from theirs except in one respect. He had a higher opinion of the Finnish people at large than they did, a belief that he also shared with the poet Leino. He got on well with the servants and work people at Järvenpää, although their views were largely 'red'.

Sibelius's brother-in-law Arvid Järnefelt still retained his Utopian and Tolstoyan convictions. For him, the only way out for mankind was for everyone to refuse military service: 'Rather than dying like mindless cannon fodder in the pursuit of killing your fellow men, would it not be easier to die as a martyr for your beliefs?' Because of his anti-militarist sympathies Järnefelt was brought before a local tribunal and subsequently the high court, but both the charges against him were thrown out. Later Rantala, his house in Lojo, was searched, but 'after two visits, the gendarmes left me in peace. In Russia practically all writers have been imprisoned. Why shouldn't I be?' He did not have long to wait.

Paradoxically, Sibelius was much impressed by Järnefelt's uncompromising and combative religious beliefs. He saw it as something magnificent, perhaps even thought of it as analogous to his own lonely symphonic struggle; perhaps even a reproach, in that, more than usual, he had been forced to compromise with the demands of the wartime situation and produce small trifles. 'As long as the war goes on, I have to make compromises, it would seem,' he told Carpelan.[2] Unlike Gallen-Kallela, however, Sibelius was so completely at the mercy of the categorical imperative that he was able to cocoon himself from the outside world. The critical political situation was not his major preoccupation during the first months of 1917 – his thoughts were centred on the Fifth Symphony and the completion of the projected *Humoresques*.

– 2 –

Sibelius began the New Year in exactly the same way as he had begun the last: 'Am reworking *mirabile dictu* Symphony 5 for Stockholm (Armas).' (Diary, 1 January 1917) But only a few days were to elapse before he was writing to Armas withdrawing the new work:

> I am very unhappy about this. When I was composing my Sym. 5 for my fiftieth birthday, I was very pressed for time. As a result I spent last year reworking it, but am still not happy. And cannot, absolutely cannot, send it to you. Try and invent some excuse: for example, that I cannot possibly risk sending my only copy of the score, or something like that, since in my experience J. S.'s judgement in this matter does not err. Perhaps you could perform Sym. 4. It has been hailed in America, England and by Oskar Fried as epoch-making. Muck has given it in Boston and New York four

times with great success. Also Busoni, Fitelberg and others. (6 January 1917 – mistakenly dated 1916, as so often at the beginning of a year)

A diary entry of the same day reads: 'Must forget the 5th symphony and work on. Perhaps the sun will one day shine on me.' But the sun did not come out so soon: 'I am sick at heart. And there seems no end in sight. How have I got myself into this position? Many reasons. My path as far as composition is concerned has reached a cul-de-sac. Must take things in hand and push ahead . . . As so often, I have the wind really against me and not, as so many assume, with me.'

Cross winds did not make life easier. He returned later to the subject of Kajanus, who had pointed out some mistakes during the rehearsals of the second version of the Fifth Symphony in December 1916: 'And that is not surprising, when all the players are poor and the conductor nervous. How often have I not had occasion to correct him as far as his ear was concerned? But I have never done so publicly in front of the orchestra, as he did to me. Well, that's the difference in our natures.' (Diary, 11 November 1917)

There had apparently been some tension between Sibelius and the orchestra. Perhaps Kajanus had tried to mediate, as he had done twenty years earlier at the première of the *Lemminkäinen Suite*, and pointed out inaccuracies of intonation in their playing? Oblivious of these small recriminations, Kajanus suddenly announced that he would be paying a visit to Ainola. Sibelius was immediately on his guard: 'No doubt he will want to take advantage of my popularity – to my own detriment?' Kajanus arrived and outlined plans that he and the impresario Fazer had drawn up for a tour of England and France with the orchestra playing Finnish repertoire. Obviously Kajanus saw this as a valuable propaganda exercise. Whichever way things went for the Russians, it was important to build up goodwill with the Allies. Naturally Sibelius understood all this, but the actual plan itself did not appeal to him. Kajanus, he noted, 'wants to make propaganda for Palmgren, Madetoja and himself. I am there on the side, as it were, and can't believe that my pride will permit this. Have outgrown them in stature. I can't see anything good coming out of this Viking trip.'

Undoubtedly Sibelius's role was an ungrateful one. To have one piece in a whole Finnish programme of otherwise only moderate interest from an international perspective would hardly have advanced his cause in the two great capitals. But on this occasion he need not have exercised himself. Kajanus's trip came to nothing. A diary entry some days later shows him to have been ashamed of his earlier mistrust: 'My nerves are bad. My view of life jaundiced as usual. I must really free myself from these suspicions and so on concerning Kajanus. Let him be, in God's name, and go his own way.'

A touch of paranoia also surfaced during an otherwise happy visit to Ainola by his childhood friend Walter von Konow. Sibelius took offence when the question of his genealogy came up and Walter touched on the question of his own noble birth. Small genealogical errors, bagatelles really, also irritated him in Nyblom's highly respectful monograph published in Stockholm. The names of his peasant ancestors were mixed up: 'All this messing around with my ancestors – now even in Sweden. But I must confess that I have myself tried to cultivate an aristocratic tone at all our watering holes.'

He had promised Ida Ekman some new songs, but doubted whether he would have any of them ready: 'If I can only ride out the storm and go my own way – always alone? But is it so essential to possess friends? One dies alone after all! It's best to cultivate solitude. This is only possible by means of intensive work.' But whatever way he turned, it was somehow the wrong one. At home in solitude he turned in on himself too deeply. If he went with friends to a restaurant in Helsinki, his high living became the subject of gossip. He reproached himself for making Aino's life so miserable: 'She has such a terribly hard time now and this pains me enormously. In my heart there is a sad, intimate melody. I see how we love each other. Aino longs for death as a relief.' (Diary, 4–5 September 1916) But other days began with 'sunlight and clear winter air, fragrant as in one's youth'. And as in their youth, Aino and he took their walks on new paths and he had new musical plans. The *Humoresques* for violin and orchestra were beginning to take shape within him.

Aino needed a change of scene. Even if she was reluctant to leave home at this juncture, she made a journey, presumably after much thought, to Petrograd – as St Petersburg had now become – to visit her daughter Eva and her husband Arvi Paloheimo, who had a comfortable apartment in the centre of the city. 'Let's pray that she has a safe journey. The beloved creature is worn out.' (Diary, 10 September 1916). Perhaps she should not have left him alone: 'Went into town yesterday and the day before. Heavy drinking and afterwards much depression. Terrible this state. Particularly as my weakness for alcohol damages me in my own and others' eyes. At home here some furtive drinking to get my nerves in better condition.' (Diary, 16 September 1916)

A few days later came news that the Accademia di Santa Cecilia in Rome had conferred honorary membership on him. It was surely Toscanini's performances of *En Saga*, *The Swan of Tuonela* and *Finlandia* that had laid the foundations of his reputation in Italy. The honour appealed to his feeling for antiquity: 'The very name Rome has always exercised a strangely powerful fascination over me.' He felt inspiration: 'A little light shines on my work. About time, as my coffers are empty. Bills etc. Unpaid.'

On 14 February the first *Humoresque* was ready. The numbering was later changed, the original *Humoresques I–V* becoming *II–VI*. The following day he went into Helsinki and sold it to Blomstedt for 2,000 marks. While in town he could not resist the opportunity of calling in on Kajanus's rehearsal, where Madetoja's First Symphony and a new piano concerto by Ernst Linko were being rehearsed and Kajanus was putting the finishing touches to *The Oceanides*. However, he was careful not to stay in town. He was sensitive to the general opprobrium that his excesses excited. Back home he took stock of the situation: 'At the rehearsal, so nervous for a time that I thought that all thought of conducting in the future would be impossible. In the evening it was better. Whatever it is, I mustn't let it get me down so much. Must look things straight in the eye – and lead my own life. Must cut back on drinking and high living.'

But the next day found him slumped into depression. His future lot was old age and neglect: 'Youth has a right to make its voice heard. One sees oneself as a father figure to them all. And they don't give a damn about you. Perhaps with reason.' Had he perhaps met Madetoja, with his pale, faraway mien, at the rehearsal? He looked forward to days filled with remunerative work, but still did not know how he was going to manage.

He continued his internal monologue a couple of days later: 'Sunshine. Working after a fashion. Missing Aino. But how will life work out for her with me in my present joyless state now that everything is so unpredictable? Must suffer other things as well . . . to rely on my dear countrymen, Katila, Kajanus; that is something I have never done. And must continue to avoid. Polite but *noli me tangere*! Feeling horribly unwell. I expect my nerves weren't improved when I played *Elektra* of Strauss from a piano score.' (Diary, 8 October 1916)

In Paris six years earlier he had, in spite of himself, been fascinated by *Salome*. At that time he was at the height of his expressionist phase. Now he reacted negatively to *Elektra*. No doubt this was in part due to the fact that he was now, with the Fifth Symphony, going through a more classical period.

Aino returned from Petrograd. Some days later Sibelius disappeared to Helsinki to go on the tiles with the painter Favén and others. The next day Aino was so bad that Sibelius feared 'the worst. Oh God.' He was full of self-loathing: 'I can't carry on in this fashion when I see what the consequences are.' It was in this frame of mind that he composed a *Religioso* for violin or cello and piano, which he dedicated to his brother Christian. But the atmosphere at home did not lighten. It must have been transparently clear to Aino that after a lapse of nine years Janne was well on the way to his old habits where Bacchus was concerned, and this drove her to despair. There were heated exchanges, which are reflected in his diary: 'It's strange how there are moments in life when it is as though a searchlight illuminates our future and we see distinctly and clearly our misery. This evening with Aino such a moment. We ought to separate but lack the courage and spirit. And then what would our lives be like? But are we locked together? Is it not possible to rebuild our lives? Impossible to think clearly.' (Diary, 3 November 1916)

He suffered every bit as much as she did, as he fully realized that his drinking would damage them both. His composing was for her a sacred mission. What would happen to the Fifth Symphony and the Sixth, which was beginning to take shape, and all his other great plans if things went on as they were? Her desperation was also his. But there must have been moments when her single-minded fanaticism, iron will and rare but devastating outbursts of anger followed by periods of resigned silence frightened him. Perhaps it was to free himself from such an atmosphere that he wrote such speculations about separation.

Matters were not helped by the knowledge that his Fourth Symphony had been given the previous day in Stockholm by the Konsertförenings Orkester conducted by Schnéevoigt. Peterson-Berger surpassed himself in denouncing the symphony with 'its Wagner-inspired philosophizing', and his destructiveness stands out in the strongest possible contrast with Stenhammar's letter (5 February 1913) after the repeat performance in Gothenburg:

> This symphony has fasted in the desert for forty days or rather wandered for forty years in its zealous search for the promised land of living music – and after a promising beginning, emerges as an emaciated Buddhist saint, tormented by visions of musical starvation, which at times take the form of *Parsifal*-like gestures or – though less often – Hagen's dark, menacing chords in *Götterdämmerung*. But always in a curiously watered-down and ascetic form, which poor duty-bound commentators, condemned in advance to embrace its delights, would regard as the height of spirituality – if by this time they can remember what that is.
>
> As a whole the symphony has a certain, architectonic line: but that attribute is purely formal. Spiritual qualities are first touched on in the third movement, while the strength of the remaining movements resides in an impassive calm from which anything clear and comprehensible is pushed to one side by subjective self-satisfaction. The second movement's aphoristic form and conclusion would also have a certain effect if it possessed any fathomable content – there is no great skill in trying to be witty or involuntarily being a source of humour: one's thoughts turn to a lunatic who sits quietly muttering to himself and sniggering, indistinct and confused.'

A year earlier Peterson-Berger had laid into the Violin Concerto, which was included in the same programme. Now as then, it was Olallo Morales who showed insight and understanding. He was prepared, albeit with some caution, to agree with the author of the programme notes, Kretschmer, that the Fourth Symphony showed 'a certain spiritual kinship with Debussy's impressionism . . . without, however, discerning a stylistic change in Sibelius's art other than it becoming more inward-looking and more keenly personal, it has lost some of its superficial Finnish colouring in favour of a more international stance.'

Discussing the first movement, he speaks of the religious mysticism of 'this symphonic *Voces intimae*, which arouses expectations that are later unfulfilled. The voices register as solitary fragments, each one unaware of its connection with the others . . . seldom coming together in a harmonic framework. It relies on line rather than the pure impressionistic colours of Debussy. Suddenly the voices are silenced as in a suspended conversation and the listener is left facing uncertainty.'

Thus Morales grasped its linear strength without speaking of expressionism. It is quite clear that he did not want to put the symphony into any pigeon-hole. Sigurd von Koch, a young composer, wrote of the symphony's 'powerful fascination' but was doubtful about any relationship to Debussy: 'Rather I would say that Sibelius more than ever establishes his own world'.

These reviews were reprinted in a prominent position in *Hufvudstadbladet* under the heading 'From Stockholm's Concert Halls: Richard Strauss and Sibelius'. Although he must have seen them, he made no reference to them in his diary.

In March he had once again to take Aino to hospital. She was soon home again, wept for a day – and recovered. She was overjoyed to welcome Eva who, with her small daughter, had left Petrograd after rifle bullets had riddled the ceiling of their dining-room. The February Revolution had broken out.

– 3 –

'*Svoboda, svoboda!*' ['Freedom!']

Eva's greeting resounded from the hallway at Ainola. There, as everywhere else in Finland, the February Revolution was greeted with joy. Sibelius wrote: 'Great things have happened in Russia. Can we here mould our own fate? That's the great question. A heavy weight hangs over Finland.' (Diary, 15 February 1917) He was expectant, sceptical, bewildered. On the political front all seemed to bode well. As a result of the provisional government's decision to lift the wartime Tsarist restrictions, Finland was once again autonomous. Those Finns who were held on political grounds in Russian prisons, or who had been deported further afield, were released and returned home. Nevertheless there were far too many imponderables for there to be unguarded optimism: 'Great things are happening these days. Liberty, equality, fraternity!' The exclamation mark no doubt betrays irony.

Katarina Sibelius, who had recently turned fourteen, went into Helsinki from time to time for her piano lessons and could witness at first hand the revolutionary atmosphere. In the first flush of euphoria she rejoiced that Finland was again 'as free as it was earlier, in Alexander I's time. We have all gone wild with joy. On Thursday the whole town was bedecked with flags – not the hated Russian one – but Finland's white and blue flag.' From Petrograd she had heard rumours that 'the soldiers – and presumably the whole of the aristocracy – were said to be for the revolution'. At the Senate Square in Helsinki, Maximov, the commander of the Russian Baltic fleet, addressed the crowd in Swedish: 'I salute free Finland'. But once the initial enthusiasm had cooled, Katarina could view the situation more critically: 'Can one rely on Russia? That only the future can say. But even if the situation in Finland were to become even worse than it has been in the past, I am sure that we would manage ... Every country has its mission and Finland will fulfil its mission on the day that it is even freer.' There speaks the father's daughter!

At the end of March Katarina, with her uncle Eero Järnefelt and his daughters, waited on the station platform at Helsinki to witness Svinhufvud's triumphal return from Siberia. Järnefelt introduced her to the future Head of State and President and she shook his hand – another example of how close were the links that Sibelius and those around him enjoyed with the ruling circles. The same day she tried to catch a glimpse of Kerensky, who had arrived in Helsinki a few hours earlier. Katarina also heard of the violence that the revolution unleashed. The majority of the Russian Baltic fleet and army was stationed in Helsinki, and both sailors and soldiers rebelled. Katarina's sister Ruth and her cousin Heikki Järnefelt had seen with their own eyes how Russian officers had been shot in the open streets. One of her friends had had to take cover when the street where she was walking was riddled with machine-gun fire. In general, Katarina's reactions harmonize with those of her father, as recorded in the mid-1930s in Karl Ekman's biography:

> The Russian revolution made itself felt even in our peaceful Järvenpää. Since the beginning of the war the district had harboured a strong military force. Now the men began to settle accounts with their officers. The murder of officers was a daily occurrence here, as in Helsingfors and other large military centres. Shots were heard all day long. The growing arrogance and savagery of the working class made things look bad for us too. Workmen's riots, unrest and strikes during the summer, which even the Järvenpää district was not spared, gave us a foretaste of what was in store. A horrible time.

In spite of the war, Sibelius had to get on with life and composing. As he told Axel Carpelan, Aino was very poorly, the children too were not well and he himself 'succumbed to the 'flu, which took its toll on my good spirits and resulted in – the *Humoresques* for violin and orchestra. As usual I still have great plans in my head for orchestral works.'

The dramatic events in Russia elicited a letter from Carpelan with some Cassandra-like portents: 'Fate has placed us in a vulnerable geographical position and we can expect to suffer on that count. I see dark nationalist Slavonic clouds rising on the horizon and who knows when they will settle on us. Perhaps earlier than we even suspect. I expect nothing good to come from the constitutional assembly with the new form of government in Russia. If Petrograd decides to continue with the war, it will mean a victory of nationalism over the socialists. Perhaps it will all turn to red-hot anarchy – but then a reaction will be the necessary corollary. Even without all that, we will be sucked into internal social tyranny for some time to come.'

Carpelan predicted the Bolshevik revolution, Russia's peace agreement with Germany as a result of the socialist victory, and its 'corollary' of the White Russian alliance with Western interventionists. On the question of Russo-Finnish relations, he touched on a sore point when he mentioned in a later letter 'the gruesome logic of geography which has placed Petrograd at only three hours' distance from the border.' In the autumn of 1939, during the fruitless Fenno-Soviet negotiations that preceded the Winter War, Stalin said much the same thing to the Finnish delegation when he told them that they could not escape the logic of geography.

The 'internal social tyranny' to which Carpelan alludes concerns the attempt by the Finnish socialists, through their majority in the lower house, to impose their new social programme. It is not impossible that Sibelius was influenced in some measure by Carpelan's views. He must have reflected on the fact that Carpelan's intuitive understanding and gifts in so many areas never strictly speaking found the wider expression they deserved, but were directed only to him. Carpelan was a very private person.

No one could have been further removed from him in temperament than Sibelius's brother-in-law Arvid Järnefelt, whose energies were dedicated to spreading his Tolstoyan philosophy. He did not have high hopes of the February revolution: 'Now the Girondins are in power in the government, when can we expect the Jacobins?' In the presence of several thousand followers and in defiance of the clergy, he swept into Berghälls Church at the end of the ordinary service, proclaiming the Tolstoyan gospel. His sermon included a sensational confession:

> I belong to the upper class . . . and can thus speak as their conscience. We confess that our culture has suffered a breakdown. We believed that we could enlighten you and lead you towards a future happiness but . . . we have achieved nothing save terror and destruction. Now that we are stepping down from our commanding position, we beg you not to follow our example and not to exploit your understanding of our downfall, but put your understanding in the service of Love.

The Järnefelt case became an overnight sensation. Most people thought, as did the newspaper *Helsingin Sanomat,* that he was unbalanced. But voices were raised in his defence: the poet and humanist Eino Leino thought his speech 'a cultural-historical event of the highest importance', and Elisabeth Järnefelt consoled her son: 'Janne understands you also and says that the church is everyone's church; the priests have merely laid siege to it and assumed self-proclaimed rights to the household.'

Sibelius himself was scrupulous in following the demands of social convention in his public demeanour, and was nearly always meticulous in their observance. But in private he admired people of stature who broke conventional barriers and spoke out for their convictions. Society, however, thought otherwise. In September Arvid was taken off to Helsinki where he spent the night in the cells, from which the following morning he was transported to court in a closed prison van together with six ladies of the night. The case was postponed and he returned home.

— 4 —

The high hopes that the February Revolution might bring freedom for the Finns were soon dampened. The Provisional Government in Petrograd was willing to grant Finland a greater autonomy that came close to, but fell short of, complete independence. In May Kerensky returned to Helsinki, and in an address to the Russian fleet and troops uttered a note of caution: 'Here in Finland we must proceed with great caution, for our magnanimity and goodwill could be interpreted (and not only by the Germans) as weakness or impotence.' His words were doubtless a warning both to the Finns not to press their luck too far and to his own forces not to conspire with radical socialists in Helsinki. Unlike Kerensky, Sibelius presumably thought that the Finnish authorities were not exerting sufficient pressure on Petrograd, but on the other hand he naturally viewed with concern the possibility of Finnish socialists linking up with Russian soldiers and radicals. 'Are we really ready for freedom?' he wondered anxiously on 28 April. A few weeks later his anxiety had deepened: 'At present we are engulfed in complete anarchy.'

May began with snow, despite the spring sun. 'My nerves are in tatters. A terrible depression. Another title for the *Humoresques*. *Lyric dances*? Am impossible with people. Can't bear to see them. Become a misanthropist in the end. Me – who was at one time the most companionable person in the land.' In the end he retained the title *Humoresques*. The second, later to become No. 3, was finished on 3 May. 'There is still ice everywhere. No birds.' But four days later the thrushes were to be seen and also some star-lings. Sibelius blamed the squirrels rather than the starlings for the damage to the trees surrounding Ainola. 'Am working on something for Pelle Wester-lund as I need lots of money now.' The next day he completed his *Rondino* for violin and piano, Op. 81, No. 2. This and the *Humoresques* fetched 2,800 marks. Even so, he was worried that his income would be insufficient to meet his outgoings, which soared sky-high with every month that passed.

One day a packet shaped like a violin case arrived through the post. It turned out to be not a violin but a leg of smoked lamb. It came from the architect Torkel Nordman in Björneborg, an enthusiastic *a cappella* singer. The gift not only aroused the recipient's taste buds but stimulated poetic associations, prompting the composition of *Fridolins dårskap (Fridolin's folly)* to words by Karlfeldt's. He called it a joke, but in its simplicity it has a captivating charm and a whiff of the old male-voice quartet tradition. He sent the song to Nordman with his thanks for *le délicieux violon*. From Karlfeldt's Värmland he turned to Runeberg and another early romantic,

Frans Michael Franzén, and chose six poems with flower motives from their output, three from each poet. These were to form the basis for his Op. 88 collection, a bouquet of songs for Ida Ekman that he completed on 16 June.

On 10 June he and Aino had celebrated their silver wedding anniversary with a delightful family gathering in the summer's warmth. Some high points were needed in a situation which was becoming more and more frightening. At the beginning of July he went to Helsinki and returned quite shaken: 'A dreadful uncertainty everywhere. Whatever will it lead to? The young will live to see better times, but you, glorious Jean Sibelius, will be resting in your grave before then. How infinitely sad it all is. And there is no, *no* light.' The sight of a mass joint demonstration by Finnish socialists and the Russian soldiery gave him a further reminder of the imminent proletarian revolution. 'Seldom has there been a time so totally without spiritual values as ours. A composer is completely out of the picture.'

In early July Sibelius became a grandfather for the third time: Ruth had a son, Eva having a month earlier also given birth to a baby boy. But neither of these happy events lifted his spirits for more than a fleeting moment: 'See everything in the future as black, that's to say concerning Aino.' Night frost in July was followed by a warm August, and Sibelius was able to bathe in the lake right into September. 'Aino – the beloved creature – is again better.' Work on the *Humoresques* continued. In early September he worked uninterruptedly at them and by the 18th, Nos III, IV and V (IV–VI in the definitive numbering) were ready and were sent off to Lindgren. In all, he got 6,000 marks for them – not an unreasonable sum in those days.

In Helsinki important events were unfolding. The Finnish socialists' attempt to concentrate power in the lower assembly and to press ahead with plans for a Finland separated from Russia had prompted Kerensky, now prime minister, to prorogue the assembly. Fears of a socialist dictatorship were so strong that the right and centre parties did not dare risk an open break with Petrograd. Divisions within Finland increased. The compromises made with Petrograd probably displeased Sibelius and stimulated the activist in him. But he tried to lead as normal a life as possible.

[20 September 1917) Walked. Beautiful autumn day. The neighbours are digging up their potatoes. Yesterday I stayed in bed. My nerves! Had been on a celebratory bout in Helsinki, but a splendid time.

[21 September] Katarina went to school in Helsinki. She's left home – my heart bleeds. They want me to conduct in Kiev. Impossible now. I'm torn to pieces with doubts over my new work's form. I'm finding things really difficult now. The cranes have flown away. Autumn is coming.

The crisis point in the war was past. Finnish exports were down, as the main trading partner, the Russians, could no longer afford to print their newspapers on Finnish paper or decorate their walls with Finnish mats. Russian defence work relating to their Finnish garrisons came to halt. The country was afflicted by unemployment, food shortages and inflation, to which Sibelius himself testified: 'Expensive times. Bitterly earned money melts away like snow.'

His sister again came on a visit. 'The first day all right. But then melancholy consumed me. Impossible to do any work. A couple of days ago composed a *Berceuse* for violin and piano, Op. 79, No. 6, together with *Bellis* for piano, Op. 85, No. 3 [later to become No. 1].' An admirer sent him some excellent Havana cigars which gave him almost childish pleasure. Not long after, other plants began to blossom in his output, including *Aquileja*, Op. 85, No. 4. This idyllic miniature, with its touch of Schumannesque melancholy, might be seen as an instance of a composer's music being unrelated to his immediate personal circumstances, for his diary of these days records another particularly depressing entry: 'Peace is further off than ever. How will this all turn out? Oh my poor country with all its dissension.' (Diary, 14 October 1917)

− 5 −

The situation had deteriorated. In the elections of 1 and 2 October the socialists had lost their majority in the lower house. Their bitterness mounted and the radical socialist faction increased its influence. Armed Red guards and White defence corps sprang up all over the country. The diary shows how, as disaster approached, Sibelius would have preferred to immerse himself in the symphony if only circumstances had permitted. But to meet his debts he was forced during the late autumn to compose one miniature after the other. He had no appetite or time for any political involvement, unlike his friend Gallen-Kallela, who threw himself into the political fray, busily campaigning for an end to the language war, denouncing the government leaders in a letter to Ståhlberg for compromising with the Petrograd government: 'It is clear that we will have nothing whatsoever to do with Russia as soon as we get the hooligans out of here.'

Sibelius inhabited a less nationalist and in spite of everything, more realistic world. Moreover, he had had enough of what Gallen-Kallela called the *Realpolitik* of the ruling party. They possessed a certain rigidity of outlook and 'foolish wisdom' which, according to Rydberg's *Dexippos* – from which Sibelius had taken the text for the *Song of the Athenians* – was rewarded with the leaden yoke of slavery. Never would he allow himself to be drawn into active political life. But if he could perhaps make another contribution similar to the *Song of the Athenians*, then he would. An opportunity soon presented itself. One day in October he was telephoned by his ear specialist Wilhelm Zilliacus: could he come into Helsinki to talk over an important matter? Zilliacus was one of the organizers of the Finnish Jaeger movement, and reported that 'our boys down there [in the Gulf of Riga] are in low spirits and in great need of encouragement from home.' The Finnish Jaeger

Battalion had obtained its military training in Germany, with a view not so much to shedding its blood on Germany's Eastern front, but rather to striking a blow for Finland's independence. Rumour had it that the German authorities were planning to disband the battalion – its very existence could be in an irritant to the peace negotiations with the Russians. Where were they to go? In Finland, opinion was by no means united in their favour, and the Russian government regarded their activities as treasonable.

During his visit to Finland, Kerensky had warned activists and extremists to refrain from 'criminal enterprises' and took up the question of the Jaeger Battalion itself with the Finnish authorities. At their camp in Libau (Liepaja) the Jaegers had plenty of time to ponder over their plight and their rootlessness. To keep up their spirits they organized a competition for the best words for a marching song, and the winner was Lieutenant Heikko Nurmio. Zilliacus asked Sibelius if he would be willing to set it and his response was an unhesitating yes. The music was copied and sent in great secrecy to Libau, and though the copies bore neither Sibelius's nor Nurmio's names, they did for some reason bear the date of Sibelius's birthday. In doing this, Sibelius was putting himself at some risk. Finland was still in the power of the Russians and Kerensky was still prime minister. In the event of revolution and chaos breaking out in Finland itself, to have written this, thus betraying White political sympathies, would always be a handicap. And given the fact that the composer in this instance happened to be Sibelius, he could be absolutely certain that his identity would sooner or later be made public. The *Jaeger March* was originally designed as encouragement for a small group of Finnish troops who were stranded far away from home. Sibelius would not have thought of possible implications. He may well have imagined its use as a marching song if, in the absence of an acceptable agreement with the Russians, a war of independence were to ensue. Never could he have imagined that it would eventually become so closely identified with one faction in a Finnish civil war!

As October drew to a close, Helsinki society made the most of the last autumn days. The champagne flowed, particularly after Maikki Järnefelt's anniversary concert, at which Sibelius was present: 'She has preserved her voice in a remarkable fashion. The odd exaggeration in expression was always there. My *Rapids-Riders' Brides* still makes a strong effect . . . Palmgren looked insignificant. Met Kajus who had his *beau jour* . . . Pleasantly drunk, but I paid for it. My God! Always this. What do I never learn?' Sibelius's hand is affected by the champagne. His writing becomes rounder and broader, as are the entries themselves – repetitious rhetorical questions and exclamation marks. Palmgren's 'insignificance' could allude to his stature as a composer or to his appearance. On the stage he cut a slight figure by the side of Maikki's domineering diva personality and fiery temperament. 'You sang like a devil,' Christian Sinding had declared after her interpretation of his song *En kvinna* in Christiania. Bis was highly enthusiastic: 'In *The*

Rapids-Riders' Brides Mrs Järnefelt rose to the highest level of artistry, an overwhelming interpretation of which only she is capable.'

Four days later Ida Ekman in her turn gave an anniversary concert. Sibelius and Aino were among the audience, and as the singer came on to the platform, Sibelius rose and walked to the podium where he handed her a garland with a card inscribed 'Congratulations and thanks for your marvellous interpretations of my songs.' She began her programme with the new flower songs – whose sensitivity and finesse aroused Bis's enthusiasm – and such favourites as *Säv, säv, susa, Demanten på marssnön* and *Var det en dröm?* After the concert they repaired to a supper party which went on until six in the morning. Sibelius felt quite exhausted: 'There must surely be an end to these anniversaries. +6°C. Moonlight. In Helsinki, champagne, wines etc. What a wonderful country!'

In between these two recitals a twenty-six-year-old composer, Bengt von Törne, gave a concert of his own compositions. A year earlier Kajanus had introduced him to Sibelius at a rehearsal of the Fourth Symphony. Here is how von Törne described the occasion:

> 'I think,' Kajanus said, 'that Monsieur de Törne would like to submit something to you.' Sibelius asked whether it was a composition, and, on my confessing this, he remarked: 'Do you know, I have had some unfortunate experiences with young composers showing me their scores.' His look expressed the utmost melancholy. 'No sooner do I say anything about their compositions than they lose their tempers. And they have no difficulty in persuading me that they are perfectly right, whereas I am completely wrong to venture even the feeblest criticism of their work.' Kajanus now replied that he thought he could so far guarantee the placidity of my temperament, and I chimed in protesting that I only hoped for severe criticism. At that, Sibelius opened his arms and smiled broadly. 'If so,' he said, 'you are *my* man. Depend on it, you will get the criticism in so many words!'
>
> Thereupon he shook hands with me, asking me to come and see him one day of the following week at the hotel where he usually put up when he came in to Helsingfors from the country.

Von Törne's sensitivity and wit made a good impression on Sibelius, and for a number of months the young man, who had only just left the Music Institute, took lessons from the composer, until the latter suddenly declared during the course of a lesson that this would be the last: 'I can teach you no more.' Nowhere in his diary does Sibelius mention von Törne, and he did not attend his concert. According to Bis, von Törne's instrumentation showed that he had had 'the good fortune to benefit from a master in this field . . . Two things were yet to come: inspiration of the highest quality and a really personal voice.' Presumably Sibelius had realized this the previous spring and gently and diplomatically broken off the lessons. In later years von Törne was to become better known as an essayist and cultural historian than a composer. His encounters with Sibelius formed the basis of a book he published in English twenty years later as *Sibelius: A Close-up*. This devoted and somewhat naïve bagatelle chanced to fall into the hands of Theodor Adorno, whose hatred of Sibelius grew during his exile and found expression in his rabid *Glosse über Sibelius*.

Musical life in Helsinki continued as usual at the beginning of November. Musical connections with Russia were unbroken: the Maryinsky Theatre's star soprano Elise Popowa and the violinist Miron Polyakin performed with the Helsinki Orchestra. But in the political arena things were less happy. On 7 November the Finnish Secretary of State Carl Enckell, together with the Russian Governor-General, took the night train to Petrograd to deliver new proposals to Kerensky concerning Finland's relationship with Russia. When they arrived next morning at the border, they were greeted by the news that the Kerensky government had been overthrown.

The October revolution unleashed unrest in Finland itself, though Sibelius makes scant reference to it in his diaries. During November there are only four entries: first on the 11th, noting that he had added *I bröder, I systrar, I älskande par* to words of Mikael Lybeck to the Op. 86 songs and *Campanula* to the Op. 85 piano pieces. On 13 November he touches on the political situation: 'A general strike is threatened. Eva and Arvi are here with the children. We are expecting Ruth's boy too. We have a full house. And are very happy. Difficult to get at my orchestral pieces when everything is so uncertain in the headlines. Everyone's attention is focused on the war and its consequences. Erik [Eero] was here yesterday. Had a good time. Rainy +6°C. Even took a walk without an overcoat today.' He shuts out the world around him and concentrates on his main problem: the symphonic form. Should he use the title 'symphony' or 'fantasy'? As on so many other occasions when the house is full of people, who are more absorbed by the current news than Sibelius and his music, he feels that he is taking a back seat.

The general strike, a type of event he remembered from 1905, had, despite some setbacks, been a demonstration of national solidarity, a protest by the whole people against Tsarist repression. But now the country was rent by factional division. The Finnish Social Democrats were inspired by events in Petrograd and enjoyed the sympathy of the Bolshevik government. 'Rise up, rise without delay and concentrate power in the hands of the organized working class,' was the greeting from Lenin conveyed to the Social Democrat leadership in Helsinki. But the Russians stressed that any initiative must come from the Finnish side.

In Helsinki a central revolutionary committee was formed which called for a general strike on 14 November. It was this that Sibelius feared most: would it lead to revolution? In his article 'Red Week', which Sibelius could have read in his *Helsingin Sanomat*, the poet Eino Leino describes the days that followed: 'Finland's largest party sets about its own countrymen with foreigners' bayonets. Are we witnessing a dreadful nightmare or is the terror really happening? House-to-house searches, arrests, the suppression of free speech, the most elementary civil rights trampled under foot, blood, bodies and looting.' But the socialists did not go so far as to exploit the situation by attempting to seize power. On 19 November the strike was called off, but the committee proclaimed that 'the revolution continues'.

Three days later Sibelius's diary records: 'Saw a swan today. It was rocked by the waves at the edge of the ice. Terrible developments concerning the socialists, whose progress is crushing us patriots. What can be done?' He is mistrustful of the chances of peace or compromise between 'patriots' and 'socialists'. In *Helsingin Sanomat* his friend the writer Juhani Aho voiced strong opposition to the idea of granting an amnesty to the Red perpetrators of atrocities, while Eino Leino, on the other hand, recognizing the restraining hand of the social democrats, did an about-turn: 'Where would we be without the Social Democratic movement? In the middle of complete anarchy, compared to which what we have recently suffered would be child's play.' Lay down your weapons, say yes to a possibly long-term amnesty and tame the wild animal that has been unleashed in the Finnish people's soul: that was the substance of his appeal.

However, the grim November drama had already reached the point of no return, when events are driven by their own dynamic. Sibelius confided to his diary: 'There are moments in life when everything is blacker than black – darker than night. Time, it's said, heals all wounds. But what of those that can't be healed? On the other hand, life is so short that one must hold out. Surely, but the struggle is hard. Aino, the beloved creature, so inexpressibly loved, who shares my struggle, how I feel for her from the bottom of my heart. So little joy she has had from me and so much bitter sorrow. Am terribly worried. Strange that I am always the source of all my suffering.'

In so far as he could, Sibelius cut himself off from politics. At the end of November, at the Social Democrat Party congress, Stalin gave assurances of unconditional Bolshevik support in the struggle for self-determination in Finland, promised fraternal help and encouraged the revolutionary leadership to take decisive action, to use the tactics of Danton. Meanwhile, the newly-elected Senate, with its chairman Svinhufvud at its head, prepared a declaration of independence that was approved by parliament, with the Social Democrats voting against it, on 6 December. Sibelius's diary does not mention the fact, but records that he was working on the Fifth Symphony. Two days later, on 8 December, Kajanus telephoned with birthday greetings, which gave him pleasure. 'He conducted my Third Symphony very well. And Madetoja has written a particularly fine review, which is something to bear in mind.' Madetoja called it 'a nordic Pastoral Symphony' and wrote with particular admiration of the masterly transition from the *Andante*'s pensive atmosphere to the finale's bold and energetic theme. Two days later, Sibelius wrote to Carpelan asking after his health and reporting that he was working on big orchestral projects: '*Hier schreibe ich Noten in Nöthen.* Yesterday I was fifty-two but the day passed without a trace of melancholy. I have quite adjusted to it. *Ein Lebenszeichen von Dir wäre mir sehr, sehr lieb.*' Was it with his big orchestral projects in mind that his thoughts turned to Breitkopf & Härtel and German – the language that linked with the larger world outside?

Christmas was fast approaching, but he did not feel well and stayed in bed for a few days: 'I got up today but I'm still not back to normal. Is this the beginning of the end? Anarchy reigns. My poor country. Have been miserable. Not least on account of my encounters in Helsinki. Aino has gone to town to do the Christmas shopping. I see everything in the blackest terms at present. Misery and barbarism. And I fear that things are never going to be better. Have Symphonies VI and VII in my head, together with the reworking of Sym 5. If I become ill and can't work any more, what will become of them? (Diary, 18 December 1917) This is the first occasion on which he expressly mentions the Seventh Symphony. In the sketch block which contains the Fifth and Sixth symphonies, the latter from the autumn of 1916, there are no ideas that can be specifically linked to the Seventh.

During December, Sibelius worked on new songs for Ida Ekman to words of Runeberg. At this dark hour he drew for sustenance on the poet to whom he felt closest. *Morgon (Morning)* was ready on the 4th, *Sommarnatten (Summer Night)* and *Norden (The North)* on the 12th; *Hennes budskap (Her Message)* was finished in its first version on the 12th, *Fågelfångaren (The Bird-Catcher)* on the 22nd and *Vem styrde hit din väg (Who Brought You Here?)* on the 28th. He re-worked *Hennes budskap* several times, and it did not reach its definitive form until 2 January 1918. With it, his Op. 90 set was complete – and to all intents and purposes so was his output in this genre. Right from the *Seven Songs*, Op. 13, Runeberg above all others had been his guiding star:

> En gång min första kärlek frågte jag
> Min lefnads stjärna, säg, hur tändes du,
> och vadan äger du ditt milda ljus?
> (Once I asked my first love:
> 'My life's star, say how you were lit,
> And to whom you owe your gentle light?')

Sibelius once planned to set these lines, which precede Runeberg's epic poem *Hanna*. Runeberg was his first love in the world of the Swedish lyric, and it is somehow fitting that in his last set of songs he should return to him.

On 22 December, Christmas preparations at Ainola were in full swing. The ritual had to be followed, if only for the children's sake. But the situation at large was anything but festive: 'Dreadful terrorist excesses. The socialists are on the march. Axel is going through a rough time in Turku.' The diary annotations show that Sibelius was following the news with concern. Two days earlier, *Hufvudsbladet* had reported disturbances in Turku, and carried a report from *Izvestia* that the commander of the Russian forces had sent fraternal greetings to the Finnish proletariat urging them to overthrow their bourgeois masters. Concerning the world war in general, Sibelius remained as pessimistic as always: 'Peace is further off than ever.' No, it was far more reassuring to read that Adolf Paul had enjoyed a success in Germany with his somewhat sensational play *Lola Montez*. In Stockholm there were plans afoot. Schnéevoigt, who was now conductor of the Konsertförenings Symfoniorkester, had founded a Symphony Choir and was planning a performance of *Snöfrid*; the celebrated Madame Cahier had devoted half of one of her recitals to his songs.

During the Christmas holiday Sibelius worked on the Runeberg settings – 'Feel much better now and think I'm ready to go out' – but his spirits didn't hold up for long. His diary entry for New Year's Eve finds him cast back into the depths of gloom:

> You grieve to see others paying off your debts and are ashamed to receive charity. A nature like yours should not have to go through all this. But you have never asked for anything, not even a stamp! They come to you asking you if they can do anything. That's the difference – and head high. That your reputation is damaged when you go into Helsinki is clear. But should you bother your head with the pack in Helsinki – glorious JS? That Axel Carpelan no longer writes to me I can understand, but it mortifies me, pains me dearly. None of my old friends, Armas and so on, can really understand me at heart. But how to go on? There's always, as they say, a bullet in the temple, but then I am thinking solely of myself, not of Aino and the children. That Aino is also beside herself with despair, that I can see. Isn't it more manly to tough it out for a few more years? – life won't last much longer. To work and get my musical ideas moving is difficult in my present frame of mind. That it should all end up like this – so insufferable, not to say appalling. Is it wise of me to cut myself off so completely? It's nearly a year since I heard an orchestra. I've not met anyone, in fact, but how can it be otherwise? And Aino is more withdrawn than ever. That the one you love cannot speak of what it is that is paining her. For weeks now no smile or laugh. Always tears and tears. Her whole life thrown away. And it could have been very different! Since I am convinced that this is our only life and that there is nothing afterwards, I must ponder the consequences – and this presents me with a terrible picture. End of 1917. Can anything be more awful?

One can only wonder at what occasioned this outburst. Had he infuriated Aino by indulging in too many glasses of wine, and was this some kind of expiation? Perhaps he dwelt on his personal miseries rather than speculate on what horrors the New Year would bring. Be that as it may, as he penned these lines important events were in train. At the Smolny Institute in Petrograd, Lenin and his government recognized Finnish independence.

CHAPTER EIGHT

Civil War

'Finland a free country – in the making. How strange it seems! After fifty-two years have difficulty in taking it in, particularly when one's political aspirations have been so often disappointed before.' Sibelius had good cause for scepticism. The country was already divided between White and Red forces and clashes between the two were not uncommon. Moreover, the presence of Russian contingents in Finland was another factor to be reckoned with. How would the continuing peace negotiations in Brest–Litovsk between Russia and Germany affect the situation in Finland?

Sibelius was naturally keen to see what would happen after Lenin's recognition of Finnish independence. Although his diary does not make direct allusion to it, it is obvious that like most Finnish patriots he would have followed events closely. Others were not slow to follow Russia's example; first came Sweden and immediately afterwards France. By 7 January 1918 he notes in his diary: 'Germany has also recognized our republic. Problems in connection with a Finnish concert in Stockholm. Lindberg [chairman of the Helsinki music council] telephoned to say that too much of the programme was in minor keys. But *que faire!* That is part of our temperament.'

Right from the beginning Sibelius's music served as a kind of national symbol for the new country. At the Independence Concert in Stockholm, *Finlandia* was the centrepiece of the programme. And Sibelius's music had over the years served to fashion an image of Finnish national self-consciousness which contributed to the speed with which countries like France hastened to extend recognition. Of course there were political considerations too: Clémenceau was anxious that Finland should not be drawn any further into the German sphere of influence, but the fact of the matter remained that, thanks to the Finnish Pavilion at the Paris Exhibition of 1900 and to the visit of the Finnish Orchestra, the French had a distinct concept of Finland as a national entity. When the Russian Ambassador in Paris, even after the October Revolution a Kerensky appointee, had insisted on the indivisibility of Russia, the French politely replied, 'Yes, naturally, but Poland and Finland are of course another matter.' Behind those words, and making their contribution to national awareness, was the music of Chopin and Sibelius.

German recognition had come a day after the French announcement, but was accompanied by a mitigating explanation that the decision had been taken two days previously. For Sibelius, recognition was particularly welcome because it would enable him to restore contact with his old publishers Breitkopf. But the Anglo-Saxon countries were slow to follow suit: 'Uncertainty and anxiety about our independence. England and America are hesitating.' Sibelius seems to have grasped the fact that, however strong their attachment to Finland, the English and Americans would not allow sentiment to stand in the way of their political objectives. These were to ensure that Russia remained in the war. If Lenin remained obdurate, the possibility remained of his being replaced by a White general, who could well insist on the integrity of the old Imperial borders. Petrograd was only three hours from the border. Finland had become a card in the Great Powers' hands, and not only at Brest–Litovsk.

A respite from all this came with some domestic news that delighted Sibelius. Eva's son, Martti Jean Alfred, was named after him. But his pleasure was soon overshadowed by his creative problems, and his diary jottings record renewed anxieties about the progress of the new symphonies and some resentment at the composer's lot: 'Finnish independence has been celebrated in Stockholm and Schnéevoigt, who conducted *Finlandia*, has scored a great triumph. How little attention people pay as a rule to the composer! The main attraction is always the performer. This always gets me down. I find it all difficult to bear.'

Perhaps he foresaw our own age's cult of the conductor that was to grow with the LP and the CD, when one would speak of Sibelius's Fourth Symphony in terms of 'Beecham's Fourth' or Karajan's, Barbirolli's or Bernstein's! Perhaps he recognized that his own interpretations would – with the sole exception of the *Andante festivo* – die with him.[1] However, he could console himself with the thought that his 'most powerful weapon' – the printed scores – would always survive. Unlike his yeoman Kajanus he need never fear that he was some kind of artistic chauffeur.

It was not long before Carpelan admonished him to leave Järvenpää with the family as soon as he could. He forecast the most brutal anarchy on the Bolshevik model 'which we do not have the means to restrain. Socialists, hooligans have at last achieved their goal, and are getting supplies from the East, and all that awaits us is pillage and massacre since we don't have the means to protect ourselves. With those people there is no question of building a free country. We don't have our own militia, and even if we did, they would still be powerless against such odds.'

Carpelan refers to a heated debate in parliament on a motion to set up a special security force to be placed at the government's disposal. This was seen as a virtual declaration of war by the socialists, but after a stormy all-night session the measure was passed, in the face of bitter opposition from the left. After this, according to the historian Erik Hornborg, the outbreak of civil war was only a matter of time. But Carpelan grasped the position right from the very first. Sibelius noted: 'Axel very despondent on account of the dreadful mess we are in.' A few days later he wrote a note congratulating him on his sixtieth birthday: 'It's said that at our age one can see things coolly and clearly; that we go into the world bearing the truth. May I then, with the privilege of age, assert the following: that we don't speak of beginning the evening of life at sixty but rather of daybreak, since life up to then has been full of pain and strife. *"Es genügt das Grosse gewollt zu haben"* – that applies well enough to what each of us has done. . . . When I thank you Axel, I do so with joy and pride; joy at having possessed your friendship, pride that so singularly rich a spirit as yours should have taken care of me.'

Sibelius had given voice to similar sentiments at the beginning of their friendship, in a letter written from Italy seventeen years earlier: 'I count myself doubly rich when a soul such as yours draws closer to me.' It was through his devotion, understanding and clear-sightedness that Carpelan had won Sibelius's friendship. Of those works he had foreordained, the Violin Concerto and the String Quartet were already in existence, *The Tempest* and the 'Forest Symphony' were hidden in the mists of the future. The weaker Carpelan became and the less able he was to battle for Sibelius, the more Sibelius feared his loss. As a composer Sibelius was wholly centred on himself, and the isolation of the war years did not make matters any better. He became if anything even more self-absorbed, dissecting his relationships with the small circle that surrounded him. It was his ego that dominated relationships; with Carpelan there was an important difference, the pleasure of losing himself in a friendship.

Sibelius was going through the usual agonies and indecision in his composition: 'I am working on a new [E flat struck out and changed to] E major symphony. Nothing of the old Fifth. Perhaps I'll change my mind.' Five days later he speaks of a symphony VI in E major, first movement. As we shall see later, he now planned to write a completely new first movement for the Fifth – but was he really planning a completely new movement to replace the D minor opening of the Sixth that he had already sketched? His indecision induced further gloom: 'My years are running out. Others are forging ahead. Soon I shall be forgotten. And how could I live with my lifeblood drained?' He worked on heroically as society around him seemed on the verge of collapse and revolution imminent. In the circumstances he thought the Independence celebration at the Finnish National Theatre on 13 January inopportune or *'malapropos'*; even Juhani Aho spoke of it as premature.

Six days later the press announced in bold headlines that the Finnish *Jaeger March* would be sung at another independence celebration at the university, at which most of the leading dignitaries of the new Finland would be present. But the battle lines were already being drawn: the social democrats had declined an invitation, saying that 'their place was alongside our Russian comrades'. There was a strong German presence: the Jaeger Battalion's colours were strongly in evidence and the Finnish lion figured at the centre of a light blue iron cross surrounded by German eagles. Professor J.J. Mikkola's address was highly nationalist in tone, and called for the Finnish borders to be extended to the Arctic and the White Sea: 'Our Scandinavian culture is dear to us and German culture is surprisingly close to us too.' His words were framed by Sibelius's *Finlandia* and the *Jaeger March,* which was sung in Swedish, encored, then followed by *Die Wacht am Rhein.* The whole ceremony bore the character of a demonstration in support of the Jaeger movement and Germany, so much so that the French consul demonstratively walked out in protest half-way through. In the second half of the proceedings the *Jaeger March* was sung in Finnish; not even the imminent threat of war could bring the Swedish and Finnish-speaking student groups together! 'To judge from the speeches and poems', wrote Aho, 'you would have thought that it was our Jaegers who had defeated Russia, admittedly with some assistance from the Germans!'

Sibelius did not attend the ceremony. He had originally refused to put his name to the *Jaeger March,* ostensibly so that any royalties could benefit the men themselves. Perhaps he also thought that, unsigned, it would fall outside his agreement with Breitkopf & Härtel. In any event the press reports the following day revealed his authorship. On the brink of civil war he appeared publicly as aligned with the Whites – his march their symbol – and as a supporter of the Finnish-German alliance. His gesture on behalf of a group of Finnish volunteers on the Gulf of Riga had turned into something quite different and quite out of proportion.

On the same day, Finnish envoys in Berlin were negotiating with Ludendorff for the return of the Jaeger Battalion and permission to purchase German arms and weaponry. The Finnish Reds were receiving arms and equipment from Petrograd. In Viipuri, Red Guards seized power with the support of Russian soldiers, disarming government troops and taking a number of hostages from among the city's White sympathizers.

After the independence demonstration Sibelius received offers for the *Jaeger March* from various publishers. 'The orchestration,' he wrote, 'has taken a lot of time . . . smoked a lot, which is not a good thing. Feel terrible in spite of taking plenty of rest. Drinking but not too heavily. Aino is still [after six days] in Helsinki with the children.' He finished scoring the march on 25 January and sent a piano reduction to Breitkopf via a friend in Stockholm, but it appears never to have turned up.

His cellar was empty and wartime regulations restricted its replenishment. Accordingly he turned for support to his doctor, Elmgren, who had been the first to operate on his throat tumour, and applied to the Senate's Department for Supplies for permission to purchase privately ten litres of sherry. Presumably his request was agreed, for three days later he wrote to

Societets hus, a well-known restaurant in Helsinki, to this end, but supplies were short and he was too late.

On 27 January 1918 Katarina played at a concert of Martha Tornell's pupils. Many of them had stayed away for fear of the street fighting that was expected to break out. The following day Sibelius noted: 'Street disorders in Helsinki yesterday. Red guards with their Russian companions. What disgrace for our people and our country! Worked on Sym VI – 1st mvmt.' Sibelius's indignation reflects a common attitude among the Whites: the Reds were not merely revolutionaries but also traitors, since they were allies of the Russian army still in Finland.

During the early hours of 28 January, Red Guards in Helsinki seized power. At the same time, White forces under the command of General Mannerheim began an operation designed to disarm the Russian garrisons in Österbotten (Ostrobothnia). The civil war and the war of independence had begun. Immediately after the coup, the Red authorities sent a telegram to the Bolshevik government in Petrograd informing them of developments and announcing the formation of a 'Socialist People's Council' in Helsinki. The White Senate set up its headquarters in Vaasa, leaving Finland split in two. The southern part of the country, including the four largest cities – Helsinki, Åbo (Turku), Viborg (Viipuri) and Tammerfors (Tampere) – was in Red hands. Ainola lay deep in Red-controlled territory; Gallen-Kallela's home, on the other hand, was on White soil, though quite near the front lines. Presumably Sibelius was unaware of developments in Ostrobothnia. His diary entry of 29 January goes on: 'The Red Guards are in action. General strike, arson, murder upon murder. This despicable scum. Went to the Westermarcks today [a neighbouring family]. Everyone is worried . . . Aino is still in bed. Can't get on with my work. When will we ever get peace and quiet for such things? A glorious day. Sun and 3 degrees above zero. Nature is flourishing while people are worse than animals. Bought a wooden sledge for a lot of money – totally useless. Daren't worry Aino with it. Study Charpentier's *Louise* which at one time impressed me. Not so much now. How one changes with the years . . . No more news of the world outside. Everything in Red hands: telephone, telegraph, railways etc.'

The newspapers that Sibelius was accustomed to read – the Swedish-language *Hufvudstadsbladet* and *Dagens Press*, the Finnish-language *Helsingin Sanomat* and *Uusi Suometar* – were all banned, and he had to content himself with the Red newspapers *Työmies (The Worker)*, and *Kansanvaltuuskunnan Tiedonantolehti (The People's Herald)*. From them he learnt that Trotsky, in Brest–Litovsk for the peace negotiations, had telegraphed his greetings to Finland's heroic working class: 'The news of your victory sends a signal of hope to all countries and brings us new strength in the struggle against war and capitalism . . . Our common proletarian brotherhood has forged new bonds between the new Finland and the free Russia.' In his tense state Sibelius had not noticed that neither this nor other declarations made any mention of Russian military help to the Finnish Reds – the Bolsheviks had no intention of jeopardizing the peace talks. Volunteers, weapons and supplies could have been a possibility, but not direct military intervention. Russian troops were war weary and unwilling to become involved in internal Finnish affairs.

Although time was not on the side of the Reds, they enjoyed some immediate advantages. In fact, things were particularly critical for the Whites during the first weeks of the war. The Red press claimed that 'the whole of southern Finland has been cleansed of White butchers', and among other things that in Kerava, near Järvenpää, White security forces had been defeated. In Ainola Sibelius feared for his life, as he reported to his diary on 2 February: 'Murder after murder, and not only combatants in the struggle; no one of education is safe. Proletarian power grows like a rolling snowball. My turn will come as soon as they discover that I am the composer of the *Jaeger March*. Mikko Slöör, [Gallén's brother-in-law] has met his death. Must have been murdered. Money can only be paid by the banks to 'workers'. The only thing in store for us is death, sooner or later. Should I get on with my symphonies or concentrate on smaller things which do not take so much time? That's the question. Went to Westermarcks this morning. Only women there and they in a state of terror. The intrepid Eva is here with money and to get a certificate from the workers testifying that it will be put to their use.'

The Red authorities in Helsinki, however, nursed no ill feelings towards Sibelius. Indeed, for a variety of reasons they were keen to see that he came to no harm. Nor had he anything to fear from the Reds in Järvenpää, where there was some local pride in his presence. Moreover, he enjoyed a reputation as being a kindly and generous person. He might have been in danger had they discovered that he had composed the *Jaeger March*, but who among them knew? The sisters Jenny and Karin Wasenius, neighbours from whom the Sibeliuses collected their milk, recalled their mother saying that his life was for a time at some risk. Of course, under civil war conditions things can easily get out of hand. Danger was more likely to come from undisciplined Red Guards from other districts. Under desperate conditions, for instance during a retreat, class hatreds could tempt them to settle accounts with the composer. Whether or not he had written the *Jaeger March*, his White sympathies were well known.

Katarina found the atmosphere at home full of gloom: 'Mamma cries every time she thinks of the massacre in Kerava. Papa goes around whispering in German, the children [Margareta and Heidi] get on everyone's nerves, and I have to keep them occupied. Otherwise, it's just like being in prison.' Sibelius did not dissent from his daughter's view. During the next few days tension increased and his anxieties mounted. A curfew was introduced.

[5 February 1918] Forbidden to go out for a walk. If only I could get away from all this misery. A must. The days are warm – one degree above zero. The fighting is getting nearer. No longer think of my own concerns about mortality. The main thing is for me to realize the hopes I have of myself.

[6 February] Another day of sheer misery and grief. This uncertainty is unbearable. Work on at the symphonies. With misgiving and hope. + 1 degree. Mild and misty. Aino is in a depressed and nervous state. How will all this end?

[7 February] Everyone is nervous and on edge. The atmosphere in the house suffers as a result. The wildest rumours are circulating here. Yet again have altered my plans for the symphonies. *Sic itur* – !

Mindless atrocities continued to outrage him. In Helsinki, Dr Gösta Schybergson had been seized at the hospital while he was conducting an operation, taken away and shot. The Swedish envoy in Helsinki lodged a sharp protest to the Red authorities, and the outrage was condemned even in the Red newspapers. Immediately after the war ended, Sibelius set two of Schybergson's poems, *Ute hörs stormen (Outside the Storm is Raging)* and *Brusande rusar en våg (Surging The Wave Rushes Forward)*, for male voices. The songs were presented to his family on 30 April.

[9 February 1918] Worked since yesterday on Sym V, 1st mvmt. It has nothing to do with the earlier one. Walked in the sun – 6 degrees below. Wonderful atmosphere! Shot in the far distance. The murder of Dr Schybergson has shaken me deeply. Then the outrages and murders in Kerava.

[10 February] Worked on the first movement of the symphony. A good day's work. Aino went to the Halonens to congratulate them on the baby girl. In Helsinki everyone is on edge because of these fearful times. Walked in my home tracts when I received a 'warning'. Heavy snow – 6 degrees.

Sibelius and his family naturally read the Red newspapers in the absence of anything else. But although the sixteen-year-old Katarina found many of their opinions 'objectionable', according to her diary she could not help wondering at times whether they had some measure of justice on their side. But no doubt in the light of their excesses, and out of loyalty to the family, she immediately put such ideas out of her mind. News from the White side circulated on typewritten reports that reached Järvenpää, serving to strengthen morale and plead the justice of the White cause. Not that Sibelius had any doubts on that score; in his eyes a Red victory would have spelt disaster for Finland. At the same time it is not impossible to imagine that Aino, with her Tolstoyan sympathies, could have nursed some sympathy with the working masses. But even had this been the case, she was possessed of the same belief in the vision of an independent Finland that the Whites espoused and in which her husband believed. Compromise was foreign to her nature, and unlike her brother Arvid she became a zealous White. For Arvid, his human sympathies embraced both White and Red; his children continued to play with Red youngsters in Lojo. This did not happen at Ainola or with Eero Järnefelt.

On Shrove Tuesday, 12 February, Ainola was searched by Red Guards looking for weapons: 'Coarse, brutish faces. Would I, at fifty-two, ever be able to fight? My nerves would never stand it.' Katarina also thought that they looked villainous, and that their rifles and other weapons could not have been more out of keeping with the peaceful ambience of Ainola: 'Papa can't put them out of his mind. Nor I.' According to Sibelius's recollections in the 1930s, they were not from the Järvenpää locality and they had no idea who he was. They behaved menacingly and were brusque in their manner. But he kept his nerve: to calm the two youngest daughters, who were crying, he sat down at the piano and played for them. The Red Guards, who were in the kitchen, said to one of the servants: 'It must be nice working in a house where you can hear such lovely music.' The servants had some Red sympathies and thought that one should not judge people by appearances; they wondered what the small girls had been told about the Red Guards to make them cry. At the same time they were loyal to the family and assured the Guards that there were no firearms in the house apart from a saloon rifle and an old pistol, which Sibelius had mentioned before the search. Having satisfied themselves they left. One of the servants, Rinne, had produced the old pistol; he kept quiet about the revolver he knew Sibelius had hidden in a drawer in one of the lower rooms. Sibelius was suffering from shock: 'I thought I would not live long enough to get down on paper what I had in my head, and that symphonies V, VI & VII would never be finished. O what terrible times we are going through! Pity our poor country.' All the same, he didn't forget to mention that, as was the time-honoured custom on Shrove Tuesday, Aino had been out tobogganing with the children at twenty degrees below zero. Juhani Aho, who stayed in Helsinki throughout the civil war, learnt of the house-to-house searches in Järvenpää, not only at the Sibelius's but at the Järnefelts, and at the Hjelts in Lepola: 'They are not allowed even to telephone one another and at every road junction there is a sentry post.' When Sibelius took his usual morning walk he had to stop and show his pass to whatever riff-raff happened to be on guard duty.

A day later six more Red Guards, this time local men, came to Ainola. The search, which Eva Paloheimo later described as routine, concerned the Sibeliuses supplies of foodstuffs and so on, and the whole house was turned upside down: 'What ignominy for my house! I could hardly hide my shame as I was forced to open cupboards for them so that they could see our poor home's "treasures". A gang of bandits armed to the teeth and I a defenceless, nervous composer. "Yield to force", the saying goes. So be it. But it is much more difficult when one's own home is being defiled.' Apart from the indignity, the search brought home to him how modest were his circumstances and how simple was the home he had built up over the course of a twenty-five year marriage. 'Bandits, Thugs, Scum.' Sibelius – cut off from the outside world, imprisoned in a fashionable area and harassed by uncouth militia, a potential object of class hatred – resorts, unusually for him, to invective. When would the next patrol come, and what would happen when it did? In Helsinki, Juhani had relative freedom of movement and could go to the railway station and see the Red Guards on their way to the front: 'Among them you could see many coarse features and hooligan types . . . but there were also decent workers, fathers in their Sunday best who were on their way to fight for the "cause", for the proletariat, for the proletariat in all countries, and at the same time for Finland; their Finland a workers' republic. It is moving, and has a certain splendour.' But by choosing violence and mayhem, these workers had placed an impregnable barrier between themselves and Aho; despite his human sympathies, he regarded them as rebels. Sibelius, on the other hand, had caught no glimpse of the human side of the enemy, but merely went in fear of his life; it was only when he had moved to the relative security of the capital that his outbursts ceased.

On 15 February their housekeeper and cook Helmi went to Helsinki to buy medicine and cigars: 'Let's hope her visit goes successfully. Without some sacrifices of cigars my gods will not be appeased. It's ten degrees below or thereabouts. Clear and with a new moon. The development is now in the making. It is pretty well the height of *naïveté* to think that symphonies matter . . . Can't make up my mind about my hair. Shall I have it all cut off and look like a caricature of Nero or a small-town actor? Rather a splendid idea.'

'Yet more murders, among others Aminoff, which dismays me and enrages us. Brother Christian imprisoned but is now released.'(Diary, 17 February 1918) Christian was chief doctor at Lappvikens Mental Hospital in Helsinki, and he had refused to reserve beds for the Red soldiers who had suffered shell shock at the front. His hospital was already full, and he is said to have told the Red authorities: 'Anyway, you are all barmy, the lot of you.' He was promptly put under arrest for a day or so.

'One thing is certain, these murderous gangs must be disarmed. If they are not, Finland will lose any vestige of civilization. Things look blacker than ever and there's no sign of hope. Six degrees below and wonderful winter weather; the moonlight yesterday was quite magical. I'm working on Sym V. It is – *post tot discrimino rerum* – going to be really good.' Alexander Aminoff, a neighbour of Gallen-Kallela's in Ruovesi and a kindly figure who had always treated his workmen with humanity, had been taken away during the course of a search for weapons and shot. This outrage drew a strong protest from Aho; indeed, each and every occasion when one of their number was murdered or threatened drove the beleaguered middle and educated classes closer together. Aminoff's fate sent a special chill down Sibelius's spine.

Perhaps he even toyed with the notion of joining up, though the idea was obviously totally impractical. Apart from the fact that he would have been arrested had he tried to leave Järvenpää, his tremor and his general disposition would have rendered him unfit for service at the front. Had he ever succeeded in getting anywhere near the front, General Mannerheim's first order would doubtless have been 'Go away and compose another symphony!' Gallen-Kallela had joined Mannerheim's forces; he had ski'd from his home to the White front and had fought there for two weeks before his presence became known at Mannerheim's headquarters, to which he was instantly moved. 'His life is far too precious to be sacrificed at the front' were Mannerheim's words, and the general's response would doubtless have been identical had Sibelius presented himself. Gallén spent the rest of his time designing ensigns, flags and medals.

By this time Sibelius's position at Ainola was worrying his Helsinki friends. Kajanus sought an audience with the effective commander of the Red Guards, Eero Haapalainen, who was minister of war in the People's Council, and explained that Sibelius was in some danger. Haapalainen furnished him with a letter to the local command: 'I hereby authorize Professor Robert Kajanus to proceed to Kerava and Tuusula with the purpose of making arrangements for the protection and security of Professor Jean Sibelius in Tusby or to organize for him and his family's removal to Helsinki, and I instruct the appropriate officers of the Red Guard to render Professor Kajanus every assistance to this end.' But Haapalainen was not really prepared to take responsibility for Sibelius's safety, even if special protection was organized; he told Kajanus that it was best for him to come to Helsinki.

On the following day, 19 February, Kajanus set out for Järvenpää with an escort of Red Guards. While the escort sat in the kitchen smoking their evil-smelling Russian cigarettes, Kajanus did his best to persuade Sibelius to leave Ainola and settle down in Helsinki for the duration of the war. Sibelius was at first obdurate and Kajanus was forced to appeal to his patriotism. Eventually he gave way; they packed their bags and the next day five sledges laden with their belongings set out in procession to the station. Kajanus, resplendent in his furs, directed the cortège, his every move watched by an adoring Katarina: 'Kajanus was magnificent – I admire him. Our departure was sad; Helmi and mamma wept, papa was agitated, mamma was angry; the children pale and Kajanus organized everything.' It was a dark day for Sibelius. He recognized several of the Red Guards who were on duty at the station. Before, they had always greeted him and had often exchanged courtesies. Now they stared resolutely into the distance. Suddenly one of them met Sibelius's gaze, and for a brief moment they made contact. Then the Guard looked the other way. The chasm opened again and could not be bridged.

'From the depths of my heart,' confided Katarina to her diary, 'I felt sorry for Aunt Nelma [Christian Sibelius's wife] when we all overran her orderly home. I don't think that our unkempt family is really suited to town life. Papa and mamma slept in the furthermost room, Maija [Christian's daughter Marjatta] and I in the nursery. We sat up talking half the night. Piiu [Margareta] slept in the dining room and Heidi in the bedroom together with Aunt Nelma, Uncle Kitti [Christian] and Christian the younger.' Food was not so easy to come by. White sympathizers staying at the hospital, even the doctors, were worse off than the others. The hospital staff favoured the Red patients from the front that had eventually been billeted there, and gave them the lion's share of what small rations there were; the others, including the doctors, had to be content with what was left over. For instance, Christian Sibelius and his family had to manage on a single loaf among them for the whole week! During the two months Sibelius was in Helsinki he lost twenty kilos.

He had word from Carpelan, a short card: '. . . am an optimist in spite of all that is going to happen. I was right in my prediction and my warning.' Sibelius answered: 'The flowers here are thriving famously, that's to say, the rouge; for other colours we shall have to wait and see.' Sibelius's floral image was doubtless prompted by the knowledge that his letters would be subject to Red censorship. Prompted by Sibelius's need for a quiet working environment, the family split up. The daughters, possibly also Aino, lived at various times in Eero Järnefelt's comfortable town flat, and at others with Eva's father-in-law, K. A. Paloheimo, in his wooden house on the outskirts of the capital. Everywhere they were welcomed with open arms, but Sibelius suffered from 'herabgesetztes Selbstegefühl'! 'It's not easy to be a guest when the family is in three different places. Particularly when food is so desperately short. But what can one do other than beg?' He had never been able to afford a flat in town like Eero; nor could he pay inflationary prices for food. His only luxury during the war months was two kilos of herring!

What other course was there but to borrow or beg – and compose? The nationalistic Helsinki youth choir, which subsequently became Kansal-liskuoro, the Finnish National Choir, had commissioned a cantata from him. He finished this piece, Oma maa (Our Native Land), to a text by the nineteenth-century poet Kallio, while he was staying with Christian at Lappviken. The terms were hardly generous: the choir bound themselves to give him a deposit of 1,000 marks, which was to be returned when the composition was sold to a publisher. 'In other words, they get it for nothing. But I haven't the heart to say no.'

The war left few in Sibelius's circle untouched. The deaths of Schyberg-son, Aminoff and young Erik Hernberg, to whom Katarina was attached, diminished them all. And although their ranks were largely White, sharp differences of opinion could arise. Eva's mother-in-law, Kerttu Paloheimo, and Erik Hernberg's aunt had Red sympathies, though the latter's husband and eldest sons were forced to hide for fear of their lives in Red-held

Helsinki. Katarina lived for a time with the Paloheimos, where there could be quite heated discussions at the dinner table.

Sibelius had to make the painful adjustments necessary for living away from home. He had to put a brave face on it when his sister-in-law Nelma arranged a coffee reception for the family circle. His diary continues: 'Eero has painted an excellent portrait of K.A. Paloheimo which ought to be very good. Lucky man! *Terque beatus*. Aino's eye is troubling her and Kitti [Christian] is confined to bed most of the time. He's not going to get any better. And so all those who care about my art are struggling along on low power. I have been vegetating for nearly four years – even though I have been composing. But who knows about that? And at such dramatic times all I can put down on paper are daily banalities.' What did Sibelius really know of these dramatic times? Presumably the same as, for example, Juhani Aho, who read the White underground papers such as *Vapaa Sana (Free Word)*. As early as 25 February it was rumoured in Helsinki that the draft peace proposals at Brest–Litovsk had included a clause calling for the withdrawal of Russian forces from Finland. And on 6 March reports were circulating of a German landing in Åland. 'It is great news that the Germans at least have a presence in Finland,' wrote Aho, and both he and Sibelius would have watched with joy the heavily-armoured ships of the Russian Baltic Fleet steam out from Helsinki on course for Kronstadt.

'They speak of a conclusive turning point in a matter of days. Perhaps even tonight. Bombardment etc.,' he noted on 20 March. According to the underground press, White troops were advancing on the northern front and fierce fighting raged around Tampere, which was still held by the Reds. But the turning point for which Sibelius hoped was slow to come, and his spirits plummeted. Nor were matters helped by his precarious finances: 'Still no money [for *Oma maa*]. Starvation! Went for a walk as usual and imagined what it must be like in southern latitudes, longed to be in Italy again. Still no sign of a success. We have never had more wonderful weather than in this February and March.'

'Defeat stares us in the face. The enemy is at the gates' was the headline of the Red newspaper *Työmies* in early April. On 3 April a German expeditionary force landed at Hangö and made for Helsinki. Sibelius sat in a hotel room and composed two small pieces for violin and piano, the *Aubade* and *Menuetto*, which he later added to the Op. 81 set. He received 2,200 marks for them, albeit 500 of it in counterfeit notes! By 11 April the Germans had already penetrated the outskirts of the capital. 'The thunder of cannon fire. Airships dropping proclamations. Rifle shots to disperse crowds and so on. In spite of all, in an optimistic frame of mind.'

Katarina's diary records the collapse of the régime with some measure of compassion: 'O these unhappy Reds – their leaders have abandoned them; their governing People's Council has gone ... I feel more sorrow than hatred for them. The latter I reserve for Whites rejoicing at their sufferings.

But there's no point feeling too much sympathy. What mercy would they have shown us had they been the victors?'

While Katarina had been visiting her sister Ruth in Tölö there was the sound of gunfire, and from their window she caught a glimpse of Red Guards running and shooting at random. Then a small group of soldiers in green uniform suddenly appeared. Germans with gleaming helmets and rifles. People rushed into the streets waving white handkerchiefs. On the following day she could report crowds thirsting for vengeance, Reds being rounded up, and at Lappvikens Hospital a dinner being organized for the German officers. 'Maija [Christian Sibelius's daughter] must have her hands full.' But she did not fall over herself to make a fuss of them.

At the market place she witnessed the columns of Red prisoners boarding ships bound for Sveaborg: 'They filed past with their hands on their heads; I could hardly bear to watch it. What a dreadful humiliation for them – to file past as prisoners through the ranks of White spectators. And I was on the point of losing my temper when some demoiselles pointed their fingers at them derisively.' She also saw the White prisoners, including Erik Hernberg's comrades, rushing out of the lycée where they had been held prisoner. Among them was the composer Aarre Merikanto. When darkness fell, people emerged with their flares to give food to the Germans in their bivouacs. 'It's wonderful to think that they are there to defend us. But the Reds have great spirit. They are fighting to the bitter end. In that one recognizes the Finnish character. As stubborn as the devil himself!'

Helsinki's musical life had stopped during the civil war, and there had been no concerts while the Reds were in control. On 20 April, while fighting still raged in many parts of the country, the Helsinki Orchestra gave a *Huldigungskonzert* for the German High Command. Kajanus conducted works by Haydn, Beethoven and Wagner, and the last part of their '*Grüss Finnlands an Deutschland*' programme began with *Die Wacht am Rhein*, after which Sibelius mounted the podium and conducted the *Jaeger March*. 'There rang out tones of courage and confidence in victory but in a completely Finnish spirit. It was a war song of primitive strength and folk-like character,' wrote Bis in *Hufvudstadsbladet* the following day. At a similar concert five days later Sibelius finished off the concert with *Finlandia*.

At about this time Sibelius returned to Ainola with Aino and their daughters. By the turn of the month a White victory had become a virtual certainty. Eero Järnefelt's son Heikki returned home safely and came to visit Ainola; Sibelius's pride in him knew no bounds. But if the war in Finland was over, the hatred and bitterness was not. The Reds had made a fatal mistake in seizing power and starting the civil war, but the Whites showed neither wisdom nor moderation in its closing stages. Now Sibelius had suddenly become a cultural symbol for the Finnish–German military alliance. Even though he had been flattered by all the official attention, he felt distaste and alarm at being drawn into the centre of controversy. He was suddenly seized with fears of Red vengeance: 'Will I survive all this without being murdered? While I have now shown where my sympathies lie and remain a composer, I ought to move to Germany for safety's sake. But they say things are even worse there. If I could give up composing and were rich, my choice would be to lead one of our military corps . . . Oh, if only I were well. But my frailty is great and my uncertainty greater. The Reds are intent on vengeance.'

If not vengeance in this generation, then in the next. Red parents gave their children names like Voitto (Victory) and Varma Kosto (Certain Vengeance). The psychological effect of the Red Terror earlier in the year had set its mark on Sibelius. He wrote to Carpelan saying that, had he remained behind in Järvenpää, he would have been shot when the Germans landed. Gallén-Kallela, who had been sent from the White headquarters as a courier to Berlin at the beginning of April, had told Adolf Paul that Sibelius had been 'sentenced to death'. It is out of the question that Gallén could have been in touch with Sibelius before his departure, and so he must have had this information from some other source. Possibly White Intelligence had heard of this plot, or some message that was passed through the lines had been intercepted. Paul touched on the matter in a letter written at the end of May or beginning of June, but tried to make light of it: 'God knows whether what Gallén told me is true or whether he hasn't got things muddled on his way round the Bothnian Gulf with his many whiskies and sodas, dinners and glasses of punch.' Paul went on to complain that six of his plays had been banned by the censor for the duration of the war. But *Die Sprache der Vögel* with incidental music by Sibelius was about to receive its première in Hamburg.

Where celebrities are concerned, there are always bound to be rumours that are difficult to verify. But Paul's letter and the fact that he had made arrangements for a warning system with the telephone exchange lends support to them. Mimmi Holm (1873–1936), who was in charge of the exchange, told Vilho Pesola in 1918 that she kept watch on movements at Järvenpää station, which her window overlooked, and had arranged with the composer to warn him in the event of any suspicious arrival.[2]

All this could hardly have contributed to the composer's peace of mind. And in the same month there were further reminders of mortality. The death of the composer Toivo Kuula, at one time his pupil, increased his gloom. After the capture of Viipuri – which at that time belonged to Finland – Kuula, a fervent White, had become involved in a brawl. Earlier in the day he had been practising a newly-composed march with his fellow White soldiers, and accompanying Sibelius's *Jaeger March* by ear. Later on that day, after the consumption of much akvavit, he had got into a fight with some Jaeger soldiers and was shot in the head. A few weeks later, on 18 May, he died. On the day of the funereal Sibelius noted in his diary: 'Today my friend Toivo Kuula was laid to rest in the cold earth. An artist's lot is infinitely

wretched. So much work, talent and courage – and then everything is over.'
Perhaps to forget himself, he immersed himself in the Fifth Symphony's first
movement: 'Going well. It's developing in the spirit of *Klassisität* – but the
ideas require it.' Some days later his old mentor Richard Faltin followed
Kuula into the grave. Sibelius and he had maintained contact ever since the
1890s, when Faltin had tried to arrange a lectureship for him at the university. In 1912 he had written that he rated Sibelius 'highly, no, highest
among today's creative artists'. He was quite devastated by the news. It
distressed him that he couldn't go through the ordeal of attending funerals
any more, and he was seized with panic: 'Frightened that I will die before
the symphonies are finished. Misfortunes come in threes, so the saying goes.
Kuula, Faltin and ?' (Diary, 7 June 1918)

Sibelius made his services available when artists gave concerts in aid of
post-war charities for the needy. On 2 May, at a musical-dramatic entertainment at the Finnish National Theatre, he conducted his own *Karelia*
Overture. In another tableau, Eero Järnefelt's daughter Leena and another
amateur sang his duet *Tanken (The Thought)*, which they repeated three days
later at the Swedish Theatre. A professional contribution was made on this
occasion by Maikki Järnefelt with *The Rapids'-Riders Brides*. At another
charity concert, Aino Ackté had sung three Sibelius songs, *Kaiutar* and
Kyssen (The Kiss), both presumably first performances, and *Maj (May)*. The
composer went to a rehearsal: 'As usual I criticized both myself and her. I
make too ready a use of the piano's lower notes, which are not really effective in songs. My piano style too ascetic in my older pieces. Ackté's voice
too "expressive" in *May*. It should be sung with greater lightness and with
brighter tone, as well as in time. Today's singers "make too much" of every
phrase. The absolute music I write is so totally self-contained musically and
strictly speaking independent of words that it would do just to recite them.
Ida Ekman understood that, hence her pre-eminence.'

Sibelius's comments should be taken with a pinch of salt. When he speaks
of his songs as 'absolute music', he does not mean to diminish the importance of expressive diction. But those interpreters who sing Sibelius's more
intimate songs with excessive intensity or constantly changing expressive
nuances à la Schumann or Wolf are likely to miss something of their essence.

On 9 May Sibelius conducted a full-scale concert of his music in Helsinki
including *The Oceanides*, the *Devotion* and *Cantique* for cello and orchestra,
and the Second Symphony: 'My nerves were comparatively good, thanks to
the use of Bromnatrium – my brother's prescription.' Count von der Goltz
was present and, apart from the music, had special reasons to be interested in
the composer: he was married to a niece of Oskar von Hase, the chief of
Breitkopf & Härtel. Sibelius wrote to Carpelan after the concert: 'Count
von der Goltz strikes me as an urbane and cultured person – as one has every
reason to expect. He knows many of my compositions. So too do the other
German officers I have had dealings with – all of them real gentlemen. As

you know, I have always got along well with aristocrats, perhaps because they and my *Wenigkeit* have nothing to fear from each other.'

On the day of the concert Oskar von Hase wrote to him at some length: 'I have recently heard that you, even though you are no longer a young man, have placed yourself at your country's service; let me hope that you have safely weathered these arduous times.' He had, he said, 'followed the developments in Finland's struggle for independence with particular concern,' not least on account of the involvement of his niece's husband [von der Goltz]. He said that he was engaged in writing a history of the firm; he had just finished dealing with its relations with Mendelssohn and had come to Schumann, before eventually getting round to Sibelius. The letter ended by inviting him to the bicentenary celebrations of the firm on 27 January 1919. Sibelius replied: 'Those emotions I felt on shaking hands with your German heroes cannot easily be described – one only experiences them once in a lifetime.' Breitkopf was to make use of those words in its advertisements for the *Jaeger March*. But Sibelius's friends in the English musical world were beginning to make contact. As early as December, Bantock had posted a batch of reviews from Birmingham which had got through to Finland in the middle of May. A review by Ernest Newman thrilled Sibelius, and he cited it in a letter to Carpelan: 'Newman says of me – being a man of genius – not national (!) but a composer of the utmost individuality and so on. Thus a swallow already foreshadowing the truth's summer.'

The privations of the war years had already affected his powers of resistance: 'Today felt dreadful – stomach! (Diary, 13 May 1918) After thirteen days' silence he reports: 'Have been in bed for about a week with lumbago. Always ill these days. Is it always going to be like this? And what of all my great musical plans? I feel really weak and miserable.'

His symphonic projects made no progress: 'Want to get on with symphonies V & VI. But am always having to break off to write smaller pieces to earn my living. I ought to economize, but habits die hard.' (Diary, 13 May 1918) Just at the right psychological moment a letter came from Carpelan: 'Now the Reds have been defeated, there'll be a change of front, the Finnish–Swedes will be butchered, and then afer that we will succumb to Moscow – and that will be the end of everything! . . . Wishing you a productive period and hope that your great plans will be realized during the short time that remains to us. I am reluctant to question you about your plans but do so for the last time.' Sibelius answered Carpelan's 'spellbinding' letter by outlining his musical plans to keep him happy. And perhaps to straighten things out in his own mind.

CHAPTER NINE

Independence

After the victory celebrations and Mannerheim's triumphant entry into Helsinki on 16 May 1918 came the time for sober appraisal. The *de facto* state of war with the Soviet Union had not been brought to an end, and it was also imperative for Finland to give thought to its relations with Germany. The new head of state, P.E. Svinhufvud, and to a lesser extent the prime minister, J.K. Paasikivi – a school friend of Sibelius (albeit five years his junior) whose children were playmates of both Sibelius's and Eero Järnefelt's children at Järvenpää – were pro-German. Mannerheim, on the other hand, resigned in protest at the Finnish Army being virtually under German command, and to avoid compromising himself in the eyes of the Allied coalition. He also mistrusted von der Goltz, the German commander, and suspected him of interfering in Finnish affairs.

The Svinhufvud-Paasikivi plan was for Finland to proclaim a monarchy with a German prince at its head. Adolf Paul, writing from Berlin, saw Sibelius as a kind of future 'Master of the King's Music' in the new order. The Finnish music periodical *Säveletär* reported that the monarch-in-waiting, Prince Friedrich Karl of Hesse, was himself an active patron of the art and a keen amateur musician. Breitkopf & Härtel were convinced that in the *March of the Jaegar Battalion* they had found a new gold mine, another *Valse triste*! It could well be a new royal march of honour, and enjoy popularity and success in Germany itself. After receiving the handwritten orchestral score, the publisher, in accordance with Sibelius's wishes, asked Theodor Grawert, the Army's music chief, to arrange it for military band. At the beginning of June Sibelius posted a piano and voice reduction to Leipzig in its place, and a special edition in a black and gold binding bearing the Imperial eagle and the Hohenzollern coat of arms was prepared for the Finnish Jaegers. In the autumn the orchestral version appeared and an arrangement for salon orchestra was printed. A delegation of officers from the Jaegers visited Ainola and presented the composer with an enormous bouquet. He was delighted with the roses, but not entirely pleased to be reminded that he was being drawn into a political hornets' nest: 'I am very worried by the dark prospects for the future. Fear the worst. Letter from B &

H [Breitkopf]. Took a very long time coming. All of Finland is in the grip of war and militarism. No understanding in the world for a symphonist's struggle.' (Diary, 9 June 1918)

The musical situation in Finland was far from encouraging. A.O. Väisänen, the folk music specialist and orchestral musician, complained of a decline in the standards of public taste and a worsening of the general musical climate: 'With his first three symphonies Sibelius has captured at most a half of the concert-going public. The greater part of the Finnish public understand only choir songs and respond genuinely to smaller orchestral pieces. In the past our educated classes could congratulate themselves on having created a favourable climate in which Finnish music could flourish. In our own times a young Finnish composer in search of comparable conditions would find it difficult, virtually impossible, to do so.'[1] This pessimism and war-weariness was echoed by Gallen-Kallela, who returned from headquarters sickened by all militarism.

In spite of everything, Sibelius seems to have recovered his spirits and emerged from his 'long period of exhaustion and its consequent depression'. One day he even went so far as to allow Katarina to practise at home for three hours 'for Martha's sake. There is no point in her wasting her lesson.' But however much he loved his daughter, he was not in a position to concentrate his energies on developing her undeniable pianistic talents. She had made out 'quite well' playing one of her father's pieces at Martha Tornell's pupils' concert, but it never occurred to him to make arrangements for her to practise properly, let alone put her in the hands of a more distinguished teacher.

In early June he returned anew to the Fifth Symphony and a new version of the first movement. But he was momentarily seized with doubts about his classical course: 'Will it be of interest to anybody? Out of sympathy with today's taste, which has developed from Wagnerian pathos, and seems more in tune with the theatrical rather than the symphonic. I have to bear this "cross".' (Diary, 3 June 1918) At the same time he was working on the first movement of the Sixth Symphony. The days were now full of summer; the apple trees were in blossom but his mental state was very different: 'Worked on VI/I. Yet anguish is gnawing my heart. Why do I have to endure this tension and torment when I am composing? This compulsion. This compulsion to write absolutely the right thing without any compromises.' (Diary, 8 June 1918)

In the middle of all this he was infuriated by a newspaper article on 'Psychoanalysis and the Philosophy of Art' by his old friend from the Euterpe group, Rolf Lagerborg. Lagerborg hailed Freud's idea that art manifests itself as a sublimation of repressed desires: 'The artist escapes neuroses through art . . . The person who is not in a position to live life to the full seeks compensation through art.' He cites Wagner: 'If we enjoyed life fully we would have no need of art . . . I do not understand how it could occur to a really happy and fulfilled person to concern himself with artistic creation.'

Sibelius thought Freud's theories demeaned the role of the composer: 'They do not encompass the possibility that the symphonist's conflict – to divine laws for the movement of notes for all time – is a somewhat greater achievement than dying for king and country: many can do that, and planting potatoes or doing similarly useful things can be done by many more.' Sibelius refused to think of his composing as in any sense an act of sublimation or compensation. For him, his creative genius was something wholly positive which raised him above or at least placed him apart from the everyday run of humanity; even more, he viewed himself as the tool of a higher power. Even so, a quotation Lagerborg took from a monograph on Fröding, one of Sibelius's favourite poets, must have struck a responsive chord: 'Artistic creativity is above all the province of the unhappy'. Did he react so strongly because he acknowledged within himself the possibility that there might be some substance in Freud's argument? One other thing in Lagerborg's article cannot have escaped him: the author's contention that the biographer had the right to explore the artist's inner life with speculation 'which many quite improperly see as degrading, concerning the physiological or pathological springs of his personality.' Sibelius must have viewed with distaste the prospect of some biographer rummaging in his own personal life.

Now that peace had returned to the country Sibelius was more torn than ever between his symphonic imperative and dire economic necessity: 'I have had to put my work on one side while I deal with business matters – about 8,000 marks in unpaid letters of credit . . . Plan some small pieces. And feel myself thereby *déclassé*. My proud symphonic visions. Oh these depressing thoughts and moods. And all the fault of not being a capitalist . . . Have donated (!) part of my income from the *Jaeger March* to a charity for their wounded. *Difficile est non satiram scribere.*' Aino, who had recovered from her illnesses in the spring, worked happily in the garden. It pained Sibelius to see it, as he was still frightened that he might be compelled to sell the whole property.

Armas Järnefelt was back in Finland and spent a few days at Ainola: 'He charmed everyone with his artistic and sincere personality. He smiles through his tears and is always sensitive. A friend without peer. I have always had the feeling that everybody sees him as my antipode. My demeanour makes me unpopular, and I can't help feeling that people think my reputation undeserved and that I stand in the way of others. That makes me awkward and trying. In other words, I appear to be a failure by comparison with him.' He had still not overcome his Järnefelt complex, and it never occurred to him to wonder what complexes he in his turn engendered, not so much in Järnefelt as conductor but as composer.

In these diary entries about Järnefelt, Sibelius's handwriting was worse than ever on account of his tremor. The dreadful truth had dawned on him that Axel Carpelan had not much longer to live. Perhaps to disguise the truth from himself he repeated his conviction that he would die before his old friend. Carpelan was suffering from a severe hardening of the coronary arteries and had great difficult in breathing. Axel compared his own fate with that of his country: 'Unhappy Finland, a republic on top of all the slaughter! Our fate is written in the stars!' He had gone to Nådendal 'for the food, good and plentiful but expensive.' (21 June 1918)

As was so often the case, Sibelius's mood soon changed. The next day was wonderful. The clouds full of poetry: 'Powerful mood; worked on Symphony VII [still in its three-movement conception]. Have I taken on too much by embarking on all these big works at the same time? Needs must. But my bills aren't paid by symphonies. They bring in nothing and cost me so much . . . Must, I suppose, call a halt and get on with some small pieces.'

The storm clouds were gathering both literally and figuratively, in this summer of 1918, a year of famine. In the stifling and oppressive summer heat Sibelius felt that he was losing his grip on things at home, where 'fierce winds were blowing up', since he could not raise enough money to keep the household afloat. 'It would be nice to be a capitalist; they would be able to write music.' More material worries assailed him, not the least of which was the cost of installing electricity at Ainola now that paraffin was impossible to get.

Aino, who was badly in need of a change, went to Helsinki to go to the theatre and then went on to stay with Martha Tornell at her summer place. Sibelius's diary records his dread at being on his own: 'O God, why these terrible agonies, this pain in living?' He was seized with anxieties about the war: 'Have stopped believing in the end of the war. It will be a thirty years' conflict.' (Diary, 1 July 1918) At home they were still dealing with the aftermath of the civil war. Sibelius identified that 'peculiarly Finnish heartache' with the spirit of the White Army. He was reminded of it when Heikki Järnefelt, Eero's son, and his mother paid a visit to Ainola and sang a stirring army song that made a strong impression on him: 'Reminds me how Finnish I am in the depths of my being.' (Diary, 25 June 1918)

Barely a month later he got into conversation with a workman on his morning stroll, but their exchange soon became heated. 'He was emotional and full of sympathy for the innocent suffering Reds. Everybody knows that people die like flies in our prison camps. But there is nothing one can do about it. Our circumstances are impossible now.' Hunger and disease raged and took a dreadful toll in the prison camps, claiming some 10,000 victims in all. Sibelius was torn between a natural distress at the scale of this tragedy and a fear of what would happen should there be another Red uprising. Their leaders had fled and sought asylum in the Soviet Union. It would seem that his argument encouraged him to retreat into his ivory tower, though this became more and more difficult:

[20 July 1918] All these furtive, vicious glances from secret Red sympathizers. It's like walking on a volcano. There is menace and turmoil everywhere! How can one get the peace of mind one needs to work when one is torn in two? Still, I'm working with some success on this and that. Yesterday and the day before, small pieces. Also a little work on the symphonies. All around there is still chaos.'

Among the small pieces there was a scout march to words by Jalmari Finne, hardly an inspiring and certainly an all too time-consuming job. Apart from the three symphonies, there were smaller orchestral pieces in his mind, 'impromptus' on which he had begun working towards the end of July. Some days later he makes reference in his diary to 'small tone poems for orchestra'. But the news he gave Carpelan at the end of June that the Fifth Symphony was finished was evidently premature. However he tried to concentrate on work, he was conscious of the tense atmosphere in the country, and the undercurrents of 'sullen, Finnish hatred' from secret Red sympathizers. The extent of his anxiety emerges in another unusual diary entry: 'Lord, do not abandon us in this hour of darkness.' (Diary, 24 July 1918)

At the beginning of August his spirits took an upward turn. His 'dear childhood friend' Walter von Konow spent a couple of days with him at Ainola. He had written a new story, *Endymion*, which he relished. As usual, his time with von Konow brought back memories of their times together at Lahis when they had imagined tales of forest creatures and invented plays to which Sibelius improvised music at the piano. 'This agony is unbearable. It must come to an end. The days are warmer and more like late summer, in spite of rain. Now, when I have kept up the appearance of outward calm, Aino has picked up considerably. A great boon for me.'

Without giving the matter much thought, Sibelius had agreed to be a member of the State Music Council. At a meeting in August he seems to have made quite an exhibition of himself: '. . . talked, gesticulated and behaved in a generally aggressive fashion. They were all quite subdued. My colleagues must have watched the spectacle with astonishment!' Thoughts of his mortality continued to haunt him: 'Will I still be able to bring off something special even as the grave beckons? Like the Beethoven F sharp minor *Adagio*.' Did he, one wonders, compare his own creative development with Beethoven's at the time of the *Hammerklavier*, to whose slow movement he alludes. Could he sense that the Fifth Symphony, whose revision so preoccupied him, was to serve as a frontier post of a 'third period'? Again the migrating birds moved him: 'Once more I watched the cranes stretch their wings, heard their cries and once again I worship. My God, how I prize what you have given me in these oboes. Work again on new things, but I shall soon have run out of cash.'

'The political scene is blacker than ever. Parliament! The Agrarians! O this appalling boorishness. Poor Finland!' Sibelius notes in his diary for 8 August 1918. Whatever had the Agrarians done? In this rump parliament, where the Social Democrats were no longer to be reckoned with after the civil war, the Agrarians tried to delay the government's plans to institute a monarchy and put a German prince on the throne. There were many on the right of the political spectrum who saw the monarchy as the strongest force for stability and a safeguard against another wave of terror. Even Eino Leino, who was a liberal, now wrote: 'To be perfectly frank, I must confess that in my view Finland can only be saved at this time by the establishment of a monarchy.'[2] Sibelius in all probability shared this view, and the idea of a Court probably appealed to him. And now the Agrarians, upstarts at whom the Whites turned up their noses, were putting a spanner in the works! But perhaps he saw that a monarchy had its hazards, particularly in the event of Germany losing the war. Unlike so many on the right, Sibelius was not naïve enough to take a German victory for granted, though at the same time he did not envisage their total defeat. He doubtless thought, as did so many others, that the war would end with some agreement preserving to a greater or lesser extent the balance of power in Europe. No doubt much of this was wishful thinking; he hoped that Germany would not collapse as completely as she eventually did, since she served as a security shield against Finland's enemies, the Bolsheviks and the émigré Finnish Reds.

As autumn approached Sibelius must have realized that the Germans had lost the military intiative. On 8 August the Allies had broken through the German lines at Amiens and the prospect of defeat loomed. The *Jaeger March* affair was worrying him more and more. The rich poetry of the summer sky that had entranced him earlier on had darkened with menacing storm clouds. At last, foreign musical contacts were being restored. Kajanus was negotiating a Nordic Music Festival in Copenhagen, naturally with strong Finnish representation, and Sibelius was seized with anxiety that he would be put in the shadow: 'A shame that Kajus wants to compete against me as a composer for all his worth. He sees me as the fount of all evil. Above all, the man who has eclipsed him. But I can't be held responsible because I have genius – and he doesn't!'

His irritation increased when he learnt that an important Finnish concert was to take place in Berlin with Schnéevoigt conducting. Carpelan had also seen the news and reacted similarly: 'This really upsets me, since he doesn't conduct Finnish music well. What is he doing poking his nose in there? Can one not lodge a protest?' Sibelius answered that it was too late to do any-thing about it: 'Everything is arranged, for sure. It is Schnéevoigt's answer to Kajus's plan to put on a Nordic music festival in Copenhagen, which was originally *his* idea. So as you see, the old battle has been joined.' The Finnish concert in the Berlin Philharmonic was prompted by political as well as cultural motivations. A few days earlier there had been an all-Hungarian concert in the same hall. Now it was the turn of the German–Finnish cultural alliance to show its paces; though this was not entirely an ideal moment, since the German Foreign Ministry had not supported Finnish plans to annex Eastern Karelia unless the Finns ceded to Russia part of the Karelian isthmus. Carpelan supported this plan, and more to the point so did Ludendorff, who realized that the border was far too close to Petrograd to be long tolerated by the Soviet Union. However, Sibelius's Second Symphony was allowed to glisten as a foretaste of the crown that Finland was to offer its German princeling.

The tone of the reviews was warmer than the immediate dictates of political rectitude called for. The *Vorwärts* critic compared it favourably with the Hungarian concert he had just heard: 'Finland's music is a perfect expression of what is meant by nationalism . . . It is not just a matter of collecting, adapting and "reworking" folk songs. In the Sibelius symphony there isn't a single melody nor a single phrase that has not sprouted from the Finnish landscape and taken its nourishment from its soil; yet everything has been refashioned and born anew in the composer's hands.' *Vorwärts* expressed regret that the highly original Fourth Symphony had not been better received when it was first performed in Berlin two years earlier. But the *Vossische Zeitung* gave voice to those reservations so often encountered in Germany: 'On a larger canvas there is a lack of real feeling for form. Sibelius appears greater the smaller the form he chooses.'

Sibelius was bogged down in small pieces: a choral piece *Jone havsfärd (Jonah's voyage)* as a thank-you for a case of lampreys, and *Linnea*, Op. 76, No. 11, originally intended for the flower pieces, Op. 85. At the end of September he 'went on the razzle' for three days on end in Helsinki: 'Really quite refreshing. Got into an argument, not to say row.' All the same, he managed to hear Kajanus rehearse the first two Beethoven symphonies. Back at Ainola he set to work with renewed vigour on his orchestral pieces, presumably the 'impromptus' he had started at the end of July. 'See now what burdens my genius and skill enjoin! How I've squandered my life away. Terrible.' He toyed with the idea of changing the name of the pieces to 'fantasies'.

His monarchist sympathies did not colour his political judgement: 'Things are going badly for the Germans. In more than one way. At home there's an oppressive calm.' In spite of the looming German defeat, the Finnish parliament finally voted to offer the crown to Prince Friedrich Karl. Sibelius noted, somewhat laconically, 'Aino has gone into town – King elected!!', the exclamation marks denoting more surprise than enthusiasm. He went into Helsinki himself for a longer period, probably a couple of weeks, to raise money – and spend it! The Helsinki Youth League gave the first performance of his new cantata *Oma maa (Our Native Land)*, as befitted a somewhat nationalist body, and Sibelius was in attendance. Katila' wrote an enthusiastic review: 'Sibelius had found convincing expression for the beauty of Finland, and the modal character of the opening made a strong impact.'[3] Madetoja covered his disappointment by discussing everything but the piece itself: '*Oma maa* offers numerous harmonic challenges and demands good intonation, which the choir achieved with commendable security. The tone poem's ceremonial feeling comes fully into its own. The many-faceted orchestral texture could, however, have been given with greater clarity.'[4]

Sibelius was displeased with its reception. '*Oma maa* was a success, albeit not with everyone. Also, Madetoja and other critics were negative. They are starting up again. But from Katila I have received mercy!!' Sibelius must have got through something like 5,000 marks on his Helsinki trip; his State Pension was to be increased the following month to 8,000 – a year! 'Am absolutely whacked. Begin to compose small pieces to refill the coffers. Can't understand myself. Got back my old appetite and let things go. Dreadful.'(Diary, 29 October 1918)

Could the coffers be refilled? As on so many previous occasions during the war years he turned to his Maecenas, Otto Donner – but this time to no avail. 'From Donner nothing . . . without money . . . sell the horse . . . and sack the servant boy!' The rise in his pension was linked to the rate of inflation but still worried him: 'Feel oppressed by kindness and can't believe that it will last. Our Reds!' He obviously feared for his pension if the social democrats gained power or influence after the next election.

At the beginning of the autumn Breitkopf & Härtel had been optimistic in their assessment of the *Jaeger March*'s prospects. But when he saw the special edition, he was shocked by the militaristic tone of the preface. He sent a telegram asking them to pulp all copies of the *de luxe* edition at his expense, and followed it with a letter demanding that the words *'die Lügen der Entente'* be removed. By this time Germany had already signed an armistice, and Breitkopf & Härtel had written to say that it seemed unlikely that the high hopes they had for the piece would be fulfilled. The arrangement for military band had not sold at all well in Germany and the orchestral version had not fared much better. Herr Westerlund in Helsinki had only ordered ten copies.

At this point Sibelius again succumbed to the spell of his old love, the violin: 'Been enormously depressed. But why? Composed a *Humoresque*, Op. 87, No. 1 (the others will have to be renumbered), for violin and orchestra.'(Diary, 20 November 1918) As he had said on an earlier occasion about its companions, the *Humoresques* were conceived in a world of illness and misery. And so perhaps we have something of the sublimation to which Lagerborg's article on Freud alluded.

Back in Helsinki he took part in Hjalmar Procopé's fiftieth birthday festivities, which he seems to have celebrated in the style of Belshazzar himself. 'Heavy drinking and met all the gay dogs in town.' Procopé had been dilatory in providing a Swedish translation of his *Scout March*: 'I'll have to see when I can send it off to Breitkopf & Härtel. Things look black for the beleaguered Germans. The country has as good as fallen apart. Could never have believed anything like this was possible. But we live in an unpredictable world where anything is possible . . . The days are ebbing away.' (27 November 1918) Finland's protector had collapsed; the White Government in Helsinki was in a weaker position and the Reds were surfacing in Germany itself.

Fate must have played a part in bringing Sibelius and Carpelan together. Only a few months after his first anonymous letter to Sibelius in 1900, he was raising funds from his Swedish friend Tamm without which the important visits Sibelius made to Berlin and Italy in the ensuing months could never have taken place. Now it seemed that their relationship would come full circle. More than a decade had passed since Carpelan's last rescue operation. Now in November 1918 it fell to him to play an almost prophetic role in Sibelius's life. The two men corresponded assiduously during the autumn, as if both sensed that every letter from Carpelan could be the last. On 2 November, when Sibelius was worrying about the preface to the *Jaeger March* and his newly reawakened thirst, which he had assuaged in Helsinki with vintages at 300 marks a bottle, he revealed something of his inner feelings: 'I am in a terrible state of depression, see everything in the blackest gloom, not least what I have so far achieved as a composer. People are working against me. I won't name names, since it gives me great pain. My thoughts often turn to you, who have always been my well-wisher. I hope things will get better. And shut our eyes to all the banality and malice that engulf us. The only consolation is that life won't last long. But when you have others to consider, one must not think in this fashion. I believe in courage, and that is my tragedy.' As at the turn of the century, Sibelius remained faithful to the Neitzschean concept that adversity is a measure of strength.

Carpelan wrote that despite his present weakness his heart was with Sibelius, and reported that *Oma maa* had made a great impression at its performance in Åbo, that *Teodora*, 'an extraordinarily inspired song', had at last come into its own in Väinö Sola's interpretation, and that everyone in Åbo grieves for Germany's misfortunes: '. . . otherwise shortages of food and money and low spirits. The Åbo Academy is one glimmer of hope. We have already raised sixteen and a half million.'[5] The Åbo Academy was the Fenno–Swedish response to Finnish nationalism, which threatened Swedish both as the official language and as a cultural force. The name itself derives from the earlier Academy founded in 1640, which was transplanted to Helsinki in 1828 and subsequently redesignated the Imperial Alexander University, the forerunner of the present Helsinki University. In November 1918 the governing body of the Academy approached Sibelius to ask whether he would consider writing a cantata for its inauguration, which was to take place in the following spring. To this end they enlisted the services of Carpelan as an intermediary. 'The Secretary of the Academy came to sound me out on whether I would use my good offices to persuade you to compose a cantata for their inaugural ceremony,' and reminded him of his long-standing affection for the old town. With one of his prophetic touches, Carpelan added that perhaps in the future there might even be a music school associated with the *Academia rediviva Åboensis*. (Some years later a musicological institute was founded at the Åbo Academy, which possesses one of the most beautiful modern chamber music halls in Europe.)

With the same zeal that he had shown in 1900, Carpelan managed to negotiate the best possible terms for Sibelius: 'As far as your fee is concerned, I told the Academy's administrators that conditions are such that you should get three or four times more than usual, and even then that would not be too much – rather the opposite. Anyway, that was accepted.' Sibelius answered by return: 'I can't imagine that the Åbo Academy could find a more persuasive spokesman than you. The day before your letter came, I had just written to the Consistory accepting their commission. This in the hope that it would give *you* pleasure, so you see how the land lies. When I first saw the inscription Åbo Academy, I felt the same tingle down my spine as I did on the train in Italy when the conductor called out Rome. It is as if we have re-established contact with our old culture before the fire [of 1827, which destroyed much of the city]. Now it only remains for Jarl Hemmer to surpass himself. I shall certainly try and do the same.' (28 November 1918)

In the climate of new-found independence, a certain hubris was evident among the Finnish nationalists. Sibelius was naturally aware that by lending his active support to the Åbo Academy and a concept of one nation two cultures, he would encounter resentment: 'Now I'll have all the Fennomans on at me. But how could I act differently?' His approaching birthday led to the usual ruminations on life and composing: 'The important thing is to stay the course. But my way of working is unaffected by my age. I am not built to "write" music; music springs from our experience. The public here at home is no longer interested in what I have to say. But then I shall just have to accustom myself to being on my own. That is also deeply ingrained in my nature.'

This says a great deal about the kind of composer Sibelius was. Generally speaking, it is not possible to distil any rules about the relationship of a specific work to outward biographical factors or to the composer's inner life. Sibelius's diary entry reminds me of Stuckenschmidt's words in his biography of Schoenberg: 'In Schoenberg, life, the world around him, and his work form an indivisible unity. To discuss Schoenberg the man is to discover and decipher the innumerable links that intertwine in his artistic, religious and political aura; that also means that in his output, be it musical, literary or in his paintings, we find the same elements mirrored and entwined.'[6]

With Sibelius one can also proceed from a trinity: life; the world about him; work. Accordingly, it is worthwhile examining his work with a view to finding some relationship between the man and the world around him. This correlation – assuming that it exists – is infinitely more subtle than a more or less direct reflection of biographical events and states of mind, and it varies from work to work.

On 17 December, Sibelius attended the first performance of Madetoja's Second Symphony, which Kajanus conducted. Its elegiac, pastoral tone struck a responsive chord in him: 'It gives one much to think about.' Perhaps he also found some echoes of his own harmonic language and tonal colours. During the same visit he took the opportunity of meeting Jarl Hemmer to talk about the text of the cantata. Their encounter developed into something of a celebration: 'Met a huge number of people and drank wine. Difficult to live this wonderful life.' His diary records his debt to Otto Donner, who came to his rescue with 10,000 marks: 'I have lived on him for the best part of a year, for I have been (and still am) without income' – or rather, as he added for the sake of accuracy, without any income 'worth talking about'. A few days after Christmas, Hemmer finished the text of *Jordens sång (Song of the Earth)* and sent it to Ainola.

Over the Christmas holiday Sibelius was plagued by lumbago: 'It's a strange thing and I can't think how I could possibly have caught it. Perhaps my Christmas sauna. I am in low spirits because of it.' Carpelan's Christmas present had been a copy of the *Jaeger March,* but he had also spent some time poring over the Op. 72 Songs. *Kyssen (The Kiss),* to words of Rydberg, he thought 'magical in its beauty and sublime, a song which only Jenny Lind is worthy of – a shaft of heavenly light, music from another sphere. Thank you, Janne, thank you for what you have given mankind.' Carpelan deplored the fact that neither the Violin sonata (*sic*), Op. 80, nor *Luonnotar* was on sale. 'They tell me that there are fifteen large consignments waiting at Lübeck for the blockade to be lifted.'

Carpelan's letter lifted Sibelius's spirits:

> You cannot imagine how your appreciation of my songs has cheered me. I would have wished you a Happy New Year long before, had I not been wholly absorbed in the cantata. Jarl Hemmer is a youngster – and proud of it. And that is his strength. His poetry has something of Stagnelius about it, *mirabile dictu.* And I find that very congenial.
>
> I shall write shortly about my work and my future plans. Will see when I can get away into the wider world. I can't abide being so cut off. It's not so bad here in the country. But going into Helsinki and meeting all the high-and-mighty Lilliputians is so depressing.

In his postscript he added: 'If possible, I shall conduct the cantata myself. I conduct these days with reluctance, since my nerves let me down. Nowadays nearly always.'

The turn of the year found him in mixed spirits: 'The others – the young ones – seem to have overtaken me. But the last thing you should do is to assert your supremacy. No! Wait and work on steadily. Your doubts concerning the symphonies will resolve themselves one day. Not by talking about it but through sheer hard work. So for the time being, be content to remain in the background. And don't forget your great love of Beethoven. You can worship worse gods. It is the ethical spirit in his music, not the technique, which is often a little old fashioned and not brilliant enough.'

CHAPTER TEN

Carpelan's Death and the Fifth Symphony's Completion

Over the New Year holiday, Martha Tornell and her half-sister Hulda Wale-sa came to stay at Ainola. Their visit seems to have been a success: they read aloud to each other, Dickens's *Christmas Carol* and Selma Lagerlöf's latest book *Bannlyst (Forbidden)*, which 'gave us much delight,' Sibelius recorded in his diary. He continued: 'The last few days have been mild, and there is a wonderful spring-like fragrance of snow. For me this scent always has over-tones of youth and passion.' (Diary, 5 January 1919)

The New Year lamps may have cast a gentle glow at Ainola but the situation elsewhere was anything but gentle. Hard cross-winds buffeted Fin-land, every bit as much as they had during the Christmas of 1901. The readings had enabled Sibelius to forget the outside world for a brief moment, but world events continued to resonate in his being like a deep orchestral pedal point: 'The political scene is darker than ever. And my own future as a composer now looks impossible when all the talk here is of Bolshevism, for or against.' (Diary, 7 January 1919)

He needed only to open his morning paper, *Hufvudstadsbladet,* at the beginning of February to see his fears come to fruition. 'The Reds are on the march' – the headline could have been taken straight out of Sibelius's diary of 13 May the previous year! 'Bolshevik agitators arrested in Tampere'; 'Strikes in Great Britain'. In Finland itself several Red agitators were brought before the courts charged with conspiring against the state. From Kuusamo in the far north it was reported that a sixteen-year-old orphan boy had died of hunger. In Estonia the Finnish Volunteer Corps had helped to drive the Bolsheviks from the key railway junction of Valga. That is where Sibelius's fourteen-year-old nephew Jussi would have been, had he had his way. He had run away from school without telling his parents, and together with other volunteers, crossed to Tallinn (Reval) and tried to enlist but was sent home as under age.

Hufvudstadsbladet's correspondent describes the view from a table at Sibe-lius's favourite watering hole, the Kämp. 'The students and dons, the bankers, stockbrokers and insurers with folders under their arms, Finnish officers with Finnish ladies on their arms. For the first time for centuries Finland was a free country. And now the Finnish ladies come into their own. At dusk one such evening, one might see the tall figure of Mannerheim emerging from the crowd. He is dressed in the new uniform of the War of Independence, with his white fur cap shining out over the mass of people.'

On 19 January the Finnish Opera reopened in the newly-renovated Alexander Theatre. Mannerheim sat in the State box and Kajanus conducted *Finlandia,* but Sibelius was not to be seen among the celebrities. He may have felt some diffidence in attending: after all, he had not composed a national opera that could match *Aïda,* which opened the season. Perhaps he was suffering his occasional bouts of insecurity, when he feared encountering 'cold, spiteful glances'.

At the Helsinki Orchestra's Thursday Concerts, Kajanus continued the Beethoven cycle he had begun the previous autumn, which did not inhibit him, however, from conducting Sibelius's Second on 6 February. Other novelties included the first performance of Schoenberg's *Verklärte Nacht* conducted by Schnéevoigt and new works by Madetoja and Ernest Pingoud, born in St Petersburg, a pupil of Reger and much influenced by Scriabin. Willy Burmester drew full houses for his four violin recitals.

But Sibelius did not move from Ainola. He felt his own horizons shrink when he was in the company of the Helsinki establishment, whose perspectives extended no further than from the Opera House to the Opera-källaren (Opera Cellar) on Runeberg's Esplanade! 'Can't stand it any more, not to be able to go abroad.' He must have read with a sense of relief a newspaper report that Finland's independence had been recognized by the Allies.

The news proved to be premature. Even though the British Foreign Secretary, Arthur Balfour, thought that the Finnish government had handled the situation well, Britain and America delayed extending recognition, partly in deference to the White Russian leaders but mainly on account of the uncertainty surrounding the whole Russian question. Sibelius debated the wisdom of making a visit to any of the Allied countries before their relations with Finland had been normalized. He was thus all the more delighted to hear from Rosa Newmarch. In a letter written on New Year's Eve 1918, she assured him that her friendship and affection had remained wholly undiminished during the hostilities that had engulfed their countries: 'Until recently there seemed little point and possibly some element of risk in making contact with you. I have no idea how much you have suffered during these terrible events . . . But let us not go into politics or history. The future lies before us.' The Promenade concerts and symphony concerts under Sir Henry Wood had continued in spite of German air attacks and power cuts and, according to Mrs Newmarch, Wagner's music exercised a specially magnetic effect on Zeppelins and aeroplanes. 'Now it seems to me that we have an insatiable thirst for music. I want to see you here as soon as it is possible for you to undertake the journey. You know, when all is weighed in the balance, we English have our good qualities, and we are always prepared to give our old friends a warm reception.'

In the circumstances, Sibelius did not go to Leipzig to take part in the celebrations of Breitkopf & Härtel's 200th anniversary. The Director thanked him for his good wishes and reaffirmed that he and his son would continue to promote his work with the same zeal and dedication that their predecessors had given to Haydn, Beethoven, Mendelssohn and Schumann. As part of their Sibelius campaign, Breitkopf & Härtel published a small monograph on the composer by Walter Niemann in their popular series *Kleine Musikerbiographien*. It is difficult to see the reasoning behind this, since in his earlier books *Die Musik Skandinaviens* and *Die Musik seit Richard Wagner*, as well as in a long article on Sibelius in *Die Zeit*, Niemann had made no secret of his generally negative attitude to the Sibelius symphonies and had questioned Sibelius's universality. The article had not escaped the composer's attention: 'My symphonies aren't good enough for him. Otherwise he's very flattering.'

One must give Niemann credit for trying to show why he doesn't regard Sibelius as a real symphonist: 'One must remember to what little extent and how poorly the Nordic national ideas with their short-breathed phrase structures are suited to what we think of as symphonic treatment.' Sibelius's basically impressionist talent ensures him 'a position of the first rank as a programmatic composer and tone-poet and as a master of orchestral colour'. Even if Sibelius's symphonies are important for their 'ethical character, . . . when measured against Western yardsticks, they are wanting to a significant extent the fundamental prerequisites of genuine symphonic writing: monumentality of form, the organic development and inner logic and sense of consummation. The loosely gathered mosaic-like musical ideas remain in the majority of cases harmonically undeveloped and are not fashioned in a complete entity. Sibelius strives to write in the manner of Tchaikovsky's *Pathétique* in a Finnish dialect and his music clearly follows a self-evident but unstated programme that contributes to a slightly incoherent overall impression. The symphonies from first to last [the last, of course, being the Fourth] all have the same concerns: the Finnish landscape and the Finnish people's soul.' The First Symphony he nevertheless hailed in extravagant terms as 'the deepest, the most natural utterance the master has given us'. The Second and Third are the most national and Finnish, although they already come close to Western modernism, while the Fourth 'stands – fortunately not entirely – on the heights of the most modern Debussyian impressionism and Schoenbergian naturalism and expressionism'. Niemann struck much the same tone, albeit from a different standpoint, as Adorno was to do in his *Glosse über Sibelius*, though the former viewed him as moving in too modern a direction while the latter dismissed him as a dangerous reactionary. Of course, it does not help that, as in his earlier essay, he lavishes praise on the tone poems, incidental music, the string quartet and the songs.

Sibelius swallowed his pride and maintained a silence. Only when Breitkopf politely enquired in March 1919 about any suggestions he might have, did he say his piece, first concerning genealogical matters and then more important things: 'Dr Niemann's understanding of my musical personality is grounded on fallacies, and even though the book is written with sympathy, the author cast aspersions on those areas of my art which – in my view – should be valued most.' Breitkopf replied that it had never been Niemann's intention to cast aspersions on his genealogy but omitted to respond to his complaints about the symphonies.

Towards the beginning of spring came a letter from Busoni in Zürich, written this time in Swedish, a language he had learnt thirty years earlier when he was living in Helsinki:

> Dearest friend, it is now all too long since I have been able to follow your development and your growing mastery. I have very often asked about your Fifth Symphony, which much interests me, and would be very grateful if you could arrange for me to see a score. No one seems to know if the symphony has been printed or where it has been published. (26 February 1919)

Contrary to his custom (they normally corresponded in German), Sibelius also replied in Swedish:

> Over my desk is Eero's portrait of you, and when I received your very welcome letter, it was as if the picture began to speak. It has been silent for many years now but has always prompted me to work. You do me the great kindness to ask about my Fifth Symphony. It is yet not in print as I have not been able to publish anything since 1914. I am so proud of the interest you show in me.

In January work had progressed on the cantata for Åbo (*Jordens Sång*), though at half pressure. 'The days go by and little, all too little, is accomplished. In the future, as my days draw to an end, I will surely come to regret my present inertia.' His beloved Kaj (Katarina) went back to school in Helsinki, and Aino went with her. 'I'm alone here with my melancholy thoughts. The cantata plagues me, not least because the musical resources in Åbo are inadequate, judging from Karl Ekman's letter [Ekman was at that time conductor there]. And then there's the promise I made Klemetti for a work for his *Suomen Laulu*. He's no friend of my music [a judgment obviously coloured by his general pessimism] and only wants to have my name on his programme. Perhaps that's not even good enough nowadays. I am now fifty-three and – sad to say – have accomplished nothing worth talking about. I see myself and my life's work as very wanting. And judging from the papers, I really have little to show for myself. Lamentable, when I'm at the height of my powers. How fortunate it is that Aino isn't at home. But the proud vessel Jean Sibelius shall yet spread sail on the high seas – but where?'

His maritime terminology had not deserted him when two days later, while working on *Jordens Sång*, he spoke of himself as in danger of shipwreck: 'My capacity for work is not what it was. Being young and "interesting" then outweighed all the troubles and travails. Now, when my colleagues proceed at full sail, I have an almost hopeless struggle to keep going. Aino ill. In bed.' (Diary, 16 January 1919) Soon after he returned to work on the cantata, he was in good spirits and thought he 'was working splendidly'.

On 23 January Elizabeth Järnefelt, his mother-in-law, celebrated her eightieth birthday, and Sibelius and Aino went into Helsinki for the festivities. Although he did not greet the prospect of an evening with all the Järnefelts with unmixed feelings, he admired her uncompromising Tolstoyan idealism and integrity, as he did his brother-in-law Arvid. 'How I love and admire her! A very special and great personality. As for my inner plight: *"herabgesetztes Selbstgefühl"*.' The whole family assembled at her home. Armas Järnefelt came from Stockholm; Arvid had been driven from his estate in Lojo under escort – the Helsinki courts had taken proceedings against him on a public order charge, for defying a directive not to preach in Berghäll's (Kallio) Church, and had sentenced him to two months' imprisonment. The sentence was to start the following month but in the end was commuted by General Mannerheim. It goes without saying that Sibelius soon gravitated to the Kämp and the König. His revelries brought their inevitable consequences:

> [29 January 1919] Cannot work when my spirits are so low. Find how difficult it is to cope with enemies so near home. The strange thing is that those who have furthered my cause most – Olof Wallin (a choral conductor) – are most against me. Wentzel Hegelstam's outburst against me in the König, and all the others who are against me make life hopeless for me here. Not that I would necessarily accomplish much more than the little I've done here, were I living abroad. But I can't be indifferent to all this – which is what I should be at my age – and that's the hard part of it. I have lived far too egotistically in every respect and am now paying the price of having no friends.'

Of course he had many friends, both at home and abroad, who were greatly attached to him, but he was undoubtedly on target in speaking of egotism – or perhaps 'egocentricity' would have been more accurate. His reply to Busoni was a case in point. His letters to that master were almost without exception responses. It would not occur to him to take the initiative and ask what Busoni had played at his last recital, let alone what he had recently composed, or what his views were on what was going on in music. How such a letter would have gladdened Busoni as he sat in his exile in neutral Zürich!

At the beginning of February Sibelius went to Åbo and delivered his cantata *Jordens sång* for chorus and orchestra (adding in his diary a rather barbed remark about 'small-town reduced forces'). He lived it up, dined with the Rector, the distinguished sociologist Edvard Westermarck, smoked cigars and drank champagne. With Axel Carpelan he had 'a great time'. The meeting was to prove their last, and its memory left him with a pang of conscience. He had expressly promised Carpelan to visit him once again before his departure, but failed to do so. On his return he wrote to make amends. 'Unfortunately my whole being was overcome with such self-disgust that I did not want to burden you with a second visit.'

He testified that the cantata had taken its toll on him: 'Tried to work. But can't work up any enthusiasm. It is as if the old musical ideas now bore me. Now I am very much down in the dumps. Must pull myself together. Life is short.' (23 February 1919) Carpelan must have sensed that Sibelius's spirits were low and had written many supportive letters: 'Speaking of Symphony 5, I forgot to ask if you have also reworked the *pastorale* section in the *Andante*, where there were 24 bars of pizzicato at one stretch, which struck me as a little monotonous. Otherwise I was very taken with it – also with the first movement (now revised, you said). [Carpelan is of course referring to the second version of the first movement in which Sibelius had effected a transition between the *Tempo molto* section and the *Allegro moderato*.]

Obviously Sibelius had caused some offence in turning down an invitation: 'Janne, don't forget that Åbo is a very small town. Don't smoke – and don't drink – both are bad for you and affect you in the same way and make difficulties for those who are working on your behalf. Just work for dear life at your new symphonies, which will be the crowning glory of your life. And try to forget your money worries – they will work out somehow.'

Carpelan's 'wonderful letter' lifted Sibelius's spirits. 'What a friend I have in him. Caused offence in Åbo. I received 6,000 marks for the cantata, which is princely. I can now resume work on the symphonies.' But the nearer the Copenhagen Music Festival loomed, the more nervous he became. He had no new trumps to play, for he was still unhappy with the Fifth Symphony. A telephone conversation with Kajanus left him agitated: 'He was calm and assured, and took the news that I wasn't coming in his stride. In no event will I go with old works. Must politely decline. Kajus said, "You don't go to Copenhagen to perform new works." But nor should you go to be put in the shade.'

According to a letter to Carpelan (20 May 1918), it would appear that Sibelius had spoken of plans to write a completely new first movement – to be the first of four – for the Fifth Symphony. Now, during the second half of February 1919, it seemed that he had abandoned this idea. On 24 February he noted: 'Yesterday I was in a wonderful mood and revised Symphony 5, first movement. Which I thought was good yesterday.' His letter to Carpelan three days later confirms this: 'These days have been very successful. Saw things very clearly. The first movement of the Fifth Symphony is one of the best things I've ever written. Can't understand my blindness. It's strange that you've always thought it would be a three-movement piece. Presumably I have been too close to it, or have also been thrown off course by certain impractical bad notes in certain instruments. Aino sends you her greetings. We must now live in the hope that your spirit will triumph over your sufferings. More soon. Working intensively on the other movements, so everything will soon be ready. Your faithful, grateful JS.' (23 February 1919)

Sibelius never forgot that Carpelan – unlike Bis in *Hufvudstadsbladet* – thought that the amalgamation of the first and second movements of the symphony was a definite improvement. Carpelan's response had been instinctive. When Sibelius had conducted the second version of the symphony in Åbo in 1916, after the first movement he had turned to his neighbour and whispered, 'That is a magnificent transformation, formally the equal of Brahms at his best.' In his reply Carpelan quotes himself and continues: 'In the second movement, it seemed to me, some *longueurs* had insinuated themselves . . . I also felt that something was not quite right between the second and third movements. A shorter movement, perhaps a scherzo, would have given greater weight and sense of fulfilment to the whole. I can't be completely sure about this. The third movement made an overwhelming impression on me. I liked Ekman's words that the dissonances were beautiful. In all these matters I'm not absolutely sure, except for one thing that as a whole, both in form and musical substance, that the Fifth Symphony is altogether outstanding. To be frank I was apprehensive when you said that you were writing a new first movement, but didn't want to say anything, as I am lacking insight and confidence. Was very upset by Bis's review – but now I feel much calmer and happier. Now I know that it will be a masterly symphony. This has weighed on me for more than two years. All my wretched days I have put all my heart and soul behind your cause, even if it is only of limited help. That you have occasionally misunderstood me has distressed me – but this has for the main part been due to my nervous condition and heart. Dear Janne, look after yourself, take plenty of exercise, give up smoking, which induces premature hardening of the arteries. You'll soon be able to have proper coffee, but forego wine for it plays havoc with your nerves and heart. Soon the time will come when you can once again breathe European air and absorb new impressions – hope it won't be Allied air!' The letter proved to be his last.

At home in Ainola, the effects of the war years began to make themselves felt. According to Sibelius, Aino remained in an overwrought, highly strung state which prompted him to fear for her sanity. The ten-year-old Margareta was pestered by boils, which her father feared might become tuberculous. Inflation mounted so quickly that the monthly living expenses for the family reached 5,000 marks. But despite all this, life had its pleasant sides: 'An electrical engineer has been here to wire the house. The little ones give me great joy. How fortunate I am to have them here. I am very happy at home. If only Aino can manage, but she is so miserable that it worries me. She longs for company, which doesn't mean anything to me. Ought to make the effort – but for my art. And this my goal that, during such times, to work on a symphony and give up time and money for something which in others' eyes is a nothing – that is really sublime.' He worked as intensively as ever on the Fifth Symphony, even if he confessed 'open embarrassment' about confiding it even to his diary. 'But it will be really good, if I can only work on it without interruption, which looks unlikely to be the case since money will soon run out.'

On 22 March came alarming news from Carpelan's cousin Tor that Axel's condition had taken a turn for the worse. Sibelius hastened to write to him: 'You can have no idea how worried I am. But the hope that you will overcome your illness never leaves me. I believe that your strong spirit will weather the storm. It's still snowing here, but spring is already in the air. The willows have already begun to change colour. Everything is coming to life. This life which I love so infinitely, that feeling must shine through everything I compose. Do your best and pull through.'

On its way to Åbo, his letter crossed with a short postcard from Carpelan, though the lines slope and the handwriting itself is difficult to read: 'A terrible attack – or rather four – so-called dry inflammation of the heart . . . Terrible pains which cannot be alleviated by any medicine. Dear and wonderful Janne, a long farewell and thanks. God's blessing now and always. A fraternal greeting to Aino. Thanks for everything, everything.' He was in full possession of his senses to the last, and the letter was correctly and formally addressed to Herr Professor Doktor Jean Sibelius and wife and children. The news of his death soon followed:

[24 March 1919] Axel†. How empty life seems. No sun, no music, no affection. How alone I am with all my music. Even on his deathbed he still wrote the card I received this morning. Lucid right to the very end.

[29 March] Now Axel is laid to rest in the cold earth. It feels so immeasurably and profoundly sad. For whom shall I compose now?

This was Carpelan's epitaph.

Even in the case of Axel Carpelan, Sibelius remained unwavering in his resolution not to go to funerals. Aino represented him in Åbo, but he was there in his thoughts.

As at the time of Kuula's death, Sibelius saw the 'cold earth' as horrifying and hostile, not as a sweet embrace. For him death was a cruel foe, and its tragedy was not softened by any hope of reunion in a life after this.

But what did he really believe? On more than one occasion he maintained quite categorically that this life was the only one we had and that death was the end of everything. Did this perhaps disguise his innermost thoughts? He felt something of the same reluctance to define in words his feelings about life and death as he did in discussing his music. In his innermost self Sibelius believed in some kind of pantheism, the soul's union with some kind of all-embracing entity as in *Minns du en tystnad*. ('Do you remember a silence' in Rydberg's *På verandan vid havet* [*On the Balcony by the Sea*]?) To finish the symphony must be his testament to Carpelan and must now be his first objective.

– 2 –

Sibelius did not return to his diary for almost four weeks after Carpelan's death. The gap testifies to a determined and final attack on the Fifth, similar to that preceding the Fourth Symphony:

> [22 April 1919] Symphony 5 – *mirabile* (not to say) *horribile dictu* – is finished in its final form. Have battled with God. My hands are trembling so much that I can scarcely write. Oh, if only Axel was alive. His thoughts were with me right to the bitter end. Outdoors two degrees above freezing point and sun. The ice is still there. Of the migratory birds have seen only wild geese but no swans.

Six days later comes an extraordinary decision:

> [28 April 1919] Have cut out the second and third movements. The first movement is a symphonic fantasia and does not require anything else. That's where it all began. Shall I call it Symphony in one movement or symphonic fantasy, or perhaps *Fantasia sinfonica I*?

He had obviously come to the conclusion that the fusion of the first two movements had been successful in forming a complete entity, so that he could give it the same name that he was to use some years later for the Seventh Symphony. Perhaps he was fired by Carpelan's enthusiasm. In any event, a few days later he had thought better of it:

> [2 May 1919] The symphony will be as originally designed, in three movements. All are with the copyist. A confession: worked over the whole of the finale once again. Now it is good. But this struggle with God!'

Now at last he had fought himself free.

There were some small additions to the two violin opuses 79 and 81: *Danse idyll* and *Vals*. To opus 76 he added an *Affetuoso*. For the Academic Song Society he composed a rallying song, *Till havs*, while for another Swedish group he wrote *Drömmarna (The dreams)* for mixed choir. In the middle of April, the remainder of the proofs of *Scaramouche* arrived, and Sibelius thought the sheer size of the parcel 'quite imposing'. 'But the big things that I dream of, when will they be taken up? Always these commercial pieces and chores. And time runs away.' The proofs were riddled with mistakes, 'terrible', and their correction proved to be 'a dreadful strain'. Spring was late that year. Towards the end of April the ice began to darken and melt. 'Heard the cranes but did not see them.' Several days later he had better luck, and managed to see the wild geese.

The Sixth Symphony with its 'dark and pastoral contrasts' and the Seventh with the 'Hellenic rondo' lay in the future. How far he had got with them is difficult to assess. In any event, he had sketched out the basic thematic substance for the Sixth and, according to his diary, also worked on the Seventh. But he was not yet ready to turn to either of them in earnest. No doubt he needed a rest from his creative labours. Yet the fact that he had finally tamed the Fifth Symphony and surmounted the psychological hurdles that had inhibited its completion should have put him in good heart for work on its successors. He briefly flirted with the notion of a chamber work, but could not summon up the energy or enthusiasm for the genre. Perhaps the fifty-three-year-old composer was beginning to tire of his surroundings, his life-style, his friends and, above all, himself. A diary entry of 8 May reads: 'Above all I must find a more musical companionship than before. Leave my old companions and all the emptiness and despondency. Concentrate on my own inner life . . . But life is so short. Can I bear it all? Only a few more years. Don't think of your reputation, the burdens you carry and the envy you inspire – anyone of standing has these problems! But friends, you have real friends, even though the best of all has passed on.' It would seem that even now, in his fifties, Sibelius had yet to adapt to the changes time had brought and to adjust to the thought that he must plan for the future within a more limited time-span.

Signs of age were beginning to cast a shadow over the future. His tremor began to alarm him. 'It would be an easy thing for me to work if cheap and weak wines were readily to hand. These days I am drinking whisky and schnapps. My hands shake so much that I can't write.' He later notes an improvement, but it would seem that he associated his tremor with spirits. One wonders whether he in fact needed a regular intake of alcohol to steady his tremor! After his long period of temperance from 1908–15 and further enforced abstinence during 1918, his drinking and tremor became something of a vicious circle; the drinking produced a tremor, which could then be stabilized only by further drink.

World events had taken an encouraging turn. He would have been cheered by the news that the United States and Great Britain recognized Finnish independence and its de facto government on 3 May, and that France had some days earlier restored diplomatic relations, having broken them off earlier at the time of the abortive monarchy. No obstacle now hindered him from travelling to the West. The elections in March must have given him some satisfaction. The socialists did not win a majority, but the very fact that only a year after the civil war they took part in the elections showed that wartime scars were beginning to heal.

Relations between the White government and Soviet Russia had not yet been restored, and some still dreamed of 'liberating' Russia from the

Bolsheviks. At the Hotel Seurahuone (Societetshuset), one of Sibelius's watering holes, General Judenitch planned his march on Petrograd, and even Mannerheim the head of state, who had been a general in the Tsarist Army, flirted with the same notion – albeit only in return for recognition of Finnish independence and sovereignty over parts of Eastern Karelia on the part of Admiral Koltschak, the White Russian commander at Omsk. Mannerheim had not been able to attend any of Sibelius's concerts in the spring of 1918. But in the summer of 1919 he invited Sibelius, Aino and their grown-up daughters to a garden party. However, Sibelius, who did not enjoy official functions, declined. Katarina, still only sixteen, represented the family. Later on, as an ordinary citizen, Mannerheim was keen to maintain his connections with the composer, who proved an elusive guest despite his admiration for the general.

Given his lifelong devotion to the *Kalevala*, it would not have been surprising if Sibelius had succumbed to notions of a Greater Finland, incorporating those areas of Eastern Karelia where the runic arts still flourished. But although Sibelius could never be indifferent to Karelia, where he had spent much time as a newly-wed and whose people he had celebrated in his pageant music the following year, he remained unresponsive to adventurism. A corps of Finnish volunteers with the tacit blessing of Mannerheim and the Finnish government crossed the Russian border in the Aunus (Olonetz) area, but without prompting the enthusiastic popular rising they had expected from the Karelian populace. Sibelius did not approve of this venture, even though one of the participants was Bobi Sivén – the idealistic son of the Jaeger Battalion activist who had paid him a visit in 1915 – who was now much in love with his daughter Katarina.

– 3 –

The Copenhagen Music Festival was fast approaching: 'They want my Second Symphony. I would have preferred the Fifth. The Second will soon be twenty years old. And Kajanus's *Sinfonietta* is two years old. The critics, however, are bound to ordain it as having showing me the way. This and other things make me depressed – I don't know why. But probably it's the way that his friends have behaved towards me all my life that has made me like this.' The concert promoters doubtless reckoned on the Second Symphony under the composer's own direction filling the house, and thought this outweighed the musical prestige of having him conduct his newly-completed symphony. Nor did they give any thought to the possible embarrassment of a composer at the height of his creative powers having to conduct an old work in front of his colleagues.

All this became a source of irritation. 'No work yesterday or today. And an expensive journey to Copenhagen, where I will not enjoy myself and which will bankrupt me for some time to come. And all this for Kajus's ill-fated festival.' His capacity to imagine slights did not diminish with the years: 'The concert Martha Tornell's pupils gave not mentioned in the papers. A mistake that she held it at all. But little Kaj acquitted herself well in my piano pieces.' He must have overlooked Yrjö Kilpinen's notice, in which Katarina's name figured quite prominently (' . . . her pleasing talents emerged in a couple of piano pieces by her great father'). But Kilpinen also mentioned that Tornell's pupils played pieces that were beyond them and that, with some few exceptions, the general standard was 'pretty elementary'. Sooner or later Sibelius must have seen this review and must surely have realized that little Kaj was not receiving the quality of tuition to which her 'pleasing talents' entitled her. But now, as so often before, he cut himself off from the real world, even where his loved ones were concerned.

The following day he searched the papers in vain for a mention of his *Festive March* for small orchestra, which was performed at the university ceremonial on 31 May: 'Nothing in the papers. Not one of the public said a word. Only the orchestra applauded at the rehearsal. Kajanus, who conducted, wanted – this is a fact – to ruin it! He took it too fast, though I specifically asked him not to, so that all its *grandezza* was lost.' This outburst against Kajanus is absurd; his recordings bear witness to his intelligent and idiomatic grasp of Sibelius's tempi, even if there are times when he errs on the fast side, as in *Tapiola,* or is a little expansive, as in the slow movement of the Third Symphony. So it was not in the best of tempers that Sibelius prepared himself for his journey to Copenhagen. 'And now we are getting ourselves ready, Aino and I, for more critical insults in Copenhagen, where I was so badly treated some six years ago. "*Das Künstlerleben ist voll von Kümmernissen*".'

They arrived in Copenhagen on Whit Sunday, only to find the city deserted. He telephoned his friends for hours, but to no avail; everyone was away in the country. But it was not long before his spirits were restored by some wonderful black Havana cigars. He was interviewed by *Berlingske Tidende*, Copenhagen's leading newspaper:

'Why doesn't your Fifth Symphony have a title?'
'A symphony needn't have one. Why on earth should it be called anything? It's pure music, not literature!'
'What do you mean by "pure music"?'
'Musical thought.'
'What do you understand by "musical thought"?'
'Ideas that can only be expressed in music, of course. Isn't that obvious? If I could express the same thing in words as I do in music, then I would naturally have recourse to words. Music is self-sufficient and much richer. It begins where the expressive possibilities of language end. That's why I write music.'

'How would you explain then that in a symphony a composer can, for example, give a picture of a sunset?'

Herr Sibelius gets up and his hands, which have all the time emphasized his words with countless nervous movements, suddenly fly through the air.

'This sort of thing drives me mad – then it's not pure music we are talking about but something else. It's incidental music. And that can be good in terms of theatrical effect. But when music is literature, it is bad literature.'

In another article introducing the festival, Sibelius's Danish biographer Gunnar Hauch touched a sensitive nerve – Sibelius and Nielsen. Besides them, he also mentioned as the innovating forces in modern music Debussy, who would probably survive, and Strauss, whose time would surely pass. 'Sibelius and Nielsen have had the strength to overcome the crisis within Nordic music and both have striven to enrich and renew their language from Nature. But Carl Nielsen is the sculptor, the worshipper of line and form; Sibelius is the master of colour and of fantasy, and a great melodist. It is unnecessary to speculate on their respective stature; suffice it to say that Sibelius is the light which shines furthest. The whole world sees him and he is the only one that the world sees . . . it is he who has been hailed as the Strindberg of music.'

This was hardly the most diplomatic start to an inter-Nordic festival.

The previous day Sibelius and Aino had been invited to a small dinner party with Nielsen and his wife, the sculptress Anne-Marie; the only other guests were Kajanus and his wife and Wilhelm Stenhammar. The latter spoke of the occasion in a letter home to his wife Helga: 'Sibelius was in great form, calm and collected, and completely at ease, without a trace of nervous irritability. He drank one schnapps but firmly declined another, despite the persuasions of his hostess; he also refused a glass of port, and drank only a modest amount of red wine, which we others consumed as if it were water, but he was so delightful and witty that I was consumed by the thought of you ,who was not able to be with us to revel in his rich conversation. After coffee by the shore, with nightingales singing and the moon shining, we ended the evening with a delightful board game, and felt like real Vikings in our shirt sleeves.' (12 June 1919)

Sibelius would not have been so relaxed as Nielsen's guest had he sensed any friction between them. Afterwards, in his note of thanks he wrote: 'Glorious friend, my thanks and hopes that all goes well. Warmest greetings to you and your delightful wife. I often wonder how it is possible for both you geniuses to live so happily together.' Did it, one wonders, strike him that his own creative work would have suffered had Aino, like Anne-Marie, pursued an independent artistic career? Not that the course of Nielsen's marriage was always free from turbulence.

It is clear, on the other hand, that relations between the two composers had been less cordial than during his earlier visit to Copenhagen in 1912, and that he never felt the same warmth for Nielsen that he did for Busoni and Stenhammar. Their difference in outlook surfaces in their attitude towards Beethoven: Sibelius worshipped him unreservedly; Nielsen, on the other hand, went so far as to prophecy that when 'the wheels of time had made a further turn, Mozart's best symphonies will still be there, while most of Beethoven's will have fallen by the wayside'.[1]

At the opening concert on 13 June, Selim Palmgren scored a great success both as composer and soloist with his Piano Concerto *(Metamorphosis)*. Even Sibelius's most fervent supporter, Kjerulf, noted that the applause was 'almost demonstrative'. Kjerulf added: 'Palmgren is so highly (and rightly) regarded among Finland's younger composers that he is seen as the crown prince, the successor to the throne occupied with such conspicuous authority by Jean Sibelius, which we long hope he will continue to hold . . . The Piano Concerto is already scheduled for performances in Holland, Germany, Sweden and other countries.'

Sibelius himself enjoyed a great success when he conducted his Second Symphony on 18 June at the Odd Fellow-Paläet: 'His tall figure towers over the orchestra . . . his baton is a veritable staff of Moses, which parts the waves . . . As he stood yesterday in front of the orchestra, it was as if he was almost a magician, conjuring up demonic spirits. The whole atmosphere was inspired . . . and culminated in a royal tribute to the greatest name at the present time in Nordic music.'

Sibelius noted the critical opinion: 'Several reviews tore me to pieces. My old friends Hetsch and Tofft! But Kjerulf held my colours high. Much small-mindedness and great hospitality. Met among others Hauch and Ferenc von Vecsey. Hauch has written warmly about me all the time but unfortunately the other critics hate him.'

The small-mindedness to which he alludes was presumably the fact that the hospitality of the festival committee did not extend to underwriting the cost of the parties he himself gave at his hotel. By the time the bill for the champagne arrived, Sibelius took out a wad of notes and began throwing them all over the place. The pianist Ilmari Hannikainen and his brothers, who had performed the Kuula Trio at one of the music festival chamber concerts, had their work cut out crawling on all fours to recover the money, which they gave to Aino. Sibelius admired the way she kept her head throughout the visit. Without her, he would not have been able to manage either in practical matters or in keeping track of money.

The last of the Festival Concerts ended with Nielsen's Fourth Symphony *(L'inestinguibile)*, conducted by the composer himself. It fired the enthusiasm of Alfred Tofft in Copenhagen's leading daily, *Berlingske Tidende* (21 June 1919), for its sureness of purpose and its complete absence of sentimentality, and as a triumphant climax for the festival. He could have added that it was finer than Sibelius's Second, since that is what he thought, but he refrained from doing so.

At the supper party given after the concert at the Langelinjes Pavilion, Nielsen was at pains to express his delight at Finland's participation in the festival and to pay tribute to Kajanus's contribution. In his response, Kajanus struck a patriotic note: 'We must fight on and stand firm; still, we will never again lose our freedom.' The Danish composer Louis Glass paid tribute to Sibelius. On the Saturday evening, as a kind of coda to the festival, a concert was organized at Tivoli, a kind of cavalcade of conductors which ended with Sibelius conducting *Finlandia*. The famous photograph showing all eight conductors was taken outside the entrance; Sibelius was the only one in a jacket and derby hat. On the far left of the picture is Fredrik Schnedler-Peterson, a fellow student from his Berlin year, who had for a time been conductor of the Åbo orchestra. Earlier, in April of that year, he had conducted an all-Danish programme in Helsinki. Schnedler-Peterson worshipped Sibelius: 'There are few others who command my heart as he does,' he wrote in his autobiography. Kajanus, whose appearance, according to Kjerulf, resembled that of Jesus Christ, was beginning to age. A few days earlier he had suffered a mild heart attack, but had quickly recovered. Next to Sibelius stands the conductor Georg Hoeberg, with whom he went through the score of *Scaramouche* in view of its forthcoming première in Copenhagen, and beside him the Finnish composer Erkki Melartin, who had been newly appointed head of the Music Institute in Helsinki and was looking as fragile and melancholy as the *Lyric Suite for Orchestra* by which he had been represented. Stenhammar and Nielsen are standing next to each other, the former distinguished and a shade retiring, while the latter radiates a blend of vitality and Danish geniality – with perhaps a touch of wildness! The party is completed by the Norwegian conductor–composer Johan Halvorsen, who as early as 1890 had already pressed Sibelius to compose a violin concerto.

You might think that Sibelius would have felt at home among this company. But it would seem from some retrospective comments he made that he took a dismal view of the proceedings. As usual, he saves the worst for Kajanus: 'Concerning Kajus, he's looking old, and that brings the two sides of his character into even sharper focus – the one *for* me, the other *against*.' Generally speaking, his colleagues served as scapegoats for the vague feeling of dissatisfaction he felt about the reception of his music in Copenhagen. Even more importantly, he must have felt (at least to some extent) threatened by the emergence of Nielsen as a figure of international stature. The Danish capital served more as an outpost of the Continent in the north than a forum for the north on the Continent. There was already an interest in Schoenberg, which was to culminate a few years later when Schoenberg himself paid his one and only visit to the city in 1923. The following year Stravinsky came, a visit that gave an impetus to the neo-classicism which was to fascinate many younger Danish composers. Sibelius did not cut the same figure in Denmark in 1919 as he did in Sweden, where he had established a much surer position. Perhaps he felt something of the cross-wind that was beginning to gather force on the Continent and he possibly sensed that it was likely to grow stronger rather than weaker during the 1920s. But a few days after his return home, he looked back on his Copenhagen visit as thoroughly refreshing: 'Drank wine and ate good food! And have been even nicer to Aino than before.' (4 July 1919)

– 4 –

Sibelius returned to a more turbulent Finland than before. The newspapers reported an incident on the Russian border and subversive plots fanned by Bolshevik agitators. Finnish militants tried to persuade Mannerheim to dissolve parliament, form a new government and march on Petrograd, but he now firmly discouraged such notions. He was pessimistic about the immediate future and warned these right-wing elements that they were merely putting a noose round their own necks. Even if at the height of the civil war Sibelius had briefly toyed with the idea of leaving, such thoughts were impossible now. He could never see himself in the role of an *émigré*, so closely was his spirit bound to Finnish mythology, culture and life. Copenhagen had also taught him a practical lesson: 'To live abroad with my family in these expensive times would be impossible. Any illusions I may have had are now gone.' His Danish revelries had cost him 5,000 kronor. From Wilhelm Hansen he had received 3,000 kronor, partly for *Scaramouche* and partly for new pieces. 'Hansen was quite amiable, but I don't think there's much of a future there. There are others who do not wish me well.' His suspicions were groundless; whatever others may have thought or said, Hansen were keen to put their full energies behind his cause.

With Germany's catastrophe before his eyes, he was perhaps looking to Hansen as a kind of fail-safe. But he did not want to break his connections with Breitkopf & Härtel. At the Leipzig Fair, Breitkopf discovered through some of their Scandinavian business contacts that during the war Sibelius had published a large number of pieces with Westerlund and other publishing houses. In September they wrote to the composer expressing pleasure at his continuing creativity and their surprise at his behaviour. They quoted the terms of the 1913 contract with them, which bore his signature, concerning their right of first refusal. They urged him to deal with them directly. Sibelius explained that they did not fully grasp his problems, but Breitkopf were not to be so easily mollified. They anticipated no great difficulty in coming to some arrangement with the Helsinki firms, but Wilhelm Hansen was an altogether different proposition. When it came to the crunch, they were perhaps already fearful that they might lose him.

Sibelius now needed to earn enough to replenish his coffers after the expense of Copenhagen and to clear up his other debts, which he complained were mountainous. But composing was going very slowly and unsatisfactorily: 'Have been in a terrible mood. I seem to be dealing only with injustice – an unproductive state.' Towards the end of July, he was ready with some new small pieces; the *Sonnet* and *Berger et bergerette* brought him 3,000 marks from Westerlund. Besieged by thoughts of death, he feared becoming old without having achieved anything of worth. 'A terrible prospect. The days are rainy but with sunny interludes – mild. Must start work for Hansen.' But Hansen had to wait: 'Written a waltz (from *Syringa* and *Granen*) for Westerlund.' (Diary, 2 September 1919)

In September 1914 he had included the two piano pieces as Nos. 5 and 6 of his Tree Pieces, Op. 75, but the fusion of the two as *Valse lyrique* did not satisfy him and a few days later he abandoned it. 'Have torn up the waltz – the themes don't go together. All this to satisfy Pelle [Westerlund]. When will I learn to say no?' Had Westerlund persuaded him to make the two piano miniatures an orchestral waltz which could bring him wealth and fortune? In any event, Sibelius was ashamed of himself: '*O sancta simplicitas!* How dreadful. Demeaning my own talents and beliefs. What will they think, when I'm fouling things up like this?'

Two days later, on 17 August, he sent the *Valse lyrique* and *Granen* to Westerlund. *Granen* remained as an independent piano piece. He began working at an orchestral piece 'like a thief. Ought to occupy myself with bread-and-butter things, but can't help myself.' On 23 July he noted: 'Going off to Jokela [which was not far away] to see Blenner [manager of a mill who was married to Kajanus's daughter, the harpist Lilly]. Axel Gallén also there. Hope to get Aino there tomorrow.' Some note of anticipation can be detected: Gallen-Kallela had become adjutant to Mannerheim after the latter's election as head of state. The situation was highly unusual: the prince of Finnish artists as the confidant of the country's regent. He compared himself with some irony to Leonardo da Vinci at the Sforza court in Milan, but he eventually grew tired of his ceremonial duties, drawing up guest lists, designing invitations, and asked to be relieved of his post. Sibelius would certainly have been keen to hear Gallén's impressions of the Mannerheim 'court'.

These were exciting times: only four days later a presidential election was declared. As regent, Mannerheim was only a provisional head of state, and all the signs pointed not to him but his rival Ståhlberg as the winner. Sibelius and Gallen-Kallela also met later at Jokela; the latter's daughter, the cellist Kirsti, gives an eye-witness glimpse of the composer leaning against the table, tapping his foot, and muttering as she went by, 'It's just too much that some people are so pretty!'

One source of delight in Sibelius's life had dried up – Carpelan's letters. And so letters from Walter von Konow assumed a greater importance and were awaited with even greater impatience. Sibelius had not attended Walter's fiftieth birthday party, and von Konow began to reflect that they had grown far apart. Sibelius was the only friend to whom von Konow could open his heart, and this he did. Sibelius was often slow in responding and there were periods when he had maintained a stony silence. But now it was von Konow who did not write for months on end, and Sibelius who began to wonder if he had 'lost Walter, my only old friend. In heavy spirits . . . my heart bleeds.' He finally wrote an anxious letter to Walter and thought he was kept waiting far too long for a reply: 'Can't understand it. Fearful that there must be some gossip – tongue-wagging or suchlike.' Some days later came a letter: 'Never should you imagine that you have hurt my feelings! That could never be – you who have given a life-enhancing sunshine. I have experienced only joy and sympathy from you. I have been suffering acute depression and anxiety of late, and severe catarrh and fevers, so have not been in good spirits.'

Where matters musical were concerned, their exchanges could never replace those with Carpelan, but Sibelius always had a special place for his 'warm, imaginative childhood friend'. Walter's 'wonderful letter' prompted both delight and concern. He felt something of the same anxiety he had felt before Carpelan's death, and again before his much-loved brother Christian's fiftieth birthday, which fell the day before Carpelan's funeral.

The autumn opened ominously. Heidi, his eight-year-old daughter, had fallen from a horse and suffered a badly broken arm. When Sibelius visited her at the orthopaedic hospital in Helsinki, he took her some plasticine – for her talents as a sculptress had already begun to show themselves – but then suddenly remembered that she could not use her left hand and was overcome by his thoughtlessness. Heidi was the youngest, shyest and most delicate of the five daughters and had a favoured place in her mother's heart, which prompted some jealousy on the part of Margareta, the eleven-year-old. Margareta had a strong temperament which could easily flare up, but also an angelic streak which was later to become the dominating feature of her make-up.

'Am alone here. Aino is in Helsinki; Heidi is out of hospital and staying with her grown-up sister Eva in Helsinki.' Sibelius was often on his own that autumn. Eva and Ruth had long since flown the nest; Katarina was at school in Helsinki, and Heidi, who caught scarlet fever while still convalescing, kept Aino in town for long periods looking after her. Margareta was still at home, but Sibelius saw little of her as she spent days on end with his neighbours, the Waseniuses, looking after the stables and horses. Things were beginning to look up outside Finland: he telegraphed an acceptance of Stenhammar's invitation to give two concerts in Gothenberg in March 1920; he promised to send some compositions to the London publisher Frederick Harris; and instructed Westerlund to send the score of *Snöfrid* to Copenhagen, where some interest had been expressed in it. At home in Finland there remained the inauguration of the Åbo Academy on 11

October. In the intervening period Sibelius had managed to become dissatisfied with *Jordens sång*, the cantata he had composed for that occasion,
and in September set to work on its revision. By the 22nd it was ready to be
sent to his old friend Karl Ekman, who was now conductor of the orchestra
in Turku. But for the concert of his works in Helsinki in November Sibelius
planned to present the *Six Humoresques* under the title *Impromptus,* on the
assumption that the new leader Paul Cherkassky would act as the soloist. To
his delight Cherkassky agreed, and Sibelius set to work to put the finishing
touches to the set. For some reason the general manager of the orchestra,
Morck, approached him to ask him to give up these dates; he declined, but
felt some momentary disquiet: 'Who's behind it? Certainly no one important. Misunderstanding.'

Two days later, on 25 September, Kajanus opened the autumn season
with an all-Sibelius concert: *Pohjola's Daughter,* the Violin Concerto and the
First Symphony. Aino went to Helsinki while Sibelius stayed at home nursing a bout of rheumatism (or perhaps pessimism): 'Kajus performing my
things this evening. I'm quite out of the swim – can't have any dealings with
all these materialists. I'm suspicious of Pelle's keenness to put up the money.
There must be something in it for him, while as usual I'm a secondary
consideration. All this is what I hear from others. Working away, however, in
spite of all this.'

For Bis in *Hufvudstadsbladet,* the concert brought back memories of the
time when Sibelius composed the First Symphony, when 'he had at his side
Robert Kajanus, the pioneer and trail-blazer for the young Finland, the man
whose energy, experience and wide vision so encouraged the young
genius'. On reading this, Sibelius was quite beside himself: 'Bis writes that
Kajus inspired etc. my first symphony. They say that suffering purifies you!
Yes! No one showed me the way – and now I hear that from this devil.'
Could Bis's choice of words possibly have justified such an outburst? A day
or so later Sibelius had regained his equilibrium: 'It kept me awake the
whole night. It's a good job my hair isn't white! I got on top of the devil. In
any event my skin is thicker as a result. Anyway, last and finally, I'll have
peace enough when I'm dead.'

– 5 –

The inaugural ceremonies of the Åbo Academy began on Saturday 11
October at the old Academic House. Sibelius had arrived in Åbo five days
before to start choral and orchestral rehearsals for his newly-commissioned
Jordens Sång (Song of the Earth), which was the high point of the occasion. At
the banquet at Hotel Hamburger-Börs – where, incidentally, Sibelius was
not placed at the table of honour – he was acclaimed by the celebrated
sociologist Edvard Westermarck as not only a great artist but also a
great force for culture. 'However wonderful the sounds he creates from the

Finnish temperament and its wild landscape, his culture and his speech proclaim him as one of us, a source of pride for our Swedish heritage.' No doubt this was true, but it would have been equally true had the Rector been opening a Finnish-speaking university. Finland had recently introduced prohibition, but in spite of the presence of both the head of state, President Ståhlberg, and several members of the government, wine and stronger drinks surreptitiously reached the guests instead of the indeterminable juices that were served officially.

After the banquet, the Swedish journalist and diplomat Kjell Strömberg recalled, a reception-cum-literary and musical symposium was improvised in Sibelius's hotel suite: 'It went on until the early hours of the morning, and we others were in fact rather tired, since nothing had been spared in the way of drink, but our illustrious host was in the best of spirits, recounting episodes from his past life in his own inimitable fashion. At the end he sat down at the piano, which had been moved in for all eventualities, and played the fantastic finale of his newly-completed Fifth Symphony, singing at times at the top of his voice.'[2]

The next day Sibelius conducted a repeat performance of the new cantata in the cathedral. After the service, the choir gathered round the statue of Per Brahe to pay tribute to the founder of the first Åbo Academy. A large and distinguished gathering heard Sibelius conduct Pacius's *Suomis Sång* to words by von Quanten, and the anthem *Vårt Land*. This serves as a reminder of Sibelius's deep roots in Finland's cultural tradition. His father had been a pupil of Runeberg, and he himself had visited the poet when he was ill and stricken, and later placed a wreath on his grave; moreover, he visited Pacius himself during his student years in Helsinki. He also knew von Qvanten's son, who emigrated to Sweden during the war of independence, and one of his forefathers on his mother's side, Haartman, had been in charge of music at Per Brahe's old academy. One may also assume that while he was in Åbo he met Walter von Konow, who in his role as Intendant would have shown the Academy's guests over Åbo Castle. He made his farewells to his father's only surviving cousin, the nonagenarian Elin Arrhenius: 'It was as if a dark, heavy door had been closed on his Lovisa memories, the sunshine of his childhood'. Generally speaking, though, his visit was a happy one: 'The cantata scored a great success in Åbo. The festivities were unforgettable. The famous Scandinavian scientists and scholars were all friendly and accessible. Dinners, lunches etc. all outstanding. Planning the cantata's first concert performance in November. Will see if the Swedish choirs will let me.' (18 October 1919) He had planned, namely, to engage the Finnish-language Suomen Laulu in Helsinki.

A couple of days later plans were afoot for a new piece for Suomen Laulu, a setting of Kivi's patriotic poem *Suomenmaa*. But there was a change of plan and he substituted another poem, Eino Leino's *Maan virsi (Hymn to the Earth)*. Gösta Stenman, an art dealer of some standing, had wanted a piece for the opening of his new gallery in Helsinki. In the meantime, Sibelius wrote to Wilhelm Hansen in Copenhagen promising new works, not without twinges of conscience, since he had already received an advance. All this time he was anxious about Heidi, who was in danger of losing the use of her left hand. The operation was performed by Professor Richard Faltin, a member of the university quartet in his student years. The long period of anxiety was to be ended by the operation's successful outcome.

The time was drawing near for three performances of the new symphony in its definitive form, together with the *Six Humoresques* for violin and orchestra (at this time called *Impromptus*) and as a final number, *Jordens Sång (Song of the Earth)*. The first concert was given in the presence of President Ståhlberg. His rival and predecessor as head of state, General Mannerheim, was on the Warsaw–Paris express, having barely three weeks before written an open letter to the President urging intervention and a march on Petrograd – fortunately both for himself and Finland, to no avail.

A hypothetical listener who had attended the premières of the four-movement (1915) and three-movement (1916) versions of the symphony would now have undoubtedly heaved a sigh of relief. The first movement (*Tempo molto moderato – Allegro moderato*) had in its broadest outlines been largely undisturbed, save for some admittedly important retouching and rescoring. On the other hand, the second movement had been revised and emerged more richly articulated than before – among other things, the pizzicato strings now emerge naturally from the *arco* variations. In the finale, the listener would have recognized the same basic processes up to fig. N, and after that would have experienced delight in finding that Sibelius had restored the E flat minor episode from the 1915 version in a revised form. Further, that he had greatly concentrated the final paragraphs, which now finished with six isolated *fffz* chords; these, according to one of the ladies in the orchestra's administration, 'completely ruined the whole symphony'! The final chords must have caused something of a sensation when they rang out into the auditorium for the very first time, yet neither Leevi Madetoja, Erik Furuhjelm, Bis nor any of the other critics in attendance made any mention of them, though their reviews all recognized the new symphony's stature and its gain in concentration and power.

The three concerts had been an outstanding triumph as far as the public was concerned. Quite apart from his success in the symphony, Sibelius had proved a sensitive accompanist in the *Humoresques*, two of which had to be repeated. In a radio interview given not long after Sibelius's death, Armas Järnefelt was asked what he thought of his brother-in-law as a conductor. He replied laconically, 'Well, let's say he was better as a composer!' Quite so, but one would have liked to hear more about a composer–conductor who was much sought after in the outside world. Generally speaking, his countrymen were a shade condescending about Sibelius as conductor – without real justification, if the evidence of orchestral players abroad is anything to go by. The words of the German-born violinist Ernst Marcke, who was a member of the Gothenburg Orchestra, still ring in my ears: 'Sibelius – now there was a great musician. And he could conduct too, flawlessly. During the rehearsals the players immediately felt they were dealing with a skilful chamber musician who understood the art of ensemble playing. In addition, he had a good sense of humour and behaved in an endearing fashion.' And the leader of the orchestra, Fermeus, remembered him as an accomplished conductor with great presence and a stick technique that could withstand comparison with any professional colleague's: 'The orchestra admired him. He said very little during rehearsals. And when things mattered, he said, "Go to it with all your heart and strength."' As Fermeus could attest, the kind of accidents that composer–conductors could make never occurred when Sibelius was conducting.

One can say with some confidence that the Helsinki concerts of November 1919 passed off brilliantly and that he fulfilled his role as 'star conductor' in all three works. For once, Sibelius felt that the orchestra was on his side; his diaries make no mention of the nervousness that often afflicted him: 'Just back from Helsinki, where I have given three concerts to sold-out houses and spectacular applause . . . Heidi sick. Aino's spirits very low. I have been successful but now feel out of the swim. Must pull myself together and get down to work when things settle down. I'm a very good composer but as a person – hm – that's another matter! Income from the concerts amounted to circa 20,000 marks. But no sooner do you plug one hole, than others appear!' The tone of this diary entry is unmistakable: Sibelius was in the best of spirits and full of confidence. As early as September he had accepted Stenhammar's invitation to make a guest appearance in Gothenburg in 1920, and on 12 December he sent a telegram accepting the two suggested dates, 8 and 10 March.

Christmas was fast approaching. Little Heidi's absence undoubtedly cast a shadow over the festive season, but Sibelius could at least console himself with the thought that she was on the mend. Katarina returned home for the holiday, and Ruth and her husband and two children also visited Ainola. But unusually for him, Sibelius makes no mention of Christmas or the New Year in his diary. In fact, there are no entries at all between 12 December 1919 and 20 January 1920. Normally the Christmas–New Year period would unleash a wave of childhood reminiscence and nostalgia. The gaps in his diary could usually be explained: feverish creative activity, such as the final spurt towards the completion of the Fourth Symphony in the spring of 1911 or the first version of the Fifth in the autumn of 1915 and the final version in the spring of 1919. Another gap occurred when the family had taken refuge in Helsinki in the spring of 1918 or in the autumn of the same year when Sibelius had a period of heavy drinking. Of course, the gap at the turn of 1919–20 need have no special significance, for the fact is that during the 1920s the general tone of the diaries tends to become increasingly tinged with pessimism. Not that this necessarily means that his life was darker, only that he had recourse to his diary to write himself free from depression.

Thus the Christmas period could well have passed quite happily at Aino-la, while he worked away at his new commission *Maan virsi*. But a later diary entry suggests that this was not the case. After completing the piece on 28 January 1920 he wrote: 'How hard it has been to write this opus. Does it mean that I am going downhill? *Ich glaub's net!*' Had his spirits been so heavy that he could not even bear to commit his thoughts to paper? After the triumphant series of concerts in November he would have come down to earth, and as the darkest time of the year, with all its poetry, took hold of Ainola, this should have been the psychological moment when his thoughts began to turn to the ethereal world of the Sixth Symphony. Instead he had to contend with yet another commission which was more distasteful than ever. During the spring of 1918 he had had to compose not only two cantatas, *Oma maa* and *Jordens Sång* – the last of which had entailed substantial revision – but a relatively large number of shorter pieces. In the conception of a new work, a six-week break in concentration could easily break the spell of something that had been slowly forming in his mind for the best part of six years.

During the corresponding period in 1909–10 he had declined all commissions – burnt his boats so to speak – in order to complete the Fourth Symphony; similarly, the Christmas of 1914 had been devoted to the Fifth Symphony and the first sketches for the Sixth. However, at this Christmas he lacked the strength to refuse Suomen Laulu's conductor Heikki Klemetti, or perhaps it would be more accurate to say that he hadn't the heart to do so. Klemetti's wife Armi, who at the beginning of December had spent a long evening at Sibelius's side at Ainola, later summoned up her courage and wrote to him – without her husband's knowledge: 'Dear Professor Sibelius, compose a cantata for us. You seem just a little ambivalent about this project, and it distresses me when I see how anxious this makes my husband . . . If [your cantata] is missing, then our 20th anniversary will lose the jewel in its crown.'

Sibelius was sensible of his debt to Klemetti and Suomen Laulu for their devotion to his cause and for singing his choral music all over Europe. And so he agreed and set to work on *Maan virsi*, but his heart was not in it and the piece weighed heavily on him. In Gothenburg, Stenhammar celebrated New Years' Eve with a letter to Sibelius: 'Counting the days until we have the pleasure of welcoming you back to Gothenburg . . . Will you let me know how much you want [as an honorarium] so that I can tell you whether we can meet your wishes?'

Sibelius's response came like a cold shower: 'Thanks for your telegram and letter. I promised that I would answer the former honestly. But it is frankly impossible for me to think of travelling this spring. Serious matters force me to this decision. Is it not possible, perhaps, that my Fifth Symphony could represent me on this occasion?' No reason given, just a plain withdrawal at a time when he should have leapt at the opportunity of seeing the wider world again – particularly Gothenburg where he was adored! Was it possible that he had been so depressed by having to work on the cantata that he feared the journey would have further held up his work on the Sixth Symphony? With customary graciousness, Stenhammar wrote asking for some explanation: 'And if you do not wish to make the real reason public, could you please let me know what I should say officially?' Sibelius thanked him for his understanding and replied that he was working on new projects which could not be interrupted. He had given the same answer time and time again; and it was as valid (or invalid) this time as it had been before. The only commission that had been hanging over his head, *Maan virsi*, was nearing completion – he finished it two days after his reply to Stenhammar.

But something weighed him down and made him profoundly ill at ease with life. The prospect of his slowing down with advancing years and thoughts of mortality haunted him. Indeed, his fear of ageing seems to have inhibited his creativity, for it was not until the autumn of 1922 that he felt in a position to tackle the new symphony. A difficult period was in store for him. During these years he came closer to the world of Bertel Gripenberg – the poet of doubt, contradiction and longing for the past. His thoughts may have turned to Gripenberg's sonnet *Icarus,* with its images of the eponymous hero rising close to the sun, his wings singed and his eyes blinded by its fierce rays. Perhaps he himself had been blinded by the cosmic eruptions of the Fifth Symphony, on which he had fixed so long a gaze, and his wings been scorched by its fires during the long period in which he circled it. So it felt perhaps during the dark months which followed the completion of *Maan virsi.* But fortunately it was not the fall of Icarus but a different poetic image; that of a Luonnotar as she glided down to the surface of the waters to prepare herself for great creative deeds – albeit in his case the worlds of the Sixth and Seventh symphonies.

CHAPTER ELEVEN

The New Decade

The 1920s augured well for Sibelius. Since 1915 he had wrestled with the intractable Fifth Symphony. Now not only was it finished, but the four performances he had conducted in November 1919 had left him in no doubt that he had at last brought it off. He no longer needed to feel dissatisfied, as he had done after the second version's première. Two new symphonies were in the process of gestation. He had drawn up a table of themes for the Sixth and had sketched out several episodes, and a Seventh was at the earliest planning stages. However, though the way forward was paved with good intentions, he was again side-tracked by the inevitable struggle to make ends meet and provide smaller pieces that would generate income.

Behind these necessary diversions lay the struggle to realize the principle of absolute music in his symphonies. Throughout his life he had been aware of the conflicting claims of symphony and tone poem, between the absolute and the programmatic. It surfaces as early as the 1890s, when he furnished the score of *Kullervo* with the title 'symphonic poem': only later did he begin to refer to it as a symphony. In 1934 he spoke of his symphonies as having been conceived and worked out in purely musical terms without any literary source of inspiration. All the symphonies written in the wake of Beethoven seemed to him closer to the symphonic poem than the symphony, with the exception of the four symphonies of Brahms. 'This is not in my view what a symphony should be. I am not a literary composer; for me, music begins where words cease; a symphony should be music first and last.' But he admitted to Walter Legge that mental images could unintentionally pass through his mind when he was at work on a symphonic movement. 'However, the conception and growth of my symphonies proceeds along purely musical lines.'

Ernest Newman, on the other hand, took the view that almost all so-called absolute music had a programmatic element in some shape or form. Of course there were exceptions, such as the *allegro* movements of Bach's Brandenburg Concertos. Newman's view of some programmatic sliding scale no doubt has its supporters, but I would prefer to put it differently.

Take the case of Sibelius's Fourth Symphony as a starting point. As we know, the first musical impressions were conceived under the influence of a visit to the Koli mountain in 1909. The tone poem that he planned, *La Montagne*, underwent a transformation and became a symphony in which two movements (the present first and third) became *La Montagne* and *The Wanderers' Thoughts* respectively. Into the finale he integrated material from his unfinished orchestral song, *The Raven*, to words by Edgar Allan Poe. But be this as it may, the end result is incontrovertibly absolute music *par excellence*. The essential question is to what extent Sibelius was able during the actual creative process to put distance between himself and the 'mental images' which may have functioned as a primary source of inspiration and sublimate them into absolute music. This struggle towards absolute expressive musical means distinguishes his whole development. In the First and Second symphonies – and even to some extent in the Third – the listener can sense pictorial or other images as the root of its inspiration. In the Fourth, by sublimating the original inspiration and distilling its essence, he comes closer to the world of absolute music than ever before. Already from its very inception the Fifth was 'absolute' in the classical sense, with strong hints of the cosmos and of the world of nature.

The musical climate in the wider world should have provided further stimulus and encouragement for the symphony. The pages of musical history had again been turned. The era of programme music was nearing its end; pure music, unencumbered by descriptive narrative, was gaining ground. The glorious vistas of Strauss's *Alpine Symphony* and the hero's final descent from its peak proved to be its apotheosis. Two years earlier Rachmaninov had rung in grandiose fashion the death knell of symbolism in *The Bells*, which like Sibelius's own *Raven* had been inspired by the macabre spirit of Poe, the former in Balmont's translation, the latter in Rydberg's. Ravel's choreographic poem *La valse* can be seen as the death throes as much of the tone poem as of Imperial Vienna.

With his unerring sense of what was in the air, Sibelius could feel that a new dawn was breaking for absolute music. Whether a new day was dawning for his symphonies in the German-speaking world was, however, an altogether different matter. He had after all composed symphonies when the form was unfashionable, but was realistic enough to grasp the fact that the war years had left him in a weaker position in Germany. His breakthrough in Germany had come with the tone poems, with *The Swan of Tuonela* and *Lemminkäinen's Homeward Journey*. The Second Symphony had been a success, but the more classical Third had been ill-attuned to a climate in which the Strauss tone poem and the half-programmatic Mahler symphonies were dominant. This was the language of '*die Moderne*' in the first decade of the century. In wartime Berlin the Fourth Symphony fell between the two stools of the expressionism of Mahler and Strauss and the radicalism of Schoenberg.

Nor were the times auspicious for Sibelius in post-war Berlin. The Fourth Symphony was too dark and introspective for the Berlin audience, while the Fifth was not sufficiently radical or 'sensational' to shock them. These were times in which it was easy to dismiss the ageing tonal composer as an anachronism. Bruckner was at last beginning to come into his own in Germany, and enjoyed the advantage of belonging to the mainstream German tradition rather than being an outsider. Mahler would no doubt have followed him had not the Nazis come to power.

In Vienna, Weingartner had not succeeded in breaking the ice with his performances of the First and Second Symphonies and if anything, the situation was to harden during the 1920s. Similarly, Sibelius had never succeeded in establishing a foothold in Paris, and the 1920s were to see no change. Impressionism was now a spent force, but that did not lead to a renewed interest in the symphony. Equally, there was little interest in or response to Schoenberg and atonality in 1920s Paris. Satie's anti-romantic, anti-impressionist *Parade* set the tone of the period, and Cocteau and *Les six* came to the fore. The stylized world of Stravinsky and his 'pandiatonic' *Pulcinella* – neither chromatic nor romantic – was a model for them. As Cocteau put it: 'Nearly all our musicians have Stravinsky to thank for something, but Schoenberg is above all a schoolmaster standing at the blackboard in the classroom.'[1] Prokofiev fared better than the apostle of dodecaphony, though not even he had an easy time in this sophisticated, fashion-conscious world where Brahms was making slow headway and Bruckner and Mahler bored the public to distraction on the few occasions they were performed. Sibelius scarcely existed in the Gallic consciousness, save as the composer of *Finlandia* and *Valse triste* – and perhaps *The Swan of Tuonela* swimming somewhere out there in the distant haze.

Apart from the Scandinavian countries, it was Britain and America that placed Sibelius among the master composers of the time. The pioneering work had been done soon after the turn of the century and had left Sibelius as a name to reckon with in London, Manchester, Liverpool and Birmingham, as well as Chicago, Boston, New York and Philadelphia. All the same, the war years had broken the thread. English audiences had had no opportunity of hearing a Sibelius symphony since Sibelius himself had conducted the Fourth in Birmingham in 1912. It was not until March 1920 that Sir Henry Wood took it up at a Queen's Hall concert.

Unlike his American colleague Olin Downes and many other Sibelians, Newman also admired Mahler, though it was as a Wagner scholar that he was best known in the German-speaking world – and to Theodor Wiesengrund Adorno's chagrin, had served to build Sibelius's international reputation. Sibelius's Fourth Symphony and Schoenberg's Five Orchestral Pieces, Op. 16, were also a challenge for the American press. At their first performances in Boston, in 1913 and 1914 respectively, Downes compared them to Sibelius's advantage. He found the symphony 'uncompromising, powerful and imaginative'; but when the Schoenberg was performed – to the astonishment and bewilderment of the subscribers of Symphony Hall – Downes commented: 'In spite of its originality and its technical accomplishment, this music strikes us as unsound and unpleasant.'[2]

But Mahler was also anathema as far as Downes was concerned. In the Second Symphony he could not find a single bar that bore witness to a musical inventiveness of distinctly original quality: 'We believe that this music will be gathering dust on the shelves long before the memories of Mahler as a man and conductor have paled.'[3] For the rest of his life Olin Downes battled for Sibelius and against Mahler and Schoenberg. After his appointment as chief critic of the *New York Times* in 1924, his judgements carried more weight with the American public than those of any other critic. That he should later denounce Stravinsky's neo-classicism as 'sterile, feeble and melodically banal' (3 February 1942) did not make him any less controversial a figure.

Sibelius's success in America for more than four decades is in no small measure due to Downes's advocacy. And he owes the subsequent dip in his fortunes to Downes's hostility towards other great figures for whom he had a temperamental disaffinity. The very intensity of his worship of Sibelius served to stoke the fires of a reaction that was to endanger his hero's standing.[4]

At the turn of the decade Sibelius's thoughts hovered around the Sixth Symphony – in unexpected ways. In some sketches clearly from the period of the inauguration of the Åbo Academy in 1919, he added above the main theme of the first movement the title 'Winter', while above the second theme of the finale we find the words 'The spirit of the pine-tree'. Other themes on the same page that came to nothing also bear names: 'The spirit of summer', 'The Moon Goddess and the clouds' and so on. A little further down the page Sibelius has noted a theme with the title 'The forging of the Sampo' and beside it the word 'fire'. Four pages earlier we find sketches for the Seventh Symphony. These animistic titles show that in the middle of his symphonic preoccupations Sibelius had once again been drawn to the idea of composing a tone poem on a *Kalevala* theme. Indeed, in a diary entry for 4 March 1920 we find a reference to his working on *Kuutar (The Moon Goddess)*. Sibelius touched on *The Forging of the Sampo* the following year during an interview with A.O. Väisänen. When he was asked whether he intended to compose *Väinämöinen's Song* for the Kalevala Society, Sibelius replied:

'I have some sketches for the piece.[5] But the subject itself is a delicate one from a musical point of view, in that it encompasses more than one art form. The moment in the poem where Väinämöinen weeps would pose few problems; it is itself music.'

'But what of the Sampo episode?'

SIBELIUS

'I will do something about it one of these days (even though the smith
Ilmarinen is always thought of as being stupid). The beauty of the whole
thing is that no one knows what the Sampo is. The forging of the Sampo
should sound *pianissimo* – like something in the far distance. But everything will be thought through symphonically. Music must not appear to
be dependent on any literary programme. The poem is only the point of
departure.'

Even in the case of a symphonic poem, Sibelius expressly states – something
he did not do in his conversation with Legge – that the composer should
distance himself from the literary source of inspiration.

One can only speculate about why Sibelius should have given titles to the
two central themes of the Sixth Symphony-to-be five years after their conception. Did he want to return to their possible source of inspiration, which
he uncovers in his desire to achieve an animistic-cosmic tone poem? It is
possible that the winter landscape around Ainola and the whistling of the
snowstorms in the pine forests during the productive period at the turn of
the year in 1914–15 gave him those 'mental images', those fantasy pictures
which inspired those particular ideas. On the other hand, the same themes
were predestined to be the mainspring of his most abstract, purely musical
symphony. Was he considering using them in a projected tone poem, simply
because the symphony was getting nowhere? He seems to have been swinging back and forth between the two. At the beginning of the 1920s he was
finding difficulty in sublimating the mental images that he had borne so
long. But eventually the symphony claimed them and they returned to their
rightful role in its orbit. He was blown off course in January when he
thoughtlessly accepted a commission, the cantata *Hymn till jorden* (Hymn to
the earth). Work on it did not come easily to him, and Sibelius began to fear
that his powers were beginning to flag. But the idea of returning to the tone
poem slowly gathered force; the roar of the forest winds was to surface only
a few years later in *Tapiola*.

– 2 –

The nightmare of civil war was long past, and as Finland's wartime isolation
faded into memory, the doors to the world's musical capitals opened.
Finland was going through a somewhat lacklustre but necessary period of
stabilization. Typical of the period was President Ståhlberg, a principled
but uncharismatic lawyer, whose prime objective was to heal the divisions that had torn the country apart during the civil war. As a result he
enjoyed strained relations with the right wing. Katarina Sibelius was a
close friend of the president's daughter and was often at the Ståhlberg
home. Although Sibelius respected Ståhlberg's integrity and incorrup-
tibility, the man he really admired and who fascinated him most was

170

Mannerheim, the loser of the presidential election and commander of the victorious White forces.

The first days of the republic saw no new *Song of the Athenians, Finlandia* or *Jæger March*. In this respect Sibelius's active political involvement was a thing of the past, save for the fact that his country needed him as much as ever as a cultural ambassador, an embodiment of its new freedom. Ståhlberg, who had entrusted the conduct of foreign affairs to the capable hands of Rudolf Holsti, made no state visits abroad. Indeed, during the 1920s, Finland's most visible representatives abroad were Sibelius and Paavo Nurmi. Sibelius embraced this patriotic mission with fervour.

Nonetheless, there were clouds on the political horizon. In the middle of January there was a conference of states bordering on the Baltic (Finland, Estonia, Latvia, Lithuania and Poland) who gathered in Helsinki to discuss the possibility of a defensive alliance. This was not without its dangers for Finland, which had not yet concluded peace with Soviet Russia. Many in Sibelius's circle (and certainly the composer himself) would have preferred to see Finland moving closer to Sweden and the other Scandinavian countries rather than the Baltic States. However, closer ties with Sweden were hindered at this time by two factors: the ongoing 'language war' in Finland itself between the Swedish-speaking community and the majority Finns; and secondly, Sweden's claim to the Åland islands, whose inhabitants were Swedish-speaking and had voted in a referendum in favour of union with Sweden.

Sibelius kept abreast of developments, but no longer involved himself to the same extent as he had during the war years. It is surprising that he at no stage mentions the Baltic conference in his diary, but registers exasperation about an article in the Helsinki paper *Uusi Suomi* reopening the question of his genealogical background, which had been the subject of press interest four years earlier. He was outraged that the genealogist Granit-Ilmoniemi published his photo alongside that of a carpenter, Ojanen, who was a very distant cousin: 'It's not enough that I am branded as a peasant abroad, but he does his best to discredit me in the society to which I belong by education and upbringing. Here I am alone in the dark – the only one who will come to me is my sister, the madwoman, laughing.'

Sibelius's outburst may seem an over-reaction. But can one imagine Mahler, Debussy, Elgar or Nielsen having to endure the indignity of seeing their backgrounds subjected to such scrutiny in the *Wiener Zeitung, Le Temps, The Times* or *Berlingske Tidende*? Did the Austrians, the Bohemians and the Jews all compete to count Mahler among their number? Sibelius did not see his identity in these ideological terms: he thought of the Finns as one indivisible people with two different languages, and the controversy surrounding his own background, whether he belonged more to one or the other language group, was highly distasteful.

Granit-Ilmoniemi had caused something of a stir in 1916 when he discovered that Matts Mårtensson, father of Johan Sibbe, was not in fact born at Lappträsk but had moved there from Pekkala, in the Finnish-speaking area of Artjärvi. The news of this had echoed throughout the country. The newspaper *Uusi Suometar* rejoiced that Sibelius had pure Finnish blood in his veins: 'Certain Swedish-language newspapers have been at pains to emphasize Sibelius's Swedish origins and have thus perceived Scandinavian-Teutonic characteristics in his music. To our Finnish ears and sensibilities it is without question clear that the most important works of our Finnish master are purely Finnish and make this same impression on foreigners, particularly on mainland Swedes. The Fenno–Swedes once believed in the Lappträsk stories. Now that game is up, and the claims that Sibelius reflects the outlook of the coastal Swedish-speaking community can be put on one side, along with many other legends.'[6]

The obvious purpose of this article was to establish that certain characteristics of Sibelius's music are attributable to his Finnish origins. Without going into sensitive racial matters – which were to develop along such horrific lines in the years to come – it must be admitted that they did have some significance for Sibelius himself. In his blood mingled elements of Finnish, Fenno–Swedish, mainland Swedish and even more distantly, some German ancestry. His upbringing was bilingual, with all its cultural and psychological consequences. I do not exclude the possibility that the composer's genealogical background could have been reflected in the way he was pulled between the two polarities of sensibility; the Fenno–Swedish Runeberg and the Finnish *Kalevala*. One columnist writing over the signature Lucas in the Swedish language *Nya Pressen* responded with heavy irony: 'A huge sigh resounds throughout the land today. A sigh of relief, a sigh of joy: a Finnish forefather of Sibelius has been discovered.' Some of the press had a field day. 'A quarter of Sibelius was Finnish; and if another Finnish antecedent could be found, we will have half of him – and before you know where you are, he will be all ours!' wrote *Helsingin Sanomat*.

'Sibelius would not be who he is', wrote Granit-Ilmoniemi, 'were not Matti from Pekkala in Artsjärvi and Anna from Lassila part of his make-up. In the same way peasant blood flows in many of our other musicians: Kuula, Merikanto, Klemetti.' By now the composer was sick and tired of these speculations: 'Granit-Ilmoniemi is at it again. Compares me with Kuula, Merikanto and Klemetti –we're all descended from peasants. It's all there in his paper. Why bother with what was or has been 200 years ago!' Prompted by these discoveries, local enthusiasts at Artsjärvi even decided to put up a commemorative plaque in honour of Sibelius's forefathers at Oja-Pekkala. The composer declared himself greatly honoured by their decision, but no sooner had this become public knowledge than a Swedish-language paper urged Lappträsk to erect a similar memorial to honour the master's Swedish ancestors. Sibelius was also furious with himself for having relaxed his guard and spoken too freely about his aristocratic fantasies: Aino had watched helplessly while her husband gave vent to all sorts of speculations that the genealogist recorded with a naïve lack of discrimination. Of course, Sibelius was not alone among composers in his fantasies about possible aristocratic origins: Beethoven, no less, had a much stronger fixation about noble ancestry.

Sigurd Wettenhovi-Aspa (earlier known under the Swedish form of his name as Wetterhoff-Asp) had belonged to Sibelius's circle since the 1890s. A dilettante who tried his hand at painting, philology, alchemy and politics, he amused Sibelius. He was full of stories of his days in Paris with Strindberg, when they had together tried to make gold, and entertained him with his theories that the origins of the ancient world were really Finnish and Egyptian. In the spring of 1916 Wettenhovi-Aspa had argued the case for Sibelius being given a title in the Senate. When he subsequently wrote congratulating Sibelius on being given the title professor, he went to some pains to explain he had suggested a knighthood or even a barony: 'You are that already in spirit and Wirenius, that little music-loving admiral at the ecclesiastical department, shared my view. However, the vice-chairman had already stressed that there was no precedent for such an honour; no composer had ever been made a baron.'[7] While he was naturally flattered by the attentions of admirers and friends, Sibelius would no doubt have felt obliged at the time to decline such an honour from a Tsarist Senate.

In the autumn of 1919 Wettenhovi-Aspa persuaded Sibelius to make a public stand on the question of the Åland islands. The Swedish-speaking inhabitants had since time immemorial pressed their claims for union with mainland Sweden and the issue surfaced first at the Versailles Peace Conference and later at the League of Nations. This naturally aroused strong feelings in Finland, and while he was in Tampere Wettenhovi-Aspa wrote to Sibelius that he had founded a committee for the friends of Åland whose purpose it would be to counter the 'lying propaganda' of the Swedish lobby. To that end he proposed to pay a visit to Clemenceau, whom he had met in the early years of the century, to persuade him of the Finnish case. On the cultural front he planned a Finnish Week in Paris and London with, among other things, a strong musical presence. He announced all this at a well-attended meeting at Tampere's Town Hall on 19 October 1919, and had hoped that Sibelius would either come personally or send a message.

To Wettenhovi-Aspa's great delight, Sibelius sent a telegram in Finnish: 'WILL DO ANYTHING FOR OUR COUNTRY'. This sibylline message roused the Finnish-speaking audience to much enthusiasm and prompted Wettenhovi-Aspi to write: 'We must have the Åland question settled and hammer seven nails in Stockholm's coffin.' Quite apart from its naïve jingoism, his letter conveys something of the headstrong feeling among those would-be activists who loathed Ståhlberg and wanted Mannerheim as president. As a committed royalist, Wettenhovi-Aspi would probably have been happy with him as king!

Perhaps Sibelius hoped to find someone to fill the vacuum left by Carpelan. He certainly saw more of Wettenhovi-Aspi in the years after Carpelan's death, and the visits to Ainola lasted into the small hours. Aino thought him a windbag and his visits a waste of precious time. Sibelius certainly spoke freely to him, sometimes too freely: 'When Asp was here I was far too open. Revealed my soul. Regret this bitterly since I do not know him well. Incorrigible. It still covers me with embarrassment. Will I never learn!' (Diary, 28 January 1920) Their discussions were not confined to the occult or Fenno–Egyptology but extended to less esoteric matters such as money. All the same, there was no way in which Wettenhovi-Aspi could take Carpelan's place. He lacked the latter's musical insight and subtlety of mind, and in any event had his own life to lead.

In January 1920 Aino went to stay with her mother in Helsinki to look after Heidi who, while convalescing from scarlet fever, had contracted chicken-pox. Sibelius's letters radiate affection and concern:

My Beloved,
So our little Heidi has fallen ill again. Try to be brave and think of brighter times ahead. It will soon be better.
Linda has been here and was in good form. She managed to talk about other things than the past. I enclose a letter here from Paris. I wonder who it's from? I'm writing in the middle of the night. I am 'in the grip of things'. I played cards with Margareta the whole evening. She won and went to bed feeling very pleased with herself. I hope I'll hear your voice in the morning. Take good care of yourself. Cheque to follow. Much love from everyone.

The diary, however, is much darker in tone: 'Sorrow. Misery. No glimpse of light. Dishonoured.' (10 February 1920)

Granit-Ilmoniemi's article still rankled and Sibelius's general depression was not even dispelled by Aino's and Heidi's homecoming:

[14 February 1920] Aino worn out and depressed. Margareta fell ill yesterday and now her mother resumes (or rather continues) her nursely calling. I wonder why our path in life is so paved with such difficulties? Perhaps we have only ourselves to blame for it.'

The last sentence sounds like a mild reproach. Perhaps, like so many fathers, Sibelius felt a little out of the picture when Aino was consumed by her 'nursely calling'. It is not impossible that her willingness to sacrifice herself masked a desire to get away. She sensed that he was getting nowhere with his new symphonies and could not bear to see him wandering the house and in low spirits. Ever since the 1890s she had spent some periods with the children at her parent's home in Vasa, whose charged atmosphere was nevertheless easier to put up with than the tensions of Ainola. Perhaps she still felt the need to return home to her mother, and was not always able to cope with her volatile husband's swings of mood. One day would find him plunged in gloom, only to see him borne aloft the following day on a wave of optimism:

'Scored *Valse lyrique*. This orchestration has entailed enormous work, so much so that my hands tremble and I can't work at it without stopping from time to time. Only wine seems to steady me – and at present prices!'[8] (Diary, 11 February 1920) By the end of the month his tremor has eased. 'My hands no longer tremble. It feels strange to be able to write normally.' The thought that his condition could worsen and prevent him writing altogether must have been a source of real anxiety. The first years of the 1920s were difficult creatively, and Sibelius did not exactly make life easier for himself or those around him.

One can well imagine how often he returned to Ainola, dead tired and hung-over after rowdy and sometimes quarrelsome evenings with Eino Leino and others, to find consolation in his diary and the solitude of Ainola. But there were signs of life from the outer world. The Norwegian composer Sverre Jordan wrote from Bergen offering him concerts there and in Kristiania and other Norwegian cities in March 1921. Sibelius agreed, but made it a condition that Stavanger should also be included in the tour and that his fee should be at least 1,000 kronor per concert.

Plans for foreign tours lifted his spirits but were also an irritant: 'Paris concerts are being prepared. Minister Enckell . . . and Kajanus + the Sinfonietta are *nervi rerum*. Nothing from England – working on a suite for Hawkes [who maintained relations with Westerlund in Helsinki].' (20 January 1920) Kajanus's three-year-old plan to do a tour in the West was to come to partial fruition, thanks partly to the support of the Finnish envoy in Paris, Carl Enckell. But Sibelius was worried about the actual content of the programmes.

Valse lyrique for orchestra brought him much-needed money, 10,000 marks to be exact, of which 3,000 were absorbed by Pelle Westerlund in repayment of his advance. His German publisher Robert Lienau had contacted him in the autumn of 1918 to give him news of what was afoot. Paul Scheinpflug had conducted the *Pelléas et Mélisande* suite in Berlin, and Lienau urged him to try his own baton in Germany. Now in February 1920, Lienau reported further developments: Strindberg's *Swanwhite* had been put on in Munich, Stuttgart, Hamburg and Freiburg to Sibelius's music, even though Strindberg's German publisher had recommended an alternative score by the harp virtuoso Ferdinand Hummel. Ferenc von Vecsey had played the Violin Concerto with the Blüthner Orchestra and as an encore the 'Night Music' from *Belshazzar's Feast*.

Lienau professed that he had never understood why Sibelius had returned to Breitkopf & Härtel immediately on the expiry of their contract: 'That your compositions at that time did not make such rapid headway as we had both hoped was not my fault . . . I would be delighted if I were able to publish anything of yours in the future.' (4 February 1920) But Sibelius was not able to hold out much hope.

He felt a little ashamed that he had not been able to keep his promise to Stenhammar and place the score of the Fifth Symphony at his disposal, as Kajanus needed it. At the end of February Stenhammar replied: 'Thank you for your last letter. I take it for granted that I shall have your symphony in the autumn. I want to play it here, and would also like – if you are agreeable and I have the opportunity, which is as yet uncertain – to do it in Stockholm. With warmest greetings in haste, your devoted Wilh. Stenhammar.' The extraordinary thing is that Sibelius took this letter as evidence that Stenhammar was 'furious': 'How do I placate him?' (Diary, 4 March 1920) He clearly had hopes of a further invitation – though that would doubtless be followed by a long explanation as to why he would, as so often before, have to withdraw from the engagement on account of new works.

Early in 1920 a figure from his student days in Berlin suddenly made contact. Alf Klingenberg, the Norwegian pianist, had emigrated to America and founded a music school at Rochester in New York State. The founder of Kodak, George Eastman, had just bought Klingenberg's Institute as a gift for the University of Rochester and was planning to enlarge it into the Eastman School of Music, which he expected to be ready by the autumn of 1921. As the new Rector of the School, Klingenberg offered Sibelius the post of Professor of Composition: 'You stay for a year or if possible longer; you teach the up-and-coming geniuses in America to compose; their numbers are unlikely to be too onerous for you . . . my intention is that you should be sufficiently free to travel as a guest conductor and perform your own works with the many and excellent orchestras we have here in America.' (19 January 1920)

Sibelius replied that the proposal did not strike him as unattractive, but added: 'My position as a kind of poet laureate with an artist's stipend etc. is such that I could not give it up without difficulty.' In his diary he wrote: 'Decided to keep his suggestion in reserve; one does not know what the future holds. If I were rich, my new proud dreams in the way of composition could be realized. Always this dreadful problem with money. And no prospect of relief in sight.' (Diary, 28 February 1920)

Even though he complained that he was plagued by rheumatism and could not conduct at the Kalevala concert on 28 February, Sibelius was in good spirits that day. 'Wonderful atmosphere. Working on a piece for Hawkes and Co. Don't think this will upset Breitkopf & Härtel.' The previous day Carl Nielsen had written him a letter: 'I have just played your glorious *En Saga* and send you in all haste my heartiest greetings. On 3 and 4 March I shall be conducting *Finlandia* in Amsterdam with Mengelberg's superlative orchestra. Greetings from my wife to you and your sweet lady.' (27 February 1920) Sibelius responded immediately: 'Wonderful friend, my thanks. My hope is that all goes well. My warmest greetings to your delightful wife and you. I often wonder how it is possible for two geniuses like you to live so happily together.'

In March he continued work on *Kuutar (The Moon Goddess)*, and towards the end of the month he enjoyed one of his periodic spells of 'high life' in Helsinki with the architect Eliel Saarinen, then at the height of his powers. He was working on plans for both Helsinki and Canberra and was soon to win a competition for the *Chicago Tribune*'s skyscraper. His villa complex Hvitträsk, with its *Jugendstil* interior, always made a great impression on Sibelius. It was here, thirteen years earlier, that Gallén had painted his Mahler portrait. A day or so later Sibelius's diary had recorded: 'In Helsinki enemies and hostile glances. Why?' It might perhaps be better to ask why he felt they were hostile.

The winter of 1920 was full of interesting encounters. A visit with Aino to Kajanus's home made a pleasant if rare interlude, but an invitation to lunch with Mannerheim was not an everyday event either. Mannerheim had not long returned from a visit to Paris, London and Warsaw, where he had met Pilsudski and Paderewski. When his boat docked at Åbo, a choir of welcome had sung Sibelius's *Isänmaalle (To My Country,)* but elsewhere his mission was not appreciated. President Ståhlberg and the government did all they could to freeze him out; he held no official position, though that did not stop him from making controversial pronouncements on the issues of the day. Although he was zealous in emphasizing the importance of a strong defence, he was also mindful of the need to heal the wounds of the civil war. Gallén was among his confidants and he admired Sibelius, not only for his music and as a national figure but also for his personal attributes.

Sibelius's friend and champion Alexander Siloti fled with wife and son from Petrograd, with only his evening dress in his luggage. They managed to get safely over the Finnish border, and their first stop was Helsinki where, according to the 1919 edition of *Riemanns Musiklexikon*, Siloti had been murdered in August 1918! On 3 March he played three piano concertos with the Helsinki Orchestra to an audience that included Mannerheim but not Sibelius. Two weeks later he played Liszt's *Totentanz* with the orchestra, and on 30 March gave a duo recital with his Finnish pupil Ilmari Hannikainen, which Sibelius and Aino did attend. Their long programme included Schumann, Mozart, Liszt and Arensky – and as an encore, Rachmaninov's *Easter Night*, the finale from the Fantasy for two pianos, Op. 5. Is it possible that its bell-ringing could have inspired Sibelius's *Bykyrkan (The Village Church)*, Op. 103, No. 1, whose organ-like main section is followed by a cadenza in which both big and small chimes are suggested?

After the concert Mrs Mascha Travers Borgström – a legendary beauty of the day with a passionate interest in music and since 1915 the wife of Sibelius's patron Arthur Borgström – gave a supper party for Siloti at their house in Mariegatan. The ways of fate are strange. Five years earlier Sibelius had dined with Borgström's first wife Aline just before the pair had divorced. And now his hostess this evening was on the brink of separating from this her fourth husband!

Siloti's wife visited Ainola at the end of April. Her husband was continuing with his concert tour and afterwards went on to Borgå (Porvoo) to rest. He wrote (as usual in German) to his 'dear and most honoured friend Sibelius' just before the family left for Antwerp: 'It seems to me that I was so exhausted by the Bolsheviks that it is only now, when my concert tour is over, that I realize just *how tired* I am. I hope that the sea trip to Antwerp will give me some rest, as immediately on arrival I must begin my damned piano practise. I am so sorry that I did not have the opportunity of visiting you in your own home, but my affection for you is no less for that. Meeting you made me feel better, for in your person you unite goodness of heart with talent. May God permit that we can soon meet again in Petersburg, and that you there perform one of your works in my concert series!' (27 May 1920)

CHAPTER TWELVE

An Offer from America

During the spring of 1920 Sibelius went to concerts often – a symptom perhaps of creative malaise, for had things been going well, he would have been totally consumed by his work. The Slovene conductor–composer Leo Funtek programmed his own orchestral transcription of Erkki Melartin's piano suite *Der traurige Garten* and Bruckner's Fourth Symphony. Sibelius liked the suite but was less fired by the symphony. His reactions are often as much a reflection of his own creative preoccupations as of anything else. Some years earlier Bruckner's Fifth Symphony had sent him into ecstasies. At that time he had been preoccupied with his own Fifth, but now that his concerns were with the finely-wrought polyphony of the Sixth, his reaction was quite different: 'Not entirely at home with the Fourth . . . it is a bit uneven and the orchestration is ungainly.'

A little later, on Easter Sunday, 4 April, he attended the première of *Maan virsi (Hymn to the earth)* conducted by Heikki Klemetti at the anniversary concert of Suomen Laulu. Although Sibelius himself was greeted by frenetic applause, the critical reception bordered on the nonchalant. Evert Katila, newly appointed to the *Helsingin Sanomat,* dismissed it with a cliché ('the well-sounding novelty brought the programme to an uplifting conclusion') and gave almost as much attention to the fact that the choir made a presenta-tion to their conductor of an expensive silver coffee service! But matters were far worse in *Hufvudstadsbladet,* where Bis committed the ultimate sol-ecism of thinking that the new piece was the same as the *Song of the Earth* premièred the preceding year, but this time with the text put into Finnish by Eino Leino. Sibelius's reaction on reading that the piece 'with its sublime, pure music again made a deep impression' can be readily imagined, but is not recorded!

Kajanus made 1919–20 a Sibelius season and programmed all the sym-phonies, several of the tone poems and the violin concerto. By 8 April he had reached the Fourth Symphony and Sibelius himself was received with enthusiastic applause when he went on to the platform. Although Leevi Madetoja's review spoke of the symphony's depth and stature, and took its public acceptance for granted, both Sibelius and Kajanus took a more realistic view of the situation. The Fourth Symphony needed consistent and frequent advocacy if it was to make real headway with the public.

The soloist on this occasion was none other than Willy Burmester, who played the Bruch G minor concerto together with three of his own transcriptions for violin and piano, an inappropriate ingredient in a symphony concert. Listening to him would have revived painful memories of their strained relations and reinforced Sibelius's feeling that Burmester's style would not have suited his own concerto. But at least in the first years of the century Burmester was at his peak, whereas by about 1915 his star was burnt out. Not that his technical virtuosity was in doubt, but his interpretative imagination had lost its savour and he was well past his best.[1] All the same, Sibelius must have felt some pangs of conscience as he recalled how he had allowed himself to be persuaded by Robert Lienau to accept Karl Halir. It had been the final straw for Burmester, who fulfilled his vow never to play the concerto in whose gestation he had at one time played no small part. The blow to his pride had broken their friendship. 'Let Marteau play it in Stockholm,' he had written in 1903, when the question of other soloists' rights had arisen, '*werde* ich *das Concert* nie *spielen*'.

On 22 April Kajanus came to the Fifth Symphony, the first conductor to do so after the composer himself. The final piece on the programme was the Improvisation *Snöfrid*, which as usual was cheered to the echo and encored. Sibelius was present but did not take a bow![2] Madetoja wrote that the Fifth continued the path blazed by the Fourth: 'In its layout it is even more individual; there is not one bar of ordinary orchestral polyphony, that is to say the development of themes in the conventional sense, but every theme leads an independent life. Hans Richter has said that this way of symphonic thinking opens up new possibilities for the future of the genre.' (23 April 1920)

In the meantime Kajanus himself was girding his loins for an important guest appearance in Paris. On 13 May he presented a demanding all-Finnish programme with the Orchestre de Pasdeloup. Sibelius was not best pleased with his choice of programme: the whole of the second half was devoted to him, but the first itself took no fewer than seventy minutes of playing time. Kajanus had not been able to resist the temptation to open with his own Sinfonietta, a harmless enough piece of some eighteen minutes duration. Then followed a group of songs by Melartin, Madetoja and Kuula; two tone poems by Kuula; and as if that were not already enough, Palmgren's Second Piano Concerto 'The River', with Ilmari Hannikainen as soloist.

After the interval came Sibelius's Third Symphony – receiving its Paris première – *The Swan of Tuonela* and *Finlandia*. The event was preceded by a speech of welcome by Maître Alfred Bruneau on behalf of the Académie des Beaux Arts and went on until midnight! As one critic put it, a three-hour concert places a strain on the keenest curiosity and the most attentive concentration. The Salle Gaveau was, in the words of the government paper

Le Temps, 'well attended and a conspicuous success'. As to the former, it was very much an official event, and as to the latter, others begged to differ! And quite apart from the length of the programme, Kajanus should have known better than to choose the Third Symphony.

The Third had not been well received by the critics in St Petersburg, Moscow, Stockholm, New York and Berlin – even London had been relatively lukewarm. Nor was *die jünge Klassisität* to the Parisian taste. Jean Chantavoine, who was by no means ill disposed towards Sibelius, presented him as a kind of country cousin. He quoted Gounod as saying, 'Only God composes in C major', though in the Paris of the 1920s he might have added Stravinsky. 'The Third Symphony proceeds in an unaffected C major, and sings of the delights of a summer in those latitudes where even the dog-days are temperate. Let us not feel any surprise or disappointment that this joy is not overflowing, for its calm mildness is perhaps all the more touching. The gentle *Andantino* à la Brahms . . . is charming and in the finale a kind of rural chorale develops, which lends the movement a beautiful character of peaceful and healthy joy.'[3]

To crown it all, the Paris concert halls were more or less inundated by Nordic symphonies that week. As reported in the *Hufvudstadsbladet* and *Helsingin Sanomat* on 23 April 1920, another critic, Jean Poueigh, had written in *Le Parisien*: 'Even if the Nordic people's (Norwegian and Finnish) musical endeavours are deserving of support, their music, with the exception of Grieg, is lacking that ethnic identity which shines through so brilliantly in the Slavonic school.' To counter that, Sibelius's Second Symphony would have made a greater stir than the Third. As far as craftsmanship was concerned, Sibelius and the other Finns found themselves generally rated below Sinding. 'We have heard great things about Monsieur Sibelius. But the Third Symphony and even *The Swan of Tuonela* were a great disappointment both in terms of substance and form.'[4] Gaston Carraud, who twenty years earlier had praised the First Symphony, passed over the Third in silence and mentioned only the song *Höstkväll* and *The Swan of Tuonela* in the same breath as Kajanus's Sinfonietta.

Sibelius's forebodings had been amply vindicated, and his suspicions of Kajanus rekindled. On 24 April his diary records: 'All the others are represented by their latest music, I with pieces from the last century (more accurately, the turn of the century). Why? And there are many other things that are worrying, not least for Aino. That glorious woman who has hitherto only believed the best of my colleagues, now realizes a bit late in the day how things really are.'

When he saw the reviews from Paris reproduced in *Hufvudstadsbladet*, Sibelius was plunged into gloom and the summer was quite ruined! 'The Paris concert a success for Kajus's Sinfonietta and also the others. I have had no great success – exactly as I predicted. It weighs heavily. But as the saying goes, time heals all wounds. Yet time is running out for me, and what have I got to show for my life?'Only Katarina's excellent examination results sweetened the bitter pill: 'What joy that wonderful girl has given her parents.'

No doubt Kajanus set back Sibelius's cause by many decades with his Pasdeloup concert. He had a heaven-sent opportunity to break a lance for his great countryman. Indeed, with his authority he could have insisted on an all-Sibelius concert – and one of more normal proportions. *The Oceanides* would have shown the French an unfamiliar side to the composer. The Fourth Symphony might have found a responsive chord in Paris, which has always enjoyed a taste for the *succès de scandale,* and the Fifth would have raised the Salle Gaveau to the rafters.

In early May, like a voice from Sibelius's youth, came a letter from Adolf Paul. He had a practical suggestion: 'Would you do *King Christian* together with me next season in Stockholm? I shall try and get the Royal Opera and orchestra. You could have half the takings, and that could amount to a lot of money. I shall raise the capital myself and rehearse the play with first-rate actors. For once I would like us to make a showing together. If you want all the takings, so be it, as long as you are with me. Think about it – for a minute but no more – and just say yes! I have become healthy and chaste ... make money by writing film scripts. The theatres don't put my plays on, though they do at least accept them. But if you open a Berlin paper, you'll see my films running concurrently at three theatres.' (30 April 1920)

During the past few years Paul had spent a good deal of time with Armas Järnefelt both in Stockholm and Berlin, and thought Järnefelt's perform-ance of *Der Rosenkavalier* in Stockholm far superior to anything he had seen in Berlin. He doubtless hoped that Järnefelt would plead his case at the Royal Opera. Needless to say, Sibelius declined, but Paul was not so easily put off: 'It was lovely of you to have written and wonderful that you spoke from the heart so frankly. You must come and stay with us.' (23 May 1920) Paul had rented a small house on the island of Wollin near Swinemünde from which he sent him a postcard of a lighthouse: 'Come here now. You are so consumed by lunches and dinners that you aren't getting time to live properly.' Sibelius had evidently complained of the claims that his social life was making on his time: Saarinen, Siloti, Mannerheim, dinner parties after concerts and so on.

Since the summer of 1918 Paul had often written from both Berlin and from Sweden, where his family spent long periods with his brother and stoked up after their starvation diet in Berlin. They had a special connection in that Eva Paloheimo's husband Arvi was now attached to the Finnish legation in Berlin. After witnessing the February revolution in Petrograd, the young couple had gone to Berlin only to go through the November 1918 disturbances in that city. They spent many evenings at Paul's house and relived old times. He longed to hear 'Schang's' (Jean's) Piano Quintet again and even asked for a score. 'A copy is soon made and you shall have whatever it costs immediately from me as usual.'

Paul makes use of a jocular private language when he writes to Sibelius. (He uses a similar vein when he writes to Gallén and Edvard Munch.) Sibelius responded in the same spirit. Despite the unfolding turbulence of late 1918, Paul addressed himself to the subject of wine, women and song: 'That wine which you mentioned in your dear and affectionate epistle, I went out and immediately sampled a bottle on my own, as one should, and with reverence!' And referring to *En bok om en människa*, in which he portrayed his (and Sibelius's) year in Berlin,[5] as well as other autobiographical intimacies, he writes: 'People don't have to know absolutely everything. If they did – and about you into the bargain – with that long Leporello-like catalogue, it wouldn't just be a banned book, but a whole library.' The letters are full of gossip: when Arthur Borgström's new wife saw Sibelius's white bust, sculpted in plaster of Paris by Munsterhjelm in Paul's home, she fell over backwards. But his light-hearted tone often masks sheer penury. Even though he constantly published new books, they seemed to bring him little money. Only when he was working for the film industry did things seem to have picked up. It goes without saying that he asked Sibelius to write some music for one of his films and make his fortune – to an equally predictable response.

– 2 –

'This evening it's midsummer. The days are wonderful – warm and full of poetry. The 'new' begins to take shape. Much hard work. If only I were not so depressed about myself as symphonist. In fact I have no encouragement or support. A strange passion, this writing symphonies.' (Diary, 23 June 1920) His spirits were not improved by the knowledge that he could not enjoy the summer weather at Ainola but had promised to conduct no fewer than five concerts of his own music at the Helsinki Fair at the turn of the month (June–July). 'Am girding myself up for the Fair and all the rest of the torment.' The Fair was an important initiative both for the arts and for Finland as a trading nation. Trade with the Soviet Union had come to a stop, and it was important to renew commercial links with central Europe and the industrial economies of the West. Sibelius could have observed that *Uusi Suomi* published a German News Supplement every day, and that *Berlingske Tidende*, where his detested Alfred Tofft functioned as music critic, paraded itself for its Finnish readers as Denmark's largest source for advertising. The Fair was not confined to industrial exhibition halls but was the pretext for concerts, drama and opera. At three in the afternoon for nine days in a row the Helsinki Orchestra gave all-Finnish programmes. After the concerts, which were rehearsed immediately beforehand, the musicians took themselves off to the opera pit, where *Tannhäuser*, *Madama Butterfly* and *Carmen* were conducted by Armas Järnefelt. The National Theatre offered Finnish classics as well as Molière – and other stages presented *La Dame aux Camélias* and Wilde's *Salomé*. Stenman's Galleries exhibited works by Churberg, Edelfelt, Eero Järnefelt and Westerholm as well as such newcomers as T.K. Sallinen and Wäinö Aaltonen.

Sibelius was plunged into the fray right from the very beginning, when he conducted Suomen Laulu and the Helsinki Orchestra in *Maan virsi*. But the first real concert of the Fair, an all-Sibelius affair given on Monday 28 June in the presence of President Ståhlberg, was packed. The programme included *Festivo*, the Fifth Symphony, the *Pelléas et Mélisande* suite, *The Swan of Tuonela* and *Lemminkäinen's Homeward Journey*. In *Uusi Suomi*, the young radical composer Ernest Pingoud laced his toast to Sibelius with a little spice: the Fifth Symphony is 'full of brilliant moments and ideas, severe, well-hewn manliness and powerfully controlled lyricism – together with some ungainly and plain moments, without which Sibelius would not be Sibelius, such as the official conventional closing chords. And yet this is a strong, very strong piece.' At the next concert Sibelius conducted the closing work, *Maan virsi*. The fact that he was the dedicatee and had commissioned the piece in the first place did not inhibit Klemetti from reviewing it in glowing terms! But at least Bis had at last caught up with the fact that *Maan virsi* was not the same as *Jordens sång*, and spoke of 'a crescendo in which strophe after strophe grows in brilliance, in power, colour and spirit'. At the fifth concert Sibelius conducted the Suite from *Belshazzar's Feast* and *Jordens sång,* and at the last, the *King Christian II* suite, *Valse triste* and *Finlandia*. According to Klemetti, the composer distilled a potent magic from his players and showed once and for all how this remarkable piece should go. 'It is a pity that this authentic performance has not yet been put on a gramophone record. In all corners of the globe, and in countless homes, an altogether misleading picture of *Valse triste* is given.' Not even Sibelius succeeded in filling the hall at the orchestra's benefit concert, and the financial returns were small.

The Fair acquired a stronger political perspective than the promoters had originally foreseen. Peace negotiations between Finland and the Soviet Union had been under way since 12 June, but the Russians were consistently dismissive of Finnish aspirations to East Karelia and a border with access to the White Sea. The Soviet negotiating position was strengthened by events in Poland, where in April the Poles had launched a reckless attack on the Russians. They had quickly been forced on to the defensive, and by June Soviet forces were threatening Warsaw. The prospect of a Polish collapse occasioned much concern in the Baltic States. On the Finnish side, it became clear that the Russians were not willing to pay the price the Finns had demanded for the security of Russia's north-western border.

After the horrors of the war of independence and the civil war, Sibelius, like most people in his circle, had lost the appetite for foreign affairs or border disputes and had given himself over to the pleasures of life. Their world no longer resounded to the thunder of cannons but to the gentler strains of Léhar's *Red Roses in the Sunset*, which was playing to full houses at Helsinki's Brunnshus Theatre. Once the Fair was over, Sibelius was seized by twinges of conscience for what he had said about Kajanus: 'Perhaps I have been a bit hard on Kajus. He has so many pressures to contend with. And we surely have no one else to champion every Tom, Dick and Harry. Why was I so out of temper? Even in Paris, where every hand is against me, I have gained real recognition. And although they regard me as overrated etc., they can't keep me down now. It's too late for that. (Diary, 12 July 1920) However, much worse was in store for him in the French capital.

An invitation came from Ivan Narodny, an admirer in New York, asking him to write music for two ballets for which he himself had written the scenario, *Vineta* – or *Versunkene Stadt* as he called it in German – and *Girl of the Fourth Dimension*. 'Both of them are imaginative subjects and have a deep meaning and philosophy,' confided Sibelius to his diary (20 May 1920). Narodny was regarded as as 'a literary vagabond,' who wrote books on music and ballet and had good connections with Otto Kahn, a wealthy patron of the arts and a member of the Metropolitan Opera Board. Sibelius realized that he must 'get out of the American thing. Not enough time in the few years I have left,' he wrote in his diary of 23 June. He could not resist the temptation of asking for $20,000 in his reply, which he knew was tantamount to a rejection.

A little later in the summer Sibelius paid a visit to his childhood summer house in Tavastland, staying first with Walter von Konow at Lahis, and then at Annila with his daughter Ruth. He enjoyed his time there, reliving old memories and the atmosphere of the place. His spirits were much lifted by a letter from his old friend and admirer, Rosa Newmarch, who passed on an invitation from Robert Newman, manager of the New Queen's Hall Orchestra, asking if he would conduct one of his compositions on 12 February 1921, and if so, what would be his fee. Needless to say, he was eager to do so. Before his boat left Bremen for New York in May 1914, he had written to Mrs Newmarch with plans for a concert of his own works in London. Now at last the day had dawned when he could at last renew his pre-war contacts; guest appearances with a foreign orchestra in a great musical metropolis were a strong, perhaps vital, inducement to composition.

Mrs Newmarch wrote on 17 July from Geneva, where she was resting after one of her many scholarly expeditions to the Slavonic world, this time Prague. At Chesters in London she had seen 'several piano pieces which attest to your activity' – and as she cautiously put it, 'have heard that a new symphony was ready . . . I continue to work but with not quite the same energy as before. I am already sixty-two and am beginning to feel signs of my age. But they say that I haven't changed all that much.' In his reply Sibelius suggested a fee of £150 'on account of the enormous costs such a journey now entails'. Both letters were written in a mixture of French and English. He wrote in French, presumably with Aino's assistance, as he did not wish to expose Mrs Newmarch to the unpleasing prospect of receiving letters in the tongue of the hated *Boches*, though more than a year had passed since the Treaty of Versailles. Even in the future he continued with his imperfect French rather than go back to his fluent and idiomatic German. Rosa's dislike of the Germans had obviously made an enduring impression on him.

In Gothenburg, Stenhammar was planning the coming season and sounded out Sibelius on the possibility of performing his music to *Everyman* at the Lorensberg Theatre and *Jordens Sång* at one of his concerts. Neither idea came to anything, but he did touch on the question of the Gothenburg première of the Fifth Symphony, which 'we could possibly organize with the perennial question of a visit from you in person'. It was for Sibelius to come when he felt like it: 'We are always ready to put on one or two extra Sibelius concerts.' (6 August 1920) The generosity of Stenhammar's invitation delighted him: 'Concerning Symphony No. 5 and all the terrible travails surrounding it, I will write at greater length. Will come to Gothenburg with the greatest delight.' (11 August 1920) Stenhammar replied asking for further clarification of the mysterious words about the Fifth Symphony. But he was not to welcome Sibelius to the orchestra during his remaining time there. He left in 1922 to devote himself to composition, having appraised Sibelius of his intentions in an earlier letter.

Wartime hatreds lingered on. At Sibelius's request, Breitkopf & Härtel sent orchestral material to the Finnish consul in Sydney, where a concert of his music was planned, only to have the parcel impounded by the Australian customs and the consul accused of 'dealings with the enemy'. All this well into 1920, two years after hostilities had ceased. Fortunately both Sibelius and Breitkopf had a sufficient sense of the ridiculous to laugh off this particular incident. But in other respects Sibelius's dealings with his publisher were not entirely harmonious. Breitkopf had asked Sibelius for a list of works he had composed during the war years and he sent off a comprehensive catalogue on 10 July. Their reply was tinged with exasperation: 'To be completely frank, we were dismayed to discover the extent to which your new output has found its way into the hands of other publishers.' (21 August 1920)

By way of appeasement, Sibelius offered them three newly-composed piano bagatelles for 1,000 Finnish marks: *Humoreske, Lied* and *Kleiner Walzer*. They were part of a new collection, Op. 97, which was intended to number ten pieces in all. His diary notes: 'We'll see what they say. If I could count on only part of that sum I should be happy.' (23 August 1920). If his diary had recorded *Finnish* marks, his letter merely stated 'marks'. Breitkopf's director Hellmuth von Hase, who had long feared that Sibelius would defect to

Wilhelm Hansen, wished to see him return to his old house. He replied that he was willing to purchase the three pieces at 1,000 deutschmarks each. Sibelius swallowed the loss involved in the rate of exchange. The Deutschmark was at this time worth less than its Finnish equivalent.

Before the war Sibelius could have changed 1,000 deutschmarks for 1,250 Finnish marks but now the exchange rate had fallen to about 600. But such a loss was trivial by the side of the internal inflation that had eroded the value of the Finnish currency, even more than the German at this point. The 600 Finnish marks that Sibelius would now receive for his piano bagatelle had the purchasing power of fifty-two in 1914! And in that same year of 1914, Breitkopf & Härtel had bought one of Sibelius's piano pieces for 750 Finnish marks.

Notwithstanding, von Hase did all in his power to strengthen his ties with Sibelius and, it would appear, was looking forward to publishing the Fifth Symphony. On 8 September Wilhelm Hansen had offered Sibelius 3,000 Danish crowns, the equivalent of 14,000 Finnish marks, for the symphony. Sibelius doubtless wanted to remain loyal to Breitkopf and so on the 13th he telegraphed Leipzig offering them the piece for 25,000 Finnish marks. Their telegram came five days later: IN PRESENT CIRCUMSTANCES REGRET IMPOSSIBLE. No counter-proposal came. Instead of rounding the figure down to, say, 40,000 German marks, von Hase allowed the Fifth Symphony and its possible successor to slip through his fingers.

In the absence of any counter-offer, Sibelius saw no alternative but to accept Hansen's proposal of 3,000 crowns. He had the additional misfortune of doing so at a time when the exchange rates had moved to his disadvantage, so that he made only 11,000 Finnish marks out of the transaction. In world sales the Fourth Symphony of 1911 had brought him six times as much. Inflation was biting hard in Finland, and it was at least some consolation to know that he was now established in Denmark with its stable currency.

As early as the end of August, Hansen had paid a personal visit to Helsinki to meet his Finnish colleague Pelle Westerlund. Westerlund had recently acquired Lindgrens, the publisher whose lists included the six *Humoresques for violin and orchestra*, the Sonatina for violin and piano, *Laetare anima mea* and *Devotion*, three collections of songs and a large number of piano miniatures – in all, about sixty wartime Sibelius trifles. These would be of distinct interest to Hansen, particularly now that Breitkopf were out of the picture. Sibelius was following the proceedings with interest: 'There is much ado at Pelle Westerlund's. Wilhelm Hansen here presumably on a business errand. From what I can gather, Pelle will sell out and make an enormous profit from my pieces.'

Sibelius himself did not stand to make much out of them. Some, such as the *Étude*, Op. 76, No. 2, composed for his daughter Eva 'to remind her of home', he had sold outright. Others such as the *Religioso*, Op. 78, and several of the piano pieces, Opp. 76 and 85, he had accepted (indeed suggested) a fee for an edition of 10,000 copies, which naturally would not be exhausted for the foreseeable future.

– 3 –

Sibelius's temperament was nothing if not volatile. 'Have been in the best of spirits. Now in the doldrums. Up and down, up and down', reads a diary entry on 6 September 1920. He knew that the offer concerning the Eastman School that Alf Klingenberg had discussed with him would involve complex and nerve-racking negotiations. In the summer of 1920 Klingenberg had made what we would now call a head-hunting trip throughout Europe, looking for suitable talent. In September he passed through Stockholm and met Armas Järnefelt, who wrote to his brother Eero asking him to advise Sibelius not to turn down the offer out of hand but to ask for a salary of $20,000 and a guaranteed number of conducting engagements.

When Klingenberg visited Ainola later that month, Sibelius obviously took Järnefelt's suggestion as a basis for negotiation. Klingenberg outlined the situation, explaining that the position they were offering would be close to that of an honorary Director. Shortly afterwards George Eastman offered him $20,000 for one academic year. The terms of his appointment included an obligation to conduct five concerts in America, and he would not be free to accept any other engagement before or during the period in question. It subsequently emerged that this latter condition was not meant too seriously. On the contrary, the School was prepared to be reasonably flexible.

Sibelius accepted, though he asked for an advance of $10,000 to enable him to put his affairs in order, compose new works for the projected concerts and spend time improving his English. He sets out his position quite frankly in a letter to Klingenberg: 'I fully understand what you and your wife said, particularly your assurance that I would have time to compose, and appreciate that you and your wife would kindly give me every help, and that it would be possible for me to earn extra. Further thought leads me to think that $20,000 is not all that much. From five concerts alone I could make $12,500. Please do not be offended by my usual frankness.'

Back in Rochester they were by no means convinced that an advance of such size constituted sound business practice, but they were prepared to compromise and deposit that sum into an American bank account. After some further discussions and compromises, an agreement was drawn up. But Sibelius was still hesitant and full of foreboding: 'Nothing will come of this America scheme.' (4 November 1920) Klingenberg exhorted him to wire a firm acceptance, and on 3 January 1921 Sibelius's diary contains the laconic entry: 'Telegraphed . . . "Yes". And so *alea jacta est*. Let us hope that I have done the right thing.'

The Rochester newspapers and the American musical press were full of the great news. Sibelius's name figures prominently in the first edition of the Eastman School's prospectus. But Klingenberg knew Sibelius from their Berlin years and doubtless realized, given his impulsive temperament, wild changes of mood and infinite capacity for indecision, that the outcome was still far from certain.

His publishing problems gave Sibelius little peace. At the beginning of October 1920, Breitkopf & Härtel sent him an account for the period 1 July 1914 to 7 October 1920. He was once again plunged into depression. He noted yet again that the royalties for large orchestral works on the one hand and miniatures on the other bore no reasonable proportion to each other. In 1915 *The Oceanides* brought him 3,000 Reichsmarks while for the four songs, Op. 72, he was credited with 2,000 Reichsmarks.

The other sore point in the *Valse triste* contract was that the royalties were fixed once and for all at 100 Finnish marks, with no safeguard against inflation. This factor became of crucial importance in the years after the First World War. The contract had been signed in 1904, and since then the Finnish mark had lost 93 per cent of its value. The German mark had sunk even more sharply and was now even weaker than the Finnish. Thus all Sibelius's contracts with Breitkopf, as well as those with Fazer, whose rights Breitkopf had acquired, were badly hit by inflation. From the outbreak of war through to 7 October 1920, 70,000 copies of *Valse triste* had been printed in Germany, Denmark and England, which was the equivalent of twenty-three editions. The piece, with its associations with death, seems to have exerted a particularly strong attraction for the piano-playing public. But every 100 marks that Sibelius received *per edition* was worth only seven marks by 1904 standards.

Breitkopf's *Abrechnung* served as yet another reminder of how enormous the sales of *Valse triste* had been and what a fortune had slipped through Sibelius's hands both before and during the war – and he did not even have himself to blame! In 1904 he had not sold anything directly to a foreign publisher. It was with Fazer that he had dealt, and Breitkopf had taken over the contract and fulfilled its conditions to the letter. Sibelius had tried to secure changes in 'Fazer's lunacy', and through Adolf Paul's good offices had tried to persuade Breitkopf to agree to a 20 per cent royalty based on the retail price. But Breitkopf had not agreed to the percentage principle, which would have given the composer some protection against inflation. Robert Lienau, Sibelius's other German publisher, paid him a 15 per cent royalty on the Violin Concerto in its reduction for violin and piano, and 10 per cent on their collection of piano pieces, *Sibeliana*. Now the retail price of *Valse triste* soared while his already derisory royalty shrank to virtually nothing. He was gripped by a feeling of impotence and anger, but suddenly his eagle eye spotted a mistake that spurred him to action: 'Earlier your accounts have been paid on the basis of 100 Finnish marks equalling eighty Reichsmarks. But now 100 Finnish marks are worth between 140 and 170 Reichsmarks.

May I ask you to adjust the figure accordingly?' In his diary he noted: 'Have written to Breitkopf and complained about the *Valse triste* outrage. Firmly and politely. Presumably to no purpose. And poverty creeps up on me.' (18 October 1920)

Not that Breitkopf had behaved outrageously. In the general currency turbulence they had perhaps not noticed that the German mark had already in 1919 fallen below the Finnish. In their answer of 18 November, Breitkopf indicated their willingness to make an appropriate adjustment from 1920 onwards, which would be for 34,000 copies. On a supplementary Royalty Statement they list royalties on three new editions of *Valse triste* and three of his other best-seller, the *Romance in D flat*, Op. 24, at the new rate of exchange. There were further sums for three new piano bagatelles and other small pieces, which came to 6,665.14 Reichsmarks, or 3,860 Finnish marks, just over half being paid at the new rate. Small wonder that Sibelius described them in his diary of 25 November as 'more than usually meagre. But in any event I see that Breitkopf are at least trying and that they can be trusted. And that's a good thing.'

Breitkopf & Härtel's royalty statements give a rather chilling insight into Sibelius's predicament. He had to confront some unpalatable truths. Royalties on his earlier works brought in virtually nothing. For his symphonies and symphonic poems he was paid ludicrously small amounts compared with those for the shorter piano compositions, and his annuity from the State only met a fraction of his expenses. He would be compelled to write more potboilers.

Yet he was no worse off than many of his great contemporaries. Even in the great musical centres of Europe, things were little better. Mahler was not able to maintain himself by writing symphonies and earned a living as a star conductor and opera director. In Paris, Debussy fought a constant battle against penury. On the other hand, Richard Strauss had amassed a fortune both as a composer and conductor. The scandal unleashed by *Salome*, far from harming his reputation, enriched his coffers and made no small contribution towards his villa at Garmisch-Partenkirchen. It was only when copyright protection came into effect during the 1920s – in no small measure thanks to Strauss's exertions – and was extended to performing and reproducing rights that the position of composers was significantly altered for the better. Sibelius's fortunes were to be radically affected.

But at the end of October 1920 the position was still bleak, no better than it was at the time just before his fiftieth birthday when he had written: 'Poor, so poor that I have to write potboilers.' (15 August 1915) No doubt he could take comfort from the plight of other great masters: Beethoven had no less a struggle to compose his masterpieces, and was likewise forced to write smaller, popular pieces. His moods fluctuated as usual: 'Up and down!' He made scant progress with composition: 'Over the last few days I have reworked *Scène pastorale*. Now working on *Autrefois*. Will send them to

Hansen. Worried about my London concert. The programme. Will I be ready with a new piece? Always the same story!' (Diary, 27 October 1920) It is possible that he was hoping to finish the projected tone poem *Kuutar*, whose themes were eventually to finish up in the Sixth Symphony. But instead he had to exert himself and settle down to *Autrefois*. 'Is it age? *Ich glaub's net!* Composed some time ago (for Breitkopf) *Humoristisches marsch*, *Impromptu*, *Humoresk II* (Nos 4, 5 & 6 of Op. 97). For the earlier batch (Nos. 1–3) 1,950 Fmks. For the [Fifth] Symphony 11,000 Fmks.' (Diary, 27 October 1920) With these three pieces Op. 97 was complete. Instead of the original ten pieces that he had planned, Sibelius settled for six.

In October 1920 the Finnish Opera put on a production of Armas Launis's *Kullervo* with Armas Järnefelt conducting. Launis himself had written the libretto, basing it on the *Kalevala* and on Aleksis Kivi's *Kullervo*. In some scenes the libretto drew on Eino Leino's *Swan of Tuonela*. Launis had studied both Lapp *joikks*[6] and runic melodies, not only from Finland but also Estonia and Ingria, and incorporated some stylistic elements of them in his opera. At the turn of the century Sibelius had conducted a number of his fugues at a student concert at Kajanus's orchestral academy.

Järnefelt was anxious to see Sibelius and Aino at the first night, but his brother-in-law dug in his heels and would not budge: 'Armas is peeved because I couldn't go to Launis's *Kullervo* première. Always the same story. People don't think what this costs me – two to three whole days plus 1,000 Fmks. And I completely lose track of my own work. Aino could have gone on her own, but she won't because we can't afford it. Always the same story! Oh, if only things were different.' (27 October 1920) But in the end Aino and Katarina went into town for a later performance. 'They went to hear Launis's *Kullervo*, which is good', Sibelius noted on 1 November – and added with a touch of irony, 'Strange that I never tried my hand at that subject. My star is on the wane. Poverty and destitution.'

But of course Sibelius *had* treated that subject, and in a way that was to astonish the world when the symphony was performed again after his death. Did he not see that in the primitivism and archaic folk elements that formed the musical language of the *Kullervo Symphony* he had created his own legitimate, independent parallel with the naturalism of Mussorgsky or the heroic archaism of Borodin, not to mention in our own time the folk-like primitivism of Bartók and Stravinsky?

– 4 –

At Mrs Newmarch's request, Sibelius sent a list of his most recent compositions to London. But when it came to specific details about the Fifth Symphony among other works which, as the author of the programme notes, she would need to know, he was curiously reticent: 'Later on I will write and tell you about the symphonic works that are occupying me at the moment. This is all I can say at present about my pieces, and there is no expert on my music to whom I could turn for help. What are the prospects for my three concerts in February? [It would seem that the project had already become more ambitious.] Are they all–Sibelius concerts?' He no doubt placed too much faith in the optimism of the promoters.

Sibelius's reluctance to give any details about his new compositions sent Mrs Newmarch into a state of exasperation. 'It is not enough just to send a list of compositions . . . What we need, dear friend, is your Fifth Symphony. Even Henry Wood has asked me to write to you about this, as he cannot be expected to learn your work at the last minute, as if it were a Haydn symphony.' (15 November 1920) Her comment says as much about the problems posed by Sibelius symphonies to orchestras in the 1920s as it does, perhaps, about their cavalier attitude to Haydn!

As far as the Fourth Symphony was concerned, Mrs Newmarch could put Sibelius's mind at rest. The Queen's Hall Orchestra had performed it the previous season, so the score was not unfamiliar and rehearsal would pose fewer problems. It was the Fifth Symphony that was urgently needed. Only at the end of the year, after Armas Järnefelt had conducted it in Stockholm, did Sibelius succeed in getting the score off to Sir Henry.

In a diary entry of 4 November Sibelius took himself to task: 'Have come to a point of no return. In that I have based my financial well-being solely on composition – on small pieces which never give me any real measure of satisfaction – I have to take the consequences. *Autrefois* is no good . . . a re-working is necessary – oh, the ignominy of it all. How I allow myself to be led by economic circumstance! Could I, without endangering my reputation, recall the score? That's the question. A telegram. How do I go about it? Tell Aino nothing; it would be her death . . . And my new compositions absorb me completely, but it will be difficult to get them printed . . . Breitkopf will be impossible after my latest letter [concerning the rate of exchange – needless to say, Sibelius's anxiety was ill-founded, as we have already shown]. What I am doing now is unworthy of me. If only *Autrefois* were any good – but it isn't. If only I had money, then this would never happen. I can hear Aino's dead-tired steps – and imagine her melancholy eyes – I can't continue . . .' He hid the diary before she could come into the room.

He had obviously allowed these potboilers to work him up into a neurotic frenzy. He felt it was demeaning to work on these wretched small pieces, and even more so when the prospect of more ballets loomed. Next after Narodny came a request from Poul Knudsen, the librettist of *Scaramouche*, for music to his new pantomime *Skuggor (Shadows)*. Sibelius's response was to ask 36,000 Danish crowns for it, the equivalent of rejection. His calculation was not misplaced. Knudsen's backer found the fee 'rather frightening'.

The next day found Sibelius in a better, more harmonious frame of mind. Why did he allow everything to get on top of him? He wrote a conciliatory note to Hansen: 'My arrangement [of *Autrefois*] is not up to much – have no time to deal with it now. Is the honorarium [2,000 Danish crowns] not too high? I leave it to your goodness to decide.' (5 November 1920) In spite of everything, his spirits were now high. A few days later came the contract from London for his three concerts, which cheered him in spite of a bout of influenza: 'Am curing myself with whisky and have already made considerable progress. Went on a walk with Aino – a dark but atmospheric autumn day. She stops and talks with the farmers – she's interested in everything and at home with everything.' (27 November 1920) But neither the influenza nor its cure prevented him from being vigilant about the contract for *Autrefois*. 'They tell me that it is going to be a new *Valse triste*,' he told Hansen, 'but I don't believe it myself. All the same, I had to play it three times in a row at a concert.'

The note of optimism is a sign that something is afoot in his creative life. Three diary entries from November give a good indication of what:

[11 November 1920] Working on the new piece – Symphony No. 6?

[19 November] Working at the new piece with a certain dread – why?

[25 November] Doubts about the symphony or *Runes historiques*.

There are many question marks – as there are for the reader too. Is the new piece not identical with the Sixth Symphony, as the first entry might imply? Are there two works, or is *Runes historiques* an alternative name for the new symphony? Is there a connection between the *Runes* and the projected *Kuutar*? The only thing one can say with any certainty is that the Sixth Symphony as it finally emerged is to a large extent based on the material he sketched at the turn of 1914–15.

In other respects all was not well: 'Kaj has pneumonia. And Heidi is coughing. Aino, that wonderful woman, returns to her nursing and keeps cheerful. I drink whisky to protect myself against the influenza.' Rather better for his morale were greetings from Ferenc von Vecsey on his world tour: Sibelius was delighted that 'The violin concerto seems to have caught on all over South America and Europe.' (27 November 1920)

However, a new ordeal awaited him: 'Armas conducts the Symphony No. 5 in Stockholm [with the Royal Opera Orchestra].' (29 November 1920) The prospect of being crucified by the Stockholm critics induced a bout of hypochondria. 'That I have survived as long as I have continues to amaze me.' The next few days seemed unending and took their toll on his nerves. 'Day in and day out I sit and stare disconsolately in front of me and think depressing thoughts. Where will this get me? To inertia and loneliness. Poor Aino. What a dreadful fate. Alone, alone with her sick children. I cannot bear to think about it. And why? Just tell me. We have just slowly drifted into this despondency. If only I could find something to improve my nerves. My nerves are really very bad. I can't leave home – Aino would then be on her own. Though I can't see what we get out of each other's company. We are both down and she avoids my gaze and then there's that implied criticism of me in all her movements. But cheer up – death is round the corner! (2 December 1920)

Even if Aino did not articulate it, he felt the tension between them. At some stage she would lose her self-control. In the longer term the brooding tension underlying the diary entries gives some foreboding of the explosion which was to occur some years later.

On 5 December, five days after the Stockholm première, *Hufvudstadsbladet* reproduced in a prominent leading article seven of the Swedish reviews. Sibelius was at least spared the vitriol of Peterson-Berger. His paper, *Dagens Nyheter,* was represented by one of Sibelius's admirers, the composer Ture Rangström: 'The new symphony . . . interpreted Sibelius's Promethean fate with a strongly individual and compelling atmospheric power . . . The latest Sibelius, which shares with the late Beethoven quartets a disdain for the wider public, and also has some kinship with their unswerving search for original thought and sound world, does not make things easy for the listener . . . This is a man writing from the other world who preaches in his pastoral symphonies his belief in the sweet despair of illusion and resignation's manly joy.'

Another composer, Kurt Atterberg, writing in *Stockholms-Tidningen* painted a portrait of Sibelius as 'an older man for whom the future no longer holds any striving for new ideals, no new problems, nor any misgivings in life's struggle. Without any fear the composer serenely reflects on the past, on childlike, innocent play with details and lines, all enclosed in a pastoral mood. It is as if the composer has laid a game of musical patience with his impressions of mankind and nature . . . only in the last movement . . . does he throw off his previous inertia and give rein to his former radiance and expressive power. After a poignant meditation he looks at the cards again with a touch of self-irony and puts the pack away.'

In *Svenska Dagbladet* William Seymer saw the new symphony as a retreat from the expressionism of its predecessor. 'But this retreat is well concealed behind an *arrière-garde* of unrelenting lines, unresolved dissonance and (as it seems to us) arbitrary passage work and abrupt, cacophonous motivic ideas. And yet one notices that the mood lightens, that almost unobserved pastoral calls and sonorities gradually dispel the gloom, and the majestic codas of the second and fourth movements reveal an unbowed love of life. . . . To what extent Sibelius's new style, which has some vestigial parallels with Carl Nielsen, has any prospect of catching on, only posterity can tell.'

Writing in *Nya Dagligt Allehanda,* the veteran Andreas Hallén, composer of the opera *Valdemarsskatten,* did not deny the symphony's strongly individual stamp, but thought it offered all too many 'reminders of the futuristic musical language of Scriabin and Busoni, who only the few zealous adherents of our decadent times can feel and understand'. The playing itself may have given a deceptive impression: the orchestra had rehearsed in Uppsala and, according to Atterberg, the brass almost completely ruined the effect of the performance. 'One had to use a lot of imagination to understand in terms of sound what the composer wanted in the finale.'

Sibelius's spirits plummeted. 'Appalling reviews of the Fifth from Stockholm. I'm supposed to be a dead man. Ridiculous. Armas writes that he is totally consumed by the symphony. Good. Today is independence day. Was invited to dinner with Mannerheim and the French minister – and the Finnish Theatre. Aino not invited to minister Fabré so I didn't go out at all.' (Diary, 6 December 1920) On his fifty-fifth birthday two days later, Sibelius was presented with a cheque for 63,000 marks by the tenor Väinö Sola on behalf of a group of Finnish businessmen. The composer was beside himself with delight. The day was memorable in another respect: the Fifth Symphony had been published by Hansens and was reviewed in the Berlin newspapers.

After his birthday Sibelius went into Helsinki, ostensibly to hear the last concert in the autumn Beethoven cycle that was crowned by the Ninth Symphony. However, things did not go according to plan. 'Have been a week in Helsinki and now have the most dreadful qualms of conscience. I don't understand myself any more. If I could only stop these drinking bouts. But it will always remains a forlorn hope.' (18 December 1920) If the year ended in dejection, there was light on the horizon in the shape of his visits abroad.

CHAPTER THIRTEEN

Visit to England

At the beginning of 1921 Sibelius at last emerged from isolation and set out on his first post-war concert tour – to England and Norway. Aino and the girls saw him off at Helsinki and on 31 January, on the way from Trelleborg to Sassnitz on board the steamer *Viktoria*, he wrote his first letter home: 'Up to now, all is well. The journey to Stockholm was wonderful. It was very sweet of you all to see me off. Look after yourselves. I'll write again soon. I think I will put my pounds in Kaj's account. I think I probably took too much with me. The pound is strong here in Germany. I shall probably stay a couple of days in Berlin to hear new things and get the feel of the place.'

He had dipped deeply into the family savings and doubtless felt the need to make amends. Katarina's piano studies in Stuttgart would be a suitable investment. He spent a few days in Berlin, where he was elected a Member-in-Ordinary of the *Akademie der freien Künste*. He stayed with Adolf Paul, who not long before had asked him to write the music for another panto-mime: 'We'll share the profits – and will have to raise half a million Reichs-marks to take over a theatre!' He also met von Hase, whose aged father had just died: 'This was a great shock for me. They are going to revise all their contracts and readjust the exchange rates.' (7 February 1921) Thus he would get some compensation for the continuing decline in the value of the German mark against the Finnish currency.

After an exhausting journey he landed in England, where the immigra-tion officer knew who he was. 'It felt so good to be recognized and wel-comed' (7 February 1921), but he was a little anxious about whether the London public would remember him. Things had gone well for him up to the sensational first performance of the Fourth Symphony in Birmingham in 1912. But the war years had seen a hiatus in his representation in British concert halls. Older music lovers might easily have forgotten him, while younger listeners would never have encountered his symphonies. The Fourth Symphony, conducted by Sir Henry Wood in March 1920, had bored the majority of the public at Queen's Hall.

Now it was up to Sibelius to recover lost ground. This also coincided with Finland's own interests, and the Finnish envoy Ossian Donner and his staff took good care of Sibelius during his stay. 'Got to London in the evening. Marcus Tollet from the Finnish Legation immediately invited me to dinner. Today I went to Rosa's – you can imagine how it felt. My old friend. Then at the Donners, whence I am just returned. They sent me a huge basket of the most wonderful flowers. She [Fru Olly Donner] is going to put on her own concert for me when all the others are over. Isn't that magnificent! It will cost a pretty penny. Generally speaking, it's terribly dear. I would never have believed it possible. My hotel is rather miserable and yet for a room half the size of my work room and miserable to boot, I pay nine shillings! (6 February 1921)

The following day he wrote to Aino: 'Write and let me know how you are. We'll see how things go in America. I've had a telegram to the effect that the Eastman School begins in October. Rosa is totally against my teaching in America but all for my giving concerts there. I'm conducting *Valse lyrique*. They're just copying the parts. Busoni is here. We're performing at the same concert. All (i.e. many) newspapers have long articles on me.'[1]

On 10 February Mrs Newmarch organized a reception for him at Claridges. Knowing how absent-minded he was, she sent him a reminder. 'Don't forget to be at Claridge's tomorrow, otherwise it will be *Hamlet* without the Prince of Denmark. Ask the nice Mr Blom [Eric Blom][2] to take you. Bantock and Henry Wood will be there.' According to the society editor of the *Morning Post*, the guests also included 'Dr von Williams' [Vaughan Williams]. Small wonder that Sibelius didn't work out who he was! When he did, he rushed after him and managed to find him by the staircase. 'It was, however, rather a disappointing meeting, for they failed, partly through shyness and partly because their only common language was inadequate French, to make real contact with one another, though they were both full of goodwill.'[3]

Saturday 12 February was the day of the concert with the Queen's Hall Orchestra. Sir Henry Wood had done the preparatory work before Sibelius's own rehearsals on Friday and evidently on the Saturday morning. The concert began at 3 o'clock. 'It's a strange feeling after seven long years to stand in front of five thousand people. They received me with prolonged applause . . . I had what I think was a brilliant success. That No. 5 is a masterpiece. It also sounded powerful. The orchestra applauded and the audience gave me an ovation. I took five bows. The reviews haven't appeared yet. I don't give a damn about them. The main thing is that the work is good. And I have at last come to see that – not before time! Rosa told me that she was jealous of the new symphony. She loves the Fourth. Isn't that very feminine? I was very nervous but I conducted well. Rosa and Bantock, in their anxiety to take care of me, made a fuss of me before the concert with the consequence that I was quite worn out. And in the evening a big dinner party at the Donners, about 50 people, Finns. Then we went with Westmarck and Alvén home to the Alvéns.

Donner made a very good speech in my honour and I answered in my well-known fashion . . . The newspapers have had long articles on me, several whole columns. I have plenty of friends here and naturally, I hope, enemies. We'll now have to see how the other concerts go. I am missing you terribly. Am like a . . . I wanted to write "young man", but *que faire*! They want me to go to Paris now. At a reception in Claridges Hotel (London's best) they said that they are Sibelius-mad in Paris. No doubt that's an exaggeration, but there may be something in it, but there's a powerful clique against me . . . Am going to Bournemouth in a couple of days. We'll stick together until the end of our days, won't we? Kiss the children, don't forget to do that.'

The Times wrote:

Having heard M. Sibelius conduct three of his symphonies in the last fortnight, the fifth and fourth in London and the third in Birmingham, we can have no hesitation in saying that this, No. 4 in A minor, is incomparably the finest. It stands out from its companions in its absolute directness of movement and simplicity of line. Its very simplicity is baffling.

Saturday's audience was so taken aback by the abrupt ending of the second movement that there was not a hand raised to applaud it. At the end there was a little clapping, enough to satisfy the demands of decency, but no more. (28 February 1921)

On 16 February Sibelius wrote home again: 'Here I am back in the wide world. Yesterday there was a reception for me at the Royal College [where Sibelius was received by its director Sir Hugh Allen]. The students played *En Saga* under my baton. Before that there was a lunch. Donners were there. Today I'm off to Bournemouth. Tomorrow concert. And so it goes on. Now I have an offer from Manchester on 5 March, but cannot decide until I know whether the concerts in Kristiania can be postponed. My hand is terribly tired, thanks to my being out of practice with conducting. But it will come back. The reviews of the Fifth Symphony are said to be good, though I am used to the first performances of a new symphony being met by incomprehension. But the Fourth has caught on with all the musicians here. And think of the way *that* was hounded. Take care of yourself.'

The following day found him in Bournemouth. 'Shall play in fifteen minutes. After which there will be a little peace. Here there are lilacs, palm trees, blossoming hawthorn etc.' The programme with the Bournemouth Orchestra whose permanent conductor, Sir Dan Godfrey, was a Sibelius admirer, comprised the Third Symphony, *En Saga* and *Valse triste*. One of the students at a nearby music college, who went round to pay his respects to the composer afterwards, mentioned *en passant* that he could not afford to come to London to hear him conduct the Fourth Symphony. Sibelius delved into his pocket and said: 'I will give you *ein Pfund Sterling*.'

His concert schedule was very heavy. Blom felt that he was rushed off his feet, sent from one engagement to another, without having a moment to himself. From Bournemouth he took the evening train to London immediately after his concert. Friday and Saturday morning he rehearsed the New Queen's Hall Orchestra for the two Ballad Concerts at 3 o'clock and 7 o'clock respectively, which included the *Karelia Suite*, the *Romance in C major* for strings, and *Valse triste*. Immediately afterwards, accompanied by Bantock, he took a late train back to Birmingham. Bantock had prepared a long programme: the Third Symphony, *Finlandia* and *En saga*, *Valse triste* and *Valse lyrique*, the slow movement of the Violin Concerto with Alex Cohen as soloist, and four songs with Doris Watkins as singer — and Sibelius had to manage all this on one rehearsal. At the concert itself the Theatre Royal was packed to capacity: 'I conducted excellently — according to the musicians. Today a reception, tomorrow back to London. Have two more engagements, one in Manchester and another in Bradford. On Friday we rehearse the Fourth Symphony (Queen's Hall). And *The Oceanides* (for Sunday at the Queen's Hall). It still feels strange after so many years to be back in a world where I belong. Begin to be myself. Am worried over your health. Have plans. We must stop worrying about the garden etc. and think of you. From Friday onwards I am staying at Donners . . . Have a *really* big reputation. Shall pull out of America. Conducted yesterday and am very tired. On Saturday a concert in London. With Busoni too. He plays Mozart's A major concerto [in fact it was the E flat, K482] and his own *Indianisches Phantasie*; I, the Fourth Symphony. It is very popular here. Rosa and all the others love it. Haven't seen the reviews — they are a matter of indifference to me. Continuing nagging worry about your health. We must get you better. You are of such good stock. Give everyone my love and look after yourself as well you can.' (21 February 1921)

That same evening he went to a concert with Bantock's songs: 'The performance was good but the actual music does not appeal to me. Wagnerian gestures and declamation, like everything these days. Sat next to Madame Bantock and Rosa. Madame Bantock is hard of hearing but I spoke freely to Rosa and was myself with Bantock. Today he is — if this is possible — kinder than ever. He has a wonderful disposition.'

Sibelius was himself with Bantock, but it is probable that Bantock never had an inkling of what his Finnish colleague really thought of his music. Frankness of the kind exhibited by Mahler and Schoenberg would have been alien to Sibelius. In any event he felt much at home with the highly sympathetic Bantock family, in spite of the 'cold English houses . . . it's freezing cold. And you can see everyone's breath in the air.' The same letter mentions that he was invited the following day to Oxford: 'The university! They are speaking of a doctorate, and are keen that I should return every year. Genuine English! Conducted all these concerts well. Will see how things go the day after tomorrow (London and Busoni) and on Sunday.

Afterwards Bradford and Manchester. Move to Donners on Monday [28 February] but a bit worried that I am running out of shirts. They – the Donners, I mean – live the "high life".' But even though he had to wait ten days to get his shirts laundered, Bantock's daughter testified that his appearance was 'always impeccable!'

Rosa Newmarch has given a detailed account of Sibelius's visit to Oxford on 23 and 24 February. On his arrival he was received by Sir Hugh Allen in his rooms in New College, where he spent the afternoon with an exclusive group from Oxford's musical life. Mrs Newmarch had the impression that Sibelius 'whose English was not fluent, had a certain difficulty in taking part in the conversation with his usual zest'. He was completely captivated by Oxford's architecture. In the evening Sibelius was the guest at high table at the college, and the next day was reserved for sight-seeing.

At the rehearsal for the Saturday concert,[4] Busoni sat in the hall next to Mrs Newmarch and listened to Sibelius going through the Fourth Symphony, the same symphony which he had conducted nine years earlier in Amsterdam. Mrs Newmarch always remembered Busoni's lively and enthusiastic conversation. Unlike Sibelius, Busoni found London depressing. In the photo which shows the two friends standing in front of the entrance to the Queen's Hall, Busoni seems gaunt, almost emaciated, compared to the bigger-boned Sibelius, who looks at him with a certain shy affection. At his concert in Manchester the audience had been shocked by his appearance – 'Busoni looked exactly like a corpse'[5] – but he refused to accept that he was ill. Inflation in Germany continually eroded his resources and forced him to make long concert tours in England and France. Moreover, he could not even afford to turn down the hardships of provincial tours in the backwaters of England. Every moment he spent practising, every hour on the concert podium, every minute travelling was for him a betrayal of his creative mission.

The combination of Busoni and Sibelius was nerve-racking for Sir Henry Wood: 'I could generally manage Busoni when I had him to myself, but my heart was always in my mouth if he met Sibelius. I never knew where they would get to. They would forget the time of the concert at which they were to appear; they hardly knew the day of the week. One year I was directing the Birmingham Festival and had to commission a friend never to let these two out of his sight. He had quite an exciting time for two or three days following them about from restaurant to restaurant. He told me he never knew what time they went to bed or got up in the morning. They were like a couple of irresponsible schoolboys.'

On the day of the concert, 26 February, *The Times* published a long article on Sibelius by Granville Bantock, possibly a riposte against the relatively cool reviews of the Fifth Symphony which had appeared two weeks before: 'He resembles the typical figure of the Kalevala, Old Väinämöinen, the singer and magician: he seems to be always seeking for "the word of origin" which bestows power over the thing named; he is always seeking to refine away the superfluous, and to give *des idées seules,* as he says. . . . He has added a new flavour to the art of the world, and stands as the typical and representative Finnish composer.'

In the *Musical News and Herald,* Edwin Evans reported a conversation with Sibelius: 'He feels strongly that colour in music has been overdone, that music is very often overdressed . . . like an overdressed woman. He feels that there is something at the same time artificial and essentially vulgar in this, and it causes his mind to recoil in the direction of ascetic austerity. He has an objection, not quite of the same nature, to the display of ingenuity, and to sophistication of whatever kind.'

In the event Sir Henry could heave a sigh of relief when both his schoolboys were in their rightful place at three o'clock at Queen's Hall. Mrs Newmarch also kept an eye on Sibelius, sending him a stream of messages, reminders, timetables and warnings to cover all possible eventualities. The severity of the Fourth Symphony did not really strike a responsive chord. *The Times* of 28 February stated: 'After the finale there was a burst of applause, sufficient to meet the requirements of politeness but not much more.' The *Times* critic, who had heard Sibelius conduct the Fifth Symphony in London and the Third in Birmingham, did not hesitate to declare the Fourth to be without doubt the finest of the three. 'Its strength and finesse lies in its severity . . .'

After the concert there must have been some slight embarrassment. Busoni, the darling of the London public, had scored a brilliant success both as a Mozart interpreter and composer, and the ovation with which he was greeted far outweighed the thin applause for the Sibelius symphony. Yet he keenly awaited – and in vain – for any real note of enthusiasm in Sibelius's response to the *Indianisches Phantäsie.* But Sibelius never really responded to the creative side of Busoni's genius. At best he accepted the *Berceuse élégiaque* as a kind of superior incidental music. It is difficult to imagine that he would warm to the *Indianisches Phantäsie,* and even more difficult to imagine him making much more than polite and empty compliments – and impossible to imagine Busoni being taken in by them! Thirty-two years earlier Sibelius and Busoni had played together on the balcony of the Ceremonial Hall in Helsinki University and taken part in the Schumann Piano Quintet. Neither of them could have possibly foreseen that fate would reunite them in London in so spectacular a fashion, nor that this was their last personal encounter.

The next day, 27 February, Busoni, still under the spell of the Fourth Symphony, sent him a note from his London hotel: 'My thanks to you for your beautiful music on both Saturdays. Can you tell me which works of yours have been performed in Italy – and in particular Rome? Do you know whether your Second has been played there? I don't think that I will have another opportunity of seeing you in London on this visit – unfortunately for me! (*Schade für mich!*)'⁶

Sibelius's response, if he did in fact reply, is not known. He would probably not have known which of his works had been done in Italy. In any event Busoni chose the Second Symphony when he appeared in Rome a few weeks later.

On Sunday 27 February Sibelius conducted two Ballad Concerts at the Queen's Hall, including *The Oceanides*, some numbers from the *King Christian II* Suite and the *Valse lyrique*. But his English hosts did not let him off the hook. In order to fulfil his new engagements he had to postpone his appearances in Kristiania until the turn of the month (March–April). After a final rehearsal with the Queen's Hall Orchestra, Sibelius left for Manchester, where he conducted *Valse triste* and *Finlandia* to frenetic applause from a capacity audience at a Wood concert in the Free Trade Hall. On the Sunday he gave a farewell concert to London, which included *The Swan of Tuonela*, *Festivo* from the *Scènes historiques* – and of course *Finlandia*, which had to be encored.

The indefatigable Mrs Newmarch drafted his letters of thanks to conductors, impresarios and orchestras – all Sibelius had to do was to sign them once they had been typed at the Finnish legation. She looked after him like a mother; their relationship had never been anything other than platonic. But she clearly had deep feeling for him. Some years earlier, at the time of his departure from London in 1909, she had asked him to sign one of the 'melancholy, intimate photographs' that had been taken of him. 'I do not want a dedication, or any inscriptions about gratitude or friendship. There is no need for such words between us. My day-to-day life will be the poorer without you, and I indulge the hope that I will see you again in the not too distant future. I feel for you great tendresse, a feeling that is neither shallow nor wanting in propriety. In all situations in life you can count on me – whether you write great and beautiful works (which you will) or whether you do not; whether you are as noble and sagacious as you are now, or have moments of weakness – all this will have no effect on our friendship, and I believe you know that.' She was then fifty-two and he nine years younger.

By this time, her maternal and professional concerns were dominant. She was well connected in the musical world and an influential writer, and realized that Sibelius's time in England was fast approaching its end. 'You know that I have long waited for your great breakthrough here, and am now more than ever certain that it will come. But I beg you not to squander your energies in teaching young Americans harmony and orchestration *à la* Sibelius. They can find all that by studying your works. You are a composer, not a pedagogue; possibly the greatest creative musician of our times – and certainly one of the noblest and most individual. *That is your mission. Au diable les dollars!* Spend the summer in Järvenpää; don't smoke too many Corona cigars, for the sake of your finances; don't drink too often (on the advice of your Leibarzt Mme Rosa Newmarch), and compose your Sixth (on the Almighty's command). This will give your life real meaning. You do not have the right to freely dispose of those years that remain to you, which most certainly do not belong to young Americans. And don't give up your musical autographs without making sure about your future royalties.' (7 March 1921)

Only a day after his arrival in England, Mrs Newmarch had gone on to the offensive about the Eastman School, and many was the time that Sibelius had rued the day he had sent off his YES telegram to Klingenberg. The contact with the world to which he belonged, with the English orchestras and audiences, had helped him to find himself again after the isolation bred by the war years. He slowly began to realize what he had let himself in for. To compose and from time to time conduct was what he was fitted for; to teach at an academic institution would be a living death. To think that he had voluntarily committed himself to academic slavery of a kind that had entrammelled him over twenty years earlier at the Music Institute! Mrs Newmarch had, as it were, taken the words out of his mouth. He drafted a telegram to Klingenberg: 'WILL COME TO AMERICA ONLY AS CONDUCTOR AND NOT THIS YEAR.' Klingenberg replied immediately, 'TERRIBLE FOR ME,' and begged him to reconsider his decision. But by the time his telegram reached London, Sibelius had already left for Norway, so things were left in the air.

Mrs Newmarch also gave him a note for Aino telling her how Sibelius had at the beginning of his visit been upset by the noise and pace of life in London, but now seemed much better: 'I grumble at him at times for smoking and for not taking care of his health, but for the most part I think he has been very sensible during this trip. Wherever he goes, he makes friends.' (6 March 1921) The tone almost suggests an end-of-term report, but when she touches upon the offer from the Eastman School, it is in deadly earnest. 'I hope that your husband does not go to America. I cannot imagine him as a professor or giving lessons. I do not believe that his nerves would survive such a life for as long as a year. Of course, there is always the question of money, but what is the point of money if the consequence is *un homme fini*. I have seen so many artists ruined by America: Dvořák, Safonov and others. Life there is far too hectic and inartistic. Sibelius is a creative artist, possibly the greatest who remains in our world. I am horrified at the thought of him squandering those years he has left to him on teaching. A concert tour is another matter. I am certain that he will be re-engaged here for the next season . . . He is fifty-five now, a critical age in a man's life, and he would have no one to look after him in America.'

As she suggested, Sibelius would have had no Aino or Newmarch to look after him, but in her reference to his 'critical age' there is a possible hint of other dangers and perhaps a hint of jealousy. During his time in London, Sibelius had been seen in the company of the pianist Harriet Cohen, then a young and attractive rising star. Sir Henry Wood used to take Sibelius to Pagani's Restaurant, a meeting place for all who meant something in the musical world. On the walls hung signed photographs of Puccini, Ravel, Elgar, Paderewski and Chaliapin. The proprietor, Signor Meschini, personally looked after his celebrated clients, and the wine waiter Cornacchia became a confidant even in matters other than vintages.

One evening Sibelius was dining at Pagani's with the critic Edwin Evans. At another table sat the twenty-year-old Harriet Cohen with some other young people. Evans, who had taken an interest in her career, introduced them. Harriet Cohen mentioned that she knew a number of his orchestral scores. The composer sounded a little sceptical, but later in one of the restaurant's banqueting rooms she confounded his doubts by playing them both *En saga* from memory. Sibelius asked how it was she came to be drawn to his music. Her grandfather was born in Lithuania (she was of Jewish origin) and that is no more than a stone's throw from Finland. His music, she told him, filled a spiritual vacuum with its special and unusual sound world and she hungered after it. Her profile was at one and the same time childlike and a touch arrogant. The eyes radiated melancholy, her hair was parted in the middle. Sibelius told her that she reminded him of his mother, 'in particular when your hair is parted in that way'. She forbore, one trusts, to compare him to her father.

There is no doubt that Miss Cohen felt a strong affinity with Sibelius's music. She defended the Fifth Symphony against the criticisms of her musical friends and grasped its formal complexities as did few others at the time. 'You are undoubtedly one of the half-dozen people who understand my Fifth Symphony,' he told her. Perhaps he subconsciously grasped the fact that the British public had not really warmed to the piece – in spite of the fact that he had been called back five times to acknowledge the applause. According to Cohen, the work itself had been given a frosty reception.

Harriet Cohen often included his piano music in her recitals – the Sonatinas, Op. 67, the Tree Pieces, Op. 76, and the arrangement of Finnish folk songs – and maintained a correspondence with him in her charming French. 'Little Harriet with her "old-fashioned" hairstyle which you so admired is now *pianiste à vous*. Write something sad, specially for me (Finnische Nocturne). I adore your transcription of *Von Herzn lieb' ich dich*. I embrace you, you dear dear creature. If you go to Paris next year, let me know in time. I will come for a few days so that we can meet.' He was not to compose a *Finnische Nocturne* for her, or anything else for that matter; nor were they ever to meet on foreign soil, either in Paris or any other city. As she herself testifies, it was in Finland that she learnt to know Sibelius best.

Generally speaking, Harriet Cohen seems to have exerted an extraordinary fascination on composers. Sir Arnold Bax composed his masterly *Symphonic Variations* for piano and orchestra for her, and Vaughan Williams his piano concerto. Bartók dedicated his *Six Dances in Bulgarian Rhythm* to her, and she was in contact with the great figures of central Europe: Schoenberg and Hindemith among composers; Schnabel, Scherchen and Furtwängler among interpreters. She tried to interest Schoenberg and Schnabel in the Fourth Symphony – she did not need to bother about Scherchen, who conducted it in Leipzig the following autumn. However, she confessed that it was an uphill struggle: 'But I shall continue to bombard the German positions, which are still dominated by the Mahler–Bruckner line.'

Cohen's enthusiasm for Sibelius as a composer and person was not to diminish with the years. 'My friendship with Sibelius forms part of the very core of my life.'[7] While she was in Scandinavia with Bax and another friend in the early 1930s, they took the boat from Stockholm over to Helsinki. Sibelius set out from Ainola to meet them and they spent the whole day drinking and eating. A year before his death she visited him at Ainola.

During his last few days in London, Sibelius was swept up in a whirlwind of festivities, dinners and lunches. On Tuesday morning he went to the Royal College of Music, where the New Queen's Orchestra played through four English novelties – Pratt, Wilson, Erlebach and van Someren-Godfrey – either under the composers' own direction or that of Adrian Boult. What he made of them is not recorded. Of course Boult himself was to become an impressive Sibelius interpreter, particularly of the tone poems.

On 10 March 1920 the time came to embark at Newcastle for Bergen. Once aboard the SS *Venus* he sent a card to Aino, but as he saw the English coast slowly receding from view he must have felt in good spirits. It was virtually settled that he was to return the following year. Or was he perhaps already attuned to those inner voices to which his diary gives expression: *l'homme propose, Dieu dispose*? His music was to go from strength to strength in England, but he was never to return to witness it at first hand. He was never again to see his old friends Rosa Newmarch, Granville Bantock and Henry Wood or to develop his new friendship with Adrian Boult.

– 2 –

On his arrival in Bergen, Sibelius told the newspaper *Bergens Aftenblad* that he had learnt a great deal from Grieg and that they had much in common, particularly in their feeling for nature – even if Grieg had grown up in spectacular surroundings, the like of which Finland could not match. Sibelius's vitality was undiminished and he threw himself into sightseeing, visiting the Hanseatic museum and the old part of the city. A fiddle player from Vestland visited Sibelius's hotel and played him folk melodies on the Hardanger fiddle, an instrument he had not encountered before. His visitor had often delighted Grieg himself with his playing at Troldhaugen. Now Sibelius realized just how much Grieg owed to the folk musicians of Vestland and the Hardanger fiddle.

The principal work at the open rehearsal which he conducted at the

Harmonium on 20 March and at the concert the following day was the Second Symphony. The second part of the programme was given over to the usual popular numbers, such as *The Swan of Tuonela* and *Finlandia*. *Morgenavisen* wrote of his masterly conducting: 'There were no extravagant gestures. On the contrary, he conducted with economy and grace. With his elegant stick technique and expressive left hand, he succeeded in getting the results he wanted. And the orchestra was responsive to the slightest gesture. There was a precision and finesse that does the orchestra much credit.'

It was a 'great and glorious evening' and it seemed that the ovations would never stop.[8] When the laurel wreath was brought in, Sibelius was momentarily taken aback, for it seemed as if Grieg himself was bearing it. In fact it was Grieg's cousin, the architect Schak Bull, who then led the audience in three loud cheers.

After the concert there was not only a banquet in his honour, but two parties. As the dawn broke, they walked over to Grieg's home, Troldhaugen, where Sibelius laid a wreath. The festivities continued right through the day; there was another farewell banquet, which went on until the night train left for Oslo at 9 o'clock. In the sleeping car Sibelius bumped into a friend from his student years, the painter Segelcke. The two of them spent the whole of the all-night journey standing in the corridor talking loudly, to the annoyance of other passengers, and drinking the whisky Sibelius had brought back from England. Like Finland, Norway suffered from prohibition.

In Oslo itself he spent a good deal of time with the Norwegian writer Knut Hamsun. Their friendship dated back to the 1890s, when Hamsun spent some time in Helsinki. Sibelius admired his charm, wit and breadth of culture, and called him 'a grand seigneur without peer in the Nordic countries'. His three concerts there were given to capacity houses: the first included the First Symphony and the *Song of the Athenians*, but in the others *The Oceanides*, the *Pelléas et Mélisande* suite, *The Swan of Tuonela* and *Finlandia* were all represented. He was received in audience by King Haakon, who also attended the concert the same evening.

On his return to Finland, Sibelius had to face up to the difficulties he had created for himself with the Eastman School. He records his dilemma: 'How can I get out of the American trip? I can't possibly teach now. It would be a disaster for them in Rochester and for me as a composer. I can appreciate Klingenberg's position: that it's terrible for him. But is it any better for me? I don't know enough English. Nor do I play the piano. I have a big reputation, not just in Germany but all over the world. And to give up composing would be suicide.' (Diary, 24 April 1921)

He plucked up his courage and wrote again to Klingenberg: 'I can conduct my own compositions tolerably, but as a teacher – impossible! Besides this there are other reasons. Dear friend, please act accordingly and try to understand my position.'

But Klingenberg was not so easily put off. The last stages in the little drama were played out by telegram:

[3 May 1921] RECEIVED LETTER, NO TEACHING NEEDED – ONLY CRITICISMS OF COMPOSITIONS IN COLLABORATION WITH ME. ENGAGEMENTS IN VIEW WITH MANY OF THE GREATEST ORCHESTRAS. THE ENTIRE MUSICAL PUBLIC EAGERLY AWAITS YOUR ARRIVAL.

[6 May] COMING AS RESULT OF YOUR TELEGRAM. BUY FINNISH MARKS FOR 10,000 DOLLARS, DEPOSIT IN BANK. SIBELIUS.

[8 May] DELIGHTED. SEND PHOTOGRAPHS, PRESS CUTTINGS IMMEDIATELY. KLINGENBERG.

[9 May] HAVE REALIZED COST OF LIVING IN AMERICA. ARRIVAL IMPOSSIBLE. SIBELIUS.

That was the end of the Sibelius–Klingenberg dialogue. Christian Sinding was engaged instead as professor of composition. Two terms later he was replaced by Selim Palmgren.

In the spring of 1921 Busoni paid what was to be his last visit to his homeland. Earlier, during a short visit at the turn of 1919–20, he had been cold-shouldered as pro-German. But 1921 saw him return in triumph and on 1 May an exclusive audience at the San Augusteo in Rome saw what *Il Tempo* described as 'a miraculous metamorphosis: the greatest living pianist transformed into conductor and composer. In Italy we are hardly conscious of the sheer versatility of our country's great son; whereas Germany, on the other hand, is well acquainted with it.' Busoni's Violin Concerto enjoyed moderate success, and was followed by the two orchestral studies for his as yet unfinished opera *Doktor Faust*, which the public did not understand. After the interval came Sibelius's Second Symphony, according to *Il Tempo* not a work that could be easily assimilated at first hearing. Yet the symphony 'with its rich outpouring of invention made a strong impression on the audience, which was particularly taken with the melancholic and poetic nature of Sibelius's muse and his deep feeling for nature'. Busoni's interpretation was 'serene yet full of dramatic power', and he received a tremendous ovation. This was the first performance of the Second Symphony in Italy. Hans Joachim Moser in Breitkopf & Härtel's *Sibelius-Mitteilungen* No. 8 (July 1964) erroneously states that the symphony was performed by Toscanini at the Teatro alla Scala on 23 April 1907 and was also included in Toscanini's tour with the Turin Orchestra in 1905. The symphony was advertised for the Turin Orchestra's concert on 11 May 1904 but was for some reason replaced by Borodin's Second and Sibelius was represented by *Finlandia*. Toscanini had, however, conducted a number of Sibelius tone poems in Northern Italy, mainly in Turin and Milan, during the period 1903–8 and had taken up *En Saga* and *Finlandia* again in 1918. Sibelius had also been represented in Rome, where Georg Schnéevoigt had conducted *En Saga* in 1910 and the First Symphony in 1914. *The Swan of Tuonela* had been conducted by, among others, Molinari in 1915 and Victor de Sabata (January 1921). After his success at the Augusteo in 1916 with *En Saga*, Toscanini had programmed in November of the same year the Funeral March from *Götterdämmerung* and as the final number *Finlandia,* but the latter had to wait.

Sibelius again did not have much peace during the early summer. In 1919 there had been the Nordic Music Festival in Copenhagen and the following year the Finnish Fair in Helsinki had eaten into his time. Now it was Finland's turn to host the Nordic Music Festival – not perhaps an ideal time, since the dispute between Finland and Sweden over the Åland islands had not been settled. Feelings ran high, even among musicians, and the more zealous nationalists among the Finns, such as the composer Yrjö Kilpinen and conductor Heikki Klemetti, were opposed to the event being held at this time. That it went ahead at all was due, as so often, to the good offices of Robert Kajanus.

The opening concert was devoted to the music of the host country and began with *Lemminkäinen's Homeward Journey,* which Sibelius conducted himself. It is obvious from the programme that nothing had been learnt from the débâcle in Paris the previous year. Apart from the Sibelius, there was Madetoja's Second Symphony, Palmgren's Second Piano Concerto *(The River),* and Kuula's *Orjan poika (The Slave's Son).* As if that wasn't enough, there were pieces by Melartin and von Kothen and Kajanus's tone poem *Aino!* The critic Evert Katila, in a generally ill-tempered review, reproached Sibelius for allowing himself so obvious a final number as *Lemminkäinen's Homeward Journey* at the beginning of a concert.

At the other concerts during the festival Denmark was represented by Nielsen's *Hymnus amoris,* Norway by Svendsen's Second Symphony and Sweden by Alfvén's Fourth Symphony *(Havsbandet)* and Stenhammar's Second Piano Concerto. The final programme was an all-Sibelius concert which the composer himself conducted. But the music days left an unpleasant taste in his mouth. 'The Nordic Music Festival was launched as if it were on Olympus. I was forced to start but was not on good form. Perhaps the whole thing was meant to show me in a bad light. It will spoil the whole summer. But *nous verrons.*' (Diary, 2 June 1921)

Perhaps '*nous verrons*' was his way of taking a grip on things. To follow Mrs Newmarch's call '*Au diable les dollars!*' was more easily said than done, particularly when his financial affairs were in such disarray. On the contrary, the whole Eastman affair seems to have reduced him to nervous exhaustion. He had turned down $20,000 flat as well as the enticing prospect of making a career for himself as composer–conductor on the other side of the Atlantic. But he was now gripped by an *idée fixe* that having done so, it was incumbent on him for the sake of his wife and children to make good the loss by producing a whole flood of new miniatures. Or was this perhaps a subterfuge to conceal the fact that he was not in the right state of mind to fulfil Mrs Newmarch's other exhortation to get on with the Sixth Symphony? In his mood of despair he succumbed ever more freely to stimulants. The cigar smoke grew ever thicker in his study and his intake of whisky mounted.

During the summer of 1921 he offered a range of second and third-class works to various publishers throughout the world. For Chappells he composed his *Suite mignonne*, Op. 98, and sent it off to London at the end of June via Rosa Newmarch. At first Chappell refused to take the *Suite*, but later changed their minds, probably after pressure from Mrs Newmarch, and paid Sibelius £200 – at that time the equivalent of 52,000 Fmks. His relations with Breitkopf & Härtel remained warm, in spite of the fact that they had rejected the Fifth Symphony on rather feeble economic grounds. Frederic Lamond, whom they had engaged to prepare a new edition of the Beethoven sonatas and who had met Busoni and possibly also Sibelius in London earlier in the year, mentioned Busoni's pleasure at renewing old memories of his times in Finland. And in July Breitkopf wrote to Sibelius offering to double his royalties, so that instead of receiving 80 Reichsmarks for an edition of *Valse triste* he would now get 160 Reichsmarks. For the three newly-published editions he thus received all of 480 marks!

Emboldened none the less by this development, Sibelius offered his *Promotionsmarsch (Academic March)* from 1919, to which he had temporarily assigned the opus number 91b. There is no mistaking the warmth of Breitkopf's response, and their pleasure that he had turned to his old publisher. However, in view of increasing production costs, combined with the exceptional obstacles in the way of placing such occasional pieces, they asked whether he would agree to postpone both its publication and his payment.

Sibelius felt his back was up against the wall. 'My loan at Handelsbanken has to be repaid on 30 January 1922. Am completely at my wits' end. Lost an important letter from a concert agency in Germany with an offer of engagement. And more bad news. Aino is ill – dreadful cough. And that poor creature suffers. Breitkopf have rejected the *Promotionsmarsch*. Ditto from England *(Suite mignonne)*. *Sic itur!* Things are not easy for me at present.' (Diary, 2 August 1921) Fortunately Wilhelm Hansen came to the rescue and bought the piece for 500 Danish crowns though they did not publish it, as it was not a commercially viable proposition. There is some confusion here, since the piece was called *Festive March*.

At the end of summer, Hermann Scherchen conducted the Fourth Symphony in Leipzig with the Grotrian-Steinweg Orchestra. Scherchen's choice of programme was bold and unconventional, and on this occasion he included Palmgren's *Metamorphoses* along with the Sibelius in the first half and devoted the second to Tchaikovsky's *Symphonie pathétique*. His planning paid off, for the concert was well attended and the reviews were appreciative; some consolation for the composer after the hostile press which greeted the 1916 Berlin première under Oskar Fried. The *Leipziger Zeitung* wrote: 'First came Sibelius with his A minor Symphony, a rhapsodic presentation of Nordic melancholy tinged with dark and expressive feeling, with many interesting and resourceful sonorities. The foreign colouring, the rhythmic freedom, the compelling performance . . . spoke strongly for the work, whose beauty Scherchen unfolded for the public with great sympathy. The *Leipziger Volks-Zeitung* was hardly less enthusiastic: 'The severe, dark atmosphere is pervasive, fully attuned with the Nordic sensibility and feeling for nature'.

At home, however, despite the glorious weather, autumn was beginning on a melancholy note. Katarina was preparing for her journey to Stuttgart, where she was to continue her piano studies under Max Pauer. Sibelius was visibly upset: 'Kaj is preparing for Stuttgart – my hand trembles so much nowadays that it is difficult to write and impossible to conduct. What hell! Margareta and Heidi have whooping cough.' Katarina went via Berlin, where Adolf Paul met her train. Before continuing her journey she played some of her father's pieces on Paul's piano. Once installed in Stuttgart, Katarina wrote home to her mother, and one can perhaps sense a hint of jealousy in Sibelius's diary entry: 'To me the glorious girl does not write. Perhaps she thought me cold when we parted. But I didn't want to show her how upset I was. And anxious. She is now beginning her own life. Youth – new music – begins to get under way. New ideas and invention. Now that I have turned my back on everything – America and all the invitations to conduct – I will have to take the consequences.' (Diary, 7 October 1921)

Even if the tremor worried him, it did not prevent him from conducting some weeks later, nor from working on the *Valse chevaleresque* instead of making further inroads into the Sixth Symphony. On the other hand, he perhaps sensed that by drawing a line under the past he stood on the threshold of a new creative period. After the inauguration of the Swedish Academy in Åbo two years previously, there was pressure to found a Finnish equivalent. For this Sibelius had composed his *Jordens Sång*; as a national figure he naturally had to be (and indeed wanted to be) even-handed in these matters. In Helsinki he went on a spree with friends he had made at the Finnish university meeting: 'I shall steer clear of these "friends" in the future. I am always too late in realizing how empty and provincial they are. Always the same old story.' (Diary, 17 October 1921)

On 1 November he conducted some festive works at the university, including *Night Ride and Sunrise*. In his diary he discusses the orchestra in much the same terms as he thought of Kajanus at the Copenhagen Festival: 'The orchestra consists of two elements, one for me and the other against. The latter are directly unmannerly, in particular [the solo cellist] Fohström.

Shall I swallow my pride and go along with this or shall I force a confronta-
tion? The former is probably wiser since my pieces can hardly be conducted
by anyone else on this occasion where the waltzes are concerned. Am
nervous – no, hyper-nervous! Always the same when people are hounding
me.'

In Berlin, Busoni had decided, despite his failing health, to resume his
New Music concerts with the Philharmonic Orchestra that had enjoyed
such celebrity from 1902 to 1909. Their return on 2 November was greeted
with great enthusiasm in the press, and in the first concert he struck a blow
for Sibelius, whose Fifth Symphony was in fact the only novelty on the
programme. The rest of the programme consisted of Busoni's own
arrangement of a concert suite from Mozart's *Idomeneo*, a set of Monteverdi
madrigals, and finally another symphony in E flat, the *Eroica*. Karl Krebs in
Der Tag spoke of the Fifth Symphony as one of the most impressive musical
experiences he had had for a long time. 'The work is more fantasy than
symphony, completely free in its formal shape, without being bound to the
usual conventions of symphonic thinking. Sibelius clings to his dreams, sings
to himself, nobly and sensitively, without any striving for effect.' Otto
Taubmann in *Berliner Börsen-Courier* was hardly less welcoming, and noted
that once again the public who flocked to the concert were well rewarded
for their trust in Busoni, 'even if his skill with the baton does not match his
virtuosity at the keyboard'. Taubmann predicted that the Sibelius symphony
would rapidly establish itself in the repertoire. In *National-Zeitung* Siegmund
Pisling – who had studied with Sibelius's own teacher in Vienna, Robert
Fuchs – discussed Leichtentritt's programme notes, which emphasized how
the first movement grows from one basic rhythmic pattern, and wondered
whether the composer wholly escapes the charge of monotony. However,
the overall tenor of the review is positive: it was clearly something of a coup
to begin with this strongly profiled, sensitive and revealing work.

The generally positive tone of the press shows that it would not have
been impossible for Sibelius to have made headway in Berlin in the 1920s.
One could say the same for Mahler, whose First Symphony had been performed under Furtwängler only a few days before. One can only imagine
the effect the Fifth Symphony would have had on Berlin audiences had it
enjoyed the advocacy of a Furtwängler or a Bruno Walter, both of whom
later expressed interest in the Seventh Symphony. With Mahler there were
other factors, but as far as Sibelius was concerned, the highly individual and
subtle mode of motivic growth, his organic musical syntax and the Nordic
feel to his musical language proved an obstacle for the Berliners.

Because of his duties as a theatre critic, Adolf Paul was unable to attend
the actual concert, but he went to the rehearsal and sent Sibelius his impressions: 'Yesterday I heard your striking and magnificent Fifth Symphony
under Busoni. His mastery is enormously developed, he conducted like a
god, each phrase was shaped with plasticity, the textures were as transparent

as crystal and had a magnificent *schwungvoll*. After the rehearsal he came up to me and said, "*Nun hast du wieder ein bisschen von unserer Helsingfors-Zeit zu hören bekommen!*"And that was exactly the right expression. He looked young again and played with the old love and inspiration he had always had for you in the old days – just like you when you played me *King Christian*. Dear friend, thank you for this beautiful work and thank God the father who sent it you.'

A week later Busoni wrote to Paul thanking him for his loyalty and his appreciative words:

> Once again it has fallen to me to help Sibelius a step forward on his path (even though this ought not to be necessary! But such are the ways of the world!) and I am glad that everything went so well. I hope you have given him your impressions of the occasion (would really like to know what he makes of this act of devotion; he is so complex and difficult to make out, and our relationship remains one-sided).
>
> They are all the same. I know their work but none of them knows mine. I think highly of the Fifth Symphony. The Fourth is closer to my heart. The Third I don't know. The Second I performed last April [actually 1 May] in Rome. In spite of our affectionate dealings, he never seems quite at ease with me and there is at the same time a childish, ingratiating manner which makes me feel awkward. I met him last in London in February. All the same I am very fond of him. (10 November 1921)

Paul quoted this part of Busoni's letter when he next wrote to Sibelius.

In his generally depressed state Busoni was piling on new and imagined injuries. Deep down he must have realized that his feelings of comradeship and affection for Sibelius were by no means one-sided but warmly and fully reciprocated. But with his sharp intuition he discerned what lay behind the occasional uneasiness and the 'childishly ingratiating manner'. It is as if he sensed behind the compliments the feelings Sibelius had confided to his diary ten years earlier: 'Why does this great artist have to compose?' But at the moment that was the only thing Busoni wanted to do. Instead, after his orchestral concert in Berlin he had to play six Mozart piano concertos and then go on tour to Paris and London. *Doktor Faust* had to wait.

> [10 November 1921] As you know, Busoni has always been like that – doesn't feel at ease and has to put on an act. He was like that even when he was young. That one must take in one's stride . . . Cut through the ice, and there is a warm and unaffected nature with a heart of gold. Write immediately and send him a few friendly lines.

Sibelius already knew that Busoni had scored a success with the Fifth Symphony and had been greeted with 'magnificent reviews'. He lost no time in writing to him: 'I thank you from the bottom of my heart. Paul has written, captivated by your performance. Without you the symphony had remained paper and I an apparition from the forest.' (20 November 1921) This was to be the last time Busoni stood before an orchestra; his new Busoni cycle ended where it began. And fate decreed that Sibelius's letter was the last in their correspondence.

Max Pauer, Katarina's piano professor, managed to spike Sibelius's delight at the success of Busoni's concert by showing her what Sibelius found to be 'a less than appealing review in a Berlin paper concerning the Fifth Symphony. Did he think he would please her by this? Perhaps he thought it was good enough for me.' (Diary, 30 November 1921) He was still a bit worried about Katarina and whether she would be happy staying with her cousin Eva Järnefelt, Armas's daughter by his first marriage: 'They are so unlike each other.'

Sibelius had thought to tempt Chappell with a new Suite (17 November 1921). Instead, he pressed ahead with his *Valse chevaleresque*. The first draft did not satisfy him, however. 'Charming, isn't it, that it has taken so long. Is it some kind of omen?' (Diary, 28 November 1921) He decided to revise it: 'My usual fate!' (Diary, 30 November 1921) He worked through the night until the crack of dawn, congratulating himself in his diary on being still young! A little later on he sent the piece to Chappell, who turned it down immediately.

On 2 December he went into Helsinki for Kajanus's sixty-fifth birthday celebrations. These festivities began to take their toll on his health: '*Sic itur* – another spree. Influenza etc . . . And now in an hour, I shall be fifty-six. And there's nothing one can do about it. The future looks bleak. How I love life and yet how difficult it is to live it. How often I've written that!' Indeed, how often had he written of life's difficulties – certainly more often than of his love for it!

Sibelius often spoke of his brother Christian as having 'radiance'. But for his daughters so had he. They remember him as having a generally sunny temperament and being often high-spirited. He was perhaps more tolerant of their small misdemeanours and transgressions than Aino, whose strict ethical code made her less indulgent. The year's end found him in better spirits. The Christmas celebrations cheered him and his success in Norway earlier in the year had brought further recognition in the form of an honour: he was made a Commendeur of the Order of St Olaf (First Class).

CHAPTER FOURTEEN

1922 and a New Symphony

The church bells rang in a year that was to end well for Sibelius. True, at first everything seemed to be going wrong. Chappell had turned down *Valse chevaleresque*. He had run up alarming bills over Christmas, and there was nothing in the bank to meet them. Christmas had taken its toll on Aino too, and he was pained to see how she was forced to work making clothes for Margareta, who had to be kitted out for her new school in Helsinki. 'I am without money and my nerves are in tatters. We must buy wood. Night is falling.' In the end it was Aino who had to pay for the wood from her own savings.

Yet even though it pained him to send Margareta away, his spirits were soon back to normal, and there is even a touch of black humour in his next diary entry: 'Am planning new works and am in a good mood. Wonderful Jean Sibelius! Everything is becoming clearer. I shall have to put an end to it all! On the veranda? Hope they'll clean up the mess properly afterwards!' (Diary, 10 January 1922) During this period he composed an unaccompanied chorus, *Likhet (Resemblance)* for male quartet, a setting of Runeberg's poem *Liknelse* for the Musices Amantes in Åbo. 'A male quartet in the good old style – that's always appealed to me – its pathos,' he wrote in his diary of 22 January. But the conductor was slow to respond, which occasioned an outburst some days later. 'Karsten obviously doesn't like it. But these dilettantes can never see further than their noses. Let them stew in their own juice, these home-grown choryphés. Why should you bother with them, arrogant and stupid as they are!' (Diary, 29 January 1922) His honorarium arrived in due course.

On 10 January he had offered the *Valse chevaleresque* to Wilhelm Hansen for 2,000 Danish crowns: 'Perhaps I am completely off my head in sending them something so light. But it's good of its kind.' (Diary, 10 January 1922) Hansen countered by offering half that sum. 'It's a tenth of what I asked from England. Unfortunately I have to take it.' (Diary, 24 January 1922) He felt he had to 'keep Aino out of the picture. At fifty-six I have to be man enough to look the facts in the face. If only my nerves were in better shape. It all prevents me from getting on with composition, these terrible problems.' (Diary, 30 January 1922).

Aino regarded the *Valse chevaleresque* as a symbol of the dissipated Sibelius who spent hours at the Kämp drinking champagne. She loathed the piece. Naturally, as with all well-laid plans, things went awry. Aino discovered the terms of Hansen's offer when Katarina's piano teacher told her, in all innocence, the contents of Hansen's telegram. Aino was inconsolable. Not content with demeaning his talents by composing such rubbish, he had then sold it for a pittance. Sibelius tried to look at it realistically. 'The offer is all right by present-day standards. If I refuse it, I shall also lose this source of income. All this is dreadful. Writing this piece has been torture – I thought myself and persuaded Aino to believe that it would be a goldmine – and now this! Worst of all, the atmosphere at home will be dreadful for a long time to come. And I am forced to live and work here in all this.' (Diary, 5 February 1922)

Sibelius's own spirits plunged down and then soared upwards:

[12 February 1922] I must get a grip on myself. I am beginning to be afraid of fate. What will become of the family? Destitution and misery. My health is getting worse – I can't deny that.

[13 February] The day is wonderful. Sunny and mild. Spring is in the air. How the times have changed. Aino and the children have gone skiing. Wonderful day. Have thought how difficult it must be to be married to a Sibelius. Probably the same for mamma and grandmother. And perhaps it was no easier for their ancestors either. And so on and so on. But there is something that drives us onwards. Since that is what the family has done.

Now that the war was over, international artists such as Edwin Fischer, Claudio Arrau and Wilhelm Kempff were able to come to Helsinki. In February Kempff, then aged twenty-six, gave a recital in Helsinki. At his début in the Finnish capital two years earlier he had ended his programme with an improvisation on a theme of Sibelius that had been handed to him in an envelope. His improvisation had ended with a four-part fugue. Bis spoke of it in rhapsodic terms 'as recalling the days of Liszt's concerts in St Petersburg, when he improvised on a Finnish folksong' and he compared the young Kempff with Reisenauer, d'Albert, Bülow and both Anton and Nicolai Rubinstein.

Sibelius was not present either on that occasion or on his countless subsequent appearances, and it was left to Aino to bring the theme into town. The eighty-two-year-old Kempff spoke to me of Sibelius's absence from his recitals as if it were the most natural thing in the world. Instead, after his first visit on 19 January 1922, Kempff became a regular visitor to Ainola. Sibelius's diary records the evening a couple of days later: 'The day before yesterday Wilhelm Kempff was here for dinner with Ilmari Hannikainen and Martha Tornell. He played Bach unforgettably. He has all the attributes of a great artist.'

Sibelius measured pianists by one exalted yardstick: Ferruccio Busoni, who stood head and shoulders above all the others. Now another pianist of genius came into his life, whose playing, like Busoni's, was distinguished by a creative dimension. At the age of sixteen Kempff had played part of an opera he had composed to Busoni, who had spoken warmly of his talent. In old age Kempff spoke of his creative gifts with extraordinary modesty, maintaining that he had composed so as to understand better the workings of the creative mind and thus deepen his understanding of the great masters. It was this creative aspect of Busoni's and Kempff's interpretative genius that fascinated Sibelius. Backhaus, on the other hand, lacked this imaginative power and had no appeal for him. At this stage in his career, Kempff was more disposed towards the virtuoso repertoire than in later years, and during the 1920s he offered the Helsinki public Liszt transcriptions, including those of the Bach Organ Fantasia and Fugue, as well as the Brahms Paganini variations. But one of the great peaks in the recital repertoire that he brought to Helsinki was Beethoven's Op. 111 Sonata. Sibelius listened with awe to his subtle and profound interpretations of the central repertoire, Beethoven, Schubert and Schumann, and must have hoped that one day he might include the F sharp minor Sonatina, Op. 67, the pearl in his piano output, in his repertoire. This he eventually did.[1]

Sibelius didn't give up hope with Chappell, but decided to offer them a new 'suite' – this time the *Suite champêtre*. Chappell returned it with some 'tart comments'. In a way Sibelius felt relieved, and he decided that 'the suite should be put on one side. It was not worthy of Jean Sibelius. How I am going to manage for money, God only knows. Aino suggested that we sell some pictures. But they are all presents and so that's not possible.' (Diary, 25 March 1922) However, he decided he couldn't afford to destroy the Suite. In the end he offered it to Wilhelm Hansen, who bought it in April. Sibelius tried to pacify his conscience: 'No changes in the piece . . . But then of its kind it is good enough.' (Diary, 10 April 1922) This was the same kind of argument he had advanced for the *Valse chevaleresque* and it hoodwinked no one, neither Aino nor him. But he goes on: 'My health is not good, nor am I spiritually. Aino is down, very down!'

At about this time Wilhelm Hansen wrote (13 March 1922) to ask Sibelius whether he had ever considered writing a piano concerto. Sibelius answered immediately: 'I have often thought of writing a piano concerto and have been urged to do so on countless occasions – by among others Busoni. But it has always seemed to me that the world wants a piano concerto à la Tchaikovffsky [*sic*] or Grieg, but not one of *meine Wenigkeit*. All the same, I shall give the matter serious thought. I am certainly interested.' (18 March 1922)

But four days later he had second thoughts: 'I must take back my words about writing a piano concerto, partly because I am to a greater extent than ever a slave of my ideas so that I can no longer write what I want, but what I must. Thus, no promise but a hope.' (22 March 1922)

The most virtuosic piano part he had ever written was the accompaniment to *Malinconia* for cello. Even so, he had soon succumbed to clichés, not so much in the ideas themselves but in their keyboard layout. Perhaps the reason for this was that he himself did not possess a sufficiently advanced piano technique, and was therefore not in a position to write in a way that would carry the imprint of his personal style. Or even more likely is the fact that the quality of his musical inspiration itself was essentially and idiomatically orchestral, and ill-suited for the keyboard. It is after all one thing to write piano sonatinas of an intimate character with themes that might possibly have worked in a string quartet, but altogether another to write a virtuoso solo part. Even the glimmer of hope that he had held out to Hansen in an unguarded moment vanished in the bright light of day. Yet his very last set of pieces from the 1920s, the *Cinq Esquisses*, Op. 114, bear witness to a pianistic style of greater depth, richness of colour and sonority than before.

In haphazard fashion he continued to make contact with foreign publishers. He tried to place a set of *Six morceaux* (Op. 99) for the piano with Joseph Williams in London – to no avail. They were later published by Fazer in Helsinki. He also put out feelers to the firm of Carl Fischer in New York for a brand-new *Suite caractéristique*, but with similarly disappointing results. All this shadow-boxing with various publishers induced bouts of deep depression: 'My financial position is appalling. Naïve to have imagined that I could go on producing piece after piece that would bring in money – in other words to be able to live off composing. Think what you need to have behind you if you do . . . I don't seem to be able to compose and compose. My interest is waning. Difficult for me to conduct, as no one seems to believe in my powers as a conductor apart from me. Bitterly regret having turned down America, but I couldn't take it. I don't want to say anything about the reasons.' (Diary, 23 February 1922)

It goes without saying that when he speaks of not being able 'to compose and compose', he means turning out a stream of potboilers while at the same time trying to work at his symphonies. His feeling of being undervalued as a conductor may have some foundation – at least in his own country. Yet the occasional snide remark in the press or the odd murmur at rehearsal could not disguise the fact that Sir Henry Wood had asked him to conduct five times in London and that Sibelius himself rehearsed everything with the sole exception of the Fifth Symphony, on which Sir Henry had done some preliminary work.

What were the real reasons that decided him against taking the Eastman offer? His diary annotation, 'to give up composition would be suicidal,' points us in the right direction without giving the complete answer. He was not to know that his friend Busoni was in an even more desperate position than he himself. Busoni's friends realized that his health was failing and financial ruin was beckoning, and urged him to accept a splendid offer from the Argentine. But this he turned down, saying, 'I am not a commercial traveller peddling performances of *La Campanella*.' He did not give the real reason to anyone – namely that his real goal was the completion of *Doktor Faust*. Doubtless his wife suspected it, just as Aino realized what it was that kept Sibelius in Finland. Yet what a career he could have made in America as a composer-conductor!

The Fifth Symphony had set out on its triumphant progress when Stokowski premièred it with the Philadelphia Orchestra in October 1921. *Musical America* thought that the Sibelius symphony had 'struck a dour and somber tone . . . Save for a paradoxically brooding allegro in the [finale], virtually the entire work is written in slow tempi. Although by no means wanting in melody, the most obvious themes are distinctly without charm and the prevalent gauntness is accentuated by stentorian passages for the brass that can scarcely be called aught but intentionally unbeautiful.'

Three weeks later, on 10 November, it reached New York, where Joseph Stransky conducted it at the Philharmonic Society. Stransky had not enjoyed a great success with the Third Symphony and *The Oceanides*. But in the *New York Times* Richard Aldrich noted that the Fifth was more acces- sible to the public and more human in its quality than 'the problematic Fourth,' which had only been taken up once after its first performance. 'Its themes are mostly of a more obviously melodious kind; the orchestral colouring is richer and warmer; yet there is something elusive in its quality, in its manner of statement, in the abruptness of some of its contours. There is also a certain lack of contrast in the first three move- ments that does not help the total effect of the composition. But at all events Sibelius has made no excursions into the fields of modern dissonance for its own sake; nor has he abandoned the older idea of melody as something out of which to develop a musical structure. . . . He is a singular figure in modern music, standing by himself, a member of no school, uninfluenced and uninfluencing.'

On 7 April 1922 Pierre Monteux introduced the Fifth to Boston, though he was scarcely intent on building on the Sibelius tradition founded in Symphony Hall by Gericke and Karl Muck. On the contrary, he had some- what reluctantly been persuaded to take it on. Even if he agreed that it deserved to be played, he was fearful of the public reaction and for that reason exaggerated the difficulties and additional rehearsals it would re- quire. Monteux's fears were legitimate in that the 'bewildering Fourth Symphony' had damaged Sibelius's name even in Boston. But all his fears proved groundless. The public was keen to hear the new piece, which was placed at the beginning of the programme, heard attentively and applauded enthusiastically. The *Boston Evening Transcript* gave much space to the new symphony under the following headline: 'Signs, Wonders and New Music of Sibelius. His Fifth Symphony for the First Time in Charac- teristic Manner and Procedure, in New Birth of Beauty, in Final Glow of Power – A Masterpiece (as It Seemed) Revealed' (8 April 1922):

He belongs to no school, like all and sundry in Paris, like the camps of Strauss and of Schoenberg in Germany and Austria . . . no one has quite plausibly traced his antecedents as though to say that there he noted a manner and there he learned a method. Out of the failure of these cataloguing devices has come the custom to define Sibelius by Finland. This or that in his music, we are told, reflects Finnish air and lights, Finnish lakes and forests. It is an easy critical device to attribute a poet, a painter, a composer to his environment . . . Yet as a man thinks and feels in himself by himself for himself, so shall he make music . . . The secret of creation, the mainspring thereof is individuality. It abounds – and it limits – in Sibelius as, perhaps, in no other composer of our time. By it, assuredly, he has ascended to [a] unique place in twentieth-century music.

Henry T. Parker's enthusiastic review developed into a long essay whose views in some respects foreshadow those of Cecil Gray, Constant Lambert and Gerald Abraham. In terms of column-inches, it was almost a metre in length, and came into Sibelius's hands at the end of April. But as his diary shows, instead of being borne aloft by its tide of praise, he was completely blown off course by a misunderstanding. 'According to the critic in *Boston Evening Transcript* Siloti among others has been intriguing against the Fifth Symphony. But the symphony had a great success and the public was delighted. That is as it should be – all honour to it. But it is a stop on the way to my Golgotha.' (Diary, 27 February 1922)

The reference to Siloti was prompted by a complete misunderstanding. Sibelius himself, perhaps with the help of family and friends, had tried to translate Parker's singularly complex English, which clearly posed problems for them. In the review Parker says: 'Even in the chatter of the intermission where Mr Siloti occasionally *displaced domestic gossip* [my italics], there was no grouching over Sibelius . . .' Sibelius misread this as 'Siloti dispersed [or dispensed] domestic gossip about him', rather than his silencing the gossip in the concert hall. He was fearful that this had contributed to the negative attitude which Monteux and others had shown. It needed no more than that to turn the triumph into ashes, to transform a brilliant review on his way to Parnassus to a milestone on his path to Golgotha.

No doubt his lonely struggles with the Sixth Symphony were consuming him, and the whisky that he was taking 'to fight off possible symptoms of influenza' helped to cloud his judgement. 'There is something to be said for everything. Working on bread-and-butter music. We'll see how things turn out. The new work is forcing its way out and I am not happy about it. Frightened of a stroke. I don't mean a blow in the face – those I can deal with – but in the body. Still have much, indeed a lot, to say. We live in a time when everyone looks to the past. I'm just as good as they were. As for Beethoven, my orchestration is better than his and my themes are better. But he was born in a wine country, I in a land where yoghurt rules the roost.'

Not that he disliked the various yoghurts or sour milk that were a staple diet in Scandinavia. Did he not realize that something miraculous had occurred, and that his goal had been achieved? The critical bastions in London, Philadelphia, New York, Boston – and for the time being Berlin – had been overcome. He had become (to quote his diary) more than 'just a representative figure in one's own region' but had established a name for himself as an international figure in post-war Europe and America.

– 2 –

A dark thread was woven into life's pattern. For some time now his brother Christian had lost colour, and his subdued spirits and growing weakness had worried Sibelius. In May 1922 his worst fears were confirmed. 'Kitti's doctor told me today that his condition is incurable. It is only a matter of time. What this means to me is impossible to put into words. Once again one is confronted by an inexorable fate.' Christian suffered from a slowly spreading pernicious anaemia and nothing could be done to save him. Liver transplants and similar therapy lay a long way in the future.

As had been the case with Carpelan, Sibelius could not bring himself to believe that his brother would die before him. Christian was at the height of his career. He was Finland's leading psychiatrist and the previous year had been elected chairman of the Finnish Academy of Sciences. But Christian never overawed his famous brother in the way that, say, the Järnefelts and Busoni could. One wonders why Sibelius did not involve his brother, who was as near professional a cellist as makes no difference, more in his creative world.[2] Perhaps the reasons were purely practical, for the demands on Christian's time were legion. The brothers were close in spirit and their intimacy often unspoken. Sibelius could sit down at the piano in Christian's home and play some new work, and would sense Christian's response without the need for it to be articulated. With Carpelan it was another matter. He had come to know him relatively late in life and Carpelan completely steeped himself in Sibelius's creative problems.

While his brother's condition weighed heavily on him, his anxieties concerning his daughter Katarina must have seemed trivial. According to her older sister, she had become completely dispirited by her cousin Eva Järnefelt, who 'bullies her in all manner of ways'. 'Kaj has to go through all the travails I went through in the 1890s, when Kajanus and his friends were on top. I was, or rather my compositions were, a thorn in their side at the time.'

On 12 May *Scaramouche* at last received its première at the Royal Theatre, Copenhagen. The conductor was Georg Hoeberg, while Johannes Poulsen directed the performance and also played the title role. Contrary to Wilhelm Hansen's assurances, spoken dialogue had been used. Sibelius's worst fears were confirmed. The three elements of words, music and dance produced no new *Gesamtkunstwerk*. The *Berlingske Tidende* thought that you could call *Scaramouche* 'either a mimed drama or a music drama, depending on whether one set greater store by the action or the music'. But spoken dialogue was 'strictly speaking totally out of place'. Like Sibelius himself, their critic thought the action too heavily reliant on Schnitzler's *Pierrette's Veil*, save for the fact that the effects were cruder. 'The inspiring element of the performance, which justified the enterprise, was and remained the music.' The main theme of *Scaramouche* is 'music's suggestive power' over the human psyche. Sibelius's score is 'rich in invention, of radiant fantasy and an unaffected, heart-warming lyricism. With a small orchestra . . . he achieves the greatest effect. A masterpiece from beginning to end.' And the critic of *Politiken* waxed no less lyrical.

With Bakst, Larionov and Picasso as models, the painter Kay Nielsen made a strong and individual impression with the sets. Johannes Poulsen's direction was predominantly taut and unfussy, and as Scaramouche he successfully projected the Pan-demonic elements in the character. Blondelaine was brilliantly danced by the young Norwegian ballerina Lillebil Ibsen, who during the war years had been one of Max Reinhardt's leading dancers in Berlin.

Sibelius noted the success of *Scaramouche* in Copenhagen with satisfaction in his diary of 22 May. Later the following year, in November 1923, one of the directors of Wilhelm Hansen tried to interest Diaghilev in putting it on in Paris, and sent him the score. Diaghilev replied encouragingly that he knew Sibelius's music; the composer himself then wrote to the great impresario via Hansen. Unfortunately, nothing came of the idea. *Scaramouche* was put on in Oslo towards the end of 1923. Wilhelm Kempff, who happened to be playing in the Norwegian capital at the time, managed to see it and wrote to the composer the following day: 'Yesterday I went to see *Scaramouche* (with Lillebil Ibsen) and was enchanted by your music. Everything is so original and yet seems so natural. That is how it should be. *Scaramouche* has also made a great impression on my friends.' (12 December 1923)

Sibelius bore the spring and early summer of 1922 with a heavy heart. 'Christian is very bad. He won't recover from this illness. How grievously sad this makes me. Beloved brother! Today a perfect summer day. But my life is full of continued anxiety for Kitti.' His hands were trembling more than usual, which he attributed to what was in fact a trivial problem with a publisher that he had blown up to outsize proportions. Walter von Konow came and spent several days at Ainola, and they enjoyed each other's company.

In dire straits, Sibelius added two additional numbers – the *Petite Valse* (later renamed *Moment de Valse*) and *Petite Marche* – to his set of six pieces, Op. 99, and offered the lot to Joseph Williams in London. He felt he had been humiliated even before sending off the set. The publisher must have turned down the whole opus, as Sibelius finally sold them to Fazer. So he began work on his *Suite caractéristique* for Carl Fischer in New York. 'Then', he wrote, 'on to my real work.'

At the turn of the month came a letter from Adolf Paul: 'Dear friend, what you told me about your brother gave me great pain. I have always been so fond of him ever since our days at the Music Institute. I do not forget his cello playing, whose tone sings even now in my ears.' On 2 July Christian died. Sibelius's grief weighed heavily on him and Christian's passing left a terrible sense of emptiness. On his deathbed, according to his letter to Paul, Sibelius had played him the Elegy from the *King Christian II* suite. Paul hastened to send a letter of condolence and promised to pass on the sad news to Busoni. On his gravestone his colleagues inscribed the sentence, 'He kindled a light in the world of ideas', which must have struck a responsive chord in Sibelius, who always spoke of him in similar terms.

Sibelius continued his struggle to keep afloat. On 13 July he took out a loan of 10,000 marks to be repayable four months later. 'At last the suite, the little suite, is ready. The weather is cold – no summer – i.e. we've had this year one winter without snow and another with . . . If only I could win some freedom without having to do these appalling – as Gallén calls them – bread-canvases.' (Diary, 8 August 1922) By September, only two months later, he had already run out of money: 'Working on small pieces – my bigger plans will never be realized. Life like this is impossible artistically as well as financially. If only I could see a way out. But I am up to my ears in debt and, when I'm forced to compose, ideas simply don't come.' (Diary, 5 September 1922)

Early in September he finished a *Novelette*, Op. 102, No. 1, for violin and piano. He had hoped to be able to sell it to Fazer 'so as to buy some breathing space, i.e. pay off the most pressing debts'. But Fazer wouldn't take it and Sibelius sent the piece to Wilhelm Hansen, announcing his intention 'to offer a number of similar pieces under this opus number. Decide the honorarium yourself.' Hansen bought the piece for 300 Danish crowns, but Sibelius did not follow up the *Novelette* with any companions.

At about this time the composer Ernest Pingoud, who was to orchestrate some of Sibelius's songs during the 1940s, was developing an active career as a music critic. After his study years in Leipzig and Petrograd, he joined a group of like-minded Swedish-speaking radicals in denouncing musical nationalism in a cultural journal called *Ultra*. To paraphrase his argument: national art can never be the highest, since it sets greater store by colour than content. Doubtless Sibelius had himself read or at least been told about Pingoud's articles in *Ultra*, and his review of the Fifth Symphony at the Helsinki Fair in 1920 certainly did not escape his attention. When he read his latest utterances on new music in *Hufvudstadsbladet*, he did so with a certain animus: 'But he is stupid – and as is well known, "against stupidity even the gods battle in vain".' (7 September 1922)

Later the same month, September 1922, Sibelius at last felt in a position to resume work on the Sixth Symphony. 'Concert in Rome on 11 March 1923. Worked on the new piece, which must be ready by January.' (24 September 1922) And two days later: 'Worked. Felt life's richness today and my art's greatness.'

Other concert plans were also afoot. In Stockholm, Georg Schnéevoigt had suggested to Sibelius's old friend Werner Söderhjelm, now Finnish Minister in Sweden, that he should if not arrange, then actively support some concerts of Finnish music during the 1922–3 season. Söderhjelm was in full agreement, but made two conditions in a letter (8 October 1922) to Hugo Lindberg, chairman of the Music Council in Helsinki. First, 'Sibban must be brought into it – he ought to have a whole concert to himself . . . I have tried reasoning with him on innumerable occasions to come here, but he always has a thousand-and-one excuses.' The other was that there were to be absolutely no *Aino* symphonies or sinfoniettas, nor any jaded master-pieces or novelties by immature and untried figures.

The job of persuading Sibelius was assigned to Lindberg. Schnéevoigt, who claimed he understood the way Sibelius's mind worked, said that 'if you impress on him that it's his blessed duty to come, then he will.' Sibelius must have agreed that the time had now come for him to make his début as a conductor in Stockholm. But a delicate issue had to be resolved. Which of the two orchestras should have the honour of the Sibelius concert, the Konsertförening (Concert Society Orchestra), of which Schnéevoigt had been conductor, or the Hovkapellet (Opera Orchestra), where Armas Järnefelt was at the helm. Söderhjelm proposed the ideal compromise: both should have their Sibelius concert. When this solution was reached, Schnéevoigt's enthusiasm for the project became conspicuously cooler. The whole project had been his idea, and although he was no longer the Konsertförening's permanent conductor, he was anxious that Sibelius should not appear with any other, since he had been responsible during his period there for markedly raising its artistic standards. Armas Järnefelt, on the other hand, had nothing against Sibelius bestowing his honours on the rival orchestra, and promised to use his good offices with the opera management to secure the project. However, he showed a relatively tepid enthusiasm.

In the middle of October Hansen passed on a new libretto by Poul Knudsen, *Kavakami,* based on a Japanese theme. Sibelius found the text more dramatically effective than *Scaramouche,* but had the courage of his convictions and replied that his energies were currently consumed by other things. His young colleague Leevi Madetoja was to fill the gap and make use of the same libretto in his pantomime–ballet *Okon Fuoko.* Fischer's rejection of the *Suite caractéristique* seems not to have worried him in the least. He went into Helsinki for Kajanus's fortieth anniversary concert with the City

Orchestra on 5 October. The main work, Beethoven's Fifth Symphony, had figured in the original 1882 programme, while Cherubini's *Anacreon* Overture had been in the second programme. A couple of days later the Finnish National Theatre celebrated the fiftieth anniversary of its foundation. 'My music was played under a covered pit. I have grown out of those older pieces.' (14 October 1922) A few weeks earlier, both events would have occasioned some imagined insult or have prompted an outburst of one sort or another. But so totally was he now immersed in his creative world that he was conferred immunity to the pin-pricks of life, real or imagined.

A diary entry of 14 October records that work on the new symphony was proceeding apace. As usual, the diary records the swings of optimism and depression, the highs and the lows we have encountered many times before. He was seized by the fear that customarily assailed him at some stage in the process, that he would die before completing the score. By 19 October he had sketched out the basic shape of the work. 'Will I have everything ready in time for the concerts at the beginning of next year? That's the crucial question! I must!' On 12 November (though he mistakenly puts October): 'Grieve over Kitti. And find it hard to compose – hard to concentrate.' There is only one diary entry in December, a good indicator that he had been working exclusively on the symphony. It records a stormy encounter about money in Helsinki which ended unsatisfactorily for him.

The Christmas and New Year period was consumed by the new symphony and it is not until 14 January 1923 that he records progress: 'Well, movements I, II, III of Symphony 6 are ready. My tremor is bad and so are my nerves. Eliel Saarinen's well-deserved success has given me a new lease of energy. He is a magnificent artist.' Although Saarinen had only won second prize in the competition for the *Chicago Tribune* Tower, it was his design that had won the most favourable attention in professional circles. Saarinen left for America the following month and settled there. Did he draw any parallels between Saarinen and himself in the New World? The Fifth Symphony's success there was a pointer towards his future breakthrough.

The period from late October 1922 through to the middle of January 1923, during which he was engrossed in the Sixth Symphony, are not well documented as far as the diary is concerned. But in contrast to the turn of the year 1919–20, this is one of the most important creative periods in his career. The fallow years are over.

CHAPTER FIFTEEN

Sweden and the Sixth Symphony

Up to this point in his life, gaps in Sibelius's diary have been the exception rather than the rule, and it has always been possible to deduce the reasons for his silence with some degree of certainty or to fill in the picture from other sources. But from 1923 onwards the diary entries thin out, to become fewer and fewer during the remaining years of his life. In 1923 itself, for example, there is one entry in January, one in May, three in October and a similar number in the following month: about two pages in all. Their sparseness naturally precludes continuity, and makes it quite impossible to follow his inner thoughts.

Not only is it the meagre diary offerings that make things more difficult, but the flow of letters, always a fruitful source of insight, also dries up. His most important correspondent, Axel Carpelan, has gone, and so too has his brother Christian. The letters to Aino are fewer, for the obvious reason that he does not travel alone as much as he did before the war, and in any event on two occasions she accompanies him. His correspondence with Rosa Newmarch and Granville Bantock is increasingly sparse since it is not stimulated by concert appearances. His replies to the flow of letters from admirers which poured into Ainola in ever-increasing number tell us nothing, since they were usually drafted or written by his secretary. Indeed, the more his reputation grew and the more that was written about him at home and abroad, the more difficult it becomes to penetrate the wall of isolation with which he surrounded himself.

In Stockholm, Schnéevoigt had won the argument over Sibelius's appearances: he was to conduct three extra concerts in February in addition to the normal Wednesday subscription concert with the Konsertförenings Orchestra. At the beginning of January, Schnéevoigt gave him the specific dates, but the composer asked for a postponement of about ten days as he had to conduct a concert of new works in Helsinki on 19 and 22 February. 'I hope to have a new symphony ready for Stockholm. Concerning Rome [a concert was planned for 11 March], I feel a curious nonchalance, I don't know why. One weakness is that so few of my pieces are suitable as a concert ending if I don't play the symphony last.' (13 January 1923) A final plan was agreed whereby Sibelius would give two extra concerts and take part in a Sunday afternoon programme and a Wednesday concert in the beginning of March.

Werner Söderhjelm at the Finnish Legation had every reason to be pleased with the way plans were developing. Even if the venue, the Auditorium, where the Konsertförenings Orchestra was based, was not as impressive as the Opera House, the orchestra itself, as Söderhjelm told Lindberg, was thanks to Schnéevoigt 'altogether first class . . . wonderful strings and well disciplined ensemble'. Söderhjelm was a man of temperament and no stranger to controversy. Instead of highlighting the most positive and optimistic aspects of his forthcoming visit, his counsel to Sibelius was frank and realistic.

'Stenhammar', he wrote on 6 February, 'thought it essential that Sibelius should introduce the Stockholm public to his "second period" and programme the Fourth Symphony, but at the same time was fearful that he would have insufficient rehearsal time to establish his intentions.' He also 'regretted that not even one of your concerts was with the Opera Orchestra, particularly with regard to its higher artistic quality.' It would seem that Stenhammar was not altogether well disposed towards Schnéevoigt and his orchestra. But what is even more surprising is Söderhjelm's indiscretion concerning Järnefelt: 'Armas is also fearful. He says, quite rightly, that the concerts would have a completely different impact if they had taken place at the Opera. But when I asked why he hadn't been more insistent, he said it was not in his interests to be too insistent – all the same, I think he could have done it for you and his orchestra's sake.' Söderhjelm seems to have manifested a somewhat more skilful diplomacy in his handling of the Åland question than in the relations between the two brothers-in-law. The final sentence can hardly have struck Sibelius as particularly encouraging: 'That is how the situation is, and we must try to "make the best of it" [in English in the original]; it will work out well in the end.'

Sibelius took no notice of the letter. He was far too absorbed in putting the finishing touches to the Sixth Symphony. He wrote an animated response to his 'dear old friend' and thanked him for his invitation to the dinner party after the first concert: 'It will be a pleasure and an honour for us. I write "us", as I hope that Aino will accompany me to Sweden. At my second concert I will perform my new symphony – the Sixth – which I am just at this moment in the process of completing. As usual, I am ablaze with it, but the work has taken a lot out of me.' (9 February 1923)

The symphony was ready in time for his Helsinki concert on 19 February, and occupied the second half of a programme which opened with *La Chasse* from the second set of *Scènes historiques* and included pieces in a lighter genre: *Autrefois*, the *Scène pastorale*, *Valse chevaleresque*, *Suite champêtre* and *Suite caractéristique*, all from the early 1920s. It is not easy to understand what possessed Sibelius to include them alongside the symphony: the juxtaposition is almost grotesque. Did he really believe that these pieces were 'good of their kind', as he had said of the *Valse chevaleresque*? Or was he merely intent to show that he had not been idle during the last three years? The concert was sold out both then and when it was repeated three days later.

Two days after the repeat concert, Sibelius and Aino left Helsinki for Sweden and Italy. Their first stop was Stockholm, where they arrived on 25 February. Sibelius was interviewed on arrival by *Svenska Dagbladet* and expressed 'delight at being able to perform his compositions in Stockholm, where both the press and the public have shown so great an interest and understanding for his art'. Doubtless the interviewer William Seymer, himself a composer, avoided touching on the delicate subject of Peterson-Berger:

'À propos interest,' says Professor Sibelius, 'it is gratifying for me to see how my music is winning ground in the world at large. Particularly in America, where my Fourth Symphony is often performed. Elsewhere it is regarded as the most difficult to understand. However, time changes views and perspectives. Think that my First Symphony, which is now regarded as a strong piece formally, was at its first performance in Berlin denounced as chaotic from beginning to end.'

Regarding the new Sixth Symphony, Sibelius spoke with some measure of reserve:

'It is very tranquil in character and outline . . . and is built, like the Fifth, on linear rather than harmonic foundations. Furthermore, like most symphonies, it has four movements, which are formally completely free and do not follow the ordinary sonata scheme.'

'And do you think it will enjoy a great success?'

'That is not for me to say. It has always been the case that with every new symphony I have written and had performed, I have won a new following but at the same time lost some of the old. In any case I do not think of a symphony only as music in this or that number of bars, but rather as an expression of a spiritual creed, a phase in one's inner life.'

Sibelius spoke with great warmth of the younger Finnish composers, of the 'highly characterful Kuula, who died under such tragic circumstances; Madetoja, an excellent symphonist; the young Kilpinen, who only writes long song cycles to texts of Finnish poems and who could be called a Finnish Hugo Wolf; the more exploratory Raitio, whose orchestral work *Antigone* caused such a stir in Helsinki, and many others.' Did Sibelius consciously or unconsciously forget Selim Palmgren? In answer to a question about where Sibelius had been most enthusiastically received as a composer–conductor, he replied: 'My most vivid recollection is of a concert in Moscow during the old times. There is an understanding of and an enthusiasm for music which has no counterpart elsewhere. For the Slavs, music lies in their blood.'¹

On Monday evening, to judge from a letter Söderhjelm wrote to Lindberg, there was a musical soirée given by Sven Palme, director of an insurance company [presumably the grandfather of Olof Palme, the Swedish prime minister assassinated in 1983], to which Sibelius was invited. The Palmes appear to have behaved with curious nonchalance, in that 'Sibelius was left to fend for himself, even when the royal party had come and the music had commenced. Eventually the Crown Prince asked my wife where he was, and only when I had asked if I could present him was an introduction effected.' After a short and amicable exchange with him and Princess Ingeborg, Sibelius 'returned to his whisky and made an early exit'.

Sibelius's first concert with the Konsertförenings Orchestra took place on Thursday 1 March. 'This is an historical occasion if ever there was one,' wrote *Svenska Dagbladet*. 'Sibelius's music is no stranger to us; it embraces everything – worlds, centuries, the masses as well as the connoisseur. Because of that, it has the power to live through the ages and in both good times and bad give comfort and solace to mankind.'

The auditorium was filled with a capacity audience; there was not a seat to be had. Even the Crown Prince was there! Peterson-Berger² feared that Sibelius's entry might not have fulfilled all expectations. 'Many a young lady may well have attended in order to set eyes on the creator of *Valse triste* – slim-waisted, pale, handsome, fashionable and with perhaps a touch of the bohemian about him, as she might have imagined from seeing his portrait and listening to the music. But instead she beheld a rather thickset, bald-headed gentleman, who behaved indeed like a man of the world but officially on the programme bears the title "Professor". Really, how can one do that when one is after all Jean Sibelius? Such a title from the armoury that the world's vanity can bestow is enough to sober down and dismay more than just the flappers.'

No doubt Sibelius's thoughts must have turned to the baritone John Forsell, the soloist in his next concert, who once came to blows with Peterson-Berger within the precincts of the Royal Opera after reading one of his reviews. But for the most part Peterson-Berger found the 'homage and ovations that greeted him fully worthy of Jean Sibelius's artistic and cultural importance. The programme and its performance were not perhaps always on the same high level.' *En Saga*, the *Rakastava* Suite and *The Swan of Tuonela* emerged 'in what is for this orchestra unusually soft and refined colours and sonorities, undoubtedly the fruit of the conductor's attentiveness'. In his favourite, the Second Symphony, the disjointed pathos of the *Andante* 'made a stronger impression than usual', but the finale, particularly at the very beginning, was 'lustreless, almost lethargic'.

William Seymer, on the other hand, spoke in positive terms of Sibelius the conductor. He writes of his clear, economical beat and the absence of showmanship, and concludes that he had never heard the orchestra play with greater intensity. He also says that the less brisk tempo of the finale of the D major symphony only worked to the advantage of the interpretation. It is interesting to note that, according to Seymer, the initiative for the Sibelius concerts came from the orchestra.

Söderhjelm was at pains to stress that Sibelius was on his best behaviour. At the *soupée* following the concert at the Finnish legation, 'Sibban was not difficult in any way. On the contrary, he was elegant, made a nice little speech and radiated an inner satisfaction. Everybody was delighted with him, and he himself was very taken with Mrs Ragnar Östberg, the wife of the architect of the Stockholm Town Hall.'

Lunches, concert and supper parties followed one after the other. At an intimate yet brilliant party at Schnéevoigt's on the Saturday evening, he was up until four in the morning, and in spite of a fair amount to drink never reached more than an 'animated and high spirited state'. Next day, at the Konsertförenings matinée, which included a Bach and a Beethoven concerto with Edwin Fischer as soloist and a symphony by Alexandersson conducted by Schnéevoigt, he brought the house down with performances of the *Elegy* from the music to *King Christian II*, *Valse triste* and *Finlandia* 'played in such a way that these hackneyed pieces sounded completely fresh'.

On Monday, after the rehearsal for the second concert, the president of the Musical Academy, Marks von Würtemberg, hosted 'an elegant lunch attended by a cabinet minister and several important figures in Swedish music.' Sibelius presumably felt unable to decline the invitation, in spite of the fact that he was to conduct a long and demanding programme: *The Oceanides*, the Sixth Symphony and *Pohjola's Daughter*, and after the interval *The Rapids-Riders' Brides* (or as it was for so long known in English, *The Ferryman's Brides*), three movements from the *Pelléas et Mélisande* suite and *Finlandia*. Peterson-Berger overflowed with praise: 'His tone painting *The Oceanides* was totally and completely different from three years ago under Schnéevoigt . . . In this beautiful poem one really heard something of the sound of the Aegean sea and of Homer . . . ' But an even greater surprise was in store: 'The Sixth Symphony sounded not only clear and comprehensible, but was full of tasteful and individual, yet expressive and vital beauty. The last three symphonies were for me more or less a torment, thanks to the lack of concrete ideas and pure melody.' But having now heard the Sixth Symphony conducted by Sibelius himself, Peterson-Berger was gripped by 'the suspicion that were I to hear the three previous symphonies under his own direction, I should have appreciated them more'. This reinforces Seymer's judgment about Sibelius's conducting.

John Forsell, the idol of the Stockholm public, was making a comeback after a long absence from the concert platform, and sang *Koskenlaskijan morsiamet (The Rapids-Riders' Brides)* in German. 'The insistent applause was

interpreted as a demand for an encore,' wrote Peterson-Berger with some
irritation, as he regarded the piece as 'earthbound'. But for all that, he had
come to a new and positive conclusion: 'Say what you will, with all his
wilfulness and eccentricity Jean Sibelius is a real tone poet – of a higher
order than most other living composers we know'. In *Svenska Dagbladet* (6
March 1923) William Seymer wrote perceptively of the Sixth Symphony,
with admiration for its classicism, polyphony and purity of language – 'It
possesses both in its harmonic and thematic substance, a singular clarity and
distinction that one is almost tempted to call Mozartian' – and also discussed
Sibelius's powers as a conductor: 'In this respect his strong and powerful
personality had a striking influence on the orchestra'.

Afterwards Sibelius felt that Forsell had almost stolen the show, not
entirely without cause if we are to believe Söderhjelm: 'The public did not
know quite what to make of the Sixth Symphony, but it won the admiration
of musicians. The other pieces, and in particular *Finlandia,* were received
with greater warmth, but the atmosphere was ruined by the tactless, manic
applause which greeted Forsell. He was showered with flowers, weird-
looking gifts, shouts of applause and was constantly recalled to the platform,
so much so that he was forced to repeat *Koskenlaskijan morsiamet,* which I for
one have never particularly cared for. In the end he took Sibban by the hand,
and the audience then realized its blunder and applauded loudly. But the
evening was Forsell's – not a single flower for Sibban.

Schnéevoigt was probably behind the idea of engaging Forsell. 'G. S. is a
business man: he knew that he would pack the house!' But it was only after a
personal request from Sibelius himself that Forsell agreed to take part.
Without doubt Sibelius had been wise. Knowing the concert scene as he
did, he realized that after two concerts of his own music, both sold out, he
would need a big name to draw an audience for a non-subscription concert
with a new symphony as its main attraction.

The Stockholm circus continued. After the second concert there had
been a reception at the Konsertförening, and afterwards a little supper at
Forsell's which Sibelius took in his stride. The following day he exhibited all
his charm at a lunch given by Söderhjelm, after which he left for Uppsala for
another concert. His final Stockholm concert took place on the Wednesday;
as was the case in the preceding Sunday matinée, Edwin Fischer was the
soloist and Schnéevoigt conducted. Sibelius conducted the First Symphony,
which Peterson-Berger thought gave clear and distinct signals that Sibelius
could have composed a superb lyric drama if he had found the right
librettist and the right subject. Söderhjelm thought that the Wednesday
concert was 'perhaps the most successful of the lot. Never has the First
Symphony made a stronger impression and the public was really warm.'
Söderhjelm was not invited to the supper party Forsell gave, so that no
reports survive of the state of 'animation and high spirits' Sibelius managed
to achieve that evening.

Aino waited in vain for news from home. Full of anxiety, she sent a telegram to Eva in Helsinki and received a reassuring response. Even if it was the first time since their long stay in Berlin and Rapallo in 1900–1 that she had been abroad with her husband, she had a bad conscience about leaving the children and was always prepared for an immediate return home. Moreover, their stay abroad seemed to be much longer than they had originally thought. There were two further concerts in Gothenburg on 10 and 11 April, and the management of the Royal Theatre in Copenhagen had also invited Sibelius to see a performance of *Scaramouche,* but this came to nothing.

Aino wrote to Katarina that she had been committed to these new events and bravely soldiered on with the round of lunches and supper parties that went on well into the small hours, but her thoughts were back at Ainola and her garden, where the heavy snows of winter were beginning to melt. Her letters home are full of instructions to plant the tomatoes, celery and leeks in the hothouse, or to look after the indoor plants.

The next day the indefatigable Sibelius and Aino were invited to a lunch which took place at Operakällaren (the Opera Cellar), one of his favourite haunts in Stockholm, given by Viktor Hoving, a bookseller from Viborg (Viipuri) and now Finnish consul in Stockholm. Söderhjelm and Eugen Wolff, the veteran campaigner for independence, were also present. The conversation centred on Karelia, and Sibelius was so captivated by the atmosphere that he remained at table until late in the afternoon.

Söderhjelm and Schnéevoigt tried to persuade Sibelius to give two further concerts in Stockholm on his way back from Italy and to 'insist on being paid properly for them'. International copyright offered little or no protection at this period. Before he left Stockholm, Sibelius met the publisher Otto Hirsch, who had been among the founders of the Konsertförening, and sold him the Sixth Symphony for 4,000 Swedish crowns. Hirsch also wanted to come to an arrangement about some songs. Presumably this concerned the foreign rights to the two sets, Opp. 86 and 88, which had been published in Finland by Westerlund. However, nothing came of this in the end, and both sets were bought by Hansen later in the year. In his conclusions about the visit, Söderhjelm made a revealing observation: 'Aino thought that it was best that the concerts had taken place at the Auditorium, as Sibelius and Georg [Schnéevoigt] are better attuned in matters of musical taste than the two brothers-in-law.' Quite coincidentally, the very next day Armas Järnefelt conducted a performance of Mahler's Eighth Symphony, which serves to reinforce Aino's remark. Werner Söderhjelm attended the concert and so was unable to see his guests on to the night express to Berlin. The legation had experienced much difficulty in getting Sibelius and Aino off, and many telegrams and bookings were made and cancelled: 'Decisiveness is not a distinguishing feature of either of them'.

On their way to Italy, Sibelius and Aino stopped off in Berlin and managed to see Adolf Paul. He was now much taken up with his play *Die Sprache der Vögel (The Language of the Birds)*, which Arthur Borgström had translated into English and which was now to be performed there thanks to Borgström's patronage. As Breitkopf had not responded to Paul's request to use Sibelius's still-unpublished incidental music, the composer suggested that he should use the score to *Belshazzar's Feast* instead. Sibelius had left his galoshes with Paul on a visit two years earlier. They had fitted him perfectly and remained there to bring him luck, so he wrote. But alas no luck was forthcoming. *The Language of the Birds* was staged in Liverpool – without any incidental music – and was a flop. Borgström's patronage dried up and Paul's cries for help in his letters to Sibelius became more strident. Artists are not the only ones to suffer ill-fortune: it can even afflict their benefactors.

– 2 –

Sibelius and Aino arrived in Rome on Sunday 11 March – the concert had been postponed until the 18th. They had booked into the Hotel Minerva, near the Pantheon. What thoughts must have passed through his mind on his return to the eternal city where twenty-two years before he had worked on the Second Symphony, which he was now to conduct at the Augusteo? The other works on the programme were *Finlandia*, the *Pelléas et Mélisande* Suite, and '*Il ritorno di Lemminkäinen*'. Presumably he was consumed by nostalgia and a desire to rekindle the spirit of that period of his life; Aino noticed that he drove aimlessly around in a carriage engrossed in daydreams. Perhaps his thoughts turned to the days when he had arrived in Rome from Rapallo, leaving his family at the Pension Suisse. Aino had sent him a letter that expressed her enormous sorrow, and he had answered: 'You must also love, otherwise our relationship will perish.' Without batting an eyelid, Aino had sat in Siloti's box in the Marinsky Theatre while the Tsar's doctor swore profusely about the Third Symphony which Sibelius was conducting. Her skill in handling such situations was a constant support. In the summer heat of Berlin in 1908, some months before Margareta's birth, Aino had restored his faith in life and helped him recover from his fears after the first of his cancer operations. The Music Festival in Copenhagen would have been wholly insupportable without her, and their present tour had been blessed by good fortune – at least up to this point.

The initiative for the concert had come from Herman Gummerus, a long-standing friend of Sibelius who was the first Minister the newly-independent Finland had sent to Rome. At the beginning of the century he had been an activist in the independence movement and had spent some time immured in the Peterpaul fortress. He had studied archaeology in Italy and during the First World War had served as the Jaeger movement's representative in Stockholm. In addition to Latin and Greek, he spoke seven modern languages and was *un homme du monde* to his fingertips.

Sibelius's arrival for the rehearsal at the Augusteo was observed by the thirteen-year-old Gianandrea Gavezzeni, who had waited by the artists' entrance to catch a glimpse of the composer and perhaps to introduce himself. Sixteen years later he recalled his impressions in an essay: 'I saw him get out of the carozella and go past. Even then he was already very old [he was in fact no more than 58] and despite his lofty appearance, he looked worn-out, serious and old, so much so that I did not dare to approach him but went off in the direction of Santa Cecilia.' The fifty-eight-year-old must have seemed like an old man in the eyes of a thirteen-year-old boy but he was certainly not worn out.

It would seem that the picture Gavezzeni formed in his childhood coloured his view of the composer in later years. During the inter-war period he developed views similar to those of Adorno and Leibowitz, who saw Sibelius as representing 'eternal old age': 'A physical old age which coincides with the spiritual. No sense of adventure, no new experiences touched him during the years that followed. The few influences he assimilated during his student years in Germany are the things that he retained throughout life.' Thanks to a Finnish friend, young Gavezzeni had got Sibelius's autograph with a dedication and a few bars of *Finlandia*, but after the episode at the Augusteo, 'I looked at the autograph as if it belonged to a bygone world and saw my own name in the inscription with amazement.'[3]

Bengt von Törne, who was living in Rome at the time, went to the rehearsal at the Augusteo and found Sibelius sitting in a corridor waiting for his turn, while Bernadino Molinari, their permanent conductor, prepared the Augusteo Orchestra. From the concert hall emerged a flood of sound. But music was not the only thing to be heard; there were Roman birds singing in the auditorium. After the rehearsal Molinari apologized for them, but Sibelius, far from being annoyed, had been enraptured by their presence and their contribution to the proceedings.

Gummerus lived with his wife and two sons on the top floor of the sixteenth-century Palazzo Massimo on the Corso Vittorio Emanuel. The palace was full of Roman reliefs, busts and inscriptions. The drawing-room with its red silk tapestries was adorned by ornate painted ceilings and a frieze portraying the Massimo castle, fortresses and towers. As a member (No. 23) of the Accademia Santa Cecilia, an honour he shared with Fauré, Glazunov, Ravel, Richard Strauss and Stravinsky, Sibelius enjoyed some standing in Rome. He was the guest of honour at the splendid reception held at the Palazzo, to which the Minister and his wife had invited prominent members of Roman society together with Bernadino Molinari and the translator of the *Kalevala*, P.E. Pavolini.

Sibelius enjoyed life with the Gummerus family. The older son Edvard, then in his teens, recalled his impressions of a little expedition they made together to the environs of Rome, and how they strolled in the grounds of the Villa Aldobrandini in Frascati. 'It was mild and sunny, and Sibelius took off his thick overcoat and said how delightful it all was. Olle [Edvard's younger brother] gave him a laurel sprig and was rewarded with a musical autograph in his album. But for the most part he struck me as very private, a man of few words, whose heavy, massive features occasionally lit up into a warm smile. One had the impression that he lived in another world and was indifferent to the things going on around him, was alone with his creative muse. It was an experience just to see him, and he made the strongest impression of anybody on me at that time.'[4]

Thanks to Gummerus's excellent contacts, Sibelius's visit received extensive press coverage. Interviews, however, were more problematic, since most of the music critics did not speak German. 'The celebrated Finnish master', wrote Alberto Gasco, critic of *La Tribuna,* 'speaks a certain amount of French but it is laboured.' Sibelius's appearance also occasioned surprise in Rome, as it had a few weeks earlier in Stockholm. Gasco had imagined him looking like a seer or a wizard with a penetrating look and a kilometre-long beard. Much to his disappointment, Georg Schnéevoigt had told him during a guest appearance in Rome that Sibelius was a wholly normal and happy family man, whose eyes, however, had something of the mystic about them; and that he was surrounded by a brood of blossoming daughters, appreciated and loved. But in Gasco's eyes, the man himself did not correspond with Schnéevoigt's description. He gave the impression of being 'a good person, straightforward, devoid of any pretence, an impeccable gentleman of a slightly military appearance'.

In his interview Gasco started with *En Saga* and *The Swan of Tuonela,* which had scored at least ten successes in the Augusteo:

SIBELIUS: 'Ah, my brave Swan. She has drawn my ship from the Gulf of Finland to the banks of the Thames . . . Small and frail, she has battled for my cause like an eagle.'
GASCO: 'We should be all the more grateful to it, for it has revealed the secrets of Finland's mysterious soul.'

This seems to have displeased Sibelius:

SIBELIUS: 'I understand. In *The Swan of Tuonela* as in my other symphonic works, you find an expression of a national art.'
GASCO: 'Exactly so.'

Here we go again. The same story in the Latin world as in central Europe: Sibelius is seen as a national speciality, not as a universal symphonist.

SIBELIUS: 'I do want to make one point clear: that my music is not folkloric. I have on no occasion made use of Finnish folk melodies. I have admittedly composed melodies in a folk-like style, but they have all been created in my mind, or rather in my heart, as I am a devoted Finn.'

GASCO: 'So it is rather the example of Mussorgsky or Grieg that you have followed?'

SIBELIUS: 'Absolutely. I am completely steeped in the poetry and mythology of Finland and have set much of the former and found inspiration in the latter, and in particular the *Kalevala*, an inexhaustible source of inspiration for every Finnish artist who is not infected by the mania for exoticism.'

From the national Gasco went over to the chauvinistic.

GASCO: 'Are there any Finnish musicians who have succumbed to foreign influences?

SIBELIUS: 'Oh yes, far too many. Among the young Finns there is a movement towards internationalism which I find disastrous. Debussy is the tempter.'

When Sibelius talks here about internationalism he probably means epigonism. He himself had been seduced not only by Debussy but also Grieg, Tchaikovsky and Bruckner, and besides that cherished a fruitful love–hate relationship with Wagner, Mahler and Schoenberg. But he always remained true to himself.

SIBELIUS: 'In Italy on the other hand! Let us speak of something else.'

Gasco had cleverly steered the conversation where he wanted it.

SIBELIUS: 'I have noticed a tendency among some young Italian symphonists – without doubt artists of quality – towards an excessive fascination for foreign influence, and in particular Ravel.'

Did Sibelius have Respighi's *Fountains of Rome* in mind or Malipiero's 'impressionistic objectivism' – or had he Casella's fascination with Stravinsky and Schoenberg? But this impression may well be illusory.

GASCO: 'Oh, no, this is the lamentable truth. But we shall soon liberate ourselves from all foreign influence. The new Italy will have new voices. The so-called cultural crisis among our young symphonists will soon be overcome.'

Italy was in the early stages of Mussolini's rise to power, and Gasco used his interview with Sibelius, whose outlook was far from chauvinist, to develop his own proto-fascist view of musical and musico-political questions.

The concert itself does not appear to have been a complete success. Domenico Alaleona in *Il Mondo* was critical of the choice of programme: *Finlandia* and *Lemminkäinen's Homeward Journey*, which were included in the first half of the programme, were not in his view suitable for export, though he was more taken with the suite from *Pelléas et Mélisande*, which he thought 'touching and exquisite' but too short for concert use. With the Second

Symphony he was happier, but generally he thought the dominant character in these works was 'mournful and uneventful and touched by monotony in the word's etymological musical meaning (keeping to one tonality and cadence), which is without question characteristic of the composer and his country, but taken in large quantities cannot but induce a sense of fatigue among his listeners'. Alaleona thought Sibelius would have been better advised to start from the more familiar *En Saga* and *The Swan of Tuonela*, which Toscanini and de Sabata had introduced to Rome, thus establishing a relationship with his audience, which would have been enhanced by his presence, even if he could make no claim to be a first-class conductor. Afterwards it would have been easier to introduce newer works. One of his conclusions, however, was strangely perceptive: that Sibelius became more universal, the more national his utterance.

The critic of *L'Epoca* found it hard to work up more than a passing interest in the Second Symphony's musical kaleidoscope. But there were more appreciative responses: *Il Giornale d'Italia* thought he had a remarkable capacity for lending a strong expressive profile to each of the instruments of the orchestra and yet maintaining a powerful feeling for the complex texture overall. Another writer in the same paper praised Sibelius for not taking refuge in the mists which shroud Debussy's art or nailing his colours to the Straussian mast or following the asthmatic and inarticulate gasps of futurism. Like Wagner in Germany, and Rossini and Verdi in Italy, Sibelius embodies the genius of his own country's music. But the critic goes on to administer a cold shower: 'Finnish music is lacking in that expressive magnetism or inspiration that a work of art must have to arouse enthusiasm and bore deeply into the listener's soul.'

Looking at the overall picture, it is clear that the Italians did not really take Sibelius to their hearts. They saw him as a national curiosity rather than as a symphonist of real quality. The First Symphony, which Schnéevoigt had conducted, and the Second, which Busoni had given, had not made a powerful impression on Roman concert audiences. Only Toscanini could have overcome public indifference at this period, but as a conductor Sibelius hardly had a chance alongside him. One wonders why Sibelius did not take the opportunity of doing something different: why not *The Oceanides*, with its overtones of Homer and classical mythology, or the Fifth Symphony with its cosmic, heroic power? These would have given a fuller, more contrasting picture of him than the dark, *Kalevala*-inspired earlier pieces. Three years earlier Robert Kajanus had thrown away Sibelius's great chance of making a breakthrough in Paris. Now Sibelius himself followed suit. Aino's scepticism was well founded: Sibelius's star was not yet in the ascendant in Italy. All the same, one has only to glance at the newspaper headlines during his visit – '*La musica in Finlandia*', '*Giovanni Sibelius all'Augusteo*' – and look at the innumerable pictures of him that were published to realize what a service he was performing for the Finnish cause. At this period Finland was a vague linguistic–ethnographic notion for the Italians, who according to Gummerus regarded the Finns as little better than savages and upstarts. If Aino had her doubts, Sibelius himself was little short of euphoric and sent Werner Söderhjelm a card of thanks: 'Rome – vino nostro – concert yesterday. Great success – good reviews. Living life to the full. Thanks for all your support and hospitality. Aino so-so. Rheumatism! But we shall go to Capri all the same.'

After spending a week on Capri, the couple returned to Rome and on Easter Sunday, 1 April, set out on the next leg of their tour to Gothenburg where Sibelius had two concerts. They stopped over in Berlin and decided to look up Busoni at his house in Charlottenburg. According to Aino, his Finnish-born Swedish wife Gerda opened the door and greeted them with the news that Busoni was too ill to receive them. Sibelius, having taken the trouble to come so far, felt slighted and obviously had no idea how ill his old friend really was. Moreover, the stairs at the entrance of the resplendent house gave no inkling of the penurious circumstances in which Busoni found himself. As Stuckenschmidt put it, his aristocratic inclinations during his last years were in inverse proportion to his material resources. While Sibelius had his State pension and his royalties from public performances were at last beginning to come in, Busoni's income from his concert appearances was shrinking as ill-health claimed him. Busoni had long suffered from a severe illness but never burdened his friends with his worries. When, later on that afternoon, Gerda telephoned to say that Ferruccio was much better and would be delighted to see them, Sibelius declined. He had no idea that this was to be the last opportunity he would have to meet his friend: Busoni died the following year. For the rest of his long life Sibelius bitterly regretted not going.

Sibelius and Aino arrived in Gothenburg on Thursday 5 April. They stayed with Stenhammar's sister-in-law Olga Bratt, whose son Leif had just come back from Germany where he was studying conducting with Fritz Busch. The young man lost no time in showing Sibelius his Runeberg settings. After Stenhammar had given up his position with the orchestra, he had been succeeded by another composer and Sibelius admirer Ture Rangström. Earlier, while he was in Stockholm, Sibelius had received a letter of welcome from Rangström expressing his profound affection for him and his music. When the two met in Gothenburg, there should have been no lack of sympathy for they shared a common enthusiasm for Strindberg: Sibelius had written incidental music for *Swanwhite* and Rangström an opera on *Kronbruden* and dedicated his First Symphony to the great writer's memory.

The prospects for his visit could not have been better. At the same time, the actual programme exposed Sibelius to some nervous strain. In a letter from Rome thanking Olga Bratt for her offer of hospitality, he made it clear that preparing the orchestra for two new symphonies was a tall order at the best of times. Even if he arrived five days before the concerts, he would still barely have enough time to prepare them. The orchestra itself was not on top form: the post of leader had been advertised and was yet to be filled, the string section was decimated because of illness, and a number of other key players were also affected and had to send deputies. The round of social obligations also took its toll. On the Sunday he and Aino were invited to his old friends the Mannheimers; on the following day to the country home of another patron of music; and after the final rehearsal on the Tuesday, Stenhammar gave a lunch in their honour. According to a letter from Aino to Katarina, the rehearsals were going well and the nervousness which had affected Sibelius in Helsinki had gone.

The first concert comprised *Pohjola's Daughter* and the Fifth and Sixth Symphonies, and Sibelius could certainly have no cause for complaint at its reception. Julius Rabe in *Göteborgs Handels-och-Sjöfarts Tidning* called it one of the greatest days in our musical calendar: 'There was that willingness on the part of the audience to respond, to be spellbound and entranced, which lends a concert such atmosphere and sense of occasion.' Rabe speaks of the Fifth and Sixth symphonies as commanding, just as their two predecessors and the string quartet *Voces intimae* had been, with an almost abstract purity. 'In our day and age, there are few works as strong and life-enhancing, yet at the same time as sensitive as Sibelius's; one's thoughts turn to Beethoven and Schubert (the changes between major and minor in the Andante of the Fifth Symphony). In Sibelius's Sixth the majestic symphonic sweep and sense of line also embraces tranquillity and the more intimate nuances of chamber music.'

After the concert some fifty people were invited to a dinner at the Bratt villa. Wine flowed and there was much laughter, so Leif Bratt recalled. Sibelius, still in tails, sank into an exhausted stupor on the sofa in the billiard room and slept. However, he did not escape the speech that Ture Rangström had prepared in his honour. He was woken up, and Rangström gave a long and flowery oration which Sibelius appeared not to have taken in. The composer had shown iron-willed discipline during the day, and punctually at nine o'clock the following morning he was on the podium, appearing none the worse for wear, to go through the evening's programme (*The Oceanides*, the *Rakastava* Suite and the Second Symphony) with which the orchestra was at least on terms of familiarity.

Aino wrote home in high spirits: 'The concert yesterday was marvellous. Everything was excellent and the evening went on in high style long into the early hours of the morning. Papa is splendid. Tomorrow we go off to Stockholm. Everyone here is so friendly and warm, and so musical.' Everything was not quite so excellent before the concert the following day. As eight o'clock approached, Sibelius was nowhere to be found. Panic ensued but eventually, after a desperate search, the star of the evening was discovered in one of the city's best restaurants consuming oysters and champagne. With some relief Aino took her place in the auditorium, her heart beating nervously. At the appointed hour, an unruffled Sibelius took his place on the podium and raised his baton. Suddenly, so she recalled in later years, he broke off after the opening bars as if he thought he were at the rehearsal. Aino froze with horror. But Sibelius gave a new up-beat and went back to the beginning of the piece. 'For me everything sounded chaotic; I was gripped with deadly fear of what would happen next.' The audience seems to have taken the incident in its stride. The rest of the programme apparently proceeded without incident. But after he had received the usual congratulations in the artists' room backstage and the time came to make his departure, he seemed depressed and downhearted, his thoughts far away. And then, as he stood on the steps of the Concert Hall, surrounded by his Gothenburg friends, he fumbled in his overcoat pocket and pulled out a small bottle of whisky which he threw down the steps so that it smashed to pieces.

Enthusiastic though the critics may have been about Sibelius the composer, they were less unanimous about his prowess as a conductor. According to one writer, the second concert showed him to better advantage than the first, when there were two new works on the programme. Here he did not have to concern himself so much with holding the orchestra together, but could allow 'the music to flow freely under his more impulsive baton'. Julius Rabe expressed himself more cautiously, noting that during the whole visit the orchestra had not been in its best shape: 'In spite of the intentness and fervour which was evident from their playing under Sibelius . . . [as a result of its reduced complement] the orchestra did not exhibit its usual confidence. As a conductor Sibelius does not posses that special quality which great conductors command of being able to whip up an orchestra to heights that it did not know it could scale.' On his way back, Sibelius wrote to Fru Bratt from Stockholm: 'The memory of the days I have spent in your company is indelible. Your deep personality enriches me enormously both as an artist and a person.'

Sibelius and Aino were back in Finland by the middle of April 1923. At the end of the month there was a further conducting engagement to fulfil in Viborg (Viipuri), where he had last performed as long ago as 1905. There he was greeted at the railway station by a crowd of dignitaries, the Viborg Choir and a large number of well-wishers. The following day he rehearsed the Viborg orchestra, augmented for the occasion, in *Vårsång (Spring Song)*, *Belshazzar's Feast* (the flautist of the Helsinki Orchestra, Michele Orlando, had been specially engaged for the *Nocturne*) and the Second Symphony. The concert was repeated the following Sunday afternoon, after which he boarded his train for Helsinki. Viborg was the meeting point for many cultures: four languages were spoken, and its proximity to St Petersburg meant that visiting artistic celebrities were frequent. Its medieval castle had been the most easterly outpost of Swedish power; there were Hanseatic buildings, official buildings from Tsarist times and a railway station representing the Finnish *art nouveau* of Saarinen and Gesellius. As his train passed the famous castle, Sibelius's thoughts must have turned to the *Karelia* music whose *Overture* and *Ballade* it had inspired.

The sense of anti-climax that inevitably follows in the wake of concert appearances now overtook him: 'Today no meaning in life. Old age looms. Aino played through the proofs of Op. 88. What a great spirit she is. Something wonderful. In Helsinki with old friends. Wentzel Hagelstam is sixty. Gallén has become an old *diva*: fool. All are leaving me – even my nearest. Alone! alone!' (Diary, 29 May 1923)

There was a respite from gloom in the summer of 1923 when Wilhelm Kempff paid a visit to Ainola. The young pianist was much taken with Finland and had spent midsummer as the guest of Heikki Klemetti, after which he came to Ainola for three or four days, much of which were spent at his host's insistence at his Steinway. Apart from other pieces, he played the two main works he was preparing for a new recital programme: the Schumann C major Fantasy and Beethoven's *Hammerklavier* Sonata. Sibelius could never have enough of the *Hammerklavier* and enlisted all his powers, short of force, to persuade his young guest to play it – twice a day at least and sometimes into the early hours! At his last concert in Helsinki eleven years earlier, Busoni had played it for him, and Sibelius possibly saw Kempff as being in the true line of succession. Not without reason Aino dubbed him 'Wille the heroic'.

During the rest of the summer Sibelius presumably worked at the Seventh Symphony and to judge from the same diary entry, was still concerned about his finances. The German mark continued to fall: in 1922 he received 640 marks for four editions of *Valse triste,* which was worth a derisory nine Finnish marks. But in 1923 the mark went through the floor. By the end of the autumn the old golden mark was worth 1,000 million paper marks, and already in July, when Sibelius received 1,280 marks for 24,000 copies of *Valse triste,* it was not worth the smallest decimal fraction of a Finnish mark. Sibelius had relatively few profitable dealings with other publishers during the year. Wilhelm Hansen turned down his offer of *Maan Virsi (Hymn to the earth)* but accepted the *Suite charactéristique,* though this was only published in a piano reduction. But a more hopeful future beckoned. Sibelius had become a member of GEMA *(Genossenschaft zur Verwertung musikalischer Auffürungsrechte),* forerunner of the Performing Rights Society, and at the beginning of February received the sum of 1500 francs. In time that swallow made a long and handsome summer, and saw his fortunes change. But as yet his economy was far from stable.

Work on the Seventh Symphony proceeded apace but took its toll. 'Life for me is over. If I'm in good spirits and have a glass or two I suffer for it long afterwards. That dreadful depression – which Aino cannot understand but which I have inherited. It's this timidity, or the fact that I lack self confidence, that means that Aino and the children never get enough support in life.' (Diary, 3 October 1923)

Later the same month we see him going through painful birth pangs:

[23 October 1923] What unbearably difficult times I have gone through these days! Perhaps the darkest in my life.

[31 October] Working on the new piece. Am in wonderful spirits. Life is rich and profound.

Hyper-inflation continued to wreak havoc in Germany. A postcard from Adolf Paul bore a stamp for 200 million marks. It would seem that Sibelius had sent him some money, for in his note of thanks he writes: 'Had it come the day before yesterday it would have fetched 330 milliard. Today it reached 800 and I felt like a king, until I returned home to find the month's rent had gone up to 302 milliard and the gas bill 179. To get your shoes resoled cost 108 milliard. Your room is always ready and waiting, as are your lucky galoshes!'

The Kordelin Foundation had just awarded Sibelius a prize of 100,000 Finnish marks and Paul congratulated him: 'It's good that you don't live on the moon as I do here, but are in a country and among people that care about you, even if they cannot care about you as much as you deserve . . . When you come here, let us take a course at Steinach [a fashionable Berlin doctor whose elixir of youth had also been advertised in the Helsinki newspapers].' Even if postage had risen to 400 milliard, Paul still had time for his fantasies.

Early in November Sibelius went into Helsinki for Eero Järnefelt's six-tieth birthday celebrations. A diary entry recalls: 'A splendid occasion for a noble person. Am worn out and worried about my work – the new piece! Alcohol, which I gave up, is now my most faithful companion. And the most understanding! Everything and everyone else have largely failed me. Can I hold out until next February, that's the question? (Diary, 11 November 1923)

Why just February? Because he had to have the new piece ready in time for the orchestral parts to be copied for his concert on 24 March 1924, when the first performance was announced. Aino was worried that he would never get it ready in time, and Sibelius had obviously promised her to give up drinking altogether, knowing that just one glass was invariably followed by several others. But his nervous tension was so great that he was in no state to give up his 'most faithful companion', which generated constantly increasing tension on Aino's part, which in its turn made his own nervous condition worse. A day later his diary recalls 'Gradual reaction to the terrible atmosphere and strain here. As if one was in the wilderness. Misery, depression and gloom. And it's in this atmosphere I'm trying to compose. But I will simply have to make a stand.'

However, as a diary entry two weeks later makes clear, he was not able to do so, as social engagements intervened: 'Two weeks of wasted days. Eero's sixtieth birthday + Linda's sixtieth birthday and Stenhammar's visit to

Helsinki. What this takes out of me! Time is so short and I'm working on a big piece. But I *must* be there. But at what a cost. My nerves are in a state. My new piece must be ready for Sweden.' His nerves were always affected when he met his sister Linda.

Stenhammar came to Helsinki to play his Second Piano Concerto with Kajanus conducting at a symphony concert on 22 November, but Sibelius recorded nothing about their encounter. However, it was on this occasion that Sibelius gave a lunch for his Swedish friend and took him aside to ask whether he would do him the honour of accepting the dedication of the Sixth Symphony. Unfortunately the dedicatory page was mislaid at Hansen's, so the published score does not bear this inscription.

CHAPTER SIXTEEN

Fantasia sinfonica

The first two months of 1924 were completely consumed by the Seventh Symphony. 'Aino has been badly ill for some time. She is at the end of her tether. I won't get my pieces ready now. Hope that at least one of them will be finished. That is imperative. But I am on the wrong rails. Alcohol to calm my nerves and state of mind. How dreadful old age is for a composer! Things don't go as quickly as they used to, and self-criticism grows to impossible proportions.' (6 January 1924)

Sibelius alludes to two works; the first is naturally the Seventh Symphony, but one can only guess at what the second could have been. As we know, he had begun the tone poem *Kuutar (The Moon Goddess)* as early as 1920, which to some extent at least was built on ideas that were later used in the Sixth Symphony. These ideas wandered backwards and forwards between the two works until the symphony had reached completion and *Kuutar* had been abandoned. He had spoken to Väisänen of a symphonic work on a *Kalevala* theme, either the forging of the *Sampo* or *Väinämöinen's Song*, and it is even possible that he was working on a precursor of *Tapiola*. All the same, it is difficult to see why he should have complained about his working tempo. After all, he had finished the Sixth Symphony in February 1923, having only begun serious work on it the preceding October, and the Seventh was finished in good time for its Stockholm première in March 1924. After that there were two large projects: the incidental music to Shakespeare's *The Tempest*, with its richly abundant invention, and *Tapiola*. None of this supports the idea that his creative fires were burning out. Already in the early stages of the Fifth Symphony he had discovered that wonderful ideas could be strangled by his growing self-criticism. Now in January 1924 was he already beginning to sense that this could become a corrosive and destructive force?

On 2 March his diary recorded the completion of the new symphony. 'Ready with "Fantasia sinfonica I" in the night.' The first to hear about it was Mrs Olga Bratt in Gothenburg. Did he perhaps turn to Stenhammar's sister-in-law as a kind of *ferne Geliebte* who could satisfy his romantic fantasies, but at an appropriate distance? There had certainly been no lack of

243

tension at Ainola. He composed through the night, stimulated by whisky. When Aino came downstairs in the morning she would find him sitting at the dining-room table, slumped over a score with the bottle within easy reach. She would take the bottle away and he would let her without uttering a word of reproach. Indeed, forty years later she could not speak of these days without losing her composure. One morning, when she came down to find Sibelius sitting in peace and quiet drinking his morning coffee, she handed him an envelope and left him without saying a word. He opened it and was shocked by what he read. He was a useless weakling who took refuge from problems in alcohol. In case he imagined that, thanks to that, he would be able to compose new masterpieces, he was grievously mistaken; she would not expose herself again to the indignity of seeing him conduct in an inebriated condition as he had been in Gothenburg, and she therefore refused to accompany him to Stockholm for the first performance of the *Fantasia sinfonica*.

Ever since they had first known each other, Aino had always shown him understanding, had sacrificed herself for him, and regarded it as her mission in life to be a support for him in his creative work, as in everything else in life. Now suddenly, for fear of a scandal, she refused to be at his side. At last her long-suffering nature rebelled and her patience snapped. It is almost with a sense of relief that one notes this manifestation of human frailty. It is often the case that when a person of some saintliness loses patience, they do so with such violence that they do not fully foresee the consequences of their actions. This letter was rather more serious than the usual matrimonial outburst that can arise between close partners. The spoken word soon passes from the memory; the written is not so easily erased. An angry verbal exchange leaves in its wake a need for reconciliation; it rarely leaves lasting wounds. Sibelius never alluded by word or deed to Aino's note, but it undoubtedly caused him much pain as he read and reread it. He did not even show it to his oldest daughter and confidant Eva Paloheimo, with whom he shared most of his sorrows and problems. However, after his death the letter was found tucked in an envelope and addressed in the tremulous longhand of his old age to 'Eva'.

Aino was as good as her word. She did not accompany Sibelius to Stockholm, nor to Copenhagen and Malmö later in the autumn. During these tours he gave nine concerts and in each of the programmes except one he included the new *Fantasia sinfonia* (or Seventh Symphony), which makes it all the more puzzling that he never once conducted it in Helsinki – nor in fact ever conducted *any* concert of his own music in his home country. Only once, in the spring of 1925, did he conduct one or two small pieces at a charity concert in Helsinki. Had Aino's letter undermined his self-confidence? Would he have found the tension unbearable if Aino were sitting in the audience? In any event it served to deprive him of the practice he would have needed to maintain the requisite conducting technique. His concerts in Sweden and Denmark in 1924 were almost his last. There were no concert tours in 1925, and his very last appearance abroad was in Copenhagen in 1926, the year of *Tapiola*. After that there were neither concerts from his baton nor any surviving major compositions from his pen. Some of the reasons for this were quite natural. He was after all now in his sixties and age had taken its toll; moreover, his tremor had increased. However, one is in some way forced to conclude that Sibelius gave up his conducting career without compelling reason. He undoubtedly missed it and spoke on various occasions of taking it up again.

In March came his concerts in Stockholm. His first rehearsal was due to take place on 20 March, but as the ferry services between Åbo and Stockholm had been suspended because of ice, there was some talk of his going by plane. In the end he took the boat and arrived on Saturday 22 March, the only score of the *Fantasia sinfonica* in his brief case. The situation was critical, as the first performance was scheduled for Monday 24 March. That did not stop him from holding a press conference in his room at the Grand Hotel on the day of his arrival. There was little time left for rehearsal. The violinist Ernst Törnqvist, later to become the leader of the Konsertförenings Orchestra, described the atmosphere as nervous. Sibelius did not possess the professional conductor's ability to rehearse a complex work that was new both to the orchestra and the world at large in the short time available, and which he had never rehearsed before. Nor was he used to conducting the Violin Concerto, which was also on the programme. He had conducted it only three times in his life, at the very first performance of the original version and its two repeats. The day of the concert fell between two holidays, and the somewhat unglamorous Auditorium was not as well attended as expected, although the audience included the Swedish Foreign Minister. A German member of the orchestra told the Swedish correspondent of *Hufvudstadsbladet*: 'Stockholm is a curious place, you know: you can score an absolute triumph, as did Sibelius last year. But now that is all over and he is no longer a sensation.' However, this proved not to be the case, for the following two concerts were completely sold out. According to Törnqvist, Sibelius managed not only to hold the works together through his personal magnetism, but also inspire the musicians to give performances of some subtlety and richness of nuance, particularly in the new work. A mishap occurred when his right hand appeared to become in some strange way locked, but he managed to take hold of the baton with his left hand, and the audience appeared not to have noticed anything amiss.

The next day Sibelius wrote home to Aino: 'Yesterday's concert was a great success. My new work is one of my best. The sonorities and colours are powerful. There are no papers published today, so I can't report on what the so-called critics have to say. But the musicians, Armas [Järnefelt] and Stenhammar were on fire with enthusiasm and praise. I have just come from a lunch that Söderhjelm gave for me and he was very pleased at its success.

Sat between Liva [Järnefelt's wife] and the Countess Hamilton. Stockholm is its usual self. I feel though that my visit is very much a repeat of the one I made last year. I thank you from the bottom of my heart for your letter. It made me so happy – and in particularly your closing remarks. Everybody asks after you and wishes you were here. The orchestra is rather good – and they played the new piece very well. [Julius] Ruthström [the soloist in the Violin Concerto] also "good'. But as you can tell, perhaps not fully up to it! I am happy and serene. I'll soon be going out with Stenhammar, with whom I had dinner last night. They sing your praises all the time.'

It would seem from this letter that Aino had possibly regretted the tone of the note she had handed him some days or weeks before. She had obviously written to him in particularly affectionate terms, to which he clearly responds. Otherwise, one can well understand Sibelius's sense of *déjà vu*. In Stockholm and the other Scandinavian capitals he was very much an official personage and duly fêted, but even though he was delighted to be an ambassador for his country, it took its toll on his energies. Because of the holiday, the reviews did not appear before Wednesday. Wilhelm Peterson-Berger thought the new *Fantasia sinfonica* a kind of concise, one-movement symphony 'reminiscent of Berwald in form, but in atmosphere close to the composer's earlier pieces inspired by the *Kalevala*.' It was not entirely free from artificial or self-conscious touches, but as a whole possessed an impressive power. 'If the work had borne a poetic motto or a title, which would have given some hint of its poetic [*sic*] background, its impact on the listener would undoubtedly have been enhanced.' Otherwise Peterson-Berger thought that 'the orchestra did not particularly distinguish itself in terms of ensemble and clarity. But it had something of the breadth which is only to be observed when a musician of stature is at the helm.'

Sibelius had obviously seen this review. 'Have just got back from the rehearsal for this evening's concert, which began at 9.30 and went on until 12. Another rehearsal at 4 with the choir etc. [for *Snöfrid*]. Then the concert is at 8 o'clock. I hope the Fifth Symphony will go well, in spite of the fact that I have only had two rehearsals. Enclose a review by the "much feared" Peterson-Berger. How little they grasp of what I have done in this piece. But *que faire!*'

The Concert Association had, as far as one can judge, decided to make something of a stir with their regular Wednesday concert, albeit not so much centred on Sibelius. They put his Fifth Symphony and *Snöfrid* together with Adolf Wiklund's First Piano Concerto. Wiklund had just been dismissed from the Royal Stockholm Opera by John Forssell, the newly-appointed director, in rather sensational circumstances. In a wave of sympathy he was engaged as soloist in his own concerto with Nils Grevillius conducting, and so the concert was turned into a public demonstration in his support. As was the case with Forsell the previous year, Sibelius was put a little in the shade. Moses Pergament, 'whose self-confidence had made an impression on everyone here in Järvenpää' and who was now living in Stockholm, wrote in *Svenska Dagbladet* that Wiklund should have been given a concert on his own so that Sibelius's appearance could have been free from musical–political demonstrations. He spoke of the Fifth Symphony as impressionistic and told how one well-known German conductor had refused to perform it because of '*das ewige Tremolo*' – which Pergament described as a 'typical example of many conductors' incapacity to grasp the originality of Sibelius's orchestral imagination'. True to form, he could not resist the temptation to give Sibelius a composition lesson and went on to say how much better the work would have been if the second movement had been different.

Sibelius was perhaps keen to show a Stockholm audience his feeling for Viktor Rydberg by including *Snöfrid* on his programme. Surprisingly enough, the doyen of Swedish national operatic composers, Andreas Hallén, was not taken with it. Hallén had earlier been an admirer of Sibelius, but had long ago resigned himself to the view that he had become a victim of 'a decadent futurism *à la* Scriabin and Busoni'. Not even *Snöfrid* from 1900 gave him comfort: it was 'not Swedish enough'! The Wednesday concert was attended by the Crown Prince and Princess, which was more than just an official gesture; the princess, later Queen Louise, appears to have loved Sibelius's music. The *Andante* of the Second Symphony was played at her funeral in 1965.

His farewell matinée concert at Auditorium the following Sunday was filled to the rafters, in spite of the good weather, and the box office was besieged by a scramble for the last tickets. On this occasion the Royal Family was represented by the Princesses Ingeborg and Astrid. The programme opened with the *Fantasia sinfonica*, which was followed by, among other things, *The Swan of Tuonela*, *Valse triste* and *Finlandia*. The latter brought the house down.

– 2 –

'Back from Stockholm, where I've had great success. The dreadful demon in me threatens to put an end to me. To escape it is not within my power, nor in Aino's either. What can I do? If only my nerves were better. Perhaps it would be better then. But it has gone on for so many years and things won't change. Alone and with "hands that tremble". Damn it!' (Diary, 5 April 1924)

Life was flat after the excitement in Stockholm. The two symphonies that had matured in him for so many years were now behind him. Thoughts of a new tone poem on a *Kalevala* theme were beginning to surface, though the motivic ideas were slow to take shape. In the past, once a new symphony was finished he began the search for the basic mood and atmosphere of its successor. Towards the end of 1926 he began to speak of another orchestral work that was in his mind. This was obviously the Eighth Symphony. But that was almost two years into the future, and in the intervening period he was to compose three commissioned works: apart from *The Tempest* and *Tapiola*, there was the cantata *Väinön virsi* (*Väinämöinen's Song*).

And so in January 1924, like so many times before, he was torn between tone poem and symphony. The conductor Georg Schnéevoigt, who had obviously been present at the première of the Seventh Symphony in Stockholm, touched on the subject of the new symphony in a long letter: 'On the last occasion when we met, you were so magnanimous as to honour me by promising to dedicate to me your next symphony, which you spoke of as being something in the style of the Second . . . But do you really think that after all you have achieved on such completely different lines, you would want to write a symphony like No 2, with its sweeping melodies and richly coloured orchestral sonorities? However, I know that were you, as an established master, to give us a symphony along those lines, it would be greeted with joy by your innumerable admirers. I would be overjoyed if you were to decide on such an magnificent enterprise. It is my hope that in the near future you get an appointment in America, a land made for your music, but which is lacking the right apostles!' Schnéevoigt makes it clear, albeit with great tact, that he was not – at this time – wholly at home with the new world that Sibelius was exploring. Like so many other of his contemporaries, he still found the *clair obscur* and Dorian modality of the Sixth Symphony alien, though in later years he was to become one of its leading exponents.

Life at home was no more harmonious than before: 'A wasted day. This existence in the land of Death without life and light. Aino is in a bad way and miserable and depressed. All one's appetite for life disappears when its woes resound so strongly! If only I could arrange a place in Helsinki for her, things would be easier for her and I could wait for Death in some nook or cranny here in the country.' (Diary, 6 April 1924)

If Aino had hoped that things would improve after her letter, and that Sibelius would sign the pledge, she was to be quickly disabused. However, it was clear from his letter from Stockholm that he loved her as deeply as ever, and whatever idle thoughts may have crossed his mind, he wanted them to live together in the 'warm and comfortable home' they had made together at Ainola. Even now, as during their engagement, he was terrified at the thought that she would predecease him.

Sibelius's dealings with his publishers had not been going well earlier in the year. He had sent Wilhelm Hansen the *Cinq morceaux lyriques*, Op. 101, for piano: 'They can be played as a suite.' He had asked for 2,000 Danish kronor as an advance on a 15 per cent royalty on the cover price. Hansen only accepted the first piece, the *Romance*, and Sibelius responded with an angry telegram:'SEND THEM BACK INCLUDING THE ROMANCE.'However,all five pieces eventually appeared under the Hansen imprint. But this small reverse preyed on his nerves. In addition, he began to worry about how well

Hansen and his German publishers would be able to protect his copyright interests in America. The question became urgent, thanks to a proposed American tour for *Scaramouche*. 'Surrounded as I am by useless egoists – these music publishers – I have difficulty in keeping an eye on what is going on. It's quite impossible . . . The younger ones, with Selim P[almgren] at the head of the pack, will finish me as far as my income is concerned. I want to compose big works but they don't bring in the money. And these small pieces cost me more work than they should. My finances are now disastrous. And I see fewer possibilities than ever coming along. Now I have to show that I am willing to face up to things and bear the consequences of not having gone to Rochester. And I shall show that I can. That's it, Jean Sibelius. You have so little time left. Are you going to spoil what time there is left by worrying about small setbacks and the like?' (14 May 1924)

Germany had returned to the Gold Standard, which meant that theoretically the mark was worth the same as it was before the First World War, while the Finnish mark had been affected by inflation of about 90 per cent. His contract concerning the piano arrangement of *Valse triste* guaranteed him, as we have already said, 100 Finnish marks per edition, and on the same principle he received 200 for the *Romance in D flat*. But Breitkopf & Härtel gave him a pleasant surprise: his royalty was to be calculated according to the pre-war exchange rate, so that 100 Finnish marks equalled 80 German Goldmarks. Perhaps the company hoped to make amends in some small way for the purely nominal royalties they had paid during the war years. Thus for two editions of *Valse triste* and the *Romance* Sibelius received altogether 720 Goldmarks, about 5000 Finnish marks – a considerable improvement on the 600 that he would otherwise have had to settle for.

In August, Sibelius opened the Helsinki papers to be greeted by the news that Busoni had died in Berlin. The previous autumn Busoni had begun practising for a concert tour in Finland: *'Toujours recommencer'*. But enfeebled by declining health, he noticed that he had lost the feeling in his fingertips. In the spring of 1924 he worked on the last act of his masterpiece *Doktor Faust*, which the Dresden Opera was waiting to put into rehearsal. But alas his illness took a fatal turn and the last scene was left unfinished. Michael von Zadora, his favourite pupil, came to see him. On the piano lay Mendelssohn's *Venetian Gondola Song* and as Zadora began to play it, Busoni burst into tears. But among his last thoughts were his youthful years in Helsinki. A horse-drawn carriage went slowly along the Viktoria Luise Platz, on to which the window of his room opened. Busoni's eyes lit up and he whispered to his wife Gerda: 'Horses' hooves! It reminds me of Helsinki. They were wonderful times!'

In the middle of August 1924 came an invitation from Gunnar Hauch, Sibelius's long-standing Danish admirer, for him to visit Copenhagen to conduct his own works. Hauch suggested as the main works the First and Fifth symphonies. Sibelius accepted immediately, but suggested that instead of the Fifth, he should substitute the *Fantasia sinfonica*, which in an earlier letter he had also referred to as *Sinfonia continua*! Early in September he also signed a contract for a concert in Bergen on 20 April 1925. 'Rehearsal on the 19th. 1,000 kroner. Symphony No. 7, *The Oceanides, Rakastava, Lemminkäinen*. In Copenhagen 1 Oct. Rehearsals on 29 and Tuesday 30 Sept.' (Diary, 5 September 1924) One can see that he is already by this stage referring to the *Fantasia sinfonica* as the Seventh Symphony. His spirits were now high, he was looking forward to his forthcoming concerts, his good humour reflected in the fact that he mixes both Norwegian and Danish in his Swedish diary entry. The New York publisher Carl Fisher owned the US and Canadian rights of twelve Sibelius pieces which Hansens had published. Fisher had paid Sibelius $12,000 altogether, and Sibelius was not dissatisfied. 'This is something to watch in the future. I behaved stupidly in sending an all-too-formal letter in response to their friendly one. That sort of thing is important.' (Diary, 7 December 1924) Later on came a letter from Dresden asking for the score of the Sixth Symphony.

The autumn passed happily. At the end of August, Sibelius's daughter Katarina married the young lawyer Eero Ilves. A diary entry from 5 September notes: 'Kaj's wedding was delightful. Everybody was pleased. The expenses were enormous!' Ruth Snellman, her husband and their two children Erkki and Laura stayed at Ainola, and the two youngest daughters were also at home. At the end of the month Sibelius left for Copenhagen, and on Sunday 28 September he wrote home from his regular hotel, the Angleterre: 'Yesterday I was with [Herman] Sandby [the cellist] and his pianist wife. She is much older than he is. Both are very agreeable. They played my pieces the whole evening. He is a noted virtuoso. Today there will be a lunch at Wilhelm Hansen. Yesterday was with Asger [Hansen], who is married but has no children. I sat next to Nina Grieg so you can imagine how I felt. My first rehearsal is tomorrow at 9 o'clock for three hours. The concert is completely sold out – also on Saturday. On Sunday I am in Malmö. I haven't quite made up my mind what I will do afterwards. I might come home immediately after I have been to Berlin [he evidently intended to see his publisher Lienau]. Want to know what's going on. Hansen and I are curious about the production of *Scaram[ouche]* in Stockholm. It has its première tomorrow and [Asger] Hansen and his wife are going.'

The round of lunches, dinner parties and suppers resumed the very next day. The Danish–Finnish Society held a dinner in his honour, at which the Copenhagen Quartet played *Voces intimae*! According to the paper: 'The master, who sat lost in deep thought, listening to his inner voices, leapt to his feet and embraced the leader, Miss Gunna Breuning-Storm.'

Sibelius's concerts again attracted the attention of royalty. The Norwegian King and Queen had been at his concert in Oslo in 1921. Members of the Swedish royal house had gone to his Stockholm concerts and now, in

Copenhagen, the King and Queen of Denmark were in attendance. And so indeed were his Danish colleagues: the audience at the Odd Fellow Palace included Carl Nielsen, his fellow student from his year in Berlin, Fini Henriques, Peder Gram, Håkon Børresen and Louis Glass. The Danish minister of education and the ambassadors of Finland and Norway were also in the audience. The Copenhagen Philharmonic Orchestra, augmented to seventy players, took its place on stage, and a minute or so before 8 o'clock the doors of the Royal Box opened and King Christian X, Queen Alexandrine and their party took their places. Sibelius was unusually slow to take his place on the podium, and right into his old age he felt guilty about the implied, if unintended, discourtesy towards his Danish hosts. He was presented with a huge laurel garland by the newspaper promoting the concert, and the audience and orchestra broke into a storm of applause. 'The master bowed his head and placed the huge wreath by the podium. And then he turned towards the orchestra and slowly raised his baton . . . A solitary clarinet could be heard', and the First Symphony had begun. In the interval Sibelius was summoned to the royal box, where he was presented with the Order of the Knight Commander of the Dannebrogen, whose cross he bore for the remainder of the concert. The second half consisted of the new work, the *Fantasia sinfonica,* followed by *Valse triste* and *Finlandia.*

The concert was Sibelius's début as a broadcaster! The proceedings were relayed 'through the ether and by cable'. Radio Ryvang's transmitters reached over land and sea into thousands of Danish homes from Skagen to Gedser, and in addition thousands of Copenhagen telephones were linked to the concert by special cables. The broadcast was successful, and only during the opening bars of *Valse triste* was the signal too weak, causing Radio Ryvang's switchboard to be momentarily besieged. 'Has anything gone wrong? We can hardly hear anything,' was the general cry until suddenly the music reasserted itself in the concert hall. The Copenhagen papers were a good deal more enthusiastic than they had been five years earlier during the Nordic Music Days. The Fifth and Sixth symphonies had received their Danish premières in 1921 and 1924, and had turned the tide in Sibelius's favour. The commentators did not find the new work as easy to follow as the more familiar First, but its reception was generally positive. The leading Copenhagen daily, *Berlingske Tidende,* suggested that the Royal Theatre should invite Sibelius to conduct *Scaramouche,* which was still in the repertory. 'Given his popularity, it would play to full houses and top prices. And what is more important, we would have an authentic performance of this lovely score.'

The Copenhagen daily *Politiken* thought that Sibelius had 'given richly of his genius both as composer and conductor, even if he looked like a perverted Berlioz in *Valse triste* . . . If there are some aspects of his personality that belong more to the present than to eternity, the fact remains that there is so much else that justifies his being numbered among the greatest living composers of our time. Nor is he one of the masters who is content to stay still: the Sibelius who composed *Scaramouche* and the latest symphonies is different from the one we met from his youth – he has greater simplicity, purity and depth. In the Sixth Symphony, which we heard last summer, this transformation had been completed. In the completely new Seventh, which Sibelius brought with him on this occasion, he continues on this path. Perhaps the inspiration is not so powerful or as original as in the Sixth Symphony, but it is however a work of great beauty which comes directly from the heart.'

Nationaltidende, the newspaper that had sponsored the concert, had Gunnar Hauch as its critic, who argued, as American critics were to do a few years later, that the new symphony's form was related to late Beethoven: 'Now more than ever is Sibelius an aristocrat of the spirit, who does not wear his heart on his sleeve. Even if he is every bit as full of imagination and temperament as he was in his youth, his style is quite different. The epic qualities are reigned in, there is a sense of distinction and reticence, not unlike that we recognize in a César Franck, but which with Sibelius is borne aloft by a much stronger personality.'

On the Saturday he wrote home: 'Your wonderful letter has given me much joy and love . . . Today is the second concert. Tomorrow I go to Malmö, where Count de la Gardie is giving a dinner in my honour. Here it is one round of lunches and dinners. Am just off to Ambassador Idman's for lunch. Spend most of my time with Hauch, since he is my impresario from *Nationaltidende*.' On the way from Malmö to Copenhagen he found time to send a postcard to Aino: 'The concert in Malmö a great success. The day after tomorrow my third concert in Copenhagen. It sold out in an hour. Hauch is exactly like Axel Carpelan. That's a good feeling. Am sending 1,200 Swedish kronor [his concert fee] for you personally.' (Diary, 6 October 1924) However, his Swedish kronor remained in his Malmö impresario's account for a long time and only reached him five months later – in February of the following year!

At the third concert, as well as at the fourth and fifth, Sibelius inserted his *Valse chevaleresque*, Aino's unfavourite piece, between *Valse triste* and *Finlandia*. The critic of *Politiken* thought it pure salon music, as opposed to *Valse triste*, which was salon music of genius. Sibelius was convinced that Thursday 9 October, two days before the fourth concert, would be his last day: 'It has been so exhausting that Hauch took me to Copenhagen's most famous doctor, who after an examination said that I needed three to four months' rest for my heart in Italy – in Naples. You must come as soon as you can and make the right preparations for four months. Send a telegram to Hauch . . . Has Carl Fisher sent anything to Järvenpää? . . . I must give up conducting in order to calm my nerves. I tend to indulge in exaggeration, something of which the doctor was well aware.' Sibelius had already revealed on previous occasions that 'exaggeration' meant alcohol. 'As far as America is concerned, I must go there. They say here that I am the only living composer who could make a success of an American tour. Millions are at stake.'

Even if there was nothing seriously the matter with his heart, or any other important symptoms, Sibelius was distinctly shaken by his diagnosis and wanted Aino by his side. He wrote a second time the same day urging her not to be anxious and telling her that the doctor had promised he had many more years to live. He had put him on a not-too-rigorous diet and pre-scribed sleeping pills to begin with. He also reports that Wilhelm Hansen had sent off a draft for 4,000 Danish kronor to his bank. Somewhat charac-teristically, he adds: 'I have money here – but take some of the money I sent you! My pension will take care of the children and the household expenses. We'll go to Florence to start with. Don't forget that you will need a visa and that the police will want to see your passport in Sweden. *Scaramouche*, which you must see, is still playing to full houses.'

But Sibelius had reckoned without the enthusiasm of his Danish admirers. His concert on Saturday 11 October was not to be the last. That very morning long queues were forming outside Wilhelm Hansen's music shop, where tickets were on sale for 'Jean Sibelius's absolutely last concert' on Sunday. He was delighted with the success of all six concerts, though puzzled by Aino's silence. 'I'm waiting for your telegram and your decision. You must have had my letter by now. Hauch has been so marvellously kind and wonderfully efficient. I had no idea that he comes from one of the oldest Danish aristocratic families.' In *Politiken* Sibelius could have read that he had broken all Copenhagen records by drawing a full house for the fifth time 'and happily the last – for if we were to continue like this, we would have to postpone the rest of the season on account of *Valse triste*'. That little barb was sweetened by much praise, but was to presage worse to come two years later.

He could also report the doctor's latest verdict: 'Urine and everything else all right. It's only the heart that needs rest. My nerves also. Amalfi or Sorrento for five months. And as little work as possible. He then guarantees that I shall be wholly recovered. That is good news when America and its millions are beckoning. Now I am not sure whether to go south directly or to come home first and then go later in, say, December. Still no word from you. I know you haven't forgotten me, but perhaps there are troubles at home. Are you coming with me to the south? If so, I ought to come home first and organize my finances. All this and much else besides worries me. This hotel [d'Angleterre] is horribly expensive and I have to wait here. Perhaps it would be better if I went to Italy direct and you came on after, but I don't like to think of you making that journey on your own. My six concerts have been an outstanding success but have been a great strain.' Sibelius's vague plans, together with Aino's silence, support Söderhjelm's view that indecision was almost a way of life for the pair of them.

At long last, on Tuesday 14 October Aino's telegram arrived. He could expect her in about ten days. One wonders whether Aino paused to reflect that by that time he would have been at the Hotel d'Angleterre for about a month, which would have given him ample opportunity to live even further beyond his means. She would certainly have been horrified had she read what he wrote the same day to Adolf Paul in Berlin: 'You see, I need plenty of money and here in Copenhagen I only drink champagne. As usual, I can't cope with life.' Sibelius asked Paul to remind Lienau that he was waiting for an *Abrechnung* in Copenhagen. Presumably he had written to Lienau earlier and had forgotten his address. But no help was to be forthcoming from that quarter. Four days earlier he had even written to Breitkopf & Härtel, but they reacted so slowly that the money did not reach Helsinki until November.

All the same, he told Paul: 'Am coming south. Waiting for Aino. Will stop off in Berlin and will hope to press your hand.' But his letter to Aino radiates uncertainty: 'I don't know what my tax position is. If it is bad, things will be more difficult. Talk to Borenius [his lawyer] and my son-in-law. The main thing is to bring as much money as you can for the journey. Everything will be so different when you come.'

Sibelius's financial plight was pretty desperate. He had spent all the Danish kronor he had earned and had nothing to fall back on. The richly-carpeted Hotel d'Angleterre was proving too much for him, so he went off to a bathing resort at Fredensborg to take stock of the situation. On Thursday 16 October Gunnar Hauch came from Copenhagen and they had a convivial day, and on the following day he forwarded him a letter from Finland – presumably from Aino – and gave him details about the cost of second-class train fares to Rome.

Whether Aino confirmed her imminent arrival or had decided against coming is not known, but on Saturday 18 October Sibelius sent a telegram to his son-in-law Arvi Paloheimo announcing his return. His trip to Rome and Capri was not to be for another two years, when he went to Italy to work on *Tapiola*.

Back home in Ainola he could say, like Wotan in the Second Act of *Die Walküre*, '*der alter Sturm, die alte Müh*'. He found it impossible to get back to work. He wrote off to Hansen, asking when the score of the *Fantasia sinfonica* would be ready. 'I would like to take it with me on tour.' Apparently he had not abandoned plans to resume conducting. Hansen had not yet made much progress with the engraving.

News of Janne's success in Copenhagen had reached Adolf Paul and gave him a ray of hope: 'You who need only to say a word to your princely and royal benefactors could help me on my feet if you would. Tell them that Denmark should put on my *Christian II* with your music at the Kongelige [the Royal Theatre]. . . Do that, dear Janne, for my play's sake, which deserves it – and for Tali's [Paul's wife] and the children, who also need it! Perhaps it will be a fiasco – which could give you some malicious pleasure!!

And they *must* take it up in Stockholm too, if you want it. You only have to say a word – "I Sibban wish it!" – and that will settle the matter.

A Berlin company put on one of Paul's earlier plays and Sibelius wrote sending his best wishes. Paul's reply gives some hint of the tensions that were soon to surface so violently: 'The reviews in some papers were excellent, but not in the Jewish press, largely because I was once the critic of the now-defunct *Tägliche Rundschau*, which the Jews hate.' Paul was extremely right-wing and his economic troubles in 1920s Germany and treatment at the hands of German newspapers and publishing houses fuelled his anti-Semitism. During the 1930s, as a Swedish citizen, he contributed to the ultra-right-wing magazine *Sverige fritt* (Free Sweden) and also to the Nazi organ, the *Völkischer Beobachter*.

CHAPTER SEVENTEEN

Sibelius at Sixty

'The New Year has started in the usual miserable way. No one's here. The only one who has remembered me is Wentzel Hagelstam, who has sent me his new book as a New Year's greeting. Aino is totally worn out. There is a lot to say about that. We ought really to move, but we have so many ties here.' (Diary, 1 January 1925)

The social climate in Finland could sometimes feel harsh, so Sibelius was particularly appreciative of Wentzel Hagelstam's gesture. He sent him the piano arrangement of his *Valse romantique* by way of thanks. His depression may well have been heightened by the fact that he had no larger work in hand, no new symphony or the like, and his life seemed without direction. In the middle of January he received a nine-page handwritten letter from Hellmuth von Hase, head of Breitkopf & Härtel, telling him that Wilhelm Hansen had made him a large offer for the outright purchase of their Sibelius catalogue. Von Hase had refused even to discuss the matter and assured Sibelius that they would never part with his work. 'Even when I was a schoolboy I remember the enthusiasm and warmth with which my father and my brother Hermann described Breitkopf's dedication to your music. The whole world soon became used to the fact that Sibelius's music was to be found at Breitkopf's.' Then came the disaster of 1914–18 and after that the post-war inflation, during which situation the firm was simply not in a position to accept works of international stature such as his for publication. This would have been impossible, given the economic position, as well as irresponsible.

Now, added von Hase, the situation had completely changed. On his travels in England and North America, he had reopened the firm's branches in London and New York. He had even permitted himself an incredulous smile when he learnt that Carl Fischer in New York had plans to publish all Sibelius's work. It would seem that von Hase was especially irritated by Wilhelm Hansen's claim that he was the publisher of all Sibelius's later work: 'I fervently hope that you will not forget that you are contracted to our publishing house, whose activities had alas to be suspended for a time, and that you have in no way committed yourself to other houses.'

Von Hase's letter was written with feeling and sensibility, and struck a responsive chord in Sibelius's mind. He replied that he was prepared in principle to resume his old connection with Breitkopf, and spoke of an orchestral work as well as smaller pieces for piano, violin and so on. He hoped it would be possible in due time to break free from other publishers, and their correspondence ended with an agreement that they would resolve any outstanding matters when they met in person. But if Breitkopf & Härtel greeted him with open arms, Sibelius was in no mood to be cheered: 'Isn't it typical! For years now – when I work through the night – I have gone to the kitchen to get something to eat. Our cook Helmi knows that. And she normally looks after me. Last night there were only radishes and pickled mushrooms, which upset my stomach and are not good for me.' (17 February 1925)

To play the starving martyr of the family was not one of his familiar roles; a more frequent part at this period was that of the solitary drinker, as depicted by Edvard Munch in his self-portrait. Sibelius went out on his own in order to be able to think, and among other things to reflect on mortality – death was a subject which he did not touch on with others. He chose the most exclusive restaurants – the Kämp, Societetshuset, König – partly to avoid the company of musicians but also because he liked eating in style and in a civilized atmosphere. From his solitary observation post at the Kämp, the meeting place of Helsinki society, he could muse over the various guests. The times when they all sat together in an upstairs room in the late 1880s with Busoni, Armas and Eero Järnefelt and Adolf Paul had long passed from view. Now Eero sat at the 'lemon table' together with his models, industrialists, university people, doctors and lawyers. Occasionally Sibelius joined them, though the company of the successful was just as likely to make him feel like a Neitzschean superman as to fuel his inferiority complex. Aino did not approve of the 'lemon table', as she realized that it increased his morbidity as well as his intake of alcohol. In this respect she had right on her side. A diary entry from 17 February reads: 'The lemon table at the *Kämp*! The lemon is the emblem of death with the Chinese. And in one of her poems Anna Maria Lenngren writes, "buried with a lemon in his hand". That is a blessing!' He was quite obsessed with the symbolism of death and the following day he repeats himself almost literally. The winter storms howled by night at Ainola and his diary records: 'How infinitely richer are these winds than in Goethe or other poetry. I have begun to take up secret drinking. It is also a good way to kill yourself. But one or two glasses, at midnight, have a wonderful effect!' As Aino had indicated, these late night-caps did not improve his composition.

It was now two years since Sibelius had conducted in Helsinki. Only the personal intervention of General Mannerheim now persuaded him to take up his baton again, for a benefit concert held in early March at the Stock

Exchange in aid of Mannerheim's children's charity. The objective was to raise funds for a new children's hospital. Sibelius conducted his *Belshazzar's Feast* Suite and *Rakastava*, together with a novelty, the *Morceau romantique* on a theme by Jacob von Julin. It is also known under another name, *Pièce romantique*, though the composer never dignified it with an opus number. It was 'a simple waltz tune, which Professor Sibelius clad in a colourful and charming orchestral dress'. Von Julin was an industrialist who was related to Mannerheim and cut quite a figure in the Finnish wood and paper industry, as did Walter Ahlström and Walter Gräsbeck, who also belonged to Sibelius's circle. One of the two manuscripts of the *Morceau romantique*, which both the composer and Mannerheim had autographed, was auctioned, and together with the piano arrangement, which was sold all over the country, brought in a tidy sum for the hospital.

But the storm of applause which greeted Sibelius at the end of the concert did not tempt him to return to the podium. The Seventh Symphony had some time to wait before its Finnish première. Yet at the same time he pressed ahead with foreign concert tours. In February we find him writing to Hansen of his plans for a tour in England. 'I have been invited to conduct a symphony in Gloucester Cathedral on 10 and 11 September. I would particularly want to perform the new *Fantasia sinfonica* and would like you to press ahead with the printing. It is best to call it *Symphonie No. 7 (in einem Satze).*' On 11 May Wilhelm Hansen could reassure Sibelius with the news that the score was already engraved and that it had been sent to America for registration and to protect its copyright there.

In London, Rosa Newmarch had read in a Czech newspaper about Sibelius's great success in Copenhagen, and news of the invitation to the Three Choirs' Festival in Gloucester had also reached her. She wrote to him on 9 March 1925 congratulating him on his successes but bemoaning the fact that it was far too premature to fix a date for a new concert in London itself: 'Quite frankly, things are not working out particularly well for the Queen's Hall Orchestra under Chappells' management . . . You know how much I want to see you in the Queen's Hall if that were only possible. Symphonic music seems to be suffering from some sort of illness. Maybe it is a reaction against real music in favour of jazz. Or possibly the expansion of radio [*l'extension du "broad-casting"*] or perhaps a lack of conviction and progressiveness among the critics? It is difficult to say. I very much want to get to know your new symphony. I am curious as to the direction in which you have developed! Will it speak to my heart in the same way as does your Fourth?'

Mrs Newmarch suffered from diabetes and her doctors advised her to take a cure in Vichy or Marienbad. This news was not particularly encouraging for Sibelius. Four years had now passed since his last appearance in London, and there seemed at present little hope of another. But at least he was reassured on one point: the silence from Robert Newman was not because of any lack of goodwill but because of the orchestra's precarious finances. The crisis came to a head in 1927, when *Punch* published its famous cartoon showing Sir Henry Wood leaving the Queen's Hall followed by Beethoven's spirit saying: 'This is indeed a tragedy for the honour of London.' Later, when the position of the Promenade Concerts was stabilized, Sir Henry was to make Sibelius many conducting offers, each one more tempting than the last – albeit to no avail.

With Schnéevoigt's departure from the Helsinki musical scene, the number of important new works sharply diminished. Robert Kajanus favoured the French and in the mid-1920s Debussy's *La mer* and *Prélude à l'après-midi d'un faune*, Ravel's *La valse*, d'Indy's *Jour d'été à la montagne* and Roger-Ducasse's *Suite française* were found in his programmes. He also included Reger's Mozart Variations, and composers like Dohnányi and Szymanowski. But in the 1910s Helsinki had been the leading city for Mahler in the north: the First, Fourth and Fifth symphonies, as well as *Das Lied von der Erde,* had all been performed there. Now he had fallen into neglect; the spring season included only one Mahler work, the First Symphony, erroneously billed as a first performance! There had been no Schoenberg since 1918, when Schnéevoigt had conducted *Verklärte Nacht.* The other members of the second Viennese school, Berg and Webern, were unknown. Stravinsky's *Firebird* had been heard, but like Prokofiev's *Scythian Suite, Le Sacre du printemps* did not reach Helsinki until the 1930s, and Bartók and Hindemith were only names.

On 1 May Sibelius received a surprising enquiry from Wilhelm Hansen: 'Have you written any music to *The Tempest*? The Royal Theatre in Copenhagen is proposing to put on a production of the play and would possibly like to use your music.' Even if the letter did not go so far as formally to commission a score, it came close to it. In any event, it came at the right psychological moment. For more than ten years Sibelius had struggled heroically with symphonic form; now came a totally different challenge which would give his imagination a freer outlet. At the same time, Hansen's approach had something of fate about it. It was as if Axel Carpelan was speaking from beyond the grave. A quarter of a century before he had tried to interest Sibelius in Shakespeare's last plays: '*The Tempest* would suit you ideally. Prospero, Miranda, the spirits of earth and air etc.'

Initially Sibelius's response was cautious: 'Unfortunately I have not written any music for *The Tempest*.' But it is obvious that the Royal Theatre had made up its mind on Sibelius. The play was to be produced by Johannes Poulsen, who had both produced *Scaramouche* and played the title role. Perhaps that was one of the factors that prompted Sibelius to accept the commission and embark on the mammoth project in the early summer. Towards its end came a telegram from Hansen: 'CAN THE ROYAL THEATRE COUNT ON RECEIVING THE SCORE OF THE TEMPEST MUSIC BY 1 SEPTEMBER,

WHEN THE PLAY GOES INTO REHEARSAL?' Hansen was also concerned about the rights; Sibelius answered that his agreement was with the Theatre, but that all other rights were yet to be settled – and that Hansen would not want to acquire the work without seeing it?

The score was ready in time, and the première was evidently planned for the turn of the year. This is clear from Sibelius's letter to Adolf Paul on 2 November, when he reports that he cannot come to Germany before the end of the year or the beginning of January, depending on the date of the première. It was by all accounts not Sibelius's fault that it was postponed until 15 March 1926.

Perhaps he recognized himself in Prospero's words:

> I, thus neglecting worldly ends, all dedicated
> To closeness and the bettering of my mind
> With that, which by being so retir'd,
> O'erpriz'd all popular rate . . .

Had not Sibelius's 'poor lonely ego' striven to find its way into 'the unbounded recesses of the soul'? Had not his symphonies been received with lack of comprehension: 'How little the public and the critics realize what I have given them!' But in his diary he also noted: 'My time will come.' He could have said with Prospero:

> And by my prescience
> I find my zenith doth depend upon
> A most auspicious star, whose influence
> If now I court not but omit, my fortunes
> Will ever after droop.

In 1925 Sibelius's fortunes were at their zenith. The world was keenly awaiting the appearance of an Eighth Symphony, as indeed was he himself. But before that he was to compose more than thirty pieces for orchestra, chorus and solists, about which he could have said, like another Prospero:

> I have bedimm'd
> The noontide sun, call'd forth the mutinous winds,
> And 'twixt the green sea and the azure vault
> Set roaring war . . .

For Sibelius, Prospero was a symbol of the creative self and therefore of his own self, just as Ariel symbolized his inspiration and Caliban his demonic side. The music to *The Tempest* became not only Sibelius's greatest score for the stage, but also one of his foremost works, especially on account of the richness of its thematic invention, its harmonic daring and the finesse of its orchestral palette.

The director Adam Poulsen sent Sibelius a Danish translation of the play, together with his own plans and suggestions concerning the music. Poulsen's views had, in many instances, a direct effect on the way in which Sibelius's score took shape. Poulsson cut the first scene with the shipwreck and instead suggested that the storm should be evoked musically. When that reached its most violent climax, the curtain would rise and the audience would briefly see, as if in a vision, the ship go under, while Ferdinand and the sailors jump overboard. The curtain then goes down while the prelude continues slowly to a decrescendo. Sibelius followed Poulsson's dramatic conception, though rather surprisingly the Prelude begins with a mez-zoforte on lower strings and timpani – doubtless because, as an experienced man of the theatre, Sibelius would know that to begin *pianopianissimo* on lower strings would not be effective because of the external noise while the audience was settling down.

Sibelius followed Poulsen's dynamic conception in his overture. Against the chromatic surging of the strings and lower woodwind, the brass whoops like giant archaic *lures* and the piccolos whine. The whole-tone configur-ations become a symbol of the demons conjured up by Ariel at Prospero's command. The musical storm abates in a scarcely audible tritone figure, as if the first three notes of the Fourth Symphony's germ motive were played simultaneously.

> Hell is empty
> And all the devils are here.

'In the music for *The Tempest* there are a mass of motives which I would liked to have developed more exhaustively, but which within the bounds of the play I had to content myself with merely sketching,' he told Hansen after the première. But when he later extracted the two orchestral suites, he concentrated the material – not always to its best advantage. Take for example the short, dissonant *Intrada* which precedes the *Berceuse* in the suite. These few bars give only a pale impression of the powerful *Intrada* heard in the play at the climax of the last act. The *Berceuse* is played separately here. By his magic Prospero casts Miranda into a deep sleep:

> 'Tis a good dullness,
> And give it way: – I know thou canst not choose.

Sibelius asked for a harp placed high above the stage – perhaps he imagined its arpeggios as the music of the spheres. He wraps the sleeping Miranda in an atmosphere of tender melancholy. The composer has described how once, when on the border between life and death, he stood one night by the bedside of his two youngest daughters: 'They lay there sleeping, life awaiting them'.

The *Chorus of the Winds* accompanies Ariel's description of how he brought the shipwreck about at Prospero's command, and saw to it that all on board were saved:

Safely in harbour
Is the king's ship: and in the deep nook, where once
Thou call'dst me up at midnight to fetch dew
From the still vex'd Bermoothes . . .

This chorus is full of Sibelian nature mysticism – gentle winds which blow after the lulling of the storm and make the strings of the Aeolian harp tremble.

Ariel's first song, 'Come unto these yellow sands', is given the title *Naiads*, but in the original, Ariel lies at the water's edge in the guise of a mermaid; out at sea a throng of naiads play in the waves. The piece is reminiscent of *The Oceanides*, Sibelius's most impressionistic tone poem, and the chorus's dreamy chords on the vowel 'a' bring Debussy's *Sirènes* to mind.

As Robert Layton writes, Sibelius draws his portrait of Prospero with 'a Purcellian grandeur'. But behind the neo-classical mask Sibelius's own features are clearly visible. The sarabande-like rhythms and the archaic-sounding harmony mirror Sibelius's as much as Prospero's unquenchable energy, and at the same time a quality of resignation to the fact of growing old – 'as if, on descending to the grave, I shot an eagle in flight', to quote Sibelius himself.

The piece called *The Oak Tree* in the concert suite has Ariel playing the flute on stage. It derives from the producer's idea of having Ariel appear in the Second Act as a young oak tree. 'He breaks off a twig and plays on it, as if it were a flute, a sleepy melody like the sighing of the leaves at the tree-top.'

Poulsen saw Caliban as a prototype of 'raw, stupid, coarse and animal materialism'. Producers nowadays are more likely to see him as a victim of ruthless imperialism. Shakespeare's text allows many interpretations. In Sibelius's musical portrait, wild gestures of melody and rolls on the bass drum portray Caliban the monster, while the modulatory cast of the piece, in the spirit of Shostakovich, and the piccolo trills are a grotesque expression of impotence and desperation.

Before the Third Act, Poulsen wanted a short entr'acte called *Miranda*. It was to portray 'a beautiful, innocent and unspoilt girl, and the love between two young people who have never loved before – gracious, childlike and naïve'. Sibelius knew all about that: he had after all composed effective portraits of Mélisande and Swanwhite. He enveloped Miranda in a half-light of excitement and expectancy.

After this, the scene changes from thoughts of love to murderous plots and orgies of drinking. In Poulsen's production notes Ariel enters playing a clarinet and leading the drunken cupbearer Stephano and the jester Trinculo with Caliban and another bacchant in tow. As a musical vignette Sibelius writes a *Humoresque*, elegant but with dark, threatening undertones. When Caliban has succeeded in inciting Stephano to kill Prospero, the three drunkards sing a canon, 'Flout 'em and scout 'em, and scout 'em and flout 'em.' This canon, like the *Humoresque,* is in *commedia dell'arte* style.

But the portrait of Antonio, Prospero's traitorous brother and the usurper of his Duchy of Milan, is completely realistic. Antonio is waiting for an opportunity to remove his overlord Alonzo, King of Naples. 'Let it be tonight', with its arrogant Spanish rhythms, depicts Antonio's inordinate lust for power. As the tempo quickens, the music takes on the character of a *tarantella.* Only the final stretto of the piece finds its way into the Second Suite, where it is given the title *Dance Intermezzo.*

Almost all the six short pieces that follow centre around Ariel. In Ariel's melodrama the 'three men of sin', Alonzo, Sebastian and Antonio, sit down to the banquet that has suddenly materialized in front of them. Ariel in the guise of a harpy sweeps the delicacies off the table with his wings. The beat of his wings is illustrated by woodwind runs in parallel thirds. The E flat minor intermezzo between the Third and Fourth Acts is obviously intended to express Alonzo's grief over the death, as he believes, of his son during the shipwreck.

To Miranda and Ferdinand's delight, Prospero conjures up a harvest festival from antiquity. The producer has a rainbow appear in the sky and Sibelius writes an interlude *The Rainbow* as a tribute to Iris, the mythical goddess of the rainbow. Just as at the conclusion of the scherzo in the Fourth Symphony, Sibelius employs here one of the scales that Messiaen was to name *gammes à transposition limitées.* Iris's melodrama follows, in the form of a very Sibelian waltz, leading into Juno's waltz song, with wishes of 'honour, riches, marriage blessing' for the young pair. Neither is included in either of the suites. Water-nymphs enter with a graceful, minuet-like dance in which C major is followed by G sharp minor – the same succession of keys as between the first and second movement of the Third Symphony. The dance of the 'sun-burn'd sicklemen' that concludes the masque also contains rhythms reminiscent of the symphony.

One can only imagine how Sibelius empathized with Prospero's view of the artist's omnipotence. But what dread, what evil premonitions must have been awakened by the scene in the Fifth Act in which Prospero makes ready to abjure his 'rough magic'.

The only thing remaining for Prospero to do is to call up heavenly music to cure the darkened senses of his enemies; then, says Prospero:

> I'll break my staff
> Bury it certain fathoms in the earth,
> And deeper than did ever plummet sound
> I'll drown my book.

Shakespeare's stage direction calls for 'Solemn music', but Sibelius composes an *Intrada* full of strident dissonances and with an air of desperation about it. Does it portray Prospero's, or rather Sibelius's, disconsolate state of mind before the prospect of abandoning his art and leaving the island which has been the retreat of a creative artist – or does it merely portray the madness of the three princes driven in by Ariel after Prospero has finished speaking? Both interpretations are possible. Poulsen himself suggested 'a wild music which leads into a solemn melody'. Sibelius followed the dissonant introduction with a short postlude for strings alone, which had already appeared earlier in the *Chorus of the Winds*.

After Prospero's last words, 'Please you draw near', Sibelius wrote a short polonaise which is not one of the best numbers in the score. But in the autumn of 1927 the Finnish National Theatre mounted a production of *The Tempest* with Sibelius's music, the part of Ariel being played by his daughter Ruth Snellman. It was for this production that he added a short epilogue whose majestic baroque style, full of manly resignation, is connected with the portrait of Prospero. And Sibelius was right, for in the Epilogue Prospero does not address the public as an actor but remains Prospero:

> Now my charms are all o'erthrown,
> And what strength I have's mine own;
> Which is most faint . . .
> Let me not . . . dwell
> In this bare island by your spell
> But release me from my bands.

The play continues in the unknown.

By setting the Epilogue Sibelius demonstrated that, unlike Prospero, he had not broken his staff or drowned his book of symphonic wisdom. In Auden's poem *Prospero to Ariel*, Prospero says,

> We did it together, Ariel
> You found in me a desire for total devotion.

That could have been said by Sibelius to his Ariel, his inspiration. He was its slave just as much as it was his. But at this stage Ariel had not left him: he did not need to think, like Prospero:

> Why that's my darling Ariel!
> I shall miss thee.

Sibelius had long planned to avoid his sixtieth birthday celebrations by going to Italy in November, remaining there for the whole of the winter season so as to avoid the fuss that had marked his fiftieth. But in the end this idea came to nothing. Kajanus, faithful as ever, set the celebrations in train at the beginning of the season. His first concert of the season was an all-Sibelius one, with the Third Symphony, *The Oceanides* and the Violin Concerto with Naum Levin, a young violinist from Viipuri as soloist. The Society of Composers annual concert on 9 November was also a Sibelius affair, with the Second Symphony as the main work. Sibelius spent his birthday in Helsinki with his eldest daughter Eva Paloheimo. In the morning President Relander came to pay his respects and present him with the Grand Cross of the Order of the White Rose, after which other tributes, official and personal, poured in. A large public collection had raised the sum of 275,000 Finnish marks, of which 150,000 were placed at his immediate disposal. The remainder was invested and generated an income from which he benefited for the remainder of his life. Even more welcome was the news that the Diet had raised his annual pension from 30,000 to 100,000 marks. According to the papers, Sibelius celebrated the rest of the day with his family, but late into the evening he was serenaded by various groups of musicians.

The birthday photographs show that the transformation in his appearance that had begun at the time of his fiftieth birthday was now complete. The wrinkles in the somewhat ravaged face had begun to fill out, while the photos taken in 1923 in Gothenburg show an intermediate stage. The severity of manhood has begun to soften. Something of the openness and vulnerability had disappeared, but had not yet been replaced by the Olympian, timeless, granite-like features we recognize from later portraits.

One thing was missing: a concert conducted by the composer himself. The Seventh Symphony had still not been heard in Finland! The only birthday concert took place the following day, when Kajanus conducted the First Symphony, the suite from the incidental music to *Swanwhite* and the *Song of the Athenians*. No newspaper gives any indication of whether or not Sibelius attended. Generally speaking, it would appear that he avoided concerts and theatres where his music was performed, both in Finland and abroad.

CHAPTER EIGHTEEN

Tapiola

On the fourth day of the New Year, 1926, Sibelius received a telegram from New York: 'WILL YOU COMPOSE SYMPHONIC POEM FOR ME PER-FORMANCES NEXT NOVEMBER SYMPHONY SOCIETY OFFERS YOU FOUR HUNDRED DOLLARS (FOR THE) FIRST THREE PERFORMANCES OF SAME WILL PAY TWO HUNDRED IMMEDIATELY TWO HUNDRED ON RECEIPT OF SCORE.' The telegram was signed by the conductor Walter Damrosch. Sibelius wired his acceptance immediately, which prompted a quick response: 'We look forward with the keenest anticipation to the receipt of your score . . . It is, of course, understood that the choice of your subject and its form, is left entirely with you, and I would merely suggest that its length be about fifteen minutes and certainly not longer than twenty minutes.' The commission reflected Sibelius's increasing popularity in the United States. A New York publisher had just published five pieces for violin and piano, the *Danses champêtres,* Op. 106. The composer had offered the 'non-American' rights to Wilhelm Hansen (19 January 1926) and ten days later wrote asking 200 Danish kronor for each piece.

During the autumn of 1925 Sibelius had planned a foreign trip but had changed his mind several times; he had planned to make part of the journey with his childhood friend Walter von Konow. First, Sibelius and Aino had intended to go to Paris at the beginning of the year, but later dropped this idea and settled on Italy at the beginning of March. Walter was enthusiastic at the prospect of joining them: 'While you are working, Aino and I can pass the time in conversation or sightseeing in Rome.' But Sibelius was by no means certain that he would be able to compose in peace and quiet if Walter was with them. Sibelius's letter together with all his others to Walter were lost during the winter war of 1939–40, but it is clear from Walter's letters that Sibelius was not encouraging. Walter was not easily put off: 'The know-ledge that you are in the same place is in itself wonderful!!' Aino never found it easy to leave the children and Ainola. Perhaps the prospect of being shown over Rome by Walter was insufficiently tempting to outweigh her reluctance to leave house and home.

At last, on 20 March Sibelius set sail from Åbo for Stettin on board the

Oihonna, specially strengthened against the ice. It is puzzling why he did not go a few days earlier and stop off in Copenhagen for the première of *The Tempest*. But its world lay behind him, and what was now on his mind was the new work. On the way south from Stettin, Sibelius stopped off in Berlin to see his friend Adolf Paul and his publisher Robert Lienau. Paul was in dire straits and could not join Sibelius in town as he had pawned even his everyday clothes. Sibelius redeemed them and then went to Paul's home. 'The children, in particular Holger, are well brought up and delightful. They are all so naïve and simple that one is quite captivated. Tali is remarkable. That she puts up with it all is a mystery.' He took a cabin in the overnight sleeper to Munich, where he changed trains. He sent a card to Aino: 'The *Tempest* music has aroused much interest in Berlin . . . A good night, but the next one I couldn't get a sleeping cabin. I get to Rome at 10.15 tomorrow.' On arrival he went to his old hotel, the Minerva, where the Finnish Embassy had put him five years earlier. 'It's strange being here without having to give a concert. I haven't quite got used to it.' Being off duty, as it were, did not really suit him, and at the end of the year he was to make a brief comeback as a conductor with another concert in Copenhagen. But as in London some years earlier, he was tormented by a neighbouring pianist. 'Someone here is murdering a Liszt rhapsody. I can't bear it. I must stop – this pianist is totally impossible . . . My nerves are in a bad way. I am drenched in perspiration and my whole body is sticky. This because of the pianist.'

A lady from the Finnish legation who had looked after them both during their earlier visit took care of him again, and saw to it that he remained incognito, since Rome was 'crawling with Finns'. His next letter to Aino was written in pencil, as the table in his room was unsteady and the ink impossible. It is obvious that his tremor had not eased. He had to wait several days before his trunk arrived, which was worrying him as it contained the sketches for *Tapiola*. 'The church bells began ringing at 6 o'clock in the morning,' he told Aino. 'Everything is full of atmosphere. And everything in life is going well.' Even though the trees were already in leaf and in blossom, Rome was still chilly at the end of March and Sibelius would not have been comfortable without his fur coat. Walter von Konow turned up on 27 March.

Aino had obviously been concerned by some press reports about *The Tempest*. Sibelius's letter expresses surprise at the impression she had formed: 'They are some of the best reviews I have ever had – Shakespeare and Sibelius, the two geniuses, have found each other! They must have translated them badly [in the Finnish newspapers] or they have left out bits . . . We celebrated Walter's [sixtieth] birthday yesterday. In some ways he wears me out. And I am trying to cut myself off so as to work.' Von Konow was becoming something of a problem. Having no other company, his attentions were wholly focused on Sibelius. As he did at Ascona thirty years

before, when he chatted up the peasant boys, he frequented the less salubri-
ous parts of town, in which Sibelius did not feel at all comfortable.

It is obvious that he rather regretted the irritation he had betrayed at
Aino's reaction to *The Tempest* reviews: 'I have forgotten all that business
with *The Tempest*. It was a mistake to go along with Poulsen. He himself is
probably all right, but the actual production itself – as you wrote – poor.' All
the same, both *Berlingske Tidende* and *Politiken* wrote that its success was due
primarily to the incidental music and the decor!

Sibelius continued: 'I share your views about *The Tempest* music. I think it
would be better not to publish any of the stage music but to make a number
of small really good pieces. Try and rest – it is absolutely *imperative*. I understand more deeply than you realize what you have gone through. But I see
the future in a positive light. Today there is a *sirocco* and it is humid and hot.
As it is in August at home just before a storm . . . I love my room here and
the service is excellent. Last night I took one bath after another. Would it be
impossible to have such a bathroom built at home? – I would love *you* to
have one. I went yesterday to look at a room with Liisi Karttunen.
Uncomfortable and sordid. Impossible, although it's cheap. If you can't get
enough rest at home, go somewhere for a couple of weeks and have a bit of
peace. Don't worry about the cost – you spend all too little on yourself and
always have done. But life is so short!' He certainly was not worrying about
the cost – and decided to stay on at the Hotel Minerva.

Generally speaking, the tone of his letters rather than their content
reflects the way in which his work is progressing. Now, when *Tapiola* is
consuming him, he writes (4 April 1926): 'My nerves are much better and
work is going well . . . It is Easter and the church bells have been ringing all
day.' He tells of his plans to make a trip to Capri with von Konow. His
letters also make clear that if *Tapiola* was making progress, it was slow. 'But
then there is no great haste. Hansen is terribly keen on *The Tempest*. Telegraphed me again yesterday.' Sibelius was evidently dissatisfied with the
latter's offer: 15 per cent on every copy sold, with a 2,000 kronor advance. It
still rankled that Hansen had only agreed to take one of the five *Danses
champêtres*, of which Fischer had bought the American rights. 'They want
me to go to Copenhagen and I could make a stop over there on my way
back to Helsinki. And could then talk to Norrie (the head of the Royal
Theatre) about the contract and payment.'

What transpires from his correspondence in early April is that he had
already planned to rework several numbers into concert suites. Of course he
was drawn to Copenhagen by the prospect of seeing *The Tempest*, which was
the talking-point of the musical and theatrical world. But at the same time
he felt an even stronger reluctance to see anyone else conduct it. He was
afraid that the Danish musical public would see his absence from the pit as a
sign of old age. In the event, he went out of his way to avoid the Danish
capital while either *Scaramouche* or *The Tempest* were in production.

Sibelius's trip to Capri, which he called 'a wonder', proved a success, and in his letter to Aino he even floated the idea of spending the winter together there. 'It's rather cheap and the climate is perfect. It is high summer here, the roses are in full bloom etc. My pension, or hotel, is modest but *very* comfortable – very much in your style – except for the modest part.' The heavenly surroundings appeared even to have had a calming effect on Walter, whose company Sibelius now found 'harmonious'. After about a week, the two friends returned to Rome, which they reached on 19 April in time for Walter to catch the train to Finland the following day. Sibelius stayed on in Rome for a few days, and his letters show him to be in good spirits: '*The Forest* [Aino's suggestion?] is a good title. Perhaps I'll send [Damrosch] an explanation of what the name "Tapiola" stands for.' And two days later, on 21 April, he wrote that it was going to be excellent, that the Paris edition of the *New York Herald* had mentioned the new piece, and that *The Swan of Tuonela* and *En Saga* had been given that season. The day before his departure, Sibelius was invited to a dinner by his old friend Rolf Thesleff, the Finnish envoy in Rome. He had politely declined the offer of the official formal dinner which Thesleff had proposed in his honour, and suggested a more intimate family affair – 'an equally great honour' for him. Sibelius had put on full evening dress, which was the custom among his circle at Järvenpää even as late as the First World War. His host was not prepared for that, but forewarned by his butler, nipped upstairs and changed into his tails, and even went so far as to put on his decorations. In this he managed to trump his guest, who had left his at home! Their evening was animated.

By now Sibelius's thoughts were turning northwards, and on Saturday 24 April he took the train for Berlin, leaving the Eternal City behind him – for good.

– 2 –

On his way home from Rome, Sibelius stopped off in Berlin for a meeting with Hellmuth von Hase, who had come specially from Leipzig to see him. This set the seal on their earlier correspondence and led to the resumption of their long and friendly relationship. Sibelius was obviously pleased and promised him *Tapiola*. 'I can see they are keen to have me back,' he wrote to Aino. 'Hardly surprising, although I am sixty. *Tapiola* is already a *fait accompli* – though I work on it surely but slowly. Here in Berlin I am in a mood for work. The hotel . . . is quiet and pleasant. Another thing is that I have no piano, which at the present stage of its development is best.' This meant that Sibelius had begun working in full orchestral score. And he went on to say that he had to have the score ready by the end of June. He went off to Breitsprecher, the fashionable shoemaker, to order new shoes and ordered new shirts. By the middle of May he was back in Finland.

While he was away, his cause was being advanced on the other side of the

Atlantic. On 3 April 1926 Leopold Stokowski and the Philadelphia Orchestra introduced the Seventh Symphony to America and followed it up by a second performance a couple of days later. During the current season he had also given the Fifth Symphony no fewer than five times. *Musical America* described the Seventh as 'bleak, austere, solidly wrought, freighted with characteristic atmosphere and, on the whole, more cryptic than the Fifth Symphony, now becoming popularized'. At the end of the same month Stokowski and the Philadelphia Orchestra were ready to present the Sixth for the first time. This took place on 23 April and was repeated the following day. *Musical America*'s reviewer appears to have grasped its essential character: 'Eccentric modern idioms are renounced and the harmonic and contrapuntal treatment has the nobility and unsensationalism of Brahms . . . The effect of the score as a whole is that of "pure music", defying the most ingenious interpretations of the program commentator.' (1 May 1926)

On 10 August Sibelius was alarmed to receive a telegram from Breitkopf & Härtel demanding the immediate delivery of *Tapiola*. Sibelius finished the score a couple of weeks later and sent it off to Leipzig. It was now important for them to get the score and parts engraved as quickly as possible – and they reacted with despatch. As early as 8 September they sent Sibelius a telegram saying that *Tapiola* would be ready by 15 October. Now the composer was gripped by a steadily increasing anxiety and irritation. On Friday 10 September he made a long diary entry, the first of the year!

'Am worried about *Tapiola*. B & H have the score, but they are taking their time. I happen to know that my biographer W. Niemann is one of their advisers. If only one could get rid of this know-all who has done me more harm than anyone else. *Tapiola* – well, if Runeberg had been forced to deliver *Kung Fjalar* in the month of March he would have turned in something completely different. I'm sorry I accepted this 'commission'. *The Tempest* and [the cantata] *Väinön virsi* are also commissions. Am I really cut out for this sort of thing?! . . . Cannot be on my own. Am drinking 'wisky' [sic]. My system can't cope.'

On 17 September Sibelius sent a telegram to Breitkopf & Härtel asking them to return *Tapiola* and warning them that he proposed to make some cuts. Breitkopf replied with a touch of irritation that the score was already engraved and that they were working on the parts, which would now have to be held up until they received his changes. They sent the score by air mail on the 21st together with two sets of proofs. They also included a warning that on no account was he to send the manuscript direct to America! At last Sibelius held the *Tapiola* score in his hand. In his heart of hearts he must have realized that the work was already in its final form. But seized as he was by doubt and anxiety he had managed to talk himself into believing that more work had to be done on the score.

But all the many worries that besieged him sprang from the same concern: the first performance of *Tapiola*. Up to this point he had conducted the premières of all his major orchestral works from the autograph score, the only exception being the tone poem *Night Ride and Sunrise*, which Alexander Siloti conducted in St Petersburg at a time when he was recovering from his throat operation. In these circumstances, he had always been in a position after the rehearsals and première to make alterations or even refashion the whole score. *Tapiola*, on the other hand, was to be conducted by Damrosch and from a definitive printed score. And he had given up – voluntarily – the possibility of making further changes. Yet suppose that after he had actually heard *Tapiola* he was not satisfied with it? Even if his 'inner ear' was well equipped to imagine the aural effects he had created, there was always the possibility that the actual sound would bring to light some surprises or miscalculations. Would it then be possible to make changes, by which time there may have been performances in other cities? Breitkopf would probably agree to reprint the score, but the whole episode would be embarrassing for a composer of his standing. Would his self-esteem have survived the cries of delight of his detractors? And was Walter Damrosch, a sound, cultured Brahmsian, really the right man to bring *Tapiola* into the world? Its wild atmosphere and its magic spells called for a Toscanini, a Stokowski, a Koussevitzky or the young Furtwängler. All in all, the New York première filled him with foreboding. He must have felt that *Tapiola* was slipping out of his hands before its time and was beginning a life of its own.

All this was fraught with danger. Did he not reckon with the possibility that his powers of self-criticism would reach the impossible level he had come to acknowledge, and assume a destructive role in his creative life? In such a frame of mind he might well discover small weaknesses in the score that would loom so large in his consciousness that they would overshadow everything else. He could have imagined flaws and failings that existed only in his feverish imagination. What would have happened to *Tapiola* had his judgment failed him we can only surmise. Admittedly in the 1890s, after several successful performances, he had withdrawn three important pieces, *Kullervo*, *Lemminkäinen and the Maidens of the Island* and *Lemminkäinen in Tuonela*. They were hidden away in a drawer but would in their time re-emerge to make their way into the concert repertoire and the recording catalogues. It was the growth of these doubts that cast light on the fate which was to meet the Eighth Symphony.

Breitkopf & Härtel's parcel with *Tapiola* arrived at Ainola just before Sibelius left for Copenhagen, where he was to conduct a concert of his music. His faithful Danish supporter Gunnar Hauch and his countless admirers at *Nationaltidende* and all over Copenhagen thought the time was ripe for a repeat of his triumph two years earlier, particularly in view of the fact that President Relander of Finland was to make a state visit to Denmark. Sibelius's concert would make a festive climax. Hauch suggested 3–6 October for the concerts. Rather surprisingly, in view of the fact that he had turned down invitations from Gloucester and Gothenburg and had pulled out of his engagement in Bergen, Sibelius accepted.

No sooner had he done so than doubts began to surface. Two years earlier the critic of *Politiken* had written that he had stolen the show and the whole season with his *Valse triste*! For his admirers, a two-year wait for a return visit was too long – not long enough, however, for his detractors! Moreover, the situation was rather more sensitive than before. Hauch had mentioned that the Danish Concert Society founded by the composer Louis Glass would be celebrating its twenty-fifth anniversary in mid-October with a series of concerts of Nordic music, with Johan Halvorsen and Robert Kajanus among the guest conductors. Sibelius suddenly realized that his concerts would to a certain extent put these in the shadow, and telegraphed his withdrawal: 'MY PROMISE TO COME WAS TOO HASTY.' (13 September 1926) He developed his reasons in a letter the following day, saying that one should perhaps consider the claims of the 'lesser lights'. Hauch was panic-stricken: he had already reserved 8 October as the most suitable date – unaware that the presidential visit was to culminate in a gala performance at the Royal Theatre! He immediately sent off a telegram pleading with Sibelius to think again and suggesting 2 October as a suitable date which would avoid any clash with the Concert Society's celebrations. Sibelius agreed to come, presumably out of loyalty to Hauch, a fine writer on music, who had made his career in the Copenhagen criminal investigation bureau and set great store by his encounters with great musicians in general and Sibelius in particular.

The first rehearsal was on 30 September, the day on which Sibelius arrived in Copenhagen. As he was taking his morning coffee at the Hotel d'Angleterre, his eye alighted on an article in *Politiken* with the provocative headline 'Danish Concert Society's Anniversary Concerts – Sibelius'. He could read Danish without difficulty. The article was by Louis Glass himself, who on an earlier visit had made a speech in his honour. Glass was beside himself, and put the blame for what he feared would now be the failure of the Anniversary Concerts firmly on Sibelius's shoulders: 'The precarious financial situation here will certainly have its effect – after the Sibelius concerts are out of the way.' To put on a Sibelius concert in honour of the Finnish presidential visit struck him as quite bizarre. If the King of Denmark were to visit Helsinki, could you imagine the Finns sending for Carl Nielsen? Anybody who proposed such an idea would be thought of as out of their mind. It would surely be Finnish music which the Danish King would want to hear. But the real reason for his outburst was rather more obvious: concerts of new music from the Nordic countries seldom drew full houses.

Yet why was it so bizarre to organize a Sibelius concert a few days before the presidential visit? It was (and still is) far from uncommon practice on such occasions to arrange concerts and exhibitions in the host country.

Indeed, how warmly Carl Nielsen would have been welcomed had he come to Helsinki a week before King Christian's visit in May 1928! Even though Glass's article was primarily directed against Hauch and Sibelius's backers at the *Nationaltidende*, Sibelius did not fail to note the dangers.

Not only the timing of the concert but also the programme itself bore the marks of improvisation. Hauch had suggested the Fifth Symphony (Sibelius had in fact conducted all his symphonies in Copenhagen, with the exception of the Third), the *King Christian* suite and *Finlandia*. Between the last two pieces Sibelius was free to insert a work of his choice. Quite astonishingly he chose one of his least successful pieces, the rather nondescript *Impromptu*, Op. 19, for female voices and orchestra to words by Viktor Rydberg. Even though the chorus had been well prepared by the young Mogens Wöldike, the full rehearsals took their toll on Sibelius's nerves and absorbed far too much valuable time that could have been spent polishing the symphony. The second half of the programme had the undoubted character of a popular concert. The composer could surely have included the Prelude to *The Tempest*, whose score and parts would have been available from the Royal Theatre's library (only a couple of months later Wilhelm Furtwängler conducted it in New York). When the day of the concert came, Sibelius mounted the podium to be met by a sea of faces: there was not an empty seat in the hall. His pleasure must have been touched with *Schadenfreude*; at least the Copenhagen musical public had rallied to him, whatever Glass might write! The performance of the Fifth Symphony went well enough – though not, it would seem, as successfully as it had two years earlier. The orchestra had only played it once before, and in Europe at this time, though not in America, the piece was regarded as difficult. One would have thought that his experiences in London and Stockholm would have taught him that the final climax and the dissonances before the very ending of the symphony were at that time considered too 'modern' to unleash the storm of applause which would have greeted the finales of the First and Second symphonies. And so it proved: the audience reacted politely but without enthusiasm once the six last chords had resounded. Sibelius was hurt, so much so that he went backstage to his room and threatened to abandon the rest of the concert, though he inevitably yielded to the persuasions of his friends and appeals to his professionalism. Of course, the *King Christian* suite won over the public, and the *Ballade*, which depicts the bloodbath in Stockholm when the rebellious Swedish noblemen were massacred, would doubtless have given particular satisfaction! The *Impromptu*, Op. 19, made no great impression either on the audience or on the press. The choir sang in a dilettantish fashion and pronounced Rydberg's text in anything but an authentic manner, so that the overall effect was both 'confusing and unconvincing'. However, *Finlandia* sealed the concert's success and found Sibelius at his most charismatic; as an encore he conducted *Valse triste,* which he had to repeat! And with that he brought what was to be his last concert appearance to a triumphant close.

The *Berlingske Tidende,* which had published Glass's article, was lyrical in Sibelius's praise, but none of the Danish critics seem to have really understood the true character and significance of the Fifth Symphony. On this occasion there was no question of repeating the concert, and in any event the visit had left an unpleasant taste in Sibelius's mouth. He had had his doubts about Hauch's plans, but had not followed his intuition. He more than anyone might have been expected to realize what the dangers of disobeying this inner imperative would be. More was at stake than just a guest appearance, since he secretly hoped that the Copenhagen concert would launch a new career for him as composer–conductor that would embrace Boston, Philadelphia and New York as well as London, Berlin and Vienna. But his signal was neither sufficiently carefully prepared nor sufficiently strong to get him anywhere.

Sibelius made his way home. Gunnar Hauch accompanied him as far as Malmö. When Hauch returned to Danish soil, he spent a few days resting at a coastal resort by the Öresund. All the excitement and controversy of the Sibelius concert had taken its toll on Hauch and evidently upset him more than it did the composer himself.

When Sibelius arrived home at Ainola on 6 October, the manuscript of *Tapiola* and the two sets of proofs clamoured for his attention. With the stimulus and excitement of Copenhagen he had almost forgotten his *idée fixe* that this commission was in some way below par. Now that he had sufficient distance between *Tapiola* and himself, he could look at it with a different perspective. The revision work occupied him for barely a week, and it is obvious that it involved no more than the kind of editing that he had done fifteen years earlier after the first performance of the Fourth Symphony. He certainly made no drastic changes, to judge from Breitkopf's subsequent acknowledgement of the score on 18 October, which announced that the actual printing would begin within a matter of days. They expressed pleasure at receiving the composer's prose explanation, which they had turned into the familiar quatrain that adorns the score, and sought his approval of it. More to the point, they promised to send an honorarium of 3,000 Reichsmark. It is obvious that Sibelius's anxieties about *Tapiola* were totally unfounded.

As usual, he had returned from Copenhagen without money. As his honorarium for *Tapiola* did not cover his current expenditure, he asked Breitkopf whether they would be interested in taking the *Danses champêtres.* But unfortunately they could not come to terms with Fischer, who had the American rights, and eventually, as we have seen, the pieces were published by Wilhelm Hansen. Sibelius's finances were still in a parlous state. Much though he would have liked to, he was unable to come to the aid of his friend Adolf Paul, who was in even more desperate straits: 'I have been very sorry that I quite frankly could not send you anything, my old friend. But many promises made on my sixtieth birthday have gone unfulfilled. For example, many international figures sent me a splendid telegram from New York with a promise that I would receive a birthday gift. The telegram came through our General Consul in America. When the news of my State Pension became public, everyone in America thought that I was getting 100,000 dollars [in fact it was 100,000 marks, worth about $2,500 at that time] and everything dried up – I received nothing. From the other funds, I shall receive only the interest, about 10,000 marks in a year or so. When I next come to Berlin I will give you all the details.'

The score and parts of *Tapiola* reached Damrosch as early as November, and the first performance was scheduled for Sunday 26 December at a New York Symphony Society concert at Mecca Temple, not the ideal acoustic. As was his wont, Damrosch prefaced the performance with a short introduction: 'We see and feel the infinite, dark green forests; we hear the howling winds, whose icy sounds seem to come from the North Pole itself. Through all this we glimpse the ghostly shadows of gods and the strange beings that belong to Nordic mythology, whispering their secrets and making their mystical dances among the branches and trees.' Not long after the première Sibelius received a telegram from New York, 'TAPIOLA ENORMOUS SUCCESS ENTHUSIASTIC CONGRATULATIONS DAMROSCH', and some days later a letter: 'I consider *Tapiola* to be one of the most original and fascinating works from your pen. The variety of expression that you give to the one theme in the various episodes, the closely knit musical structure, the highly original orchestration, and, above all, the poetic imagery of the entire work, are truly marvellous. No one but a Norseman could have written this work. We were all enthralled by the dark pine forests and the shadowy gods and wood-nymphs who dwell therein. The coda with its icy winds sweeping through the forest made us shiver.'

All the same, *Tapiola* did not make a really strong critical impact. And although Olin Downes in the *New York Times* wrote of its mastery, its strong atmosphere and sense of vision, he noted: 'The melodic material is undeniably sparse ... Sibelius creates a powerful atmosphere and evokes with extraordinary mastery the deep mysteries of the wilderness, the visions and special signs which the mythological eye is able to discover among the shadows of the primæval forest. Sibelius's melodic invention in later years has never reached the level of the earlier tone poems and symphonies but ... as far as form is concerned, his music has become steadily more fascinating and acquired an increasingly exciting and individual stamp.'

Later on, in April 1927, when he was making his customary round-up of the season's programmes, Downes spoke of *Tapiola* as to some extent a disappointment – 'a work of style and manner rather than inspiration'. Lawrence Gilman in the *New York Herald Tribune* was no more positive, and yearned for another work of the stature of his 'great masterpiece', the Fourth Symphony. A third critic found 'signs which indicate that Sibelius's powerful imagination is beginning to run out'. He found the main idea not only weak but sterile. 'Only towards the end are we reminded of the voice of the master from the North who made so indelible an earlier impression.' Much of this might have been due to Damrosch's conducting.

It was only with Serge Koussevitzky and the Boston Symphony Orchestra some six years later that *Tapiola* came into its own. Koussevitzky had been slow to come to Sibelius, and had seen it as too 'dark' – perhaps surprisingly, when one remembers that he was born in Vishny Volotchok in very similar terrain. He won his greatest fame with the Russian repertoire and the French impressionists, as well as Richard Strauss. The critics were captivated by his brilliant virtuosity, rhythmic vitality and the iridescent quality of his interpretations, which were regarded as unsurpassed in America. When he ventured into the symphonies of Beethoven and Brahms, doubts could be voiced, but there was no doubt about his charismatic and magnetic personality. During his period the Boston Symphony rose to be one of the world's very greatest orchestras. In his Koussevitzky biography the German musicologist Hugo Leichtentritt ranks the leading conductors of the day as four in number, Koussevitzky, Toscanini, Walter and Furtwängler – and among the up-and-coming maestros were Szell, Klemperer and Artur Rodzinki. But of Koussevitzky as Sibelius conductor Leichtentritt waxes eloquent: 'Koussevitzky holds the key which opens the door to the heights and depths of Sibelius's Nordic music. It is arguable whether we will ever experience more authoritative and flawless performances of the Finnish master's music than those conceived during Koussevitzky's era at Boston.'

Koussevitzky had 'discovered' Sibelius in the mid-1920s, though he had conducted one of the symphonies (probably the First) in Russia in 1916. Not without reason, Koussevitzky called the Seventh 'Sibelius's Parsifal', and so powerful was his performance that for many conductors it remained a model. At the beginning of January 1927 Koussevitzky and his orchestra brought the symphony to New York after having given it in Boston. The new piece received a mixed reception and found Downes still unreceptive to Sibelius's later style: the Seventh Symphony is, he said, 'less original in musical substance than the Fifth. Sibelius has succumbed at times to the great enchanter of Bayreuth; he has even sent his soul to Paris and has yielded to the persuasive magic of Debussy.' (9 January 1927)

Lawrence Gilman in the *New York Herald Tribune* wrote with enthusiasm: 'Sibelius handles with uncommon mastery the system of thematic evolution which Beethoven sets as the difficult model for all future symphonists; and his application of the principle is conspicuous in this new score. Thematic motives, which seem bare and unpromising, are made to yield an astonishing richness and variety of tonal speech.' Henry T. Parker had also become aware of a link with Beethoven: 'One grows conscious in this music of a curious Beethoven kinship. Mr Gilman very properly detected in the scherzando episode a similarity of mood and matter to the "Eroica". And shortly after the A minor opening there comes a broad and bardic song in the strings, which as it mounts and unfolds in an almost religious mood, discovers some of the very spirit and quality of the later Beethoven adagios.'

But the reaction against Sibelius was already beginning to surface. Leonard Liebling quoted the celebrated verdict on Richard Strauss and thought this could be applied to Sibelius: 'He was a talented composer who used to be a genius. Much of the same estimate falls into the mind when contemplating the case of Sibelius . . . He arrived at a time when symphonic creation seemed to have ended with Brahms and Tchaikovsky, and that made the welcome to Sibelius a warm and universal one. He deserved it richly, too, on the basis of individual merit. As the years wore on, however, Sibelius sang his song over and over. He found no new note, no variety of expression, no vitally compelling subjects or forms . . . The Seventh Symphony has isolated moments of nobility, of charm, of glowing passion, and consistently it shows the practised hand of a symphonic expert, but the work as a whole lacks sustained interest and cumulative power . . . His message was delivered long ago.'

The year 1926 ended on a generally happy note, however. A letter Sibelius wrote to Olga Bratt in Gothenburg gives an idea of his mood:

I bless my orchestral pieces since they brought me the delight of receiving so kind and warm a letter from you [some of his orchestral pieces had just been performed in Gothenburg] . . .

My thoughts turn to you so often. When I am writing and composing, your image is always in the forefront of my mind. That is not in itself remarkable – but natural. I mention this only as a reason for my so-called diligence.

The well-being and happiness of those who are dear to you is always close to my heart – although I am barely acquainted with Mr Leif . . .

Stenhammar's illness is a great sorrow for me. I am so very fond of him. He fortunately has his wonderful wife, your sister, and so is very fortunate in being so well related.

The expression is *das Streben tut leicht das Leben schwer.* And in this way my life has gone. I am burning the candle at both ends. Perhaps it is a tallow candle, for they burn to the bitter end – so long as the scissors permit.

My own dear ones and those around me are a great joy to me, and are so understanding. (20 December 1926)

The new work that was now occupying Sibelius was obviously the Eighth Symphony. It had presumably been in the planning stage for some time, but two commissions had come in between: *The Tempest* and *Tapiola*. Now he should have been, as it were, in open water, but he was still preoccupied by the job of reworking *The Tempest* into two concert suites. Although the news of Stenhammar's illness cast a shadow over the festive season, he was otherwise in good spirits over Christmas. The new work had him in its grip. At the end of the autumn Gunnar Hauch had been to Germany and spoken to Furtwängler about Sibelius and in particular *The Tempest,* whose repute had reached the German conductor. Hauch persuaded the Royal Theatre to send him the score of the Prelude, and Furtwängler decided to take it to New York, where he was to conduct the Philharmonic Society's Orchestra. According to Hauch, he was also eager to conduct *The Bard*.

CHAPTER NINETEEN

1927

Sibelius enjoyed Heine, not least because his cycle of poems *Nordsee* brings so vividly to life the Greece of antiquity with its gods and myths. Among these poems can be found *Der Gesang der Okeaniden*, which prompts the question of whether Sibelius's tone poem was directly inspired by Homer or whether he had Heine's poem in mind. Sibelius could find parallels in the Heine poems with his own ideas of musical metamorphosis: the sea glistens like liquid gold in the moonlight and against the light-blue, starless sky, 'the white clouds hover like giant marble shimmering gods, in constantly changing forms'. But false, deceiving tongues have cast the eternal gods to destruction:

> Und die armen Götter, oben am Himmel
> Wandern sie, qualvoll
> Trostlos unendliche Bahnen,
> Und können nicht sterben
> Und schleppen mit sich
> Ihr strahlendes Elend.
>
> *(Sonnenuntergang)*

At the beginning of 1927 Sibelius stood at the height of his creative powers. Four of his very greatest works had been completed in as many years (1923–6), and before that period had ended, he had already embarked on an eighth symphony. But the years immediately after *Tapiola* posed entirely different problems. Judging from the documentation that survives, there is no question that from 1927 for the next six years, and perhaps even longer, Sibelius worked intensively on the new symphony. He was the only person in the world to see the sketches he had made and, apart from his copyist, the finished score of the first movement, and possibly the remaining movements of the work. So we are faced with the problem of describing a long period of work without actually being able to turn to the actual results. Of our three central concerns – the life, the surrounding world and the musical works – the third and most important remains shrouded in mystery.

The internal balance of the biography is disturbed. Of course, we do know one thing which Sibelius himself did not know, or even at this stage suspect, that neither he nor anyone else would ever hear the symphony performed and that no sketches would be permitted to survive.

As a conductor he had made a come-back after a gap of two years. In spite of a less than ideal programme, all too little rehearsal time and a hostile salvo from the press, his Copenhagen visit had been a success. America beckoned like some Eldorado. He could with good reason take heart, as in the good old times: 'Glorious Ego, what are you waiting for? *Man lebt nur einmal!*'

$-2-$

At the turn of January-February 1927, Sibelius and Aino set off together for Paris. He badly needed a change of scene and atmosphere, to hear foreign orchestras playing new music and to see new faces. Doubtless he hoped that he would hear some late Debussy and some newer French music that would stimulate and renew his spirit. They booked into the Hotel Voltaire, which is on the Left Bank at the corner of Quai Voltaire. Here Wagner had composed *The Flying Dutchman* and both Baudelaire and Oscar Wilde had been among the clientele. From his window he could see the dark waters of the Seine and on the opposite bank the Louvre. But instead of pressing on with the Eighth Symphony, Sibelius occupied himself with work on *The Tempest* suites. The forthcoming American première of its Prelude no doubt preyed on his nerves, and on 11 February he wrote to Hansen asking him to send the score to Paris. Four days later he wrote to the Royal Theatre to find out whether it would be possible to see *The Tempest* either at the end of March or beginning of April in Copenhagen. 'It would be of great value.'

The score of the Prelude arrived in due course, but the Royal Theatre was slow in responding to his question. It was not until the end of March that they wrote that there would be a performance of the play on 8 April at his request. At the end of February Sibelius gave an interview to the Paris correspondent of the Finnish newspaper *Suomen Kuvalehti* in which he expressed his interest in contemporary French music: 'I am listening to a great deal of modern French music for my own pleasure – I don't think I have ever gone so often to concerts as I have here. There is enough here to last a lifetime: even on my deathbed, I will want to know in which direction music is developing. One of the most surprising facets of new French music is the great technical resource and sureness of touch as well as its openness.'

Sibelius's interest extended beyond such classics as Debussy, Ravel, Florent Schmitt and Erik Satie to the younger generation, Milhaud, Roussel and Honegger. He expressed surprise that concert programmes would juxtapose the classical repertoire side by side with the newest music, for example Mendelssohn's *Fingal's Cave* Overture alongside a symphony by Roussel. The latter, presumably the Second, made a strong impression on him. 'And also one hears much older, one might say forgotten, masters such as the Italian, Monteverdi . . . ' Present-day listeners must find it difficult to understand how seldom Sibelius and his contemporaries had the opportunity of hearing early music. It was the growth of broadcasting and the gramophone which was to bring the baroque and renaissance repertoire, as well as non-Western music, before the public. Debussy had already gently tapped these sources, and Sibelius himself in the Sixth Symphony gives evidence of having steeped himself in Palestrina. From Monteverdi, Sibelius turns to Stravinsky, who is one of 'those composers who swings back and forth from Bach to the latest modern trends'. The interview touched on how much exposure his music was receiving in France – a sensitive topic, for the contrast between Paris and New York could hardly be more striking. In America he was performed by conductors and orchestras of world class, whereas in Paris he was met by a wall of incomprehension. As we have mentioned, Stokowski had conducted the Fifth, Sixth and Seventh Symphonies in Philadelphia in 1926, and Damrosch had premièred *Tapiola* in New York. Koussevitzky had given the Seventh in Boston and the following January took it to New York. In France not a single Sibelius symphony was performed in 1927. Kajanus and the Helsinki Orchestra had brought the First Symphony to Paris in 1900, and in 1921 Kajanus had conducted the Pasdeloup Orchestra in a concert that included the Third. Chevillard and Rhené-Baton had both included *The Swan of Tuonela* and *En Saga* in their programmes – and that was about all!

Sibelius and Aino appear to have been captivated by Florent Schmitt's *Three Rhapsodies* – one French, one Polish and one Viennese – for two pianos. 'A pianist and his wife [Robert and Gaby Casadesus] played them altogether marvellously,' wrote Aino to Katarina. 'I nearly fell off the chair (Papa was also delighted, not just me) and one's pulse really quickened. Papa immediately rushed out the following morning to buy them for you.' Sibelius was, according to Aino, in excellent spirits and avoided all things Finnish like the plague. When Sibelius worked back at the hotel, Aino went to the theatre on her own and saw Sarah Bernhardt. When Aino wrote later, it was obvious that the enchantment of new French music was beginning to wear thin. The couple had heard the Bach Triple Concerto and Mozart's E flat Symphony, which was the best thing they heard in Paris: 'We felt as if we were *purifiés* of the noise of car horns' and all the other features of modern city life. It would seem too that they had tired of the sonorities favoured by French composers: 'The sound appears to well up from oriental springs, and then comes the celeste, "*flûtes gémissantes*" and muted trumpets. Papa will not say what he really must think, out of pure politeness, but they are very full of themselves, and new composers crop up everywhere writing in every conceivable form. But superficiality is the quality that they all have in common.' The musical climate took its cue from pieces like Milhaud's *La Création du Monde*, Honegger's *Pacific 231* and Poulenc's *Mouvements perpetuels* and his song-cycle *Le Bestiaire*, a world that Sibelius would scarcely have found wholly congenial – at least not in the longer term.

In 1927 the commanding figure on the Parisian scene was Stravinsky. He was the last word in fashion, and by his side even Prokofiev had been put in the shade. In any event, by the time Sibelius had arrived in Paris, Prokofiev had already left for his first triumphant concert tour of the Soviet Union. In a sense the Sibeliuses' Paris trip was ill-timed. The spring season had not got fully into its stride; had they come a few weeks later they would have heard Stravinsky conducting the première of *Oedipus Rex* and seen Diaghilev's production of Prokofiev's *Le pas d'acier*. In her last letter to Katarina, Aino speaks of their travel plans: 'Probably on Thursday or Friday the 25th we will come home via Berlin. We won't after all be going to Copenhagen, but will probably come back through Sweden and will be home by the beginning of April.'

In Berlin, Janne and Aino stopped off to see Adolf Paul. They decided that the date of *The Tempest* performance (18 April) would have involved them in too long a delay and too much expense. And so, although it was the talk of the theatre world, Sibelius never saw Johannes Poulsens's famous production nor heard the score in its original setting. On Sibelius's return, his cough, which had worried Paul while they were in Berlin, developed into influenza.

– 3 –

On 25 April 1927 Robert Kajanus and the Helsinki Orchestra gave a concert that presented three Finnish first performances – the Seventh Symphony, *Tapiola* and the Prelude to *The Tempest* – along with the *Rakastava* suite. Nowhere is there any evidence that Sibelius attended the concert, though it is possible that he was still recovering from his bout of influenza. It is all the more strange that only a few days later, on 2 May, when Kajanus gave a concert of Finnish music during the Nordic Music Week in Stockholm, none of these was included. The concert, believe it or not, lasted the best part of three hours, during which Madetoja conducted his Third Symphony, and at the very end Sibelius was represented by an insignificant piece, the cantata *Song of the Earth*. This was the only Sibelius played at the festival. The contrast with the Danes could hardly have been stronger: Nielsen was represented by his Fourth Symphony, which formed the centrepiece of their concert! Needless to say, Sibelius was put totally in the shade. And yet, although Sibelius had conducted the Seventh Symphony in Stockholm, both the Prelude to *The Tempest* and *Tapiola* would have been first performances. Peterson-Berger vented his spleen on the Finns: for him Aarre Merikanto's *Pan*, Erik Furuhjelm's *Exotica* and Väinö Raitio's *Nocturne* were 'internationalist cacophony'; Madetoja's symphony showed little sense of form, Kajanus's new *Overtura sinfonica* was 'kapellmeistermusik without ideas'.

The Sibelius was a 'hastily put-together commission job where some moments of inspiration shine through the mass of sequences and other facile repetitions'. The only piece to which he gave any credit was Selim Palmgren's *Suite Pastorale*. Even though the *Song of the Earth* found greater favour with Kurt Atterberg and, surprisingly enough, Moses Pergament, it was Peterson-Berger's tirade which infuriated Sibelius. Curt Berg in *Stockholms Dagblad* was hardly better: 'In spite of the evening's endurance, one was a little curious as to what Finland's, yes, perhaps the world's, foremost living composer would have to offer. But the great man had been disadvantaged by the programme . . . the cantata is on the whole plain and monotonous.'

The choice of programme had caused surprise and embarrassment in Finland itself. The Finnish-language *Uusi Suomi* added: 'When a persistent rumour has it that . . . Sibelius's choral piece was inserted in the programme without even consulting the master himself about which of his works he would like to represent him or asking his permission to perform the choral piece, the whole event appears in a very disturbing light. Why was such tactlessness directed just against Sibelius?' The selfsame day found the composer in the depths of depression and fury, as we see from his diary, which he had not touched for eight months.'

[8 May 1927] Isolation and loneliness is driving me to despair. Not even my wife is talking to me. Life has been tremendously difficult because no one thought to consult me about the choice of my composition at the Stockholm Music Week. There were many factors at play, not only objective considerations. In order to survive, I have to have alcohol. Wine or wisky [*sic*]! And that's where all my troubles begin. Am abused, alone, and all my real friends are dead. My prestige here at present is rock-bottom. Impossible to work. If only there were a way out. A sad but deep truth: *when things go well*, I have plenty of friends and am happy. When things go badly, *everyone* leaves me alone.

Must make the best use of the time I have left. Written to Hansen concerning *Scaramouche* etc. The cellist Kindler . . . wants me to write him a piece for cello and orchestra. Well, we'll see. Tried to have an alcohol-free day, despite the fact that there is so much annoying me and no one to talk to. Aino said I have only myself to blame for losing all my friends. I lost some when my reputation abroad began to soar, and others faded away when I was no longer young and all the rage. In reality, all they want is to bask in my reflected glory. Perhaps it is all my fault.

In his summing up in *Dagens Nyheter*, Peterson-Berger pulled no punches: 'I cannot call to mind any other musical celebration where the participants have behaved like such old women in their over-sensitiveness, given rein to such irritability and exhibited such hunger for praise. We know from the experience of the participating countries that three are known for their highly-developed self-admiration, and for the superior and pitying glances they cast on the fourth, their host country, which is known to admire everything foreign . . . But obviously no one dared touch on the really sensitive issue, that there is no point in celebrating something if there is nothing to celebrate.'

When Sibelius opened *Hufvudstadsbladet* on 11 May he was greeted by Kajanus's grim and staring gaze. 'P-B was right in many respects,' he said. 'The Music Week was a guiding principle for us . . . Every country except Denmark made the mistake of allowing its programmes to be dominated by ultra-modern tendencies . . . ' There was not a word from him about the widely-reported comments in the other Scandinavian countries, as well as in Finland, that Sibelius had been shabbily treated in the Finnish programme. Sibelius seethed with anger:

[11 May 1927] Beautiful day, though cold and windy. Went for a walk. Find all his self-promotion [Kajanus's interview] so pathetic. He and his supporters want to dethrone me. And then what? After them there will be others. He conducted my new pieces as if he hated me. He is no longer jubilant, he is triumphant!

Of course, in his innermost self he knew this was not the case. Kajanus was imperious and conscious of his worth as a composing conductor. But when he conducted Sibelius's music, it was the composer who sat in the triumphal coach, while he – to use his own words – merely served his humble role as the 'coachman'. Sibelius diligently kept his diary during May and June 1927. And it is the last time one is in a position to observe the everyday events in his life on an almost day-to-day basis.

[9 May 1927] Began the day with a sauna . . . Am tired and shaky. There's not a part of me that's really functioning. Aino has gone to town. Windy. 8 degrees above zero. No alcohol. But smoke far too much. How can I escape from it? Would dearly like to compose, but can't; my hands won't keep steady.

[10 May] Aino's name-day. Played duets. Cold – 3 degrees above zero. No alcohol. Nor anything else. The tremor is less troublesome when the atmosphere at home is better. These things torment the life out of me. Am far too over-sensitive! Worked a little on the *Tempest* suite. My hands are better in the evening, as is obvious from this.

His dentist had found something that prompted an X-ray examination:

[12 May] Went by limousine to Helsinki. X-ray Institute. No alcohol. Left home at nine and at home by half-past twelve. The shortest visit I have ever paid to town.

[13 May] Compose a little – presentiment of cancer. Perhaps imaginary.

A pity to worry Aino about it. Very trembly. No alcohol. In the evening my hands are all right. Strange.

[14 May] Went for a walk in wonderful weather. Am in a bad temper. Better in the evening. No alcohol but tobacco instead . . .

[15 May] Went for a walk. Worked in the evening until two. No alcohol. I can't get that insult out of my mind. Am in a temper.

[16 May] No alcohol. Work a bit. Cold but beautiful.

[17 May] Struggling on. But it is still not clear. No alcohol. Invited to conduct 'Sibelius' in Stockholm and Gothenburg. Aino and Heidi are in town. The *Tempest* Suite torments the life out of me. It's like having to do your homework all over again.

[19 May] Worked on a chorale and on the suite. Went for a walk in the morning.

The next few days proceed along similar lines:

[27 May] Worked all day. Bad weather. 9 degrees Celsius. Aino at home. Smoked. *Sine alc.*

[29 May] A Wisky. Kaj is here with family. Raining.

[30 May] *Sine alc.* Walked a little. Aino gone to town. Worked a bit.

[4, 5, 6 June] *Sine alc.* Changeable moods. Work also.

[10 June] Celebrated our thirty-fifth wedding anniversary with punch, wine etc . . . Kaj came and played so sensitively.

[11 June] Weather cold. Rain with some sun. Work on the suite. Boring. Sent off the chorale [*Väinön virsi?*], which is not up to much. Must really turn down all work on commission.

[13 June] The day went 'under the influence'. Depression.

[19 June] Alcohol now and then. Good weather. Worked.

[22 June] Worked these last few days. My intake of alcohol very moderate!

Hansen had informed Sibelius that the Royal Danish Ballet would be performing *Scaramouche* in June at the Théâtre des Champs-Elysées in Paris. The composer was worried about its première, 'particularly as its success is dependent on other than purely artistic factors'. He wrote to Hansen of his misgivings on 9 May, and particularly deplored the inclusion of dialogue. In his diary an entry for 26 June records: 'The failure of *Scaramouche* sent me and Aino into depression.' Early in July he wrote to Hansen: 'That

Scaramouche did not meet up to expectations in Paris did not surprise me. It would be useful to see the reviews.' *Le Courier Musical* wrote without enthusiasm of Sibelius's score, but it is not clear from the reviews whether the dialogue was omitted or not.

At the beginning of July, Sibelius told Hansen that he could soon expect to take delivery of the First Suite from *The Tempest*. He suggested a cash advance of 1,500 Danish kronor, and promised to send the Second Suite for smaller orchestra when it was ready. This occupied him for the best part of July, and was sent off to Copenhagen at the beginning of August. Sibelius even toyed with the idea of transcribing the suite for piano, and indeed, later that autumn sent Hansen piano arrangements of three numbers – *Miranda*, *Dance of the Nymphs* and *Prospero* – adding: 'As you see, I want them to be transcribed simply. These three are the most awkward to arrange. The others are much easier.' He made no further transcriptions himself.

– 4 –

A dynamic figure now entered Sibelius's life: Olin Downes, who had been the music critic of the *New York Times* since 1923. Admittedly they had once met briefly before, in 1914 at Norfolk, Connecticut, for Downes had championed Sibelius's music from as early as 1911. Now, on 18 April 1927, he wrote sounding him out about the possibility of a concert tour of the United States the following season. He was at pains to point out that he was only acting as an intermediary for William Brennan, manager of the Boston Symphony Orchestra. Downes himself was planning a European tour, and proposed staying in England, France and Germany up to the first week in August. 'About that time I expect to visit Finland and hope that I can then have the privilege of calling upon you.'

Once again Sibelius was covered in confusion: torn between on the one hand the lure of welcome dollars and the possibility of conducting great orchestras, and on the other his doubts as to his capacity to do so after so long a gap. Indeed, it took some time before he made up his mind. On 16 June he telegraphed Downes, who was staying in Paris: 'CLOSELY ENGAGED WITH NEW WORKS REGRET BEING UNABLE AT PRESENT MOMENT DECIDE FOR TOURNÉ ... WISHING YOU WELCOME TO FINLAND.'

Downes did not make contact again until 17 August, when he notified Sibelius that he would be arriving in Helsinki on 5 or 6 September. With his usual vitality and enthusiasm, he overwhelmed Sibelius with various requests, and as his knowledge of German was minimal, asked if he could invite an English-speaking friend to act as an interpreter. As a romantic nature-worshipper he even entertained plans to buy a small cabin by a lake, where he could fish and enjoy the solitude of the forest:

I have dreamed for many years of Finland – ever since first hearing your music, which I knew could only come from a wonderful northern country, where there was room to be alone and a grand nature about – and have also dreamed of seeing you in your own country, and finally have dreamed of catching a large salmon! Or a sturgeon, if there are no salmon running, would do! Or are there sturgeon in Finland? I think so.

Indeed, I have even wondered if it would not be possible, in some place in the Finnish woods where there are few people, by a lake with fish in it, to buy very cheaply a small wood cabin for myself, where I could come every year or every other year for a month, to be by myself, have a few books, a fire, perhaps even, at last a piano, and be completely happy . . .

We may not be able to talk much, and since you are an older man than I am, I doubt if my company will interest you. But I have talked to you often through your music; whether we communicate personally or not is without importance. I know best many people to whom I have never said a word; in fact, I prefer that kind of company . . . Therefore, if our meeting is not comfortable or interesting to you, and I realize that it is best to go on quickly, don't misunderstand me. I wish to see you only for a little while, to remember you as a man as well as artist, and there will never be walls between you and me in your music. It is the only great and *noble* music that I hear being produced today.

As in his reviews, Downes goes straight to the point. His views on Mahler, Schoenberg and the later Stravinsky were decidedly negative. But his strength lay in the liveliness of his writing and the effective depiction of the music, the composers and interpreters who caught his fancy. George Marek paints a sharp vignette in his Toscanini biography.

Downes apparently did not enjoy the company of musicologists, and towards the end of the 1930s he spent an evening with Paul Henry Láng, author of *Music in Western Civilization*, and some other scholars. The discussion became heated, and it was obvious that Downes and his companions did not speak the same language and Downes left the company in anger. The following day Láng wrote him a charming letter: 'Downes may not be a scholar but he is a gentleman, was the conclusion of our little get-together after last night's dance recital. I thought that I should tell you that all who disagreed with you one time or another are unanimous in considering you a damned good sport and I should like to add that if anyone else ever toes into you I will be the first to get on your side.'

Presumably Sibelius awaited Downes's visit with a mixture of curiosity and apprehension, but received him with his customary hospitality. They spent hours and days together, both at Ainola and in Helsinki. Sibelius gave him an inscribed copy of the Sixth Symphony, but for the rest he left his son-in-law Arvi Paloheimo to show him the sights.

During the journey home, on board the Compagnie Générale

Transatlantique's elegant liner *De Grasse*, Downes wrote a letter of thanks: 'I hope that you, so great a man and artist, will not feel it amiss if I address you as my very dear friend . . . I feel a great fear and sense of weakness, even dread, in going back to my place of work and living, and the happiness and torture which wait there. It is really going into battle, and in some ways my summer in Europe, passed a great deal alone, has made me weak and soft and most unwilling to go back to that place. But – I do retain as a priceless memory the strength, the spirit and the *reality* – the marvellous *reality* which your music, and now yourself, hold for me . . . But whether we ever meet again or not, I shall know that you are always near and for that life will be less lonely.'

Downes also mentioned that he discussed the sensitive matter of the new work:

Can you tell me a little about the Eighth Symphony? Is it already finished, or when will it be ready?' Sibelius answered nervously that two movements were already written down but that the rest was still in his head. He did not want to hurry it or to let the score out of his hands until he was completely sure that he had done all he could to get it right. This should have been sufficient to stop me. But I pressed on: 'Could you not tell me generally more about it? How many movements there will be, how large an orchestra you have used, and in which form roughly speaking it is conceived? The wider American public would find it of the greatest interest.' He understood my reasons for asking, and would want to oblige a friend, but he became very uncomfortable. He muttered a few inconsequential words. His face assumed a most unhappy expression. Then he turned to me in frustration. '*Ich kann nicht!*' burst out in German and he gave a deep sigh. He will not speak about his work before it is ready.

When Downes returned from his Finnish forests and lakes to the reality of New York, he was overcome by a certain melancholy. All the same, he must certainly have begun to miss his stall at Carnegie Hall and his box at the Metropolitan Opera. Conversely, he must have been aware of his wider musical mission and in particular his Sibelius campaign, which was to unleash many musico–political storms. After his visit, Sibelius noted laconically in his diary: 'Olin Downes from New York was here with me. An extraordinary critic.' (12 September 1927)

– 5 –

Armas Järnefelt was enormously active at this time both as a composer and conductor. In May 1927 he had conducted the première of a new cantata in Åbo. Sibelius declined his invitation to attend and wrote wishing him all success. 'I would willingly have come to Åbo for the cantata, but had

I done so, my role would have been to dress up and go to formal dinners, just the sort of thing I deride in others.' As we have already mentioned, Järnefelt was to perform *Tapiola* in Stockholm and the Prelude to *The Tempest* and sought the composer's guidance. Sibelius responded that the main theme 'should be played very *espressivo*, almost as a dilettante would play it.'

Nor did Sibelius go into Helsinki in October to hear the Swedish composer Ture Rangström conduct a concert of his music, but contented himself with writing some friendly greetings and his apologies. His thoughts were concentrated on a closer Swedish friend, Wilhelm Stenhammar, whose health had long given cause for anxiety. In November he received the news of his death from Olga Bratt. 'In my long life I have never met an artist of the nobility and idealism of Wilhelm Stenhammar. I feel happy and privileged to have been his friend. He has done so much for my art! How totally empty it feels now that he has gone,' he wrote in his reply. He goes on to tell Bratt that he had been busily composing – and speaks misleadingly of 'a number of cantatas and other commissioned pieces', presumably thinking of *Väinön virsi*. 'Because of them I have had to put off my "real" work. Now that I am as good as free of them, I am feeling much happier with my music.'

After the funeral, Stenhammar's widow Helga wrote to him: 'Sten [as she used to call her husband] once whispered secretively to me: "Do you know that Sibb sets great store by my A minor Quartet, and that he always keeps it on his night table." That you always set great store by this work, which at that time he thought was his finest, brought him the most complete happiness that life can give an artist.' Now, as he had reason to do from time to time in the following years, Sibelius's thoughts turned to a line from one of his long-departed poet friends, Karl August Tavaststjerna: 'It is becoming so silent around me.'

CHAPTER TWENTY

The Eighth Symphony

When on 12 February 1928 Sibelius checked into the Hotel Excelsior in Berlin, among the first things he did was to write to Aino. His journey, he could report, had gone well, even if he did not meet anyone in Stockholm. His brother-in-law Eero Järnefelt was in Nyköping and his other friends were out of town. He found his hotel terribly expensive and set about finding another one. He could report that *Tapiola* had just had its Gothen-burg première under Armas Järnefelt in early February and received a mixed press, and that Kajanus was to conduct it in Stockholm. All seemed to be going well with Adolf Paul and he was in funds, though only two months later he had got through all his money again. Sibelius's letter bears witness to his need for contact, and he enthuses over a new Hamsun novel he has just bought. He tries to give some idea of his work but avoids going into detail, for he always believed that music was like a butterfly, whose wings, once touched, lose their lustre.

A few days later Sibelius changed hotels and moved to his old standby, the Hotel Moltke. On 16 February he went to hear Florizel von Reuter playing the Paganini Caprices, which was 'a great experience . . . But one has to be a virtuoso of divine gifts, if you can make music like that remotely satisfying.' Perhaps his thoughts turned to Willy Burmester, who at the turn of the century had made his breakthrough in Berlin with a Paganini recital – but that was long ago and Burmester's star had long since waned. 'I hope that my nerves will return to normal. How pleased I shall be to have the new works finished and ready.' He speaks of works in the plural, so one wonders whether he is thinking of the three sets of instrumental pieces, Opp. 114–116? Or more probably, as had so often been the case before, was he working simultaneously on another big orchestral piece as well as the Eighth Symphony?

'My nerves are settling down, and up to now I'm happy with the hotel. Heard Schumann's E flat Symphony from the Philharmonic under Kun-wald. Nothing to write home about.' Aino went into Helsinki for a few days, from where she replied. Sibelius responded a few days later: 'I can see you were a little melancholy, but when you get back to the atmosphere of our lovely home, things will be better. I will stay on here for two or three weeks, and then I will return home with pleasure. I am working well here, even though I have no piano, but I miss you terribly. You are the one who understands me most and can get me to work best . . . Piiu's [Margareta's] idea about England is excellent. I approve it thoroughly. And wonderful Oxford! My delight! There's not a great deal to hear here if you compare it with Paris . . . Paul is still the same old good friend, but we haven't seen as much of each other as before. But at least he hasn't asked me to lend him money. My new work will be wonderful. It is going well, but there is no hurry!'

The fact that Sibelius speaks of working without a piano indicates that the Eighth Symphony was at a fairly advanced stage. The early planning, during which he would try out ideas on a piano and improvise, was over; he would now be ready to write directly into short or even full score. The generally affectionate and conversational tone of his letters remains much the same as always; indeed, they could have been written at the turn of the century, save only for the handwriting.

A letter dated 1 March (though the postmark shows that Sibelius had forgotten 1928 was a leap year and should have written 29 February) shows him in continued good spirits. 'I would like Paul to do a text for *Scara-[mouche]*. Wrote to Hansen and received the piano score this morning.' His letter records that he had lunched with his old publisher Robert Lienau, newly returned from a visit to London, at their old watering hole the Restaurant Habel on the Unter den Linden. They were never short of conversation, and Lienau would recall how in 1909 they would meet for an early lunch at 11 o'clock and not notice the passage of time until, with some difficulty, they would rise from the table between 4 or 5 o'clock in the afternoon. But Sibelius's ties with Breitkopf and Hansen were now too strong to allow of a resumption of their old professional relationship.

The same letter reveals that he had gone through the score of Stravinsky's *Oedipus Rex*. 'I could not afford to throw away three or four hundred marks for a ticket for the première.' Twenty-one years later he wrote on a scrap of paper dated 20 November 1949: 'Mr Stravinsky says that my craftsmanship is poor. That I take to be the greatest compliment I have had in the whole of my long life!' But he was too outraged to let it go at that: 'Mr I. S. is always imitating someone. I like his *Oedipus* best where he is imitating Gluck. Technique in music is not learned in school from blackboards and easels. In that respect Mr I. S. is at the top of the class. But when one compares my symphonies with his stillborn affectations . . . !'

In September 1961, when Stravinsky conducted a number of Sibelius's works in Helsinki, he paid a visit to Ainola, where he laid a wreath on Sibelius's grave and kneeled while he made the sign of the cross. When he returned to Helsinki he told his companion Robert Craft that he had heard the First Symphony in the company of Rimsky-Korsakov, who had said: 'Yes, I suppose that is also possible.' Stravinsky liked Sibelius's *Canzonetta* for string orchestra from the incidental music to *Kuolema*. 'I like that kind of Italian melody gone north. Tchaikovsky did too, of course, and through him the taste became an important and attractive part of St Petersburg culture.' Two years later, when Stravinsky was awarded the Wihuri Foundation International Sibelius Prize, as an act of homage he transcribed the *Canzonetta* for four horns, two clarinets, harp and double-bass. When I visited her in New York in 1974, three years after Stravinsky's death, his widow Vera received me in her beautiful apartment. After admiring the impressionists on the wall, I asked her where Sibelius could have read or heard any pejorative remarks attributed to Stravinsky. Mme Stravinsky was obviously surprised, and after a pause for reflection she said: 'My husband had no special feeling for Sibelius's music, but he respected him as a composer.'

Sibelius postponed his departure from Berlin in order to hear Ferenc von Vecsey playing his Violin Concerto with Furtwängler and the Berlin Philharmonic on 9 March. He had only recently heard Furtwängler conducting Berlioz's *Symphonie fantastique* and was full of admiration. 'My concerto [conducted] by Furtwängler is worth more than ten of my own [concerts]. He is a conductor of great stature. Klemperer is also here.' Klemperer had recently conducted the Seventh Symphony in Wiesbaden, and later, during his American tour, included the Second and Fourth. In the spring of 1973 a Sibelius concert with Klemperer and the New Philharmonia Orchestra, in which the Fourth Symphony was included, was to be advertised in London, but the conductor's health gave way and he died shortly afterwards. Some years earlier he had summed up his view of Sibelius in a conversation we had in Zürich : 'His achievement was to create an altogether new music with completely classical means.'

Luise Wolff, widow of the celebrated concert manager Herman Wolff, sent Sibelius a ticket for the Fürtwangler concert in Berlin. 'This is the most prestigious concert series – and the continuation of the Nikisch concerts. When I have some new works, I shall give concerts again.' Sibelius's ambitions to return to the podium were fired. Once the Eighth Symphony and perhaps another big work were ready, he would be able to realize the plans for a Berlin concert that he had so long harboured. Another request, familiar from earlier letters: Could Aino send him 10,000 Finnish marks payable through the Deutsche Bank? His last letter from Berlin, on 15 March, reports that he had heard the Klingler Quartet playing late Beethoven (the A minor Quartet, Op. 132). It is obvious too that Peterson-Berger's review in *Dagens Nyheter* savaging *Tapiola* needled him. 'I cannot take this man seriously. For a lifetime he has been attacking me. And despite his brilliant writing, still has not the slightest understanding of my music. But no doubt it will survive.'

Sibelius's last days in Berlin were spoiled by the reviews of the Violin Concerto. His expectations had been too high – all too high. He should have realized that the Berlin critical scene was largely dominated by followers of the radical Schoenbergian *Neue Musik*. One of the most strident of them was Heinrich Strobel, critic of the *Berliner Börsen-Courier*, a champion of Hindemith and Stravinsky, who later enjoyed prominence in the post-war avant-garde Donaueschingen Festival. He had little sympathy with the first number, Respighi's *Ancient Airs and Dances*, but saved most of his venom for the Sibelius concerto, acknowledging Franz von Vecsey's sure-ness and facility but finding his tone dry and hard. The concerto itself he found shapeless and monotonous, without any real ideas or idiomatic violin-istic virtuosity, accusing it of 'boring Nordic dreariness'. He ended by asking how Furtwängler could have programmed 'this anaemic concerto'. Alfred Einstein, later well known for his Mozart biography, reviewed it in the *Berliner Tageblatt* more sympathetically as 'the kind of concerto one would expect from Sibelius . . . a first movement based in an elegiac minor key, but which shows the violin in a consolatory F major; which is not quite certain whether it wants to be in concertante or symphonic style. [This is followed by] a slow movement with a full-throated and gripping cantilena with its chaste dreams of love; and to finish with a dance-like, rhythmically pregnant, somewhat Nordicly-coloured [set of] variations. All in all, a conventional piece despite the virtuoso figuration: a study in technique from Mendelssohn to Max Bruch. The concerto is dedicated to Vecsey, whose technical freedom makes him a model for every master class in violin playing.'

The anonymous critic writing in *Vossische Zeitung* thought that Vecsey put his complete soul as well as his masterly technique into the concerto, which he did not think, however, could be numbered 'among that sympa-thetic master's finest works'. Reading these reviews, one wonders to what extent Vecsey's playing affected their judgments. It was not until Heifetz recorded it with peerless virtuosity under Sir Thomas Beecham in 1935 that the concerto came into its own. True to form, Sibelius concentrated solely on the most negative elements in the reviews.

One wonders how Sibelius really reacted in his innermost self to these Berlin critics. Did they have a damaging effect on his inspiration? One must say that only a very few composers of stature have received such contro-versial reviews after having reached sixty. In general, composers of that age are showered with the praises of their admirers, while their detractors tend to treat them to polite, innocuous phrases. The closer they reach the biblical three score years and ten, the more they are placed on a pedestal. In Sibe-lius's case, things were different. From the 1920s through to the outbreak of the Second World War, the higher his reputation in the English-speaking world the stronger the reaction in the German and French-speaking worlds. Moreover, he lived long enough to witness the beginnings of a reaction against him in America and among certain English critics.

The chorus of disapproval in Sweden and Berlin was counterbalanced by a mounting interest in his music in America. Boston had had a strong

Sibelius tradition from the very beginning: Gericke introduced him, Karl Muck fostered him, Monteux returned to him, and under Koussevitzky he blossoms – or so wrote Henry T. Parker in the *Boston Transcript* after the première of the Sixth Symphony. Now Koussevitzky had 'discovered' the Third, which had actually been turned down by Muck, Max Fiedler and Monteux. On 9 November 1928 Koussevitzky introduced it to Boston. The *Boston Post* headlined its review 'SIBELIUS THIRD, MUCH AHEAD OF ITS TIME IN 1907, NOW MODERN' and its critic Henry T. Parker asked: 'Did Igor the Great invent the rhythms that set the hands clenching and the blood tingling? They have beaten from 1907 in the first movement of this Third Symphony of Jean Sibelius, biding his time in the remotest Helsing-fors . . . [Then, speaking of Strauss's early operas] The old lion's paw still strikes out orchestral colours to stir the listening senses. Yet there is not one, even in the work of his noon, that more seizes the imagination than that blackish-grey which Sibelius conjures into tones from rock-bound lakes under leaden skies.'

Leonard Bernstein once described to me how during his youth he had studied the Sibelius symphonies, in particular the Second, Fifth and Seventh, with Koussevitzky. When our conversation turned to the first movement of the Third, he mentioned one revealing detail that reinforces the rhythmic power that must have distinguished Koussevitzky's reading. When the second subject returns in the recapitulation, Koussevitzky emphasized the rhythmic accompaniment in the woodwind to almost percussive effect.

About a month after his performance of the Third Symphony, Koussevitzky wrote his first letter to Sibelius:

> I have long intended to write to you but there have been so many demands on my time that I have scarcely had a minute to myself.
>
> It would presumably interest you to know that we have given your Third Symphony with great success in Boston. The work made so strong an impression that I was asked to repeat it, something that I also propose to do in New York at the beginning of January, and later in Boston. Again, during the coming season I shall be playing your Seventh Symphony, which I conducted two years ago. I should be very pleased if you could send me a few lines and let me know whether you have any new works which have not yet been performed. Do you not think that it would be an excellent idea if you came to America? In view of the great sympathy that is felt for you here, you would be received with the greatest delight.

Every word radiates Koussevitzky's enormous admiration for Sibelius – and his determination. As interpreter of the Sibelius symphonies and tone poems, he and his orchestra gave of their utmost. In Sibelius, Koussevitzky had found a composer who, in much the same way as Tchaikovsky, Scriabin and the impressionists, struck powerful resonances in his artistic soul. Koussevitzky and the Boston orchestra not only drew the best out of Sibelius's work but found that these performances surpassed their own best. Indeed, the Boston Symphony's legendary reputation was closely related to the quality of its Sibelius. Small wonder that Koussevitzky was anxious to lay claim to future works from his pen. This appealed to Sibelius, who saw Koussevitzky as his Court Kapellmeister – in much the same way that Koussevitzky thought of him as his Court Composer!

At the beginning of December, Wilhelm Hansen made a specific inquiry concerning the Eighth Symphony to which Sibelius responded on 17 December: 'My Symphony VIII is still in my head. But when the time is ripe I will be delighted to discuss it with you.' At this stage his replies were polite, but as time wore on, year after year, he answered with growing irritation. For now, he was still optimistic about delivering it.

The Fourth Symphony was given in Stockholm. The reviews plunged him into gloom: 'How difficult it is to swallow destructive reviews when you get older. Peterson–Berger regarding my Symphony IV: "bloodless, colourless, lacking in temperament and devoid of ideas". What more can one say?' (Diary, 6 December 1928) If nothing else, Peterson–Berger managed to ruin Sibelius's birthday. But his diary entry reflects an ephemeral concern, and too great a significance should not be read into it. News of Koussevitzky's triumphs in Boston presumably reached Sibelius shortly before Christmas and must have given him some consolation over the holidays. On 28 December he made his second and last diary entry for the year: 'How infinitely difficult it is to live this our only life! Symphony III has had great success in Boston under Koussevitzky. Will I always be cursed with being so oversensitive? Dreadful.'

Sibelius answered Koussevitzky's letter concerning the success of his Third Symphony immediately and with obvious delight: 'It was with great pleasure that I received your letter, which has great significance for me. I can only regret that I was not present at the concert, and thus did not have the opportunity of hearing and admiring you. It is impossible for me to come to America at the moment. But there is still a great deal of time. I shall soon be publishing new works.' Again we notice that he speaks, as he had in his letter to Aino from Berlin, about works in the plural. But he rather regretted his last sentence, and in another letter to Koussevitzky written on the same day but incorrectly dated, he says: 'My new work is far from finished, and I cannot say unfortunately when it is likely to be ready. I regret that I mentioned the matter. The only thing I can promise is that you, dear Maestro, will be the first to have any news.' And so the year's reckoning is typical: brickbats in Berlin and Stockholm, bouquets in America. But now with Koussevitzky in Boston, the sun is at last shining.

Olin Downes had not forgotten the short visit he paid to Ainola in 1927. It had obviously made an indelible impression. In the spring of 1929 he made a long trip to Europe, also planning to include the Soviet Union in his itinerary. By mid-May he had reached Leningrad and sent a telegram to Sibelius, asking him if he could receive him in Helsinki. Sibelius would certainly have received it with surprise – for at that time Finnish citizens were unaccustomed to receiving telegrams from the Soviet Union. Among his long list of requests was one for the whereabouts of Ilya Repin (1844–1930), whose output includes a celebrated portrait of Mussorgsky and whom he believed was living in Finland (in fact he lived just outside Leningrad.)[1]

Downes presumably visited Sibelius at Ainola and the composer seems to have been in the best of humours. A little later Sibelius sent him a signed photograph, for which Downes thanked him: 'It is so really *you* and it cheers me to look at it – that *you*, with all you know and have experienced and with the knowledge of a great spirit, should look so happy – indeed, like a boy, and a rather bad one! And I hear you say again all those wonderful things that sometimes made me laugh so, and always gave me happiness and courage. And also I hear you say "life is simple"! That's wonderful, you know, and if *you* say it, it's true . . . And if I ever feel childishly, egotistically sad again, I shall think of "*les traditions*" and look at your picture and *laugh*, a very happy laugh, if only in imitation of a great man with the wisdom and experience of his greatness, who can also laugh. God bless you, and also may He, or the Devil, or whoever or whatever produces good music, bless the new work – the great *Mystery*, which you properly keep to yourself, on which you are engaged.' In the last lines one can sense Downes's impatience. Some years later he was to give it more direct expression.

The letters Adolf Paul sent Sibelius from Berlin also lifted his spirits, when they did not irritate him: in any event, they were never boring. As usual, he hides something of his real predicament. 'The oysters are still tempting at the Kempinski, the white wines are flowing and only your chair is empty.' He asked for Sibelius's help in placing his latest novel *Königsmarck* with a Swedish-language publisher in Helsinki, and in securing a commission for another from the noted patron Amos Andersson. In the summer of 1929 Paul again found himself in dire straits and Sibelius sent him 500 marks. But in November the same year Paul was invited along with other writers and intellectuals to Spain, where he and his companions lunched with Primo de Rivera. He sat on the dictator's left. 'In Cervantes' hostelry in Toledo I raised my glass to you,' he wrote. In Andalusia he listened to gypsy singers, 'whose pastoral songs, desert songs and the cries of wild birds, produce an atmosphere that was heart-rending in a way that only your music is. You were with me then'.

The eight concerts Sibelius conducted in 1921 at the Queen's Hall in London and on tour in the provinces would in normal conditions have been enough to ensure further engagements. That they did not can be ascribed to the Depression, which had taken its toll on English musical life. The London orchestras, in particular the New Queen's Hall Orchestra, were fighting for their very existence, and in addition competing for public favour with that new phenomenon the wireless. Rosa Newmarch could not find strong enough words with which to deplore the closure of the Sunday Concert series at the Queen's Hall. There was even talk of turning the hall itself into a cinema or an orphanage. Chappells the music publishers had stopped promoting concerts in 1926, complaining that it was no longer able to compete with broadcasting. Even Sir Thomas Beecham complained that if things continued as they were, 'our concert halls will in a few years' time become a wilderness'.

But by the autumn of 1929 the situation had improved. And in both London and the provinces there was renewed interest in Sibelius, a fact reflected both in the composer's correspondence and in the guest book at Ainola. In September 1929 Sibelius received a letter from Basil Cameron, then conductor of an orchestra at the spa resort of Harrogate. This announced that he had been invited to conduct the Fourth Symphony at one of the Royal Philharmonic Society's concerts at the Queen's Hall in January the following year. The letter continued: 'I would very much like to make the journey to see you in the hope that you would be willing to go through the score with me ... I am naturally anxious to give the best possible performance of the Symphony and one which accords with your wishes. I had the pleasure of playing violin in the Queen's Hall Orchestra under your direction some years ago – I believe in 1910 [1909 in fact] – when you conducted some of your compositions at a symphony concert.'[2]

Cameron arrived in Helsinki in the middle of October. To judge from his letter of thanks, the visit was a great success and he expressed the hope of returning in the near future. After beginning his letter in English, Cameron changed to German and invited Sibelius to conduct at the Hastings Festival from 22 to 25 January. The programme he suggested included *The Swan of Tuonela* or *En Saga* and, above all, the Prelude to *The Tempest*. At first Sibelius accepted, but then got cold feet and got his son-in-law Arvi Paloheimo to send a telegram: 'PROFOUNDLY REGRET PROMISE OVERHASTY SIBELIUS CANNOT COME THIS TIME.' Three years had passed since Sibelius last stood on the podium. Now when an invitation was forthcoming, his nerve failed him. Hastings could have been a suitably low-key entry point for his come-back as a conductor. There was not the glare of London or New York, nor even Stockholm or Copenhagen. And moreover he would have had the opportunity of meeting Sir Henry Wood and possibly Sir Thomas Beecham!

On his return, Cameron happened to meet Cecil Gray, the composer and writer who was at this time music critic of the *Daily Telegraph*. The meeting inspired Gray, already a great admirer of Sibelius's music, to extend his projected visit to Tallinn, and cross the Gulf of Finland to meet the celebrated Finn. A few years earlier, in 1924, Gray had published his *Survey of*

Contemporary Music, which made quite a stir at the time, not so much because he spoke in unflattering terms of such fashionable figures as Stravinsky and Scriabin, but more because of his unstinted praises of Sibelius, Bartók and somewhat more surprisingly, Bernard van Dieren, with whom he had studied composition. In his book Gray was at pains to point out that at the time of writing these three composers were practically unknown, which in the case of the first two was (to put it mildly) something of an exaggeration.

Gray had been planning to spend Christmas with Sergei Mamontov, the director of the Estonian Opera, with whom his wife was connected. Gray had many international contacts, and knew his Russian music well. When on New Year's Eve he boarded the ferry to Helsinki he did so with some trepidation, as he had been informed that Sibelius regarded *homo diurnalis* – journalists – as the lowest form of life. They met at the Hotel Fennia, where Sibelius was staying for a few days. Their conversation began haltingly, in a macaronic jumble of French and German, until Sibelius suddenly exclaimed: 'But Mr Gray, you are not a journalist – you are a musician! Why did you not say so at the start?' Whereupon Sibelius produced a bottle of whisky from the cupboard, and from that moment onwards, all went well.

The next day they met again for lunch at the Hotel Fennia, and remained at the same table until it was time for dinner. They broke up at seven the following morning.

> Not only did he prove to be the perfect host in all that pertains to the table, but the intellectual feast he spreads before his guests is even more magnificent, if that were possible. Most musicians are apt to have one-track minds. However interesting their conversation may be in speaking of their art, and particularly in speaking of themselves and of their own achievements, they are, as a rule, singularly uninteresting and unilluminating on other topics.
>
> Sibelius exhibits precisely the opposite tendency – of himself and his work he speaks diffidently and unwillingly. One quickly realizes that he prefers to discuss any and every other subject on earth, and does – literature, philosophy, psychology, painting, politics, science . . . To give any adequate idea of all the wisdom and wit – enigmatic, gnomic, aphoristic, paradoxical –which flows from Sibelius on such occasions would be impossible.[3]

When Gray launched a bitter attack on British foreign policy, Sibelius ventured to disagree: 'If we sometimes criticize your foreign policy it is on quite different grounds: because it is so subtle, so astute, so far-sighted, so Machiavellian. Today the world is passing through what is perhaps the most critical phase in all human history. It may be difficult for you in your island to realize to what an extent the peoples of the world look to England. If England fails, all is lost; England is the lynch-pin of civilization. When the crisis comes, as come it will, England will find herself again, and will save the world for civilization as she has done before.' This was Sibelius speaking in January 1930!

Influenced by Sibelius's life-style, Gray completely lost his sense of what time of day it was. And was not even sure what day of the week it was. He wondered if all Finns lived like this, and whether they ever did any work.

– 2 –

Gray's visit was to have important consequences. Two months later, in March 1930, he wrote that Oxford University Press had asked him to write a book on Sibelius's music. It was to be the 'definitive and official' biography. 'Having thought over the matter, I have agreed – *je vais me mettre à l'ouevre*⁴ – immediately but with due regard, as I would want the book to be really good.' Gray said that he blushed with shame for much of what he had written in his earlier book: among other things, he had called *Night Ride and Sunrise* a mediocre piece. He blamed these stupidities on his youth and expressed the hope that Sibelius would overlook them. With a view to the needs of English readers, the book would also contain a biographical section, but it need not necessarily be extensive. 'This, I know, will not be to your liking but the wider public and therefore the publishers require it. Do not for one moment imagine that I will be indiscreet.' Had they perhaps in their cups discussed the question of Sibelius's genealogy, politically sensitive at that period of the language war? Gray's letter mentions in passing that Sibelius's old friend and champion Granville Bantock had been knighted in the New Year's honours of 1930.

Sibelius's response was positive, and Gray proposed to leave the biographical section of the book until after his next visit to Finland. He had recently read Niemann's little book on Sibelius, which he thought 'quite good, but it appears to me that Niemann exaggerates the national elements in your work, and that what he has to say about your symphonies is, speaking frankly, ludicrous'. Gray's insights and good judgment undoubtedly gave Sibelius much satisfaction. The man who was to write his biography understood him and his music, and above all appreciated that the symphonies were the cornerstone of his output.

Gray's biography was published in 1931. It is brilliant in style and provocative in content, and betrays a commanding knowledge of the symphonic literature. From Sibelius's own point of view, it was as flattering as it was embarrassing to be placed not alongside Beethoven but at times above him. Gray at the same time argued that all German symphonic music after Beethoven is – unsymphonic!

In a purely technical sense, therefore, from the point of view of formal structure, it is true to say that in his later work Sibelius takes up music where Beethoven laid it down. Even in his early work, however, it is important to note that, romantic in spirit though it is, it bears no trace whatever of the influence of the great romantic composers themselves – the art of Weber, of Berlioz, of Chopin, of Liszt, has had no repercussion on that of Sibelius. His entire art, in fact, follows on straight from that of Beethoven, without any intermediary influence of any kind; one can pass from one to the other without feeling that there is an intervening gap of a century. Indeed there is less feeling of strangeness in passing from Beethoven to Sibelius than from Beethoven to Berlioz.

Gray makes short work of the remaining nineteenth-century symphonists. Berlioz's *Symphonie fantastique* and Liszt's *Faust Symphony* are not symphonies at all but 'symphonic poems in disguise' and César Franck's Symphony, with its 'cyclic form, its long-winded cloying melodies, which permit of no fruitful developments, its slimy chromatic harmonies and abuse of canonic devices, is the unapproachable model of everything that should be avoided in symphonic composition'. Even Bruckner, Mahler, Tchaikovsky and Elgar are not exempt from stricture. According to Gray, Sibelius is 'the only composer of our time who has preserved inviolate the purity and integrity of the true symphonic style.' After this, Gray launches his offensive against German hegemony. Schubert was only a 'potentially great symphonist'. Brahms was not a symphonist 'by natural aptitude or inclination', but achieved the symphonic style by 'a kind of self-immolation'.

'The Teutonic genius in music is pre-eminently lyrical . . . ' But what of Beethoven? 'Beethoven was no more a typical German than Goethe was.' The real Bruckner 'is at heart a charming Schubertian lyricist; the real Mahler is not the ambitious architect of the vast symphonies, but the composer of delicate and exquisite songs'. But in *one* respect Sibelius did not match Beethoven and the other German masters. Sibelius's symphonies often lack a really lyrical slow movement. Only the *Andante* of the First Symphony is an exception, but this is also the weakest of the four movements. Nearly all the lyrical movements come dangerously close to the borders of the commonplace and conventional. As an exception, Gray mentions the 'lovely slow movements of the Violin Concerto and the *Voces intimae* Quartet'. But he goes on: 'In no other respect can he be regarded as at all inferior even to Beethoven himself as a symphonist'. And not content with that, he does not hesitate to assert that 'in sheer constructive mastery and intellectual power not even such consummate achievements as the first movements of the *Eroica* and the *Choral* can be placed above those of Sibelius's Second, Fourth or Fifth, and not even beside the gigantic single movement of the Seventh, which seems to me to be one of the highest summits to which music has yet attained in these respects'.

Cecil Gray's book made an important contribution to Sibelius's cause in England, and the number of performances in London rose steeply in its wake, culminating in the 1937 and 1938 Sibelius Festivals. The monograph was the first study of its kind to appear on the international scene. Putting its polemic exaggerations on one side, its importance lies in placing the symphonies at the centre of his achievement and in the direct lineage of Beethoven, and unlike Walter Niemann, placing him firmly in a European context.

– 3 –

In his chatty letters Adolf Paul brought Berlin so vividly to life that Sibelius felt that he could see the sights and smell the scents in his nostrils. 'It is quiet and still here, apart from from the communists, who demonstrated noisily and marched by with their red banners. I was just coming home after having read a Christmas story I had written on the radio, and couldn't get across the road for ages – but managed to get home before the Christmas tree was lit. You surely have winter and snow; here it is just overcast and slush (that will make you homesick for Berlin?) Incidentally, I saw a horse and carriage yesterday, which is something of a rarity nowadays. But you were not sitting in it! Oysters are cheap at the moment.'

In fact, Sibelius always seems to have felt a kind of nostalgia for his student year in Berlin, the city of victories and defeats where Busoni had once lived, not far from Paul's present flat. After having written the letter, Paul went to the cinema and saw *The Jazz Singer* with Al Jolson. Somewhat to his surprise, he discovered that Warner Bros had made use of Sibelius's *Pelléas et Mélisande* in the course of the film. 'They have used the whole of the *Melisande* movement, which incidentally fits in quite well.' Needless to say, he urged Sibelius to press for damages in the event that Warners had not sought copyright clearance. After speaking to Lienau the following day, he wrote that the latter had sold the rights for a shamelessly small sum. And so the prospect of huge damages proved a mirage; early in the New Year, Robert Lienau wrote to say that his American agent had 'succeeded in placing various movements from *Pelléas et Mélisande* in sound films' and enclosed a trifling royalty of 325 German marks! Perhaps, in the Continental fashion, Lienau had forgotten a few noughts!

– 4 –

At the end of February, Koussevitzky introduced the Sixth Symphony to Boston. The work caught on, which gave the *Boston Transcript*'s Henry T. Parker reason to say that 'in Boston, and to some extent also New York and Philadelphia, no composer is more firmly seated in the saddle than Sibelius where the standard repertoire is concerned. Whenever a new or old piece by Sibelius is played in London, Paris or one of Germany's musical capitals, there is an apologetic air . . . In America's concert halls we may perhaps lack tradition. But tradition can at times serve to exclude.' He went on to say that the interest a Sibelius score arouses has nothing of the literary or pictorial about it: 'In his music he achieves a completely individual expression, in the manner of Blake's poems or Thoreau's prose.'

Another critic, who used the initials P. R., is also at pains to stress the abstract qualities of Sibelius music: 'His individuality has absolutely nothing to do with the fact that he is born and bred in Finland, but comes from an innermost human quality, which one can only call imagination, genius . . . Sibelius's name can be mentioned alongside such giants as Beethoven and Wagner rather than lesser figures, such as César Franck.' All these reviews tell the same story. Sibelius was no longer just an ethnic curiosity for the Americans. He was taken as seriously as any other composer of stature.

In March 1930 Koussevitzky and his orchestra made their usual pilgrimage to New York. The music critic of the *New York Herald Tribune*, Lawrence Gilman, was inspired to sing the praises of Sibelius's later works, and he too voices the same exalted Beethovenian comparison: 'Each and every one of Sibelius's last three symphonies reminds one of Beethoven.' And so, as we have seen, America had already noticed what Cecil Gray was later to assert in his monograph.

In the spring of 1930, while he was in Paris, Koussevitzky wrote to Sibelius inviting him to conduct three concerts – two in Boston and one in Cambridge, Massachusetts – with the Boston Symphony Orchestra.

– 5 –

Ever since he was persuaded to send a telegram at the time of the Åland Island crisis, Sibelius had taken care not to be drawn into political controversy. But his conversation with Cecil Gray shows that he took an intelligent interest in European affairs. He set store by the English as a stabilizing force in the international arena, and would have viewed the Weimar Republic's bid to improve its relations with the Soviet Union with ambivalent feelings. No doubt he would have been swayed by personal considerations. In spite of the advocacy of Breitkopf & Härtel and Lienau, his music made scant headway in Germany. True, Furtwängler had programmed the Violin Concerto, but otherwise he had few champions. Busoni was no longer there and the only German friends he had were Lienau and von Hase – Adolf Paul was a Swedish citizen. His German biographer Walter Niemann had done his cause more harm than good. In England, as we have seen, his position was growing stronger by the day. Not only were Henry Wood, Granville Bantock, Basil Cameron and Adrian Boult active on his behalf, he also had influential friends in Rosa Newmarch, Ernest Newman, Eric Blom, Constant Lambert and Cecil Gray.

In Finland itself, two problems gave him cause for concern. First, the tension between the majority Finnish-speaking Finns and the minority whose tongue was Swedish. By this time, the long struggle he had witnessed in his youth was over: Finnish had gained equal status with Swedish, but now the gradual erosion of Swedish in academic, business and cultural life worried him. Instead of regarding Swedish as a valuable resource – especially as it made co-operation with the other Scandinavian countries easier – every attempt was being made to discourage its use. A young nation such as Finland could not afford such divisive indulgences. Independence from Russia was barely a decade old.

The communist threat was a second preoccupation. After the civil war the Finnish communist party had gone underground, and its subversive activities were directed from Moscow by O. V. Kuusinen, one of Stalin's faithful henchmen, who had been secretary of the Komintern since 1921. The communists enjoyed *de facto* representation in the Finnish Diet through their surrogates, the Finnish Labour and Small-Holders' party, who mustered 23 seats out of 200. There was widespread concern that Moscow could have ready access to Finnish security secrets through them, particularly among the Ostrobothnian peasants, who had formed the core of General Mannerheim's White forces during the war of independence. Being mostly pietist, they were outraged by the anti-religious tone of the communist movement, which in their ears was the voice of Satan.

The situation came to a head in 1929. The communists had intensified their propaganda campaign and during the previous year had organized a number of strikes with a view to paralysing Finland's timber export, partly to give support to the Soviet Union's export drive in this area. When members of the communist youth movement provocatively organized a meeting in autumn 1929 at Lapua, the centre of Ostrobothnian pietism, violence ensued. In opposition to the communist call to armed struggle, the Lapua movement, as it was called, came with a diffuse programme, patriotic and religious in character, appealing for unity irrespective of class and language group.

In the spring of 1930 the government introduced legislation to curb communist agitation, but did not succeed in getting it on to the statute book. The government resigned and a new prime minister, Pehr Evind Svinhufvud, formed a cabinet. In July, the Lapua movement mounted a patriotic demonstration of some 12,000 people, who marched on Helsinki. Here they were received and addressed by prominent national figures including President Relander, prime minister Svinhufvud and General Mannerheim. Nearly all the Finnish establishment was represented (Sibelius among them), apart from the left-wing parties. Why, one wonders, did Sibelius allow himself to be drawn into this movement? No doubt its patriotic tone swayed him and others from the circles in which he moved. His experiences during the civil war had left him in no doubt as to his sympathies. The left, as well as half the Agrarian Party in the Diet, vigorously opposed expenditure on national defence in favour of social reforms. Not even with the support of the remaining Agrarians and the liberals could the right-wing government secure an adequate defence budget.

A second reason why the Lapua movement gained Sibelius's support was its apparently liberal attitude to the language war, although he should have realized that the movement included Finnish-speaking fanatics as well as right-wing extremists. It was not really as much in character for him to have agreed to attend the July rally as it would have been for Aino, who was ultra-right-wing. In spite of her generally Finnish outlook, she subscribed to an extreme right-wing Swedish magazine which had begun to appear in 1917. However, by the autumn the Lapua movement soon succumbed to extremism and violence, directed not only against communists but also some leading social democrats. There were even isolated killings, and when in October fanatics briefly kidnapped ex-president Ståhlberg and his wife, the movement lost much of its support among moderate opinion. Sibelius certainly turned his back on it.

The correspondence with Cecil Gray continued unabated, and in October the English critic returned to Helsinki to read through unpublished manuscripts, including *Kullervo*. During the year he had studied Swedish and was sufficiently *au courant* with its grammar and syntax to tackle Furuhjelm's pioneering book.

CHAPTER TWENTY-ONE

1931: A Year of Hope

On 7 March 1931 Axel Gallén, as Sibelius had always called him – though he was now officially known by the Finnish form of his name, Akseli Gallen-Kallela – died in Stockholm. His son-in-law, the ethno-musicologist A.O. Väisänen, telephoned Sibelius and asked him to compose a piece for the funeral. Sibelius allowed himself to be persuaded – and perhaps in his innermost self followed his instinctive feeling.

Of the three central figures of the 'Symposium' days, only Kajanus and Sibelius now remained – and Kajanus himself had barely two years left to live. Since the 1890s the occasions on which they had all three gathered had been few. After his telephone conversation with Väisänen, Sibelius was panic-stricken. The funeral was only a few days off, and it would be 'absolutely impossible' for him to have anything ready in time. But Väisänen remained unmoved and stood his ground: 'You have given your word. The invitations have been sent out and the programme has been printed. It says that funeral music by you will be played. Everyone counts on your music being heard in the church. And moreover you are going to be one of the pall-bearers.'

Sibelius had to give way, and the result was *Sorgemusik (Funeral Music)* for organ. The piece is rather advanced in style, and given the fact that he produced it in record time, the idea has gained currency that he drew on material he already had to hand. The notion that he might have drawn on a theme or paragraph from the Eighth Symphony on which he was working is conceivable. Some time after Sibelius's death the composer Joonas Kokkonen ventured to raise this possibility with Aino, who admitted that she also had the feeling that it could have some connection with the symphony. Even if *Funeral music* shares the same opus as *Intrada* – written in honour of the state visit to Finland of the Swedish King and Queen in 1925 – the two pieces have nothing in common.

Sorgemusik, Sibelius's last instrumental piece, exerts every fascination in its own right, with its distinctive and individual tone colour. But the most interesting thing is that it builds on the newest elements of his sound world. For Gallén, Sibelius broke his usual rule of never attending funerals and agreed to serve as a pall-bearer. Adolf Paul, who was from time to time a guest at the Symposium evenings, wrote that his death hit him hard. 'I was glad that I had been able to see his strong, powerful figure [clearly in the summer of 1930] and relive with him a little of my youth. Never for one moment would I have suspected that ill-health would strike him down.' His letter went on to say that a rich German autograph collector was interested in acquiring a Sibelius manuscript. Nothing small-scale, he had insisted, but a larger work. And he had commissioned Paul to organize the matter. A large sum was at stake – the collection included the original autograph of Bach's *Wohltemperierte Klavier*. Sibelius appears to have made an offer, though at the time Paul sent his reply, he had not yet had a response. With Paul himself, however, things were in a bad way. He was no longer in a position to keep the handsome apartment in Joachimsthalerstrasse in which he had lived for twenty-one years. His landlord had secured a court order for his eviction.

One wonders to what extent Sibelius was aware of the enormous potential value of his autographs at a time when his reputation was steadily mounting. *Tapiola* had presumably become the property of Breitkopf & Härtel, and the forthcoming Eighth Symphony he had already donated to the Boston Symphony Orchestra's Library. By the spring of 1931 Sibelius was intent on finishing the Eighth Symphony. The undertakings he had given Koussevitzky about his rights to its first performance and the promise to deposit the manuscript would certainly have been seen in Boston as signs of its imminent completion.

Sibelius sought the solitude and anonymity of a big city, and as usual his choice fell on Berlin. Without even waiting to hear Kajanus conducting the Seventh, Sixth and Third symphonies on 30 April, he set out on the passenger ship *Ariadne*, the Baltic flagship, for Stettin. In Berlin he registered at the Hotel Continental by Friedrichstrasse Station, from which he wrote to his old friend Georg Boldemann, whose opera libretto *Blauer Dunst* he had at one time thought of setting. 'I would very much like to see you but I am dead tired after the sea journey [he had been the main celebrity on board the *Ariadne* and had been liberally plied with the Captain's hospitality]. Perhaps you know of a room where I could work, of modest size, with nice people. And a bathroom.' Luckily, the Boldemann's son Holger and his wife Maija, the daughter of Arvid Järnefelt, were just on the point of moving out to her parents at Wannsee, and Sibelius was able to have the use of their apartment in Wilmersdorf.

This was to be the last of Sibelius's foreign trips – and the last occasion on which we have any record of his daily life or the progress of his compositions. During the next two months in Berlin, however, he makes no mention of depression or flagging creative energy. Nor does his handwriting betray any tremor, not even when he was taken ill towards the end of his stay. On his arrival he wrote to Aino asking about Kajanus's concert, discussing everyday matters concerning their garden and announcing that he would be dining with the Boldemans on Sunday. A week later he writes again:

I have now settled in. I like it here and can work better than I have done for a long, long time. I have a servant – Amalia – a Catholic who cooks well for me. I have eaten out for the last three days. There are three rooms and Amalia's kitchen. As long as there is no music. So far it has been very peaceful in that respect. I am eagerly awaiting your news. If you can't write yourself, get the girls to do it. Tomorrow, Saturday, it will be two weeks since I have been away. Yesterday I went with Boldemann to order some clothes. And I also visited Lazzi [Georg Boldemann's son Laci, who was to become a gifted composer]. Maija is quite adorable in her Tolstoyan enthusiasms. Tell that to Arvid. The Boldemanns are making a great fuss of me. Up to the present I have no instrument, but later on I shall need one. I plan to ask my publisher to make the arrangements. Now that I have got away from all the irritations of the artistic world, everything is going so well for me. It has been high summer, but today and yesterday the weather was cold. People beat their carpets and there are other noises, but since there is nothing with pitch, it doesn't disturb me.

Before Sibelius began work on a new piece, he usually sat at the piano and improvised. But once the improvisation stage was over, he would settle down with a ruler and draw some bar lines, at which stage, Aino testified, he had the work clearly in his head and was ready to put pen to paper. But there were occasions, particularly towards the end, when he would want to try out the aural effect of certain passages.

Eventually a letter arrived from Aino, to which he responded briefly. 'Here I am having a good time – well looked after by Amalia – and I can really work properly. That's why I am in such good spirits.' All his letters are couched in the most loving terms and express concern about Aino's health.

A few days later he had another letter from Aino, to which he responded: 'Have two dear letters from you. Everything is fine here. Only hope that I won't be distracted by music. To calm your nerves, you should put life in perspective. Do not allow yourself to be tyrannized by the garden. If my music tyrannizes me, that is only right and proper. But you *must* let some things be and allow, for example, part of the garden to go untended. Do you think I'm dreadful? As far as money is concerned, things are working out well, though I shall be interested to see what Voss-S. [Voss-Schrader, the head of the Fazer publishing house] has to say. Last night there was a majestic storm. I sat in the dark and admired it. Have just written to John Forsell.'

On 22 May he wrote to Aino about the Eighth Symphony in greater detail than he had done before:

I was expecting to hear from you today, but no letter came. Am worried about the political situation. How are things at home? Please write, my darling – completely frankly. Here I am living in my music. Am engrossed in my work, but anxiety about everything gets me down. It would be a dreadful shame if it forced me to break off my stay here. My plan is to stay on until the end of June. Then home. We'll see how things go. The symphony is making great strides and I must get it finished while I am still in full spiritual vigour. It's strange, this work's conception.

Money questions will sort themselves out. But just now I am in need of some. Soon some will be coming in; the symphony should bring in between 30 to 40 thousand marks. I will have other things ready later this year.

The underlying tone here reminds one of the letters he wrote home during his first visit to Italy, when he started work on the Second Symphony. In spite of his various anxieties, Sibelius was in an optimistic and positive frame of mind; he was composing in something approaching a state of euphoria. 'Lina Boldemann [Georg's wife, who was a singing teacher] has given me a coffee machine. Have just bought some coffee, or rather she has. I pay my own way – rent to Holger. Money runs away, but I am doing very well. I eat at home. Cheaper than eating out . . . I shall be needing more money soon. Have ordered a new suit, which isn't ready yet, and have been to Breit-sprecher and have had some wonderful walking shoes made. I have paid for them. I haven't yet got round to buying new collars.' Sibelius's pen flows as freely and fluently as it did in the days of his youth. But he knew his Goethe all too well: '*Himmelshoch jauchzend, zum Tode betrübt.*'

A week later Aino received an alarming telegram: 'ILL, RETURNING IMMEDIATELY. THOUSAND MARKS WHICH I ASKED FOR HAS NOT ARRIVED. SEND IT BY TELEGRAPH.' The same evening, Boldemann sent Aino more reassuring news: 'JEAN MUCH BETTER.' Sibelius had a severe stomach complaint and spent a couple of days in a clinic. Even in his present predicament he drew up an account of his expenses so that Aino could see 'the lie of the land'. The medical bills were steep: 800 Finnish gold marks to the clinic, 60 for the professor's two visits. The kindly Boldemann came to visit him and stayed to dinner. But he insisted – greatly to Sibelius's annoyance – on having the window open: 'With me in my condition and so weak. How inconsiderate! The doctor maintains that I have recently had pleurisy. Must stay here for twelve to fifteen days.' Visions of the past haunt him. 'When I lie here, I can see myself in the mirror. And I look very much like my brother Kitti when he lay there at the end. Strange, the attack of anxiety I had in the street near Paul's, whom I have not visited. Have never experienced anything so dreadful. How difficult the formalities are before you depart this life!'

He immediately regretted the self-dramatization – particularly the letter's closing 'Farewell!' – and a couple of days later he wrote: 'I should never have sent that letter the day before yesterday. But I needed to talk to you. But now I realize I should have exercised more self-control.' But he is beginning to tire of brooding over his aches and pains, and asks Aino to write: 'Tell me about yourself and your gardening. That is real poetry. They only play the classics here. And I am not interested in hearing how so–and–so takes various bits in Schubert's "Unfinished". Can't they let these masterpieces alone and be played as they are? My work is making progress, albeit slow progress. But it is going to be good!'

His very last letter from Berlin – and the last he ever wrote to Aino from abroad – dates from 10 June 1931: 'Have been forced to stop having treatment from Prof. Zuelzer. I could not have gone through with it! He injected me with a new substance – Eutonon – which is at the experimental stage. The Boldemanns and the enchanting Maija put a stop to it . . . You can imagine the kind of humour it has put me in. Now I have a good, ordinary physician, Dr Scheff, who has much of Kitti's approach to life. As he says: "Why inject poison into your body when it is quite healthy!" In any event, I am now feeling a bit better.'

What of the ever-troublesome question of money? Sibelius was looking forward to a quarterly statement from Hansen at the end of June, which he calculated would be in the order of 1700–1800 Reichsmarks. This would help to meet some bills. After meeting his medical fees and his rent he reckoned on returning straight home. 'But now that I am fit again it would be a pity to break my pattern of work. It would be best if I could stay on until Whitsun. By that time the Baltic weather would be ideal.' The letter also reminds Aino to write to Cecil Gray. 'Yesterday Paul came to dinner. Amalia cooked a carp. And I made a salad, which I can now eat once more. Zuelzer had forbidden vinegar. He is a scientist and wants to make his name with Eutonon. For him that is the main thing. My life and that of others are a secondary consideration. I am in very good spirits now. Take care of yourself, light of my life.'

– 2 –

For a whole year now Koussevitzky had heard nothing from Sibelius, even though in August 1930 the composer had given him to understand that an Eighth Symphony was imminent. Koussevitzky was on tenterhooks. The Boston Symphony's jubilee celebrations were over, but Sibelius had not sent a word, let alone a new work. And so it was Koussevitzky who took up his pen during his annual summer stay in Paris:

Paris, 8 August 1931
I have not written to you as I did not want to disturb you with my letter, but I am already thinking of the Boston season and I wanted to ask

whether your new work, which I await with great impatience, is ready. May I hope that the first performance will be given during the coming season?

Your Seventh Symphony enjoyed a great success last season, and this year I will be conducting the Fourth – I am studying the score at the moment. This symphony is close to me, I feel it deeply.

In the same letter he asks about certain tempi, particularly in the second movement and the finale. His first question concerned the tempo marking *Doppo più lento* at letter K in the second movement *(Allegro molto vivace)*: 'I understand it as applying for three bars; afterwards *Tempo primo* is restored and remains until the end. Is this not so? I must have your confirmation of this anyway. Could you also send me an exact tempo (metronome marking) for the final Allegro movement?'

Sibelius replied on 20 August: 'In the event of your wishing to perform my new symphony next spring, this will I hope be possible . . . The tempo for the fourth movement is minim=120. The last two pages of the score should be taken a little more gently. Regarding the pages at letter K in the second movement, I do not wish to oppose your intentions. In the end – forgive me if I sound so confident – one may express the truth in more than one way. Above all, I thank you, Maestro Koussevitzky, for having written to me about this matter.' As we see, Sibelius gives the conductor the freedom to shape details according to his own judgment.

Koussevitzky's reply betrays his pleasure: 'You may rest assured that I will perform your new symphony with the greatest of pleasure next spring in Boston, and also in New York, if I could have the orchestral material by March.'

No doubt the headway that Sibelius had made in Berlin earlier in the year prompted his confidence in making his promise. A further spur came from Copenhagen in the form of an inquiry from Hansen, who had already asked about the symphony three years earlier. Then as now, Sibelius replied that he had the symphony 'in his head'. It would seem that he was only now beginning to realize what he had let himself in for. On 15 January 1932 he sent off this telegram to Koussevitzky: 'NO SYMPHONY THIS SEASON HAVE WRITTEN TO CHERKASSKY' [Paul Cherkassky was leader of the Boston Symphony Orchestra and had played the Sibelius Concerto in Helsinki].[1]

In his reply, on 22 April, Koussevitzky shows no flicker of impatience. He speaks of the triumphant successes that the Second and Fourth symphonies have enjoyed in Boston, New York and other cities. And as if in passing, he once again thanks Sibelius for giving the Boston Orchestra the right of first performance of the Eighth Symphony. He finally advises him to inform his publishers of the position 'since publishers do not always follow composers' wishes'.

Clearly charmed by the tone of Koussevitzky's letter, Sibelius replied on 6 June: 'It would be good if you could perform my symphony at the end of October. This would then be a world première. I will probably send you a handwritten score because – as you say – publishers respect nothing.'

But not everyone was as tactful. Olin Downes wrote from Moscow in June 1932, announcing his intention to visit Helsinki later that month and asking him for a great favour. 'You know I have never asked you to talk about your music or about music. We have talked of other things. But now I ask if you will talk with me for publication, about your music, particularly the eighth symphony, which I understand is now finished, and your opinions on music etc. I ask this for two reasons. First, I wish to write about the new symphony in advance of its performance by Koussevitzky, whom I saw in Paris. Secondly, I wish to include this subject, and say something about my visit to you, in a radio talk I will make for America, probably from either Berlin or Vienna . . . Do you know that Koussevitzky is going to play all your symphonies next season?' Downes reminded Sibelius that Koussevitzky, who as already indicated had not understood his music when he arrived in America, was now one of his warmest admirers: 'When he tried a year ago – and in vain – to make me admire one of the later works of Stravinsky, he said, "Remember how I changed about Sibelius. You must now try to be open-minded about Stravinsky." To which I replied, "There is no comparison. Stravinsky *was* a great composer, Sibelius *is* a great composer."' Downes continued: 'Is the Eighth Symphony in print? And if it is printed, may I have a copy to take with me to America?' A year earlier he had cabled the selfsame request: 'PLEASE ASK PUBLISHER FORWARD IMMEDIATELY SCORE YOUR EIGHTH SYMPHONY MY EXPENSE.'

Sibelius had not realized what a Pandora's box he had opened in confiding to Koussevitzky that he would soon publish new works. On 2 July came a letter from Koussevitzky in Bad Gastein: 'I look forward with the greatest of pleasure to performing your new symphony in Boston in October. In November I will also play it in New York. It would be best to send the handwritten score to Paris, where I will arrive in about two weeks and where I will stay until 15 September. If it were possible, therefore, for you to have the material sent to Paris before September 14, I could take it back to America myself.'

Six years previously Breitkopf & Härtel had warned Sibelius against sending the *Tapiola* manuscript to Walter Damrosch. Now the tables were turned, and it was Koussevitzky who was warning him about sending the score of the Eighth Symphony to Breitkopf! A few days later Sibelius was writing to Koussevitzky with news of another postponement:

14 July 1932
Unfortunately I have mentioned October as the month for the première

of my symphony. But this is not certain, as I have had all sorts of interruptions. Please do not advertise any performance.

In a rough draft of the letter he expressed himself with even greater caution: 'October is uncertain and certainly too early. When it will be ready I do not know.' But Koussevitzky remained unperturbed and ignored Sibelius's doubts:

5 October 1932
This season I intend to perform all of your symphonies in Boston. My plan is to include one of your works in the programme of each concert. Now I should like to know whether you approve of the symphonies being played in chronological order. I urgently beg you to let me know whether I could have your Eighth Symphony within one-and-a-half to two months. If this is not possible by the end of December, I will arrange my programmes so that your symphonies are performed in every other concert and that the season ends with the first performance of your new symphony.
   I also beg you to let me know whether I will receive the score in the form of orchestral parts or only as a handwritten score. In the latter case, we can write out the orchestral parts ourselves here in Boston.

The drama was nearing its climax. Sibelius answered later the same month:

26 October
Dear Maestro,
I thank you with all my heart for your letter of 5 October with its particularly important information. I feel that giving the symphonies in chronological order is the best way. I just do not know if I can send the work by December. I shall try.
   Unfortunately I was forced to promise the Royal Philharmonic Society in London the first performance in Europe. This will take place after your world première.
   And so: either I will send you the handwritten score in December or the printed material a couple of months later.

On the evidence of the early deadline Sibelius gave himself, this was the most concrete suggestion he had made to Koussevitzky – with the sole proviso that he could not be absolutely sure that it would be ready in time.
   The contact with the Royal Philharmonic Society had been made in the summer of 1931, after Sibelius's return from Berlin, by Basil Cameron, who had visited Finland two years previously. Cameron had been invited to conduct some RPS concerts in October and November, and was full of enthusiasm: 'Mr [Cecil] Gray told me that you have perhaps written a new symphony. Would you in that case allow me to give the first performance in London?' Obviously encouraged by Sibelius's reaction, Cameron went

straight ahead: 'Could you . . . give me some information about how the symphony should be advertised. Which key it is in, how long the playing time, and what you would advise us to play within the framework of the same programme?'

Sibelius was clearly alarmed, and his reply was apparently such that Cameron felt obliged to apologize for his intrusion. But he soon returned to the attack. Cameron wrote from Bayreuth – where he had just heard Toscanini conduct *Parsifal* – that he had shown Sibelius's first letter to the RPS Secretary, who was delighted at the prospect of being able to advertise a new work for the coming winter season. Cameron hoped to present it at his last RPO concert on 3 December.

Sibelius sounded a quick retreat, as is clear from the fact that as early as 29 September he was worried that the new symphony would not be ready in time. So he clutched at a final straw: could he possibly conduct the symphony at his guest appearance in San Francisco the following March? Meanwhile, Koussevitzky was continuing his triumphant survey and it was thanks to him that *Tapiola* achieved a breakthrough in November 1932. 'Conductor, orchestra and audience . . . all felt the wingbeats of a masterpiece,' wrote Henry T. Parker in the *Boston Transcript*. The same paper published Sibelius's portrait under the headline 'Strength of ten men'. The caption read: 'Jean Sibelius, the composer placed above all others at the symphony concerts during the present year.'

On 7 November Koussevitzky sent a telegram to Ainola: 'TAPIOLA TWICE IN BOSTON EXCEPTIONAL PUBLIC AND CRITICAL ACCLAIM. COMPLETE SYMPHONIC CYCLE BEGINS THIS WEEK WITH SYMPHONY I.' The *Boston Post* stated quite explicitly what could be read between the lines: 'The 8th symphony will receive its world première here next spring.' Koussevitzky now had the bit between the teeth. His New Year telegram to Sibelius finishes: 'AM WORRIED. HAS THE SCORE TO THE 8TH SYMPHONY BEEN SENT?' Ten days later he repeated the question more emphatically: 'AM VERY CONCERNED PLEASE ADVISE.' Sibelius's reply followed on 17 January 1933: 'REGRET IMPOSSIBLE THIS SEASON, HAVE WRITTEN TO CHERKASSKY 2ND JANUARY, GREETINGS SIBELIUS.'

Even if Koussevitsky should by now have been prepared for a rebuff, he took it hard and wrote to Sibelius on 1 February: 'Your telegram greatly discouraged me but I perfectly understand that you cannot release a composition until you feel satisfied with every single note you are giving to the world. This, naturally, does not change my plans, and I am continuing the cycle of your symphonies . . . I still hope in my heart of hearts that the 8th Symphony will come. Even if you send it at the end of March, I could give it in Boston and New York in April.'

Sibelius had to reconcile himself to the fact that the long-awaited première was regarded as newsworthy material in the world's press. In London the *Daily Telegraph* wrote: 'The advent of this symphony has excited world-wide interest. Last summer Basil Cameron saw Sibelius in Helsingfors and the composer told him that the symphony was complete – in his head.'

Koussevitzky was by no means the only champion of Sibelius in America. In one week in November 1932 the Fourth Symphony had been given in New York under Stokowski, *En saga* by Toscanini – 'which gave many listeners a new view of Sibelius' – and the First Symphony by both Rodzinski and Koussevitzky! It is less well known that conductors more readily associated with the Viennese classics and the German tradition also performed him in New York: Klemperer the Seventh and Second symphonies, Bruno Walter the Seventh and *The Swan of Tuonela* and as we have said, Furtwängler *The Tempest* Prelude. A little later Eugene Ormandy came into the picture.

After having performed the complete cycle in Boston during the 1932–3 season, Koussevitzky brought the Seventh to London for a guest appearance with the newly-formed BBC Symphony Orchestra. Their performance at a concert on 15 May was recorded. In a letter to the composer on 7 June Koussevitzky reported: 'I have heard the records and cannot say that I am perfectly satisfied with the tests: some of it is good, but some details and phrasings are not as clear as they should be. However, these records possess one distinctive quality: they are "alive", and in this respect come out better than when recorded at special sessions. Nevertheless it is for you . . . to judge whether the enregistration is good enough to have the discs appear . . . if they do not please you, they will be destroyed.'

This early live recording more than holds its own today. 'It may interest you to know that the symphonies 4, 6 and 7 left the deepest impression, the 5th aroused the greatest enthusiasm in the audience; as to the 1st and 2nd symphonies, they always win the largest success and popularity. As regards myself, the artistic joy I experienced in performing your works is beyond any words . . . any hope to have your 8th Symphony for the coming season, and may we still have the privilege of its first performance anywhere?'

Sibelius answered on 3 July: 'I find it hard to express the joy I experienced when I listened to you, dear Maestro. Admittedly only on record. Everything was full of life and natural, and I cannot thank you sufficiently.' Then came the bitter pill. 'I beg you not to advertise the new symphony. I shall write about it later.' Koussevitzky wrote again at the New Year, renewing his hope that he would see the Eighth Symphony before the end of 1934.

The relationship between Sibelius and Koussevitzky continued on another plane, without the play of demonic forces behind the scenes. A final vignette was Koussevitzky's visit to Helsinki in September 1935, some three months before Sibelius's seventieth birthday.

A certain nineteen-year-old student (the author of this book) smuggled himself into the balcony of the University's Ceremonial Hall to watch Koussevitzky's rehearsal. The conductor had finished the first movement of the Second Symphony and had raised his baton for the second. He conjured up an almost ghostly sonority in the introductory pizzicato bars, and all was proceeding well until he came to the first ritenuto marked in the score, where he indicated a rubato. But alas the ensemble between cellos and violins broke down and there was suddenly an air of confusion. Koussevitzky's colour changed to a crimson red; storms threatened. He broke off, and a deathly silence engulfed the whole auditorium. His otherwise sonorous tones rose in an angry shriek: 'But gentlemen, *das ist doch gar nicht schwer.* Please *nur so*: tum, tum, tum, tum . . . *Bitte!*' But in vain. His musician's German fell on deaf ears. The musicians sat there like a glowing fire. But with psychological skill Koussevitzky put everything right, and when he raised his baton and lowered his voice the tension disappeared.

Koussevitzky's mastery showed when he turned from the romanticism of the Second to the spirituality of the Seventh. What a vision of space he achieved with the trombone theme, and with what conviction and majesty he paced the serene Olympian motto theme that forms the symphony's credo! And then when the score of the Seventh Symphony was replaced by *Tapiola*, the Olympian figure on the podium was transformed into a sorcerer. He brought forth from the orchestra everything that *Tapiola* has to offer in terms of spells, magic and atmosphere. The concert itself took place on Friday 13 September, when *Tapiola* and the Seventh Symphony comprised the first half and the Second followed after the interval. The musicians were electrified and gripped by Koussevitzky's magical baton, as well as by the knowledge that the composer was in the audience.

Koussevitzky and his wife Natalie spent a week in Helsinki. In the early years of the century, while he was staying at Syväranta, not far from Sibelius's home, he had stood at Ainola's gate but not ventured further. At that time he had no feeling for Sibelius's music, but now he returned to Järvenpää as the composer's guest. The families became good friends. The language problem was easily solved: Jean and Serge communicated in German, Aino and Madame Natalie in Russian. It is not known whether the conversation touched upon the sensitive issue of the Eighth Symphony, though the telegram Koussevitzky sent on 21 November on his return to America does not allude to the matter. He does thank Aino for the apples she sent from Ainola's garden: 'We were touched by your warm thoughts.'

In a subsequent letter Koussevitzky said that the hours that they spent together left an indelible impression which would stay with them all their lives, and the composer in his turn replied in similar terms. However close they were on that occasion, however, Sibelius did not permit Koussevitzky admittance to his *jardin secret* to catch a glimpse of the new symphony, though that was permitted to his copyist of many years, Paul Voigt – a German by birth who had once been leader of the second violins in the Helsinki Orchestra. It is worth noting that Voigt had already received some of the Eighth Symphony a couple of years before Koussevitzky's visit. When he returned the finished score he enclosed the following note dated 4 September 1933:

Most Honoured Master!

I hereby deliver the completed work and hope, Herr Professor, that you will be satisfied with the result. I also wish to draw your attention, Herr Professor, to page 2, as it is not clear in the bassoon and cello parts where the bass clef should be inserted. The price is 8 marks per page, 23 pages = 184 Finnmarks.

On the back of the letter Sibelius drafted his reply, also in German:

My best thanks.
Please do not bind the copy yet.
Title: Sinfonia 8.
At the end: fermata.
The Largo continues without a break.
The whole piece will be roughly eight times as long as this.
As for your honorarium, I beg you to accept at least 10 marks per page.
With best greetings etc.

From Voigt's letter and Sibelius's reply, it is evident that the first movement of the Eighth Symphony existed and was followed after a *fermato* – *attacca* by a Largo movement, and that Sibelius calculated that the whole symphony would be on the scale of the Second, thus adhering to the original design he had discussed with Schnéevoigt in 1924.

During the many conversations it was my honour and privilege to hold with Aino Sibelius after her husband's death, I learned that she and Sibelius together had either taken to Voigt or fetched from him a thick bunch of manuscripts. Sibelius's daughter Margareta Jalas also visited Voigt on the same errand. This supports the view that several movements, and perhaps the whole symphony, had been completed or had neared completion.

Sibelius's diary entries, which are in any event scanty after the 1920s, tell us very little. One entry on 18 December 1931 reads: 'Working on my 8th Symphony and am pure youthfulness. How to explain this?' Only four months earlier, as we have seen, he had written to Koussevitzky in encouraging terms, presumably because work had progressed so well in Berlin the preceding May.

As late as the critical year 1933 he noted on 4 May: 'It is as if I had returned home. In my art. Am writing, i.e. forging the first movement. Take everything in another way, deeper. A gypsy came today. Romantic.' But after this it seems as if the composer's optimism begins to flag. He entered the most oppressive period of his life. Ten years later, however, it would appear that his creative fires were again alight. In a letter to Georg and Lina Boldemann, who had moved to Sweden to escape the Nazis, he wrote: 'Am now consumed by my new work and am curious to see whether it will be finished before I go to the final silence.' He told his son-in-law Jussi Jalas in January 1943 that his life would soon be over and that he would regard everything as having been in vain if he had not finished the symphony that was in his thoughts.

Why did it all end this way? The evidence would seem to point to the fact that his self-criticism had gained the upper hand and had become totally destructive. He had after all composed four great works during 1923–6, and there is nothing to suggest that his mental faculties were in any way diminished. One thinks of his youth, when he consulted an ear specialist and learned that in the course of time he would become completely deaf. He reacted strongly at the time in a letter to Aino: 'A musician who cannot hear. Now I shall ensure that I listen to orchestral music above all else as long as I can still hear; then later, when the hearing has gone, one will be able to imagine the sound better . . . Do not tell anyone of this. I simply cannot bear the thought of people saying it sounds like that because he is deaf.' (5 November 1891) Perhaps a factor in his reluctance to release the Eighth Symphony was that he could not bear the thought of people saying, 'It sounds like that because he is old.'

After his death Aino Sibelius told me: 'In the 1940s there was a great *auto da fé* at Ainola. My husband collected a number of manuscripts in a laundry basket and burned them on the open fire in the dining room. Parts of the *Karelia Suite* were destroyed – I later saw remains of the pages which had been torn out – and many other things. I did not have the strength to be present and left the room. I therefore do not know what he threw on to the fire. But after this my husband became calmer and gradually lighter in mood. It was a happy time.'

In his English-language book on Sibelius, the composer's secretary Santeri Levas wrote: 'In August 1945 he told me that he had destroyed the whole work. "My Eighth Symphony", he said, "has been 'ready' – ready in inverted commas – many times. I even went so far as to put it in the fire."'

CHAPTER TWENTY-TWO

The Silence

[29 April 1933] Here is the *vita nova* I have dreamt about. Must make something of the years which are still left me.

[3 May] Concerts (radio) in Vienna. *Radiozeit* [the Austrian equivalent of *The Radio Times*)] – a wonderful article on me. Clearly Cecil Gray's doing, or rather his book's . . .

[16 November] How does one achieve this peace of mind that Pekka Halonen talks about? Kajanus's death caused the scores of *Lemminkäinen* to be sent to me . . . R. K. held on to them for thirty-five years. But why? Strange, the workings of the human heart.

The Swan of Tuonela and *Lemminkäinen's Homeward Journey* had been published by Breitkopf & Härtel as early as 1901. Sibelius had however withheld the two other movements – *Lemminkäinen and the Maidens of the Island* and *Lemminkäinen in Tuonela* – and forbidden their performance. In 1920, faced with a financial crisis, he deposited the manuscript of the whole of the *Lemminkäinen Suite*, as well as *Luonnotar* and three movements from the *Scènes historiques,* in the Kalevala Society's archives. The Society's secretary, A.O. Väisänen, signed a receipt on 15 December 1920.

Even though the receipt stipulated that Väisänen had the original manuscript 'in his custody', he spoke of it in the society's next Yearbook as a 'donation'. As a direct consequence of their correspondence, one can read in Väisänen's summary of the year 1933 mention of the 'enormously valuable *gift*' (my italics): two movements from the *Lemminkäinen Suite*, namely *Lemminkäinen and the Maidens of the Island* and *Lemminkäinen in Tuonela*. So it remains a mystery how Kajanus's death could possibly have affected the 'rediscovery' of these movements one way or the other.

When the Kalevala Society celebrated its centenary on 1 March 1935, it did so with a concert in Helsinki under Schnéevoigt's baton, at which the great novelties were *Lemminkäinen and the Maidens of the Island* and *Lemminkäinen in Tuonela*, receiving their first hearing since the 1890s. Their reception, by the press and more particularly the public, was rapturous.

[22 November 1933] Depressed by a review in *The Chesterian* concerning my Symphony III. That it is 'Tschaikoffski [*sic*] indebted'. A lie! But how can I learn to disregard these constant pinpricks?

[4 April 1934] Heard concert from London on the wireless. Goodwill and good wishes from the English world. But how little they understand that here! Our coarseness – which has increased to an alarming extent since they have dropped everything Swedish – our self-congratulation because of these sporting successes [the European finals in Turin]. Uneducated, our claims to be civilized are far too premature – it's all part of the same thing – the language war.

Another youthful work, the *Kullervo* Symphony, was allowed to resurface, even if the public could only glimpse its central movement, *Kullervo and His Sister*. This did not kindle the same enthusiasm. According to the critic Evert Katila, this was in some measure due to the unsuitability of the soloists.

The great event of 1935 was Sibelius's seventieth birthday, which in some respects has neither precedent nor parallel among musicians. Sibelius and his wife left Ainola for the capital and settled into an apartment there. On the birthday morning all the Helsinki newspapers appeared as Sibelius editions and reprinted the flood of congratulatory telegrams that had poured in from all over the world. From Richard Strauss, Ralph Vaughan Williams, Ottorino Respighi among composers; Felix Weingartner, Wilhelm Furt-wängler and Otto Klemperer among conductors. The latter's tribute is of particular interest: 'Jean Sibelius is one of the most beautiful and heart-warming phenomena among living composers. Without glancing either to left or right, without following trends or fashions, he has pursued his own path and composed music, always music . . . As early as the Second Sym-phony he reveals himself as fully fledged. What freshness and power! . . . Sibelius follows the traditional forms of the classical symphony, but he always builds up his music with living, life-enhancing material. We con-ductors thank him from the bottom of our hearts for the great works he has given us.'

No mean tribute from one of the most celebrated interpreters of the classical symphonic repertoire! These words must have warmed Sibelius's heart, particularly in view of the dismissive tone adopted by so many Ger-man critics. More than once in later life he was to remark that in Germany his music was liked only by conductors!

From Denmark there was an unexpected telegram: 'Long live the beloved great master, long live the people and the landscape that has given us Sibelius. Feodor Chaliapin.' Most unusually, *The Times* honoured his birth-day in its hallowed leader columns, a rare tribute which Sibelius himself could read in the *Helsingin Sanomat* on the birthday morning. The festivities culminated in a gala concert that evening in the New Exhibition Hall. At a time when menacing clouds were beginning to build up on the international horizon, the Finnish authorities were keen to emphasize Sibelius's standing as a national symbol. Among the guests in the first row were all the former presidents of Finland – and even a president-to-be in the person of the speaker of the Diet, Kyösti Kallio. Unfortunately, President Svinhufvud was incapacitated by illness. But as if that were not enough, the prime ministers of Sweden, Norway and Denmark were also present. And Hitler had conferred on Sibelius the Goethe Medal, Germany's highest honour in the arts, doubtless a politically-motivated gesture.

For the concert itself the two Helsinki orchestras, the City Orchestra (now known as the Helsinki Philharmonic) and the Radio Orchestra, joined forces to make up a 100-man ensemble, which was conducted, appropriately enough, by Armas Järnefelt. As a Sibelius conductor, Järnefelt had few peers and was steeped in the musical atmosphere and thought of the repertoire. To *Finlandia*, which opened the concert, he brought nobility and confidence for the future, and to the First Symphony vision. The first part of the concert was relayed by wireless not only to Finland itself but to America as well. The second half comprised some of the most powerful numbers from *The Tempest* music, the *Intrada*, *Berceuse* and the *Storm*, as well as an early work, *The Captive Queen*, which like *Finlandia* has strong patriotic overtones.

After the concert there was a banquet at the Grand Hotel, where a surprise awaited them: the *Tafelmusik* which came from the loudspeakers in various parts of the hall was in fact a concert relayed direct from New York. The New York Philharmonic conducted by Otto Klemperer played two movements of the Second Symphony, and though the first bars were drowned by atmospheric disturbance, this was soon eliminated. The deafening applause of the American public must have warmed Sibelius's heart. It was the last occasion on which he agreed to celebrate his birthday in public, but in its scale the event must be unsurpassed. Abroad, Sibelius had done well during the autumn season: Sir Thomas Beecham in London, Koussevitzky in Boston and Toscanini in Vienna.

With England, Sibelius had enjoyed a special relationship right from the early years of the century, when he had conducted his own works in London and made the acquaintance of Henry Wood, Rosa Newmarch and Granville Bantock. Apart from the war years and a period in the 1920s when the London concert scene was afflicted by the Depression, the English concert-going public had followed his development with greater interest than almost any other.

Throughout the 1930s his name was frequently to be encountered in concert programmes, but the year 1930 itself was decisive in establishing Sibelius in another and in some ways more important sense. The advent of electrical recording had transformed the gramophone industry in much the same way as the advent of the long-playing record, stereo and the compact disc were to do in more recent times, and London was its main centre. Plans to record the complete symphonies began to surface. A start was made when the Finnish government decided to subsidize recordings of the First and Second Symphonies, an enlightened and at this time unprecedented gesture considering the fact that Finland was so small and young a country. It was quite simply a measure of the unique importance Finland attached to Sibelius as a national figure. In Denmark, for example, there was no comparable effort to promote the Nielsen symphonies, and their appearance on record was a post-war phenomenon that was not completed until 1952. By this time Elgar himself had conducted both his symphonies for the gramophone and both Rachmaninov and Richard Strauss had made important recordings. The choice of conductor was left to Sibelius, and in May that year Robert Kajanus went to London to record the symphonies for the Columbia label. The orchestra was largely drawn from the London Symphony, which could not be named for contractual reasons. Even today, these recordings show us something of Kajanus's mastery and nobility, and his ability to draw from his players a special Sibelius string sonority. They convey what one senses as a special authenticity.

Two years later His Master's Voice launched the Sibelius Society, a subscription series of records which would encompass all his major works and culminate in the forthcoming Eighth Symphony. Walter Legge, who was also responsible for other, similar ventures, such as the Hugo Wolf Song Society (to name only one), had invited Kajanus to return to record the Third and Fifth symphonies as well as *Tapiola*, *Pohjola's Daughter* and *Belshazzar's Feast* with the London Symphony Orchestra. Only his death in 1933 prevented Kajanus from completing the enterprise, but in June 1934 Georg Schnéevoigt and the Helsinki Orchestra paid London a visit to give concerts and make recordings. Legge reported that these concerts were regarded as something of a Sibelius festival. And at Sibelius's express wish, Schnéevoigt recorded the Fourth and Sixth symphonies together with *Luonnotar*. It is evident that Sibelius was anxious to see that the two most difficult of his symphonies, which had not yet gained wide public acceptance, should be put on record. The demanding soprano part in *Luonnotar* was entrusted to Helmi Liukkonen.

Already in the early 1930s Legge had tried to interest Sir Thomas Beecham in Mahler but without success; even *Das Lied von der Erde* Beecham dismissed as a 'monstrous afterbirth of the illicit amours of *Tristan and Isolde*'. However, he approved of Sibelius, 'partly because the great Finn had become a box-office magnet and partly because he knew that I wanted to record several works for the Sibelius Society – and at that time he seemed the best choice [more sessions for T.B.'s orchestra!].' The indefatigable Legge wrote to tell Sibelius that Beecham had been chosen for the orchestral recording as 'during the past winter, [he has] given magnificent performances of your First, Second, Third and Fourth Symphonies, the Violin Concerto and *Tapiola*,' adding that 'your music is now the sensation of London'. Legge's letter must have given Sibelius pleasure, but one is struck by a cryptic note he scribbled on it: 'Beecham, whom they have chosen, must be treated with great caution.' Why this cloud in what was otherwise blue skies and sunshine? Quite simply the inevitable Eighth Symphony, which Legge wanted Beecham to record – and which Sibelius had already promised to Boston.

From the surviving correspondence it is clear that Legge kept Sibelius well abreast of the progress of events. In January 1935 he wrote in his good but at that time not wholly idiomatic German: 'Beecham conducted your Fourth Symphony at the end of the month. He has already had three rehearsals and has worked like a dog with the Schnéevoigt records, but there is much on the records which do not correspond with the score. Sir Thomas has asked me to put a number of questions to you.' Beecham's queries mostly concerned matters of tempo and dynamics. At the end of the letter Legge asks for metronome markings for the whole work. A few days later a telegram arrived at Ainola: 'BEECHAM BROADCASTING YOUR FOURTH SYMPHONY TONIGHT 8.15 PLEASE LISTEN HE AND I WILL AWAIT CRITICISM WITH GREAT INTEREST.'

A couple of years later Beecham made his famous recording of the symphony and the tests were sent to Sibelius for approval. The composer sent a handwritten response four pages long, with a number of detailed points concerning tempi and other points of interpretation. When Beecham heard this he telephoned Sibelius in Finland and spoke at such length that Sibelius, whose English was hardly extensive, was quite worn out! He sent a telegram: 'DISCS BY SIR THOMAS ARE EXCELLENT CANCEL LETTER 28.11 GREETINGS SIBELIUS.' The next day when Legge and Beecham met face to face, one waving Sibelius's letter and the other his telegram, Beecham said: 'You win this round, my boy. We'll do the whole damned piece all over again and I'll pay the orchestra. I'll take the symphony on a provincial tour and you will be at every rehearsal with the score and the old cove's letter in front of you.'[1]

By a stroke of fate Sir Henry Wood had been reminded of his old love of Sibelius. Georg Schnéevoigt had been engaged to conduct a Sibelius concert at Bournemouth, but was taken ill and Sir Henry stepped in to replace him. The programme included a novelty, the two *Lemminkäinen Legends*, whose performance Sibelius had until recently forbidden. Sir Henry was fired with enthusiasm and told Sibelius: 'They really went home and were greeted with acclamation by an audience that was filled to the last place. I am so taken with them . . . that I would dearly like to include them among the "novelties" in the forthcoming season of Promenade concerts at the Queen's Hall in London.' (26 February 1937) So enthusiastic was he that he decided to do not only them but all the seven symphonies, the Violin Concerto and a number of smaller works in six Sibelius concerts during the next season of Promenade Concerts, a phenomenon which at the time had no precedent as far as living composers were concerned. This did not meet with universal acclaim, and prompted some pretty bizarre reviews. *The Times* reproached Sir Henry with setting 'education versus entertainment' and the *Observer* commented a little sourly: 'As far as we can remember, only Liszt has been so honoured in recent years.' In the circumstances of the day, it is not surprising that some of the works Sir Henry conducted still puzzled both audiences and critics. To include the Sixth Symphony in the context of the Proms was undoubtedly bold. But none of the reviews seem to have grasped its essential character or even its modality.

Classical symphonic form is indivisible from major–minor tonality, and this emerges most strongly in the Sixth Symphony's closing cadences. In this respect *The Times* critic compared the symphony with the D major fugue from the second book of Bach's *Das Wohltemperierte Klavier*, while the *Observer* saw parallels with the first movement of Beethoven's *Waldstein* Sonata 'which is built on similar thematic ideas – especially five-finger exercises'! Indeed, according to the *Observer*, it appeared that Sibelius was preoccupied 'with material that could be smuggled comfortably into other men's passage-works . . . The symphony ends in a near whisper and the audience hesitates: is it time to applaud?' The Fourth Symphony, on the other hand, had a better time of it, and although there were one or two unenthusiastic reviews, there were more that were perceptive and thought-ful – at least indicating a desire to 'understand' and come to terms with it. The Violin Concerto was another matter. *The Times* was fairly dismissive – 'truth to tell it is a poor work' – and the work was accused of superficiality and lack of shape. Part of the blame for this must be laid at the door of Sir Henry's soloist, Emil Telmányi (Nielsen's son-in-law), who lacked the tech-nical brilliance for which the concerto calls. Only two years earlier Jascha Heifetz had made his pioneering records with Beecham for HMV's Sibelius Society, and no contemporary could begin to match him in virtuosity and beauty of sonority. Even *The Oceanides* had a rough ride, but curiously enough, the melodramatic *Ferryman's Brides* (*The Rapids-Riders' Brides*) sent *The Times* into something approaching ecstasy. Surprisingly enough, it was the correspondent of the French musical journal *Le Monde Musical* who focused attention on one of the most remarkable works of the season, the symphonic poem *Tapiola*. A few months earlier London had also heard an electrifying account of the Second Symphony which Arturo Toscanini conducted at a guest appearance with the BBC Symphony Orchestra; it took London by storm. News of these and other events in the London musical calendar did not go unnoticed in America and elsewhere.

A year later, in August 1938, came a letter from Sir Thomas Beecham: 'I think you have been informed that I am giving a Festival of your music next autumn here in London.' And so on 27 October Sir Thomas inaugurated a series of six Sibelius concerts at the Queen's Hall. As *The Times* reported: 'They were all packed out, partly because Sibelius is the big name at the moment, and perhaps because Sir Thomas Beecham does not put on a festival devoted to a single figure unless that composer has made a deep and personal impression on him. This bodes well, for we can expect to look forward to some performances of exceptional distinction.'

Beecham's programmes went further than Wood's in sheer ambition and comprehensiveness. In addition to all seven symphonies and the Violin Concerto, they comprised all the tone poems including *Luonnotar*, two of the *Lemminkäinen Legends*, both of *The Tempest* suites, the *Serenades* (with the Finnish violinist Anja Ignatius as soloist), the second set of *Scènes historiques*, *Pelléas et Mélisande*, *Swanwhite*, *In memoriam*, *Finlandia* and *Valse triste*. In addition to this, another concert was devoted to the chamber and chamber–orchestral music: *Rakastava*, the string quartet, *Voces intimae*, a group of songs (with Aulikki Rautavaara no less), the C major *Romance* for strings and the *King Christian II* suite. Sibelius had never before enjoyed such comprehensive or distinguished exposure. *The Times* still found difficulties with the Sixth Symphony, which it thought the least successful of the cycle, but Beecham's masterly interpretation of the Fourth won its admiration, and his performance 'surpassed everything Sir Thomas achieved in his interpretation of the Seventh Symphony [at the same concert]'. The Violin Concerto, again with Telmányi as soloist, still produced only modified rapture. However, it got off more lightly than in the preceding year: *The Times* contented itself with saying that it 'perhaps hardly belongs to the great line of violin concertos . . . Mr Telmányi played it with a consistent earnestness and a complete accomplishment of style . . . ' They added that 'The colourful *Night Ride and Sunrise, opus 55*, sounded almost Byronic in its romanticism.'

Both Wood and Beecham had competed to lure Sibelius to London as a guest of honour, but the composer declined both invitations, pleading his advanced years. His eldest daughter Eva Paloheimo was present at one of the Beecham concerts, and Sibelius himself was kept abreast of events by telegram, and was able to hear some of them on the radio. The great question for everyone, however, was still the Eighth Symphony. All his symphonies were to be included in the Festival. 'The long looked-for No. VIII still tarries, but it is rumoured from Finland (with what truth we cannot say) that already a ninth is in the composer's mind and that some of it may already be on paper.' All this attention (save for the speculation about future compositions) must have given Sibelius pleasure, but a letter from Wood after the Beecham Festival was over showed his hurt pride. 'It is very extraordinary to me today to scan the papers here and see that SIR THOMAS BEECHAM [his capitals] is giving a so-called 'SIBELIUS FESTIVAL'. The fact seems to be unaccountably overlooked that during the strenuous Season of Promenade Concerts in 1937, I gave *what was indeed a* SIBELIUS FESTIVAL, [his italics] and through the Season did your Seven Symphonies. It seems to me, because this great undertaking was carried out in the stride of these Series of Concerts that it may have passed un-noticed and un-recognized.

This has hurt your friend extremely. Never mind, I hope with all my heart that I shall be able to produce your *EIGHT* [sic!] *SYMPHONY* and more Symphonies to come.'

Other, more serious matters were preoccupying Europe in 1938. The *Anschluss* had taken place at the beginning of the year, and the Munich crisis followed in the summer. Hitler's seizure of the rump of the Czech state, which the Munich agreement had guaranteed, deprived Europe of the hope of 'peace in our time' that Chamberlain had promised them. The collapse of the negotiations between Britain and France on the one hand, and the Soviet Union on the other later that year – and more ominously, the signature of the Nazi–Soviet non-aggression pact only a few days before the invasion of Poland on 1 September 1939 – set the seal on the catastrophic events that were soon to unfold.

The Nazi–Soviet agreement had divided eastern Europe into spheres of influence. The eastern part of Poland fell under Soviet hegemony, and on 17 September, barely three weeks after the Nazi invasion had begun, Russian troops entered Poland. Also included in the Soviet sphere of influence were the three Baltic States, Finland and, in the Balkans, northern Bukovina. One after the other the Baltic States were incorporated into the Soviet Union, and in November came Finland's turn. A Soviet ultimatum, whose demands included the leasing of the naval base of Hangö and other territorial concessions, was delivered in Helsinki and rejected. On 30 November the Red Army attacked Finland, Soviet planes bombed Helsinki and other Finnish cities and the 'Winter War' began.

News of the war naturally prompted anxiety for the ageing composer's safety. Offers of asylum poured in, but he declined them. 'I am too old. I want to remain in my own country.' His friends in England, including Cecil Gray, sent offers of help, but it would have been inconceivable for the composer of *Finlandia*, the symbol of Finland's identity and independence, to have left, whatever his age. The absence of serious hostilities between Germany and the Allies meant that the spotlight was on Finland, which enjoyed wide international sympathy and support. But even the considerable material aid that was sent was insufficient to stave off the Soviet onslaught; in March 1940 Finland sued for peace and had to reconcile itself to considerable loss of territory. Sibelius would have followed the Nazi invasion of Norway and Denmark and the fall of France.

In June 1941, Hitler launched his surprise invasion of the Soviet Union and hostilities were resumed. Anticipating that the Finnish government would seize the opportunity of recovering the territory lost to the USSR after the Winter War, Soviet planes attacked Finland. The Finns were careful to proclaim themselves co-belligerents rather than allies of the Germans, but it was not long before the territories lost during the Winter War were regained. Whatever gloss the Finnish government might put on it, the fact remained that, to the horror and dismay of its friends, Finland was now to all intents and purposes allied with Nazi Germany. Feeling was particularly strong in the United States, though America was still officially a neutral country and had not yet entered the war. Nor did the Americans ever declare war on Finland, though some months later, under pressure from the beleaguered Russians, Britain did so.

Immediately after the 'continuation war', as it is known in Finland, had broken out, the Finnish government turned to Sibelius and asked him to use the goodwill he enjoyed in the USA to explain Finland's case. Sibelius's appeal was sent to the Associated Press and appeared the following day in the American papers. A typical headline was that of *The Philadelphia Inquirer*: 'Sibelius asks the Americans to understand the Finnish War':

> In a statement to the Associated Press today (12 July) Jean Sibelius, the ageing Finnish composer, appealed to the American people to understand Finland's difficult position. The composer, who is in good health, lives quietly in the country 30 miles north of Helsinki.

Sibelius's appeal did not go unheeded and he received many letters from America in response, few of them sympathetic to the Nazis even though they may have expressed some understanding of the Finnish position.

> 'In 1939 my fatherland was attacked by the Bolsheviks. Enlightened American people then realized we were fighting not only for our freedom but for all Western civilization and they gave us valuable assistance.
>
> Now that the barbaric hordes of the east are again attacking us in their attempt to Bolshevize Europe, I am convinced that freedom-loving, intelligent people will rightly understand and appreciate the present situation, realizing that the Bolshevization of Europe would annihilate freedom and civilization in this continent.'

The Finnish government did not, however, limit its objectives to the restoration of the *status quo ante* and halt its advancing armies at the pre-war borders, but joined the German assault on Leningrad.

Sibelius's discomfort and anguish during the war years is clearly visible in a diary entry from 1943. As we have seen, fewer entries survive as the years advance. There are some in 1926, the year of *Tapiola*'s composition, and some for the following year. But after that, entries are only sporadic and made on loose pages, and from the period 1935–43 – from his seventieth birthday through to the closing phase of the war – there is nothing. There are, however, some regular annotations from the autumn of 1943 through to January 1944.

> [6 September 1943] This primitive way of thinking, anti-Semitism and the like, is something that at my age I *cannot* condone. My upbringing and

breeding don't fit in with the times. That is an understatement – exceptionally badly put.

[12 September] *The tragedy begins.* My heaviness of spirit paralyses me. The reason? Alone, alone. I cannot let myself tell of my great sorrow. Aino must be protected. My ——— [has been?] fateful for me and my art, my life. But am I to blame? No.

[13 September] Am better when I face up to life's meaninglessness. The Symphony is in my thoughts. Our critics here are beneath contempt. Only very few understand what I have done and want to do in the world of the symphony. The majority have no idea of what it is about. The German radio only plays old music so as to 'improve' public taste. But these things are usually only historic curiosities. A talent like mine, not to say genius, can't be nourished on yoghurt etc. Other ingredients are necessary!

[15 September] What hell I have had to go through! My oversensitivity and all the pain I have involuntarily caused Aino, my beloved wife. She tries to be brave and cheerful and not show how these things affect her. *Das grosse Unglück.*

[16 September] I am in no way what I should be in today's world. Neither by descent, nature or temperament. My descent – God knows what these racial theorists have dreamt up![2]

[17 September] Am full of anguish. My legacy to the children. I am not guilty. What is to be done! What dreadful agony! People must surely realize the injustice of predestination.

[19 September] In certain countries like Germany, 'the Aryan paragraphs' are used to get rid of the intelligentsia. Otherwise 'racial purity' couldn't work. Aino quiet and sad. She has her views too.

[20 September] Out of this chaos perhaps something saner, truer and better will emerge. How can you, Jean Sibelius, possibly take these 'Aryan paragraphs' seriously? That is a great advantage for an artist. You are a cultural aristocrat and can make a stand against stupid prejudice.

[22 September] Everything seems to me so petty. These puerile *Rassenbestimmungen* [racial laws] which are humbug. I am an artist and certainly have the advantage of profiting from the good in all my antecedents.

[30 September] Yesterday a great moment – like a caress from a sunnier world. Heard the symphony that Vaughan Williams has dedicated to me.[3] Listened to it from Stockholm under Malcolm Sargent. Civilized and humane! Am deeply grateful. Williams gives me more than anyone can imagine. A tragic fate has befallen my country. We have to live with barbarism [the Nazis] otherwise we shall go under [the Communists].

[1 October] *Niente!* Three enemy planes fly over us today. A beautiful day in my view. Not in other's. Pompeii is in ruins, as it always has been – everything of value destroyed.

[5 October] Heard this evening a 'Europe concert' from Germany. All the composers were represented by their best works – I by *Finlandia.* They look on me as a has-been or *fait accompli.* Am very down, as Adolf Paul, my friend since our youth, is dead. The critics here – as also in Sweden and Germany – are reserved when my symphonies are played. Quite different in the English world. As a symphonist I am not for these people at home. Life is soon over. Others will come and surpass me in the eyes of the world. We are fated to die forgotten. I must start economizing. I can't go on like this.

[7 October] Went for a walk in the windy weather. Wonderful.

[23 October] The *Sibelius Gesellschaft* has given a concert in Berlin with Aune Antti, with a programme of other Finnish composers with me tagging along.

[6 January 1944] To aim high – that is life's challenge. To learn to do this – if it is not inborn – that is what life is about.

[14 January] Ever since Karl Ekman's book on me came out in 1935, the book has embittered my life and only brought me misery. How many sleepless nights Aino and I have had as a result cannot be numbered. K. Ekman has put things into my mouth which I have not said. And on top of that it is tendentious. Ida Ekman begged me to allow Karl [her son] to write and publish his book on me. Otherwise, as she put it, Karl would go under. I have had enough of being a target.

After these scribbles there is a shopping list and some undated and indecipherable notes. But the last entry reads: 'What enormous musical possibilities the *Kalevala* offers.'

Wartime privations were no less acute for Sibelius than for anyone else. There were acute food shortages and provisions were strictly rationed. Sibelius's plight was eased in one respect. His old friends Lina and Georg Boldemann, who had looked after him so well during his time in Berlin in 1931, had eventually fled from the horrors of Nazi persecution and taken refuge in Sweden. Their devotion took the practical form of sending Sibelius and Aino food parcels, which were more than welcome. Their letters of thanks give some picture of conditions during the war years.

From Aino's letters and from a photo taken in 1944 we learn that Sibelius had lost weight. The reported loss of some of his manuscripts, including *Luonnotar,* during the bombing raids on Leipzig had depressed him, but his concerns were more for the serious developments that were threatening Finland. In 1944 the government had put out peace feelers, and the German 'co-belligerents', mainly concentrated in the north of the country, became enemies.

The post-war years saw little change in Sibelius's relative position in the English-speaking world and on the Continent. His reputation in England seemed unassailable and his position among the classics was taken for granted. His music occupied a dominant role in the concert hall and on the BBC. More importantly, the gramophone continued to further his cause. Immediately after the war Beecham recorded *Tapiola* and the Sixth Symphony, and later re-recorded *The Tempest* music and the Violin Concerto with Isaac Stern; he also made his first recordings of the First Symphony and some of the *Scènes historiques*. In America, Stokowski recorded the First and Second symphonies, Ormandy the Second, Fourth and Fifth, and Koussevitzky continued to champion the symphonies in the concert hall and re-recorded the Second.

The early 1950s saw first recordings in the new LP format of all four *Lemminkäinen Legends* in their correct order, placing *The Swan of Tuonela* second, from Thomas Jensen and Sixten Ehrling. It also saw the first one-man cycles of the symphonies from Anthony Collins and Sixten Ehrling. Walter Legge again endeavoured to persuade Sibelius to come over to London, either to conduct a cycle himself with the Philharmonia Orchestra, which he had founded immediately after the war, or at least to supervise one. Sibelius yet again pleaded his great age. In September 1954 Legge wrote:

> Some time ago I wrote and told you that we had recorded your Fourth and Fifth Symphonies as well as *Tapiola* with Herbert von Karajan and the Philharmonia Orchestra. As I believe I have already told you, Herbert von Karajan is, in my view, of all the leading conductors, the one with the greatest insight into your music. If you are completely happy with his performances of these three great works I would be deeply grateful if you would write and tell me so, because if Herbert von Karajan's performances satisfy you, it is my intention to record all your symphonies to be published in time for the celebration of your ninetieth birthday. If you have any criticisms, no matter how small, do please let me have them.
>
> You have probably forgotten, but in 1937 you kindly sent me new metronome markings for the end of the Fourth Symphony. These were an invaluable guide to us in recording and it has particularly gratified me to see that several American critics have commented that for the first time in their experience the wonderful two last pages of the Fourth Symphony are revealed in an entirely new light.

In the margin of Legge's letter Sibelius pencilled a draft of a telegram to

Karajan: 'As before, I have always admired your Symphony IV and deep insights and great artistic grip. My grateful thanks.' And a little later he was to tell Legge in person: 'Karajan is the only one who really understands my music.' In the end Karajan recorded the last four symphonies and *Tapiola*, the first three having already been recorded with Paul Kletzki.

At home in Helsinki, a Sibelius Week had been started in 1951 – and in the beginning it was devoted almost exclusively to him. Visiting soloists had included David Oistrakh and Isaac Stern. Conductors included Sir Thomas Beecham, who conducted two all-Sibelius concerts, both with the same programme: the Sixth and Seventh symphonies, the incidental music to *The Tempest* and *Tapiola*. In the late 1920s Robert Kajanus had also given the same programme, save for the Sixth Symphony, but the public at that time was not ready for Sibelius's later music, and the critics too had shown a striking lack of understanding and enthusiasm. Now, when Sir Thomas conducted these pieces, the climate was wholly different. His effect on both the orchestra and the audience was electrifying, something to which the author of this book can testify. Beecham like no other was completely attuned to the Sixth Symphony's modal style, just as he also made the Palestrinian polyphony in the first part of the Seventh grow into an ecstatic threnody.

The eighty-eight-year-old composer heard the concert on the radio and on the following day received Sir Thomas at Ainola. The latter described his visit in an entertaining Home Service broadcast to mark Sibelius's ninetieth birthday, when he mentioned that the composer had asked him to record *The Oceanides*. 'I don't know why. But of course, I shall do that thing.'

On 18 September 1957 Sibelius returned from his customary morning walk. That autumn he had not yet seen the cranes on their flight to warmer, more southerly latitudes. How eagerly he had watched and how intently he had listened to the cries of these magical creatures in earlier years! Now at last he was to be granted another glimpse of these extraordinary birds, which awakened almost mystical feelings in him. Aino Sibelius described how he became gripped by a growing feeling of ecstasy: 'Here they come, the birds of my youth!' The day was heavy with clouds and the cranes flew so low that he could see them clearly with his own eyes. Suddenly, one of them changed course towards Sibelius and circled over Ainola, before trumpeting its cry and rejoining the flock.

The following evening Sibelius spoke on the phone to Sir Malcolm Sargent, who had come to Finland to conduct the Fifth Symphony at one of the Helsinki Orchestra's Friday concerts. Aino was a little concerned by the fact that Jean seemed eager to go to bed earlier than usual instead of waiting up, as was his habit, until the late-night news from Swedish Radio, which was broadcast at 11 o'clock Finnish time. Her anxieties were not misplaced, for the next day, Friday 20 September, he suffered a cerebral haemorrhage while seated at table for lunch. Aino hurried forward to support him, meanwhile leafing through the telephone directory for help. A doctor was soon on the scene. Sibelius was still conscious when his daughters Eva and Katarina arrived at his sickbed a couple of hours later. Eva said: 'Pappa, here are Eva and Kaj', to which Sibelius weakly responded: 'Eva and Kaj.' Those were his last words before he lost consciousness and his general condition deteriorated. When the broadcast of Sargent's concert was due, Aino wanted to turn on the radio in the hope that the sound of the Fifth Symphony would bring him back to consciousness, but decided against it. An hour later, at 9.15 p.m., the doctor confirmed that death had taken place.

E come i gru van cantando lor lai
facendo in aer di sé lunga riga [4]

Sibelius's body was taken from Ainola to Helsinki Cathedral. Seventeen thousand people filed past in procession to pay their respects to the composer whose songs were part and parcel of every Finn's Christmas since childhood, and whose tone poem *Finlandia* had resounded through the world at times of national crisis and celebration. Sibelius was accorded a state funeral that was attended by people from every walk of life, from the president of the republic down to the ordinary citizen. The music included the Prelude to *The Tempest* and as a contrast, Prospero's lullaby for Miranda, as well as the Oaktree, whose mysterious flute overcomes the powers of darkness. The orchestra conducted by Tauno Hannikainen played the slow movement of the Fourth Symphony, perhaps the deepest and most revealing of his musical utterances, and *The Swan of Tuonela. In memoriam* was played as the coffin was borne out of the church. Sibelius had once commented: 'Strange to think that this will presumably be played when I am a corpse.' (23 October 1909)

Aino and the remainder of the family bore the coffin home to Ainola. The students formed a guard of honour in the centre of the city and a long way into the countryside. Thousands of people lined the streets, and schools were closed for the afternoon. When they reached Järvenpää they were greeted by another guard of honour stretching for the best part of a kilometre. On Aino's wreath the inscription read, 'With gratitude for a life which has been blessed by your great art. Your wife.'

As dusk fell, candles were lit in windows throughout the land, and during the course of the evening they gradually burned out. But what was it that England's great composer, Ralph Vaughan Williams, wrote in his tribute to Jean Sibelius on his eighty-fifth birthday? 'You have lit a candle that will never be put out.'

Notes

CHAPTER ONE

1 Leopold Schmidt, *Beethoven: Leben und Werk* (Berlin, 1924), p. 214.

2 *Nya Argus* (16 December 1914).

3 *Hufvudstadsbladet* (24 November 1914).

4 *Helsingin Sanomat* (26 June 1910).

CHAPTER TWO

1 Since these words were written, James Hepokowski has published his splendid monograph on the symphony, to which readers are referred [Tr.].

2 A whole generation of music-lovers in the English-speaking world have grown up with Tovey's telling image in his penetrating analytical note, and I have retained this as a means of identifying the theme [Tr.].

3 It is also related to what was to become the finale [Tr.].

4 Philip Barford, 'Beethoven as Man and Artist' in *The Beethoven Companion*, ed. Denis Arnold and Nigel Fortune (London, 1971), pp. 21–38.

CHAPTER THREE

1 As reported in *Uusi Säveletär* (1915:2).

2 Dated 23 July 1915.

3 Letter to Wilhelm Stenhammar (11 January 1915).

4 *Göteborgs, Handels-och-Sjöfartstidning* (26 March 1915).

5 Sibelius incorrectly put 'Nuori Suomi 1892'. However, on 29 September he sold them to the publisher Apostol, but notes in his diary that he must rework them. A week later, he notes he has 'composed or to be accurate revised the *Romance* and *Epilogue* (which the *Perpetuum mobile* now became) as Op. 2a, b.' By this means he managed to get rid of the Rondo for viola and piano, which in its turn had removed the A minor Quartet from his 1909 catalogue. Confusion has certainly reigned over his glorious song, *Arioso*, Op. 3.

CHAPTER FOUR

1 *Dagens Nyheter* (23 April 1915).

2 *Hufvudstadsbladet* (28 April 1915).

CHAPTER FIVE

1 Rosa Newmarch, *Jean Sibelius: A Short Story of a Long Friendship* (Boston, 1939; London, 1944), p. 38.

2 5 July 1915.

3 It eventually appeared in 1981 [Tr.].

4 Nyland's Student Corporation.

5 *Uusi Suometar* (8 December 1915).
6 *Helsingin Sanomat* (19 December 1915).

CHAPTER SIX
1 *Dagens Press* (10 January 1916).
2 Martin Lamm, *Swedenborg* (Stockholm, 1915), p. 14.
3 Op. cit., p. 65.
4 Op. cit., p. 272.
5 Op. cit., p. 272.
6 *Hufvudstadsbladet* (3 March 1916).
7 *Dagens Press* (31 March 1916).
8 *Dagens Nyheter*, quoted in *Hufvudstadsbladet* (24 February 1916).
9 Edward J. Dent, *Ferruccio Busoni* (Oxford, 1966), p. 230.

CHAPTER SEVEN
1 10 August 1916.
2 Letter of 1 September 1916.

CHAPTER EIGHT
1 His New Year 1939 performance of the *Andante festivo* came to light in the Finnish Radio Archives, but until recently the performance in circulation was the preparatory rehearsal conducted by Tauno Hannikainen, not Sibelius himself.
2 *Uusi Maailma* No. 24 (3 December 1975) pp. 68–9.

CHAPTER NINE
1 A. O. Väisänen, *'Musiikillisen viljelyksemme tulevaisuus'* in *Säveletär* (1918).
2 *Työn Valta* (17 July 1918).
3 *Uusi Suometar* (26 October 1918).
4 *Helsingin Sanomat* (26 October 1918).
5 21 November 1918.
6 H. H. Stuckenschmidt, *Schoenberg* (Zürich & Freiburg, 1974), p. 7.

CHAPTER TEN
1 *Levande musik* (Swedish edn.), p.22.
2 Kjell Strömberg, *En gammal parisares minnen* (An Old Parisian's Memoirs) (Stockholm, 1969), p. 60.

CHAPTER ELEVEN
1 'Nevertheless I take leave to suggest that Schoenberg is not the mere fool or madman that he is generally supposed to be. May it not be that the new composer sees a logic in certain tonal relations that to the rest of us seem chaos at present, but the coherence of which may be clear enough to us all some day?' Ernest Newman, 'The Case of Arnold Schoenberg', *The Nation*, 1912; reproduced in *Testament of Music*, ed. Herbert van Thal (London, 1962), pp. 163–4.
2 *Boston Post* (19 December 1914).

3 *Boston Post* (21 January 1918).

4 Readers are referred to Glenda Dawn Goss, *Jean Sibelius and Olin Downes, Music, Friendship, Criticism* (Boston, 1995), p. 274. Professor Goss offers a comprehensive and exhaustive survey of Downes as standard bearer of Sibelius's cause [Translator].

5 'All'Overtura' from the first set of *Scènes historiques* was originally composed for a tableau in which one sees Väinämöinen seated on a cliff, singing and playing the *kantele* while people from Kaleva and Pohja listen enraptured. Probably Sibelius consciously 'forgot' to mention this relatively short piece, which neither in style nor ambition measures up to the *Kalevala* theme.

6 *Uusi Suometar* (20 May 1916).

7 Letter dated 19 April 1916.

8 Prohibition had been introduced during the early months of independence, and naturally served to increase the price of alcohol.

9 This would seem to have been its first performance in Denmark.

CHAPTER TWELVE

1 Joachim Hartnack, *Grosse Geiger unserer Zeit* (Munich, 1967), p. 46.

2 *Hufvudstadsbladet* (23 April 1920).

3 See vol. I, pp. 100–1 [Tr.].

4 The high-pitched musical cries made by the Lapps to call their reindeer.

CHAPTER THIRTEEN

1 Letter to Aino (7 February 1921).

2 Eric Blom was later an influential scholar–critic and editor of the fifth edition of *Grove's Dictionary of Music and Musicians* (London, 1954).

3 Ursula Vaughan Williams, *R. V. W: A Biography of Ralph Vaughan Williams* (London, 1946), p. 139. It would seem unlikely that Sibelius had at this stage heard any of Vaughan Williams's music, though he might possibly have seen *A Sea Symphony*, which was published in vocal score in 1909.

4 26 February 1921.

5 According to an earlier Sibelius letter, Busoni had been in London as early as 7 February. Besides the Fourth Symphony, he could also have heard either the Fifth Symphony (12 February) or the three shorter pieces (19 February), but the fact that later the same year he conducted the Fifth in Berlin would suggest that he had heard it in London.

6 Harriet Cohen, *A Bundle of Time* (London, 1969), pp. 63–5.

7 *Bergens Tidende* (22 March 1921).

CHAPTER FOURTEEN

1 He played it for the first time in Halle on 6 October 1937.

2 He had, of course, written a couple of cello pieces with him in mind [Tr.].

CHAPTER FIFTEEN

1 *Svenska Dagbladet* (27 February 1923).

2 *Dagens Nyheter* (2 February 1923).

3 Gianandrea Gavazzeni, *La vecchiaia e la fortuna di Jean Sibelius* (1939), reproduced in *Musicisti d'Europa, studi sui contemporanei* (Milan, 1954), pp. 9–10.

4 Erik Gummerus, *Palatset med kolonnerna* (Borås, 1974), p.188.

CHAPTER SEVENTEEN

1 The Finnish parliament. Before 1917, Finland's elected body was the Senate, and after independence this became the Diet. Unlike Sweden, which has a bicameral parliament, Finland's is unicameral.

CHAPTER NINETEEN

1 In her excellent study *Jean Sibelius and Olin Downes, Music, Friendship, Criticism,* Glenda Dawn Goss cites a report published by a fellow staff member at the *New York Times.* Downes, it seems, was met at the border by a written greeting from Sibelius, whom he discovered anticipating his visit in the lobby of the critic's hotel. There ensued a long and remarkable evening during which Downes had his first encounter with Scandinavia's notorious *akvavit,* as well as with Sibelius's legendary capacity to consume it. Talk flowed as freely as liquor as the composer introduced Downes to a café with a bottle of Haig at each place. When the bottles had been emptied, in the early hours of the morning, Downes foggily groped his way back to his hotel, while Sibelius strode out of the establishment as 'steady as Plymouth Rock'. 'How Downes Came Up', *Times Talk*, vol. vii, No. 5 (January, 1954, 5) [Tr.].

CHAPTER TWENTY

1 He published an account of his interview in 'The Glory that was Russia – Repin, the artist who painted Mussorgsky, recalls memories of dead composers', together with 'A Visit to Sibelius', in the *New York Times* (21 July 1929).

2 Their correspondence was conducted in German..

3 Cecil Gray, *Musical Chairs* (London, 1948), p. 255 *et seq.*

4 Their correspondence was conducted in French.

5 Cecil Gray, *Sibelius* (Oxford, 1931), p. 201.

CHAPTER TWENTY-ONE

1 Cherkassky, an uncle of the celebrated pianist, had lived in Helsinki between 1917 and 1922, and had been leader of the Helsinki Orchestra as well as a soloist. Cherkassky had written in early December to report that Koussevitzky had seen it rumoured in the English press that the Eighth Symphony had been promised to the Royal Philharmonic Society. He was naturally displeased and had spoken to Cherkassky, who had reassured him that if Sibelius had promised him the première, his word would be kept. Sibelius had replied that it would. It was easier for him to correspond with Cherkassky, as they both wrote in Swedish. Koussevitzky's correspondence begins in German but by this time he used English.

CHAPTER TWENTY-TWO

1 Elisabeth Schwarzkopf, *On and Off the Record: A memoir of Walter Legge* (London, 1982), pp. 163–4.

2 As is often the case, these diary entries border on the incoherent. It is obvious from their intensity that something of importance has occurred, possibly relating to the Eighth Symphony. It is obvious also that he was disturbed by the implications of Nazi racism.

3 The original was inscribed 'Dedication to Jean Sibelius without permission and in sincerest flattery'.

4 'and just like cranes in flight, chanting their lays,
stretched out in a long ribbon in the air'
(Dante Alighieri, *Divina Commedia*, 'Inferno', Canto 5, lines 46–7)

Index

Blomstedt, Lennart, 36
Boldemann, Georg, 306, 307, 308, 316, 328
Boldemann, Holger, 306
Boldemann, Laci, 307
Boldemann, Lina, 308, 316, 328
Boldemann, Maija, 306, 307
Boosey & Hawkes (publishers), 175
Borg, Maria, 72
Borgström, Aline, 33, 177
Borgström, Arthur, 33, 177–8, 232
Borgström, Hjalmar, 37
Borgström, Mascha Travers, 177–8
Boston, 218–19, 276, 281, 294–5, 301–2, 306, 320
Boult, Sir Adrian, 205
Bournemouth: JS's concerts in, 198–9
Boutade (JS), 7–8, 74
Bradford, 200
Brahe, Per, 161
Brahms, Johannes, 48, 168, 216, 300
Bratt, Leif, 51, 237, 238
Bratt, Olga, 51, 237, 243, 277, 289
Breitkopf & Härtel (publishers), 2, 31, 32, 42, 45, 48–9, 61, 77, 111, 128–30, 137–8, 144–5, 175, 186–7, 189–90, 209, 254, 256–7, 274, 306
Brennan, William, 286
brinner på ön, Der (Fire on the Island) (JS), 12
Bruckner, Anton, 168, 179, 300
Bruneau, Alfred, 180
Brusande rusar en våg (Surging the Wave Rushes Forward) (JS), 120
brustna tonen, Den (The Broken Voice) (JS), 12
Bull, Schak, 206
Burgin, Richard, 36, 66–9, 84
Burmester, Willy, 143, 180, 290
Busch, Fritz, 51, 237
Busoni, Ferruccio, 30, 34, 199, 200, 207, 211–12, 215–16, 217–18, 237, 240, 249; JS's correspondence with, 37, 85, 145, 146, 201–2, 212–13
Busoni, Gerda, 85, 237
Bykyrkan (The Village Church) (JS), 177

Cahier, Mme Charles, 113
Cameron, Basil, 297, 312–13, 314
Campanula (JS), 110
Cantique (Ab imo pectore) (JS), 83, 128
Canzonetta (JS), 83, 292
Capri, 269
Capriccietto (JS), 7
Carminalia (JS), 47
Carpelan, Axel, 68, 74, 93, 147, 220; death, 149–50; illnesses, 76–7, 87, 90, 133, 149; JS's

correspondence with, 1–3, 6, 55–6, 63, 69–70, 72–3, 75–6, 87–8, 90, 93–5, 97, 103–4, 111, 115–16, 124, 127–9, 134–5, 138–41, 147–9
Carpelan, Tor, 149
Carraud, Gaston, 181
Casadeus, Robert and Gaby, 281
Casella, Alfredo, 84
Cassazione (JS, Op. 6), 42, 46–7
Ceremonial Cantata (JS, Op. 15), 43, 47, 69
Chaliapin, Feodor, 319
Chantavoine, Jean, 181
Chappels (publishers), 209, 213, 216, 297
Cherkassky, Paul, 160, 310
Cherubini, Luigi, 224
Christian X, King, 251
Cinq Esquisses (JS), 217
Cinq morceaux lyriques (JS), 248
Clemenceau, Georges, 114, 173
Cocteau, Jean, 168
Cohen, Alex, 199
Cohen, Harriet, 203–5
Collins, Anthony, 329
Copenhagen, 220–1; JS's concert tours, 152–7, 249–54, 271–4; Nordic Music Festival, 135, 152–7
Coronation Cantata (JS, Op. 19), 43, 46–7, 63
Couplet (JS), 7

Dagens Press (newspaper), 118
Damrosch, Walter, 266, 271, 275, 281
Danse caracteristique (JS), 87
Danse idyll (JS), 150
Danse pastorale (JS), 88
Danses champêtres (JS), 266, 274
Debussy, Claude, 3–4, 101–2, 154, 190, 235, 259, 280, 281
Demanten på marssnön (JS), 109
Devotion (JS, Op. 77 No. 2), 32, 59, 83, 128, 187
Diaghilev, Serge, 221
Dickens, Charles, 142
Dieren, Bernard van, 298
d'Indy, Vincent, 259
Dolce far niente (JS), 86
Dold förening (JS), 90
Donner, Olly, 197
Donner, Ossian, 196–7, 198
Donner, Otto, 137, 140
Downes, Olin, 168–9, 275, 276, 286–8, 295–6, 311
Drömmarna (The Dreams) (JS), 150
Dryad, The (JS), 83
Duke Magnus and the Mermaid (JS), 40

Goltz, Count Rüdiger von der, 128–30
Gorky, Maxim, 97
Gothenburg, 77, 186; JS's concert tours, 37–41,
    231, 237–9
Gounod, Charles, 181
Grainger, Percy, 34
Gram, Peder, 251
Granen (JS), 5, 158
Granit-Ilmoniemi, Eeli, 79, 171–2, 174
Gräsbeck, Walter, 258
Grawert, Theodor, 130
Gray, Cecil, 297–301, 304, 325
Grevillius, Nils, 246
Grieg, Edvard, 205
Gripenberg, Bertel, 61, 74, 95–6, 165
Gripenberg, Maggie, 1
Gummerus, Edvard, 233–4
Gummerus, Herman, 232–4, 237

Haakon, King, 206
Haapalainen, Eero, 123
Haartman family, 72
Hagelstam, Anna, 10
Hagelstam, Wentzel, 146, 240, 256
Halir, Karl, 180
Hallén, Andreas, 194–5, 247
Halonen, Pekka, 52, 68, 318
Halvorsen, Johan, 156, 272
Hamsun, Knut, 206
Hannikainen, Ilmari, 9, 69, 91, 155, 177, 180, 215
Hansen, Wilhelm (publishers), 2, 6, 32, 157, 162,
    187, 193, 209, 214, 216, 222, 240, 248–9, 253,
    256, 258, 259–60, 266, 268, 285–6, 295
Har du mod? (JS), 43–4
Harlequinade (JS), 87
Harris, Frederick, 159
Harrogate, 297
Hase, Helmuth von, 186–7, 196, 256–7, 269
Hase, Oskar von, 128–9
Hastings, 297
Hauch, Gunnar, 65, 154–5, 249, 252, 271, 272, 274,
    278
Hecht, Gustav (critic), 37
Heifetz, Jascha, 293, 323
Heine, Heinrich, 279
Helsingin Sanomat (newspaper), 69, 89, 104,
    110–11, 118, 172, 179
Helsinki: Helsinki Fair, 183–4; Helsinki
    University, 68, 138; musical life in, 33, 36, 68,
    74–5, 78–9, 83–4, 91–2, 93, 109, 126, 128–9,
    136–7, 143, 162–3, 179–80, 183–4, 191, 210–11,
    215, 226–7, 242, 244, 257–8, 259, 282–4, 320;

Nordic Music Festival (1921), 208
Helsinki Orchestra, 50, 66, 126, 143, 183–4, 320
Hemmer, Jarl, 139–40
Hennes budskap (Her Message) (JS), 112
Henriques, Fini, 251
Hernberg, Erik, 124
Herr Lager och Skön Fager (JS), 3
Hindemith, Paul, 205
Hirsch, Otto, 231
Hitler, Adolf, 320, 325
Hoeberg, Georg, 156, 220
Hofmann, Josef, 34
Hofmannsthal, Hugo von: *Everyman*, 88, 90–1,
    186
Holm, Mimmi, 127
Holsti, Rudolf, 171
Honegger, Arthur, 280, 281
Hornborg, Erik, 116
Höstkväll (Autumn Evening) (JS), 46, 86, 181
Hoving, Viktor, 91, 231
Hufvudstadsbladet (newspaper), 3, 10, 62, 81, 84,
    102, 112, 118, 126, 142, 160, 179, 194, 222, 284
Hummel, Ferdinand, 175
Humoreske (JS), 186
Humoreske II (JS), 191
Humoresque for piano (JS), 87
Humoresques for violin and orchestra (JS), 4, 99,
    105–6, 137, 160, 162, 187
Humoristisches Marsch (JS), 191
Hymn till jorden (Hymn to the Earth) (JS), 170

I bröder, I systrar, I älskande par (JS), 90, 110
Ibsen, Lillebil, 221
Ikonen, Lauri, 92
Ilves, Eero, 250
Ilves, Katarina (née Sibelius, JS's daughter), 67, 68,
    79, 87, 88, 106, 145, 152, 170, 213, 220, 331;
    childhood, 14, 38, 58, 59, 60; and civil war, 118,
    124–6; marriage, 250; as pianist, 66, 131, 153,
    196, 210; on revolution of, 1917, 102–3
impressionism, 1, 4, 53, 168
Impromptu (JS, Op. 97 No. 5), 191
Impromptu for violin and piano (JS, Op. 87 No. 1),
    61
Impromptu for women's voices (JS), 11, 21, 44, 46,
    273
In memoriam (JS), 331
Ingeborg, Princess, 247
Iris (JS), 87
Isänmaalle (To My Country) (JS), 177
*Islossningen i Uleå älv (The Melting of the Ice on the
    Uleå River)* (JS, Op. 28c), 46–7

Printed and bound by CPI Group (UK) Ltd, Croydon, CR0 4YY

19/06/2025

01903789-0001